Compensation

Barry Gerhart
University of Wisconsin

Sara L. Rynes
University of Iowa

Compensation

Theory, Evidence, and Strategic Implications

SAGE | SA SOUTH ASIA

Los Angeles | London | New Delhi
Singapore | Washington DC | Melbourne

Originally published in 2003 by

SAGE www.sagepublishing.com
Los Angeles | London | New Delhi | Singapore | Washington DC | Melbourne

This South Asia edition published in 2008 by

SAGE | SA SOUTH ASIA

SAGE Publications India Pvt Ltd
B1/I-1 Mohan Cooperative Industrial Area
Mathura Road
New Delhi 110 044, India

Published by Vivek Mehra for SAGE Publications India Pvt Ltd.

ISBN: 978-81-7829-920-4 (PB)

Contents

Introduction to the Series vii
David A. Whetten

Acknowledgments ix

1. Introduction: The Enigmas of Compensation 1
   - Objectives 3
   - Outline of the Book 5

2. Differences in Pay Level: Why Do Some Companies Pay More Than Others? 11
   - A Tale of Two Markets 11
   - The Case for Limited Discretion: Neoclassical Economic Theory 12
   - Post-Institutional Economics: Theory Meets Reality 16
   - Why It May "Pay" to Pay More 21
   - The International Dimension 27
   - Differences in Pay Levels for Particular Jobs 29
   - Research on Pay Level Decision Making 31
   - Summary 39
   - Resource 2.1 40

3. Effects of Pay Level: What Do Employers Get in Return for Higher Pay? 47
   - Theories of the Importance of Pay to Individuals 48
   - What Do Employers Get in Return for Higher Pay Levels? 59
   - Future Research 77

4. Pay Structure: Relative Pay Within Organizations 81
   - The Role of Jobs and Job Evaluation in Pay Structure 84
   - Theories of Differences in Pay Structure 87
   - Work-Life Incentives 97

Empirical Research on the Effects of Pay Structure 105
Future Research 108

5. Pay Basis: Theories of Motivation and Pay for Performance 115
Effects of Pay and Motivational Programs on Performance: Meta-Analytic Results 116
Theories of Pay-Performance Relationships 119
Psychological Versus Economic Perspectives 120
Workforce Composition, Sorting, and Personality-Based Theories 151
Future Research 160

6. Pay-for-Performance Programs: Empirical Evidence 165
Broad Policy Decisions 166
Putting It All Together: Empirical Evidence on Pay Programs 184
Summary 219
Future Research 221

7. Pay Strategy 227
Strategic Fit and Alignment 231
Beyond Generic Strategies: The Resource-Based View of the Firm 244
Beyond Direct Earnings: Total Rewards 251
Summary and Future Research 253

8. Toward the Future 257
Future Research 259
Methodological Recommendations 262

References 267

Index 291

About the Authors 309

Introduction to the Series

The title of this series, *Foundations for Organizational Science (FOS)*, denotes a distinctive focus. FOS books are educational aids for mastering the core theories, essential tools, and emerging perspectives that constitute the field of organizational science (broadly conceived to include organizational behavior, organizational theory, human resource management, and business strategy). Our ambitious goal is to assemble the "essential library" for members of our professional community.

The vision for the series emerged from conversations with several colleagues, including Peter Frost, Anne Huff, Rick Mowday, Benjamin Schneider, Susan Taylor, and Andy Van de Ven. A number of common interests emerged from these sympathetic encounters, including enhancing the quality of doctoral education by providing broader access to the master teachers in our field, "bottling" the experience and insights of some of the founding scholars in our field before they retire, and providing professional development opportunities for colleagues seeking to broaden their understanding of the rapidly expanding subfields within organizational science.

Our unique learning objectives are reflected in an unusual set of instructions to FOS authors. They are encouraged to (a) "write the way they teach," framing their books as extensions of their teaching notes rather than as expansions of handbook chapters; (b) pass on their "craft knowledge" to the next generation of scholars, making them wiser, not just smarter; (c) share with their "virtual students and colleagues" the insider tips and best bets for research that are normally reserved for one-on-one mentoring sessions; and (d) make the complexity of their subject matter comprehensible to nonexperts so that readers can share their puzzlement, fascination, and intrigue.

We are proud of the group of highly qualified authors who have embraced the unique educational perspective of our *Foundations* series. We encourage your suggestions for how these books can better satisfy your learning needs—as a newcomer to the field preparing for prelims or developing a dissertation proposal or as an established scholar seeking to broaden your knowledge and proficiency.

—David A. Whetten
Series Editor

Acknowledgments

We would like to thank M. Susan Taylor for the opportunity to do this book, her detailed and helpful comments on the entire manuscript, and her patience in awaiting its arrival. We also thank Lois Tetrick, who used a draft of the book in her doctoral seminar and provided helpful feedback to us.

Over the years, we have been fortunate to learn a great deal from our mentors, colleagues, and students at Wisconsin, Cornell, Minnesota, Vanderbilt, and Iowa about the field of compensation. We especially wish to thank Herb Heneman, Tom Mahoney, George Milkovich, Marc Orlitzky, Ben Rosen, Don Schwab, Charlie Trevor, and Caroline Weber for their contributions to the way we think about and approach the field.

To Heather and Paul

1 Introduction

THE ENIGMAS OF COMPENSATION

Little evidence demonstrates the efficacy of rewards, although much evidence indicates that rewards and their design loom large in management attention.

—Pfeffer (1998a)

I've gone to seminars where you're told that people want to be told how good a worker they are. And yeah, that's true. It does feel good. But the bottom line is money. It boils down to money. To get that big chunk at the end of the year.

—Assembly line worker at Lincoln Electric (as quoted in Jasinowski & Hamrin, 1995)

Compensation is a complex and often confusing topic. Although compensation costs comprise, on average, 65% to 70% of total costs in the U.S. economy (Blinder, 1990; U.S. Bureau of Labor Statistics, 2001a) and are likewise substantial elsewhere (e.g., European Parliament, 1999), most managers are not sure of the likely consequences of spending either more, or less, on employees or of paying employees in different ways. Consider, for example, the plight of a manager trying to distill general "best practices" from the following set of highly successful companies.

Workers at Lincoln Electric are 3 times more productive than workers at comparable companies. Lincoln workers are paid on the basis of individual piecework plus an end-of-the-year individual bonus based on ideas and cooperation, output, dependability, and quality. Size of the bonus pool is based on overall company performance for the year. Lincoln has no paid holidays, no paid sick days, no paid health insurance, no coffee breaks, and no factory air conditioning. Yet in addition to the company's financial success, Lincoln has absenteeism of less than 1.5% and employee turnover of less than 3% after the first 3 months of employment.

SAS Institute, a software company, has an explicit strategy of deemphasizing monetary rewards and stock options, which are typically the basis on which most companies in their industry compete for workers. SAS also deemphasizes hierarchy and opportunities for salary growth through promotion, focusing instead on broad benefits for everyone that have an equalizing effect on compensation. Despite this lack of emphasis on pay for performance, SAS has experienced strong financial success and is frequently found on "100 Best Companies to Work For" lists. Employee turnover is 4% in a very high-turnover industry.

Microsoft typically pays below-market salaries and often hires people away from other companies for less than they are currently earning. In return, employees receive stock options that vary by position level and performance and, in Bill Gates's words, "a chance to change the world" (Rebello, 1992). Microsoft also makes extensive use of contract and subcontract workers, who do not receive the same compensation or benefits.

General Electric (GE) evaluates employees on a forced curve and terminates the bottom 10% each year. The *GE 2000 Annual Report* says that the "top 20% must be loved, nurtured and rewarded in the soul and wallet because they are the ones who make magic happen" (p. 4). However, the lowest 10% are removed each year,

> Always raising the bar of performance and increasing the quality of leadership. Not removing that bottom 10% early in their careers is not only a management failure, but false kindness as well—a form of cruelty—because inevitably a new leader will come into a business and take out that bottom 10% right away. (p. 4)

GE makes heavy use of performance bonuses and stock options for its top performers.

Egon Zehnder International, a global executive search firm, has no individual merit component in its compensation system. In contrast to most professional service firms (which pay on the basis of billable hours and clients generated), each Zehnder partner has an equal number of shares in the firm's equity, regardless of tenure. Shares rise in value each year because the firm reinvests 10% to 20% of its profits back into the firm. The remaining 80% to 90% is distributed across partners, with 60% being distributed across the board and the rest based on years as partner. Consultant turnover is 2% (as opposed to 30% in the industry on average), and the profit pool has grown every year for 37 years.

Based on the preceding examples, what seem to be the most effective pay practices? High emphasis on individual productivity, or no such emphasis? Emphasis on stock or stock options, or not? Rewards for seniority, or constant culling of the workforce to eliminate the lowest-performing individuals?

To add to managers' confusion, researchers often disagree on many of the most central questions surrounding pay, depending on their disciplinary training, ideological beliefs, or other factors. For example, different schools of researchers disagree over the following issues:

- Whether or not pay is a strong motivator of performance
- Whether it is better to have high pay differentials both across and within job categories, or egalitarian pay throughout
- Whether or not paying high wages and salaries will induce loyalty and hard work
- Whether it is more effective to reward on the basis of group productivity, individual productivity, or some combination of the two
- Whether executive pay is too high or too low
- Whether there are general best practices in compensation or whether appropriate compensation practices depend on a variety of contextual conditions

Like others before us (e.g., Bartol & Locke, 2000; Gerhart & Milkovich, 1992; Lawler, 1971; Pfeffer, 1998a, 1998b), we believe that some general principles can be discerned with respect to determinants and effects of compensation practices but also that there are many unanswered questions. In addition, it appears that many different permutations of the general principles can be effective, as well as some pay systems that seem to confound many (if not most) of the general principles. Finally, there are questions about the extent to which effective compensation systems are reproducible across organizations, given that the effectiveness of compensation systems may be interdependent with a variety of other factors, such as an organization's history, business strategy, culture, and other human resource practices.

Objectives

In writing this book, we have consciously worked to accomplish a number of objectives. One is to *integrate theory with empirical evidence* for each of the three major compensation decisions considered in this book: pay level, pay structure, and pay delivery systems. This is very important, because theories in some areas come into direct opposition with one another. For example, some theories (such as tournament theory) emphasize the potential advantages of hierarchical pay differentials, whereas other theories (based on social cohesion) emphasize the potential dangers. Still other theories (contingency theories and the resource-based view of the firm) argue that the most effective size of pay differentials depends on other organizational characteristics. In such cases, only empirical evidence can help us to choose among theories or modify them to more closely reflect reality.

A second goal is to review theories and research about both the *determinants and outcomes* of these three aspects of pay (with somewhat greater emphasis given to outcomes).

Third, we incorporate theory and evidence from *multiple disciplines,* primarily economics, psychology, and management, but also sociology. This is an advantage because the determinants and effects of compensation are very complex and have multiple facets. Thus, a complete understanding of compensation is not possible without interdisciplinary integration. For example, economics tends to focus on average or general effects, while psychology focuses more on individual differences and variations in outcomes. Similarly, economics and psychology tend to be founded on theories of individual choice and motivation, while sociology (and "blended" fields such as social psychology and organizational economics) tend to focus on social and group relationships, motivations, and outcomes.

Fourth, wherever possible, we discuss *effect sizes and practical significance* of compensation findings rather than merely their statistical *significance.* Numerous treatises have now been written about the limitations of statistical significance testing, such as the failure of the vast majority of empirical studies to meet their underlying assumptions, the dependence of statistical significance on sample size, and the arbitrariness and lack of precision in merely reporting cutoffs between statistical significance and nonsignificance (e.g., Schmidt, 1996). Thus, wherever possible, we supplement reports of statistical significance with estimates of variance explained, or percentage change in dependent or endogenous variables as a function of meaningful changes in independent or exogenous ones.

Fifth, we *reinterpret or take a broader outlook* in areas where previous research has either been misinterpreted or found to have serious shortcomings. We believe that at least two such areas merit such treatment in this book: research on within-group pay differentials and research on merit pay. The reader will see, for example, that previous studies that have reported negative outcomes from within-group pay differentials have sometimes completely ignored other aspects of their findings that point to *positive* effects of such differentials. As such, we place entirely different interpretations than the original authors on some reported findings.

Finally, we seek to understand not only what has been learned from previous research but also the most important *issues for future research.* Although some areas of compensation have been widely studied, other very important issues have remained almost entirely unresolved. Specific suggestions for future research can be found in each of the chapters, and more general research needs are summarized in the last chapter.

Outline of the Book

The complexity of pay systems makes it difficult to organize theories and research about pay in a comprehensive yet comprehensible manner. Thus, we begin with relatively simple issues and then build complexity as we go along. For example, Chapters 2 and 3 discuss the most general pay decision made by an organization, that of *pay level* (roughly, whether to pay more, or less, than what other organizations do). In Chapter 4, we add complexity by considering the fact that organizations may have the same average pay levels but very different *pay structures* (e.g., differences in compensation across high- versus low-level jobs). Chapters 5 and 6 focus on *changes* in pay (rather than initial or starting pay) and on differences in the *bases* on which such changes are determined (e.g., organizational performance versus individual performance, or individual performance versus seniority). Then, in Chapter 7, we consider the most complex possibility of all: that the effects of pay are deeply embedded in circumstances unique to each organization and thus perhaps impossible to accurately describe as main or independent effects.

In Chapter 2, we address theories of pay level. Such theories seek to explain why, for example, Lincoln Electric and Microsoft offer lower base pay levels than their competitors, while other companies, such as Mars Candy or A.G. Edwards, offer above-market base pay. We begin the chapter with a discussion of why early theorists and researchers paid curiously little attention to this question. For many years, economists did not consider this to be an important issue because their basic models of wage determination predicted that organizations would always be tending toward the same "market wage" as other employers. However, investigations of actual labor markets by applied economists after World War II showed that pay varied widely for the same type of work across employers, even in the same geographical area. For example, Dunlop (1957) observed a differential of nearly 100% between Boston truckers in the magazine industry versus those working in scrap iron and metal, despite the fact that they were performing almost identical work and were represented by the same union.

Over time, the discrepancies between theory and reality became too large to ignore, and a variety of enhancements to neoclassical theory emerged to explain the existence of these differences (e.g., efficiency wage, rent sharing, resource dependence, and ability-to-pay theories). We close Chapter 2 with a summary of the very limited empirical evidence on how pay level decisions are made, as well as a discussion of the complexities of studying pay level decisions (and outcomes) as distinct from other aspects of pay determination.

Chapter 3 discusses theories and research on the *effects*, rather than the determinants, of pay level. We begin by reviewing general theories of pay importance, which are rather different in economics (which tends to assign a predominant role to pay in work behaviors) than in psychology (which tends to assume that pay is only one of several factors influencing work attitudes and behaviors). From these general theories, we move to contingency theories suggesting that pay importance depends on the characteristics of both markets (e.g., variability in pay across employers) and individuals (e.g., values or personality). Next, we review evidence regarding the effects of pay level on various outcomes, such as pay satisfaction, applicant attraction, employee retention, employee quality, and overall utility. Finally, we note the surprising paucity of field research concerning the effects of pay level on objective outcomes (e.g., employee attraction, quality and retention, overall utility) and call for additional research in these areas.

In Chapter 4, we introduce greater complexity by moving our discussion from differences in average pay levels across employers to differences in the structure of pay inside organizations. By structure, we mean differences in pay between the top of the organizational hierarchy and the bottom (e.g., chief executive officer, or CEO, versus entry level positions) and between one job family and another (e.g., professional versus technical). For example, we explore issues such as why SAS and Southwest Airlines deliberately restrict the number of job levels and the size of pay differentials between them, while other organizations (such as GE) pay very large differentials as employees move up the career ladder (at least when stock grants and options are taken into account).

Whereas prior to Chapter 4, we talk about jobs as an abstract concept, discussion of pay structures requires a more explicit description of how jobs are described, evaluated, and compared both within and across employers. After discussing job evaluation and other possible bases for determining pay structures (e.g., individual differences in knowledge, skills, and abilities), we turn to various theories of why employers might choose to have steeper-than-average pay structures (e.g., tournament or winner-take-all theories), flatter-than-average structures (egalitarian or cooperative theories), or structures that pay special attention to a few key strategic positions (resource dependence theory). Limited evidence on the existence and effects of alternative structures is reviewed, and suggestions are made for future research.

In Chapter 5, we introduce theories about the incentive and motivational effects of alternative pay delivery systems. Common pay delivery systems include across-the-board increases, merit pay, seniority-based pay, stock grants and options, gainsharing and other group incentives, and profit sharing.

Given the rather amazing variety of pay delivery systems or bases for pay increases (or decreases), surprisingly little is known empirically about how such choices are made in the first place. We suspect that these differences often begin with implicit theories of motivation on the part of organizational founders, which determine not only compensation systems but also other organizational features, such as structure, culture, and leadership style, and other human resource practices, such as selection and performance management. Consistent with institutional theory (e.g., DiMaggio & Powell, 1983; Scott, 1995), we suspect that these basic differences persist over time, although they may well undergo some permutations as environmental conditions change.

Despite the paucity of empirical evidence regarding the origins of pay delivery design, at least five theories, four from psychology and one from economics, have something to say about this issue. The four psychological theories discussed in this book are expectancy, goal setting, social cognition, and equity theory. Although each of these theories is somewhat unique, the fact that they share a psychological perspective means that as a group, they are quite different from the economic perspective.

For example, relative to economic theory, psychological theories place a greater emphasis on intrinsic aspects of motivation, on cognitive processes underlying motivational effects, on individual differences in tastes and preferences, on the effects of relative rather than absolute compensation, and on the meaning that people attach to money. In contrast, economic theory tends to dwell on compensation as *the* motivator, to assume that work itself is aversive rather than intrinsically motivating, and to assume that differences in preferences and tastes are generally unobservable and relatively unimportant to optimal pay solutions.

The primary economic theory for explaining when different types of pay systems should be used and how to structure effective compensation contracts is *agency theory.* We introduce basic agency concepts, such as the implications of the separation of ownership from control, the potential for goal incongruity between owners and employees or "agents," and the costs of monitoring employees to ensure that they act in the interests of owners.

We close Chapter 5 with a discussion of how the choice of different pay forms (e.g., merit pay, piece rates, gainsharing) may affect workforce composition in addition to worker motivation. That is, in addition to affecting how hard or how cooperatively employees work, different pay delivery systems may also attract and retain different *types* of workers with respect to ability, personality characteristics, and values.

In Chapter 6, we review empirical evidence regarding the *effects* of alternative forms of pay for performance. We begin the chapter by introducing three central questions that must be addressed prior to designing a pay-for-performance system: whether pay will be based on behaviors versus results, the desired intensity of pay-for-performance relationships, and emphasis on individual versus group rewards. Following this general introduction, we discuss what is known about the effects of individual pay-for-behavior systems (e.g., merit pay, merit bonuses, and skill- or competency-based pay); individual pay-for-outcome systems (piece rates and sales incentives); and pay-for-group-based outcomes (e.g., gainsharing, profit sharing, stock plans).

In Chapter 7, we introduce the full complexity of compensation choices and effects by discussing pay strategies as part of the overall organizational context. We begin by documenting organizational differences in pay strategies to show that there is room for managerial discretion in pay design despite the constraints of market forces. Second, after a brief description of the concepts of *alignment* and *fit,* we introduce three types of pay strategy alignment: *vertical* (between pay strategy and organizational business strategy), *horizontal* (between pay strategy and other aspects of human resource strategy, such as selection and training), and *internal* (between various subdimensions of pay strategy, such as pay level and pay delivery). We then note how the shift in the organization strategy literature toward "looking inside" for competitive advantage (exemplified by the resource-based view of the firm) has potentially dramatic implications for the study of compensation. For example, to the extent that the resource-based view is correct, successful pay practices are less likely to be successfully imitated by others, and main effects for pay practices (i.e., best practices) may be difficult to find. Finally, we make suggestions for future research on pay strategy.

In Chapter 8, we briefly outline some of the major conclusions and areas of controversy to emerge from our book. In addition, we suggest five substantive topics for future research and make five methodological recommendations that apply across substantive areas. These include the need for improved construct validity and operationalization of importance measures; increased use of multilevel designs and multisource, multimethod data sets; increased attention to effect sizes and practical significance; and longitudinal research to reduce selection biases and to illuminate underlying or intervening processes.

2 Differences in Pay Level

WHY DO SOME COMPANIES PAY MORE THAN OTHERS?

> *Every employer constrained by market forces must consider market values in setting his labor costs. . . . Employers are, to that extent, "pricetakers." They deal with the market as a given, and do not meaningfully have a "policy" about it.*
>
> —Spaulding v. University of Washington (1984)

> *It is naïve to talk of the "competitive wage," the "equilibrium wage," or the "wage that clears the market."*
>
> —Lester (1952)

A Tale of Two Markets

As the above quotations indicate, there are rather substantial differences of opinion about the extent to which employers have discretion in setting pay levels. Those who draw on neoclassical economic theory are inclined to start from the premise that pay levels are always tending toward equality, while those who take alternative perspectives tend to believe that there are substantial and durable differences in pay for the same work across employers, even in the same geographic area (e.g., Lester, 1952; Slichter, 1950; Treiman & Hartmann, 1981). Thus, the former tend to assume that employers are, by and large, "wage takers," while the latter assume that employers have considerable discretion to act strategically in designing pay practices. This issue is of fundamental importance in compensation research, because if neoclassical economic theory is strictly correct, there is little room for employers to manage compensation. Therefore, we begin with this issue.

The Case for Limited Discretion: Neoclassical Economic Theory

In his seminal *Inquiry Into the Nature and Causes of the Wealth of Nations,* classical economist Adam Smith (1776/1976) argued that market forces would compel employers to offer jobs of roughly equal overall attractiveness and that any short-run differences in attractiveness would disappear in the long run:

> The whole of the advantages and disadvantages of the different employments of labour and stock must, in the same neighborhood, be either perfectly equal or continually tending to equality. If, in the same neighborhood, there was any employment evidently either more or less advantageous than the rest, so many people would crowd into it in the one case, and so many people would desert it in the other, that its advantages would soon return to the level of the other employments. This at least would be the case in a society where there was perfect liberty, and where every man was perfectly free both to choose what occupation he thought proper, and to change it as often as he thought proper. Every man's interest would prompt him to seek the advantageous, and to shun the disadvantageous employment. (p. 99)

Smith's (1776/1976) analysis yields several important implications. First, workers seek to maximize *total utility,* not just wages, with total utility (and thus job choice) being a function of the "whole of the advantages and disadvantages" of various jobs. Indeed, Smith explicitly identified several components of total net advantage besides pay: agreeableness or disagreeableness of the work, difficulty and expense of learning it, job security, responsibility, and the probability of success (or risk of failure). Thus, a higher wage (or *compensating wage differential*) was presumed necessary for jobs that are less pleasant, more difficult or expensive to learn, not secure, highly responsible, or that present significant risk of failure. By the same token, however, jobs that are pleasant, easy to learn, secure, and so forth could carry lower wages and still offer the same net advantages as jobs that pay more but are less attractive on these other dimensions.[1]

Second, Smith (1776/1976) believed that his model of the labor market was accurate only when workers are free to choose and move and when mobility across jobs is not prohibitively costly. Information also plays an important role, in that workers must be sufficiently well-informed to know that there are better opportunities to be had. Third, Smith assumed that net advantages across jobs were equalized *over time,* rather than instantaneously. Thus, "If there are persistent price differentials in truly similar environments, it may only be because adjustment is not quickly brought about. . . . If allowance is made for the time necessary for the allocational process to work itself out," the model will yield good results (Rottenberg, 1956, pp. 198–199).

Although Smith clearly argued that total net advantage, not price alone, was the "touchstone of occupational choice and change," 20th-century neoclassical economists developed "more elegant systems of analysis [that] *do* use price as the instrument for allocating labor among alternative uses" (Rottenberg, 1956, p. 187). This required the adoption of an additional assumption—specifically, that all nonpecuniary aspects of jobs (e.g., responsibility, agreeableness of the work) were equal. By employing this *ceteris paribus* assumption, models were developed in which labor allocation revolved solely around wages, as opposed to overall utility.

The resulting model is presented in Figure 2.1 and is probably familiar to anyone who has taken an introductory economics course. In this model, the supply of labor and the demand for labor intersect to determine wage level and employment in occupations, industries, and firms (Ehrenberg & Smith, 1988).[2] Assuming nonwage factors to be equal across alternatives, the demand curve in Figure 2.1 reflects the number of workers who would be demanded at each particular wage rate. Analogously, the supply curve reflects the number of workers who would want employment at each wage.

As Figure 2.1 shows, at the low wage rate, W_1, demand is high, but supply is low. Thus, there is a shortage of workers. In contrast, at the high wage rate, W_2, employers wish to hire fewer workers than are willing to work, resulting in a labor surplus. Thus, neither W_1 nor W_2 is an *equilibrium wage*, meaning that neither wage enables all employers to hire the desired number of workers and all workers to find acceptable jobs.

According to Figure 2.1, W_e is the equilibrium wage rate at which the market clears, and employment is equal to L_e here. Eventually, employers offering W_2 realize that they do not have to pay so much in order to hire workers, and real wages fall to W_e over time. At the same time, workers without jobs eventually realize that they can obtain a job if they are willing to accept lower wages. In contrast, at W_1, employers realize that they must pay more to attract and retain a sufficient number of qualified workers. As a result, more workers are drawn into the market by the higher rate. Thus, although the equilibrium wage does not come about immediately, the market is always adjusting in that direction.

It is further assumed that the equilibrium rate is the one faced by all workers and employers in the market. That is, no single employer or

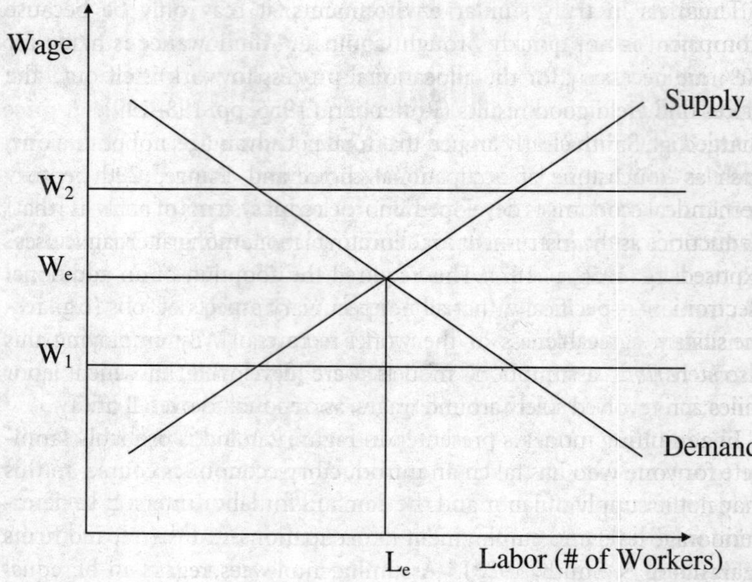

Figure 2.1 Neoclassical Model of Wage, Labor Supply, and Labor Demand

employee is assumed to be large or powerful enough to influence the overall going rate. As a result, individual employers and employees are assumed to be mere price takers, as suggested by the court in *Spaulding v. University of Washington* (1984). Moreover, in the world of well-informed and rational decision makers assumed by neoclassical economics, the observed pay policy is also the most *efficient* policy, because a firm employing suboptimal policies would soon earn less profit and eventually fail.

To put this in more concrete terms, consider what happens to an employer that pays more than its competitors. An organization that has higher labor costs than its product market competitors will, all else being equal, have to charge higher average prices for products of similar quality because organizations in a particular industry "encounter similar constraints of technology, raw materials, product demand, and pricing" (Mahoney, 1979a, p. 122; see also Dunlop, 1957; Krueger & Summers, 1988). This is likely to cause it to lose revenue and perhaps go out of business, particularly in organizations for which labor costs represent a high proportion of total operating expenses.[3]

Thus, for example, if labor costs are 30% of revenues at both Company A and Company B, but Company A has labor costs that are 20% higher than B's, we would expect Company A to have product prices that are higher by 6% (.30 × .20). At some point, the higher price charged by Company A will cause it to lose business to competitor firms such as B. Because labor is a derived demand, the reduced product demand would also be expected to reduce employment levels.[4] Reductions in market share and employment levels in U.S. industries exposed to foreign competition (such as automobiles and consumer electronics) are a case in point (Kochan & Cappelli, 1984).[5] Similarly, the sustained high unemployment rates in parts of Western Europe may also stem in part from labor costs that are higher than those just a few miles across the border (e.g., Germany versus the Czech Republic).

In addition to product market constraints, employers must also compete for employees in the labor market, where their competitors may or may not be product market competitors. Essentially, labor market competition dictates the amount an organization must pay to compete against other companies that hire similar employees, regardless of industry. For example, automobile manufacturers must compete not only with other auto companies for newly graduated electrical engineers but also with manufacturers of computers and medical devices. Labor market competition thus places a lower bound on pay levels. Employers that pay below-market rates can be expected to encounter high recruiting costs and turnover and to have greater difficulty maintaining product quality. In this way, employers are constantly pressured toward market-clearing wages that are bounded by product market competitors at the high end and labor market competitors on the bottom.

Obviously, this is a highly simplified model, a point that has been recognized for a long time. For example, Reynolds (1951) stated that "It is doubtful whether any major theorist has taken this as more than a point of departure" (p. 208). Nevertheless, the model has had a remarkably enduring effect, not only on compensation theory and research but also on employer practice. For example, employers routinely deflect criticism about "excessive" executive compensation (Crystal, 1991) or claims of pay discrimination (Rynes & Milkovich, 1986) by saying their actions are constrained and dictated by the market.

If one accepts the highly interconnected logic of the neoclassical model, then it makes little sense to talk about employers' pay policies, since the only effective "policy" is to pay what others do. Similarly, it makes little sense to empirically examine the reasons for different pay policies, since they are bound to be minor and to disappear over time. Finally, since differences in pay are always tending toward equality, it also makes little sense to examine whether some pay policies appear to be more effective than others. Thus, by starting from this model as a base, economists have been relatively slow to examine the kinds of strategic pay questions that are now regarded as most interesting among compensation researchers and corporate executives.

Post-Institutional Economics: Theory Meets Reality

Neoclassical theories of pay determination and the sanctity of the market wage went largely unchallenged until the 1940s and 1950s, when a variety of economists such as Clark Kerr, Lloyd Reynolds, Richard Lester, Charles Myers, George Schultz, and John Dunlop put the model up against empirical reality (Kaufman, 1999; Segal, 1986). To an important degree, circumstances demanded that they do so. For example, during the Great Depression of 1931 to 1940, the annual unemployment rate in the United States never dropped below 14%, peaking at 25% in 1933. With unemployment of this magnitude and persistence, it was increasingly difficult to argue that the market was clearing, as would have been predicted by the neoclassical model.

Second, each of these economists worked at the National War Labor Board during World War II, which was created to assure reliable wartime production through strike avoidance and inflation control (Katz & Kochan, 1992). In meeting its charge of settling disputes and making recommendations regarding wages, the board and its economists were frequently faced with "interplant, geographical, and other wage differentials that the traditional models of labor market operations could not readily account for" (Segal, 1986, pp. 397–398). In addition, they observed that a number of "institutional" forces, such as historical precedent, unions, equity beliefs, and ability to pay also seemed to play major roles in how pay was administered in organizations, consistent with earlier work by John R. Commons and other members of Wisconsin's "institutional school" of economics.

Kerr, Dunlop, and their colleagues have been referred to as *post-institutionalists* (or sometimes *neoinstitutionalists*) because of their balanced regard for both institutional and market forces.[6] In Segal's (1986) view, the most distinct contribution of the neoinstitutional school was to direct attention to the actual operation of labor markets. In contrast to the neoclassical school, the post-institutionalists were willing to entertain the notion that market forces did not always work exactly as suggested by textbook models. In fact, their examination of actual pay levels cast a shadow over the neoclassical construct of the market rate:

> Economists who have made detailed comparative studies of wage rates within a plant or between plants in the same labor market area are struck by the haphazard variations in such rates.... Actual wage facts seem contrary to what one might expect according to conventional wage theory. Demand and supply do not eliminate gross "inequities" or gross irrationality. Perfect competition seems to be the exception rather than the rule. (Lester, 1946, p. 152)

For example, an analysis of 2,900 occupations in 48 different areas surveyed by the U.S. Bureau of Labor Statistics in 1943 and 1944 found that the straight-time hourly earnings of males in the same occupation were on average 50% higher in the highest-paying plant than in the lowest-paying plant in a community (Lester, 1946). Dunlop (1957) observed a differential of nearly 100% between Boston truckers in the magazine industry versus those working in scrap iron and metal, despite the fact that they were performing almost identical work and were represented by the same union. Slichter (1950), too, observed that there were differences in wages for the same job across industries and that these differences appeared to be fairly stable over time. Moreover, Slichter observed that the wages of low-skilled workers tended to covary with those of high-skilled workers in the same industries, leading him to suggest that managerial policy played a role in creating wage differentials that was not captured by the standard neoclassical model. More recently, Treiman and Hartmann (1981) reported a 267% differential in the pay of forklift operators in the Newark, New Jersey labor market.

The types of differentials discovered by the post-institutionalists are not merely historical. Current data show that pay rates vary across a number of organizational characteristics. For example, organizational size has a substantial impact, with labor cost per worker being 57% higher in establishments having 500 or more employees than in companies having less than 100. Similarly, Table 2.1 shows that workers covered by collective bargaining contracts command 36% higher total compensation than those not covered. In addition, goods-producing industries (e.g., manufacturing) pay more than twice as much as retail industries (see Table 2.2). Finally, there are large differences in pay levels across nations (see Table 2.3), as well as across different metropolitan areas for the same narrowly defined occupations (see Table 2.4).

Table 2.1 Total Labor Costs per Hour Worked in Private Industry, by Establishment Size and Collective Bargaining Coverage

Establishment Size	*Hourly Labor Cost*	*Percentage of All Establishment Mean*
All	$19.85	100%
1-99 Employees	$17.16	86%
100-499	$19.30	97%
500 or more	$26.93	136%
Covered By Collective Bargaining		
Yes	$25.88	130%
No	$19.07	96%

SOURCE: U.S. Bureau of Labor Statistics (2000).

Table 2.2 Total Labor Costs and Wages and Salaries per Hour Worked in Private Industry, by Major Industry Group

	Total Labor Costs	*Wages and Salaries*
All Workers	*$19.85 (100%)*	*$14.49 (73%)*
By Industry		
Goods-producing	$23.55	$16.25
Service-producing	$18.72	$13.95
Transportation & public utilities	$25.84	$17.73
Wholesale trade	$22.12	$15.90
Retail trade	$10.99	$8.73
Finance, insurance, real estate	$26.97	$19.30
Services	$19.73	$14.93

SOURCE: U.S. Bureau of Labor Statistics (2000).

Multivariate studies using more recent data than the post-institutionalists also document the existence of employer differences in pay (Gerhart & Milkovich, 1990; Groshen, 1988, 1991; Leonard, 1990). Groshen (1991) examined sources of wage variance within six manufacturing industries. Controlling for detailed occupation codes, sex, incentive eligibility, union status, and industry (by virtue of conducting analyses

Table 2.3 Hourly Total Compensation Costs for Production Workers in Manufacturing, by Country, 2001

	Hourly Total Compensation Cost	*Percent of U.S.*
United States	$20.32	100%
Japan	$19.59	96%
Europe	$18.38	90%
Germany	$22.86	112%
U.K.	$16.14	79%
Spain	$10.88	53%
Hong Kong, South Korea, Singapore, & Taiwan	$6.95	34%
Mexico	$2.34	12%

SOURCE: U.S. Bureau of Labor Statistics (2001b).

Table 2.4 Geographic Wage Differentials

	Median Hourly Wage, 2001			
	Computer Engineers	*Carpenters*	*Registered Nurses*	*Financial Managers*
Nashville, TN	$27	$14	$23	$28
Lincoln, NE	$25	$13	$20	$27
New York, NY	$35	$22	$28	$54
San Francisco, CA	$35	$27	$32	$45
High/Low ratio	1.4	2.1	1.6	2.0

SOURCE: U.S. Bureau of Labor Statistics (2001c).

within narrow industries), she found that establishment differences accounted for 21% to 58% of the variance of pay level within industries, with the median being 30%. Groshen assumed that the detailed occupational controls would serve as a good proxy for human capital differences, but she did not directly measure or control for human capital variables.

Leonard (1990) was able to control for a set of human capital variables, as well as occupation, job level, and sales, in a study of a much different sample: middle- and top-level executives. He reported that approximately

8% of the variance in cash compensation (base plus bonus) was due to firm differences. However, we note that the category having the largest variance (64%) was "joint effects" of the variables he studied, meaning that it was not possible to separate the variance sources, because the variables were correlated. (For example, human capital is higher in some firms than in others, and these firms tend to pay more. It is not possible to tell to what degree the higher pay results from a firm effect or a human capital effect.) Presumably, some portion of the joint effects were due to firm differences. For the sake of comparison, note that the firm effect was larger than that for occupation (2.2%) and human capital (1.1%) and nearly as large as for job level (10.4%).

In addition to pay level, Gerhart and Milkovich (1990) looked at differences in *how* organizations paid managers, by measuring the ratio of annual bonus payments to base pay, and the percentage of managers eligible for long-term incentives. They used data on roughly 16,000 managers from the top six levels at roughly 200 organizations and followed them over a period of up to 5 years. Controlling for differences in human capital, job level, and organization characteristics, they found significant and stable employer differences in base pay over the 5-year period.

However, Gerhart and Milkovich (1990) found even larger stable employer differences in the degree to which their compensation was composed of a fixed component (i.e., base salary) versus a variable component (i.e., annual bonus and long-term incentive plans). They inferred that although organizations had some discretion regarding *how much* they paid, they had even more regarding *how* they paid (i.e., the mix between fixed and variable components). Their explanation for the difference in discretion used the same logic that we described earlier: that labor market pressures (paying enough to attract and retain employees of acceptable quality) set a floor for pay level, while product market pressures (keeping labor costs low enough to maintain product price competitiveness) set a ceiling. On the other hand, the same amount of pay could be delivered in a variety of ways. Haire, Ghiselli, and Gordon (1967) had made the same point a few decades earlier: Organizations may have more discretion in terms of how they pay (versus how much), because delivery systems "can be varied by a company without increasing the total salary expense" (p. 10). A key implication of this finding is that focusing exclusively on pay level (e.g., as in efficiency wage models, which are discussed shortly), probably ignores some of the most significant and most interesting differences in compensation practices and strategies.

In summary, based on their studies of the actual functioning of labor markets, the post-institutionalist economists identified a number of important limitations of the mainstream economic model of the labor market. Resource 2.1 provides additional information on these limitations and the neoclassical economics response. These contributions by post-institutionalist economists have had a major impact on thinking in compensation, where the importance of jobs, internal labor markets, and employer differences are now central. The multivariate studies reviewed above reinforce the importance of these concepts.

In contrast, for several decades, these limitations and the importance of the concepts just noted were largely ignored or dismissed by mainstream economists. However, things change. The importance of nonmarket factors such as administrative rules, internal labor markets (see Chapter 4), and employer differences are now finally being recognized by neoclassical economics. Transaction cost economics, personnel economics, and other perspectives have increasingly sought to extend the neoclassical model to understand how the market actually works. According to Boyer and Smith (2001):

> The stated mission of the neoinstitutionalists—causing simple price theory to adapt to the unique realities of the labor market—seems to be on its way to fulfillment. Neoclassical labor economists are now—at long last, some would say—addressing some of the issues that had so consumed the interest of the neoinstitutionalists. (p. 218)

We now examine how formal economic theory has begun to incorporate the findings of the neoinstitutionalists and how strategic perspectives have already done so.

Why It May "Pay" to Pay More

> A relatively high wage level has many advantages to the firm. It simplifies the recruitment problem. Even though the company might be able to get enough workers at a lower wage level, it can get them faster and with less persuasion at higher wages. It can also establish strict hiring specifications designed to fill the plant with a "nice class of worker." . . . The company may also be able to insist on better-than-average efficiency, so that higher wages do not produce a proportionate increase in unit labor costs. . . . A high wage level also has public relations value for the firm. (Reynolds, 1951, p. 232)

Efficiency Wage Theories

Drawing on the observations of post-institutionalists such as Reynolds, Slichter, Dunlop, and Lester, mainstream economists have more recently elaborated on the idea that paying above-market rates might help organizations realize increased effectiveness. This can happen in one of two ways: by generating higher amounts of effort among current employees (an *incentive* effect) or by attracting higher-quality or more conscientious employees in the first place (a *sorting* effect).

However, some firms are believed to have more incentive than others to pay high wages (Krueger & Summers, 1988). For example, organizations that put greater discretion in the hands of employees are likely to be more dependent on their efforts and abilities, and hence to pay higher (i.e., efficiency) wages. Similarly, firms that make greater use of work teams or computer-assisted manufacturing may pay more in order to generate a larger and stronger applicant pool, which permits more intensive screening and selective hiring of applicants. Alternatively, some firms may have more difficulty monitoring employee behavior because of the scale of the organization, the complexity of the work, or the geographic dispersion of employees. If so, efficiency wages might be seen as a way to spur effort and reduce *shirking* in the absence of close (and expensive) supervision.

Consider the scale or size of a firm, for example, which we have seen has a substantial positive impact on wage rates. What is the rationale for this strong positive relationship between size and wages? Take the case of highly paid professionals or executives. One efficiency wage explanation is that larger organizations are better able to leverage worker ability. Milkovich and Newman (1999), for example, note that David Letterman makes a great deal more money now as host of his own show at CBS than he used to make doing the weather at a small local news station. At CBS, he reaches a greater audience, so his ability has more value. (On this issue, see also Frank & Cook, 1995.) A top executive at a large organization will have greater information-processing demands (Henderson & Fredrickson, 1996) and greater responsibility than an executive at a small organization. The upside (creation of wealth) and downside of poor executive performance (loss of wealth) are more extreme in larger firms. For example, General Electric (GE) has a market capitalization of $455 billion as of mid-2001. Even a small hiccough in performance in percentage terms would lead to a tremendous decrease in value. Compared with the top executive at, say, a $100,000 market capitalization firm, there is a great deal more at stake at GE.

The (economic) rationale for hourly workers being paid more in larger firms is less clear (Brown & Medoff, 1989). As noted, larger firms and establishments may encounter more difficult monitoring problems and thus are more concerned about shirking. Another possibility is that larger firms use production technologies that require a higher-quality workforce. This may be more an issue of ability than of controlling shirking. However, standard human capital variables (e.g., educational attainment, workforce experience) do not fully capture differences in workforce quality, as is indicated by the fact that the size effect is large even after they are controlled (Brown & Medoff, 1989; Mellow, 1982).[7] Therefore, controlling for these standard human capital variables does not necessarily make the size effect go away, but some evidence suggests that controlling for other proxies for workforce quality may have an influence. For example, in a study of small firms (mean number of employees = 135), Reilly (1995) found that whether an establishment had access to a computer predicted wages and that adding this variable to the wage equation eliminated the impact of establishment size on wages. Likewise, Bayard and Troske (1999) report that greater productivity of workers in larger establishments accounted for half the effect of establishment size on wages. (For a similar argument, see also Idson & Oi, 1999.)

Several different variations of efficiency wage theory focus on different mechanisms by which efficiency wages spur effort or permit greater selectivity (see Groshen, 1988). The first, *sorting by ability*, argues that some employers may choose higher rates of pay as a means of hiring and retaining higher-ability employees. Conversely, this model is sometimes referred to as the *adverse selection* model, reflecting the presumption that high-ability employees will shun low-wage employers.

In focusing on ability, efficiency wage theorists drew on earlier work of human capital theorists such as Gary Becker (1975) and Jacob Mincer (e.g., Mincer, 1974; Mincer & Polachek, 1974), who argued that workers invest in their own productive capacity (through education, on-the-job training, and health care) as a means of enhancing future rates of return to their employment. Prior to the development of human capital theory, economists had paid little attention to the potential importance of quality differences between workers. Rather, labor was treated much like any other commodity in the production process and was conceptualized for the most part as homogeneous standardized units. Table 2.5 shows how earnings vary by education level and by age (a rough proxy for labor market experience and training).

However, with the growing focus on price theory in neoclassical economics, it was a natural step to focus on the question of why different workers commanded different prices for their services. In addition, human capital theory provided a means of responding to post-institutionalists'

Table 2.5 Usual Weekly Earnings, Full-Time Workers, by Age and Education Level, 2001

Age	*Weekly Earnings*	*Percent of Average*
All (25 and over)	$624	100%
25-34	$578	93%
35-44	$647	104%
45-54	$683	109%
55-64	$627	100%
65 & over	$488	78%
Education	*Weekly Earnings*	*Percent of Average*
All (age 25 and over)	$624	100%
Less than high school	$371	59%
High school, no college	$513	82%
Some college or associate degree	$613	98%
Bachelor's degree	$857	137%
Advanced degree	$1,058	170%

SOURCE: U.S. Bureau of Labor Statistics (2001d).

observations that the large differences in pay across employers seemed to exist largely as a sorting mechanism for workers of varying quality.

Of course, for this model to work in practice, employers must have an effective means of distinguishing high- from low-ability applicants. Utility theory, which will be discussed in the next chapter, is useful for showing how changes in employer selectivity interact with other factors to influence the overall utility of employing a higher-quality workforce.

The second group of efficiency wage models, *shirking/monitoring and turnover* models, posit that high wages can be helpful for dealing with the difficulty of monitoring and measuring employee performance. Because of difficulties with performance monitoring, workers are sometimes able to shirk without enduring a payment penalty (Yellen, 1984). For example, Lazear (1979) argues that without an appropriate payment system, workers have an "incentive to cheat, shirk, and engage in malfeasant behavior" (p. 1266). This view is consistent with the neoclassicists' model of the choice between labor and leisure, in which workers are assumed to prefer leisure but must work to fund their consumption of goods and services.

Thus, the work itself is not something that has motivational value to workers in the neoclassical model. Rather, the emphasis is on extrinsic reinforcers, particularly pay but also monitoring and supervision.

Yellen (1984) proposes that one way to discourage shirking is to set pay levels above what a worker can obtain elsewhere. By so doing, workers will be less likely to shirk, because they do not wish to risk losing the wage premium. The alternatives, by definition, are either a lower-paying job (with a non–efficiency wage employer), or unemployment (Yellen, 1984). Note that it is not only the higher wage but also the risk of losing that higher wage that discourages shirking. One proxy for the risk of job loss is the unemployment rate, because a higher unemployment rate implies that a worker can be more easily replaced with someone of comparable ability. In this sense, "Unemployment plays a socially valuable role in creating work incentives" (Yellen, 1984).[8]

In contrast to other efficiency wage models, the *gift exchange* variant has less of a neoclassical economics orientation, focusing more on social conventions (Yellen, 1984). Akerlof's (1984) "partial gift exchange" model suggests that "Some firms willingly pay workers in excess of the market-clearing wage," in return for which "They expect workers to supply more effort" (p. 79). Or as Yellen describes it, firms pay "workers a gift of wages in excess of the minimum required, in return for their gift of effort above the minimum required" (1984, p. 204). Akerlof cites Adams's (1965) work on overreward inequity as empirical support for this model. However, he does acknowledge that "Not all studies reproduce the result that 'overpaid' workers will produce more" (Akerlof, 1984, p. 82).

Indeed, a problem with the gift exchange variant is its assumption that perceived overreward is a compelling force for increasing worker effort and productivity. In fact, research shows that overreward inequity is very difficult to obtain and maintain, especially outside the laboratory (for reviews, see Campbell & Pritchard, 1976; Kanfer, 1990). Rather, it appears that many people who initially feel overpaid soon come to reevaluate the value of their inputs, thus restoring a sense of equity through enhanced self-concept rather than increased effort or output. Therefore, there does not appear to be a strong empirical basis for the belief that higher wages will induce greater effort simply because of overreward inequity.

Rent-Sharing or Ability-to-Pay Models

Closely related to efficiency wage theories are *rent-sharing* or *ability-to-pay* models. *Rent* is "a return received in an activity that is in excess of the minimum needed to attract the resources to that activity" (Milgrom & Roberts, 1992, p. 603). In rent-sharing models, firms with above-normal profits (due, perhaps, to monopoly power or effective business strategies) are assumed to share these rents with workers in the form of higher compensation. In other words, a rent (or quasi-rent)[9] is paid to workers, such that the pay level is higher than necessary to attract and retain workers. Presumably, the rent-sharing model rules out the possibility that higher compensation is used for other efficiency purposes, such as to control shirking and enhance effort.

A recent study by Hildreth and Oswald (1997) sought to test the rent-sharing model against the neoclassical model by examining the influence of current profits on future wages as far as 6 years into the future. In a pure neoclassical model, no relationship between profits and pay would exist, especially in the longer run. On the other hand, a rent-sharing model would predict a positive relationship. Hildreth and Oswald found a positive influence of profits on subsequent wages, even using a 6-year lag, which they interpreted as supportive of a rent-sharing model. They estimated that firms near the top of the profit distribution paid wages that were roughly 16% higher than firms near the bottom of the profit distribution, an estimate that Hildreth and Oswald noted as being quite close to that provided by Lester (1964, p. 328), several decades earlier.

Whether rent-sharing and ability-to-pay theories are really different from efficiency wage theories is not clear. For example, Krueger and Summers say the two are "intimately related" because the "reason firms share rents is presumably that failure to do so will result in their workforce not cooperating with it by quitting, shirking, or otherwise interfering with production" (1988, p. 280). Thus, they view rent-sharing as "a species of efficiency wage theory."

Coff (1999) has raised the point that competitive advantage and financial performance (e.g., profit or total shareholder return) do not necessarily go together, because different stakeholders (shareholders, managers, employees) compete for the same economic rents. In his view, the relative power of these stakeholder groups determines the allocation. Although his main emphasis was not on the efficiency implications of power as the means of allocation, he does note that employees "can often hold up other stakeholders or threaten to quit" (p. 125), which certainly is relevant to short-run efficiency and so would seem to fit with Krueger and Summers's argument.

Business Strategy

Also consistent with efficiency wage theory is the idea that because of their business strategies, certain employers may find high-ability or highly motivated workers more valuable. Recent studies conducted in telecommunications (Batt, 2001) and health care (Hunter, 2000) suggest that wages and skill requirements vary substantially within industry for the same occupation as a function of the type of market and customer that is the focus of the business strategy. Firms focusing on more of a differentiation (as opposed to a cost leadership) business strategy may need more able and motivated workers and may use high wages as one means of building this sort of workforce.

Batt's (2001) study looked at the influence of several sets of factors on earnings of sales and service workers in a nationally representative sample of call centers in four telecommunications 4-digit Standard Industrial Classification (SIC) codes: cellular, wireline, cable TV, and Internet service providers (ISPs). In addition to these industry categories, earnings determinants included additional establishment level variables (e.g., size, union status), human capital, human resource practices (e.g., worker discretion), and our main interest here, business strategy, which was defined in terms of the type of customer the strategy emphasized: large business, small business, residential, or operator services. The key finding from Batt's study was that business strategy had a substantial effect on earnings. For example, a focus on large-business customers was associated with 68% higher earnings, compared with a strategy where there was no dominant customer focus. This was after controlling for industry, union status, size, and other establishment characteristics. Adding human capital and human resource variables resulted in a substantial decline in the strategy-earnings relationship to a 19% advantage. Batt interpreted this change from 68% to 19% as evidence of a sorting effect. Establishments focusing on large-business customers have higher hiring standards in part because the human resource strategies they use (e.g., greater discretion in decision making) require more capable and motivated workers.

The International Dimension

Although there are substantial differences in pay levels between employers within countries, these often pale in comparison to differences across countries (see Table 2.3). Why is this the case? Do employers get more

Table 2.6 Gross Domestic Product per Person Employed, by Country, 1997

Country	
U.S.	128
Japan	106
European Union	90
Germany	96
U.K.	92
Spain	71
Hong Kong, South Korea, Singapore, & Taiwan	62
Latin America	25
Mexico	22
OECD Average	100

SOURCE: van Ark & McGuckin (1999).
NOTE: (OECD) Organization for Economic Cooperation and Development.

effort or output from employees in high-wage countries? One way to address this question is to compare productivity across countries. Ideally, we would like to have comparable data on unit labor costs, defined as the cost to produce a standardized unit of output. Unfortunately, such data are not available. There are, however, data on gross domestic product (GDP) per person employed, which we present in Table 2.6. These data are expressed as a percentage of most of the countries in the Organization for Economic Cooperation and Development (OECD). Although these data are coarse and are confounded with a number of factors (e.g., average hours worked per person employed), some broad-brush comparisons may nevertheless be of interest.

The United States has the highest productivity (128% of the OECD average) of any country included in the study.[10] Note that Germany is lower than the average, at 96% of the OECD average. Recall, however, that Germany's labor cost per hour was much higher than that of the United States. (Table 2.3 indicates a difference of 12% in 2001. The difference was 36% as recently as 1999.) This combination of high labor costs and low productivity helps explain the fact that the unemployment rate in Germany in 2000 was about twice as high as that in the United States (8.3% versus 4.0%). Mexico, which we saw had relatively low labor costs, also turns out to have relatively low productivity, which to some degree offsets any cost advantage it may have realized. In summary, the evidence suggests that countries with relatively high labor costs may nevertheless offer a good return on investment because of higher productivity.

We make two other observations. First, as Alfred Marshall noted many years ago, high labor costs may be less of an issue in cases where they represent a small portion of total costs. For example, if labor cost represents 15% of total cost, then despite the fact that Taiwan's labor costs are only 32% of those in the United States, the total cost of production in Taiwan would still be 90% of that in the United States. Whether this would be enough of a savings to justify locating production in Taiwan on a cost basis alone is unclear. Knowing that the average productivity (see above) in Taiwan is 62% of the U.S. average would probably argue against the cost advantage being sufficient. The important caveat to this is that if all other costs are relatively fixed and beyond the control of the company, even small differences in labor cost may be critical.[11]

Second, economy-wide data can obscure important differences in relative productivity of specific industries or of firms within industries. For example, General Motors (GM) has two truck assembly plants in Mexico that employ more than 70,000 workers, who earn approximately $10 per day, much less than the $220 per day in wages and benefits earned by comparable GM workers in the United States. However, it would be a mistake to infer from national productivity data that the Mexican plants are not competitive with the U.S. plants. In fact, one of the Mexican plants, Silao, has ranked number one in GM's internal studies of quality and is considered GM's manufacturing showplace (Woodyard, 1998).

Differences in Pay Levels for Particular Jobs

To this point, we have shown that some employers routinely pay more than do other employers for all types of work and presented theories and evidence as to why they might do so. However, in some cases, employers appear to pay above-market wages for some jobs, but not others. Although they may or may not pay a higher overall wage bill than other employers, the incidence of "special" rates for particular jobs deserves at least brief mention in this chapter, as they are undoubtedly part of the reason that market rates often vary widely for specific types of work in a given locale.

In this chapter, we discuss only a few of the reasons why employers might single out certain jobs or job families for more favorable pay treatment. More detailed discussion of these issues will be pursued later in Chapters 4 (Pay Structure) and 7 (Pay Strategy).

Differences in Pay Structure

Across all jobs, an organization may pay a wage bill that is roughly the same as that of other employers. However, within that overall level, an employer may choose alternative *pay structures*, which generally refer to variability in pay across jobs within a given organization. (This contrasts with pay level, which refers to variability in pay across employers.) Organizations that pay their executives far more than their entry level employees are said to have steep pay structures, while those with more egalitarian distributions are said to have flat structures.

Why might some employers choose to create steeper-than-average pay structures than others? One reason may be to induce greater retention of workers by offering larger incentives for promotion. This may be particularly important if the skills needed to execute an organization's strategy tend to be firm specific (e.g., Becker, 1975; Doeringer & Piore, 1971). In that case, retention of employees will be considerably more crucial to employers because such skills, by definition, cannot be "bought" on the external market. Alternatively, higher-than-average promotion incentives may be used to induce high effort by offering very lucrative "prizes" (i.e., wages) for a small number of workers who are promoted to the highest-level jobs; this is known as a *tournament model* (Lazear & Rosen, 1981).

Alternatively, employers may decide to *reduce* the payoffs to promotion and seniority relative to other employers. When this action is taken, it is usually for the purpose of encouraging greater harmony, shared vision, and cooperation among workers. A well-known example of this pay strategy is Ben & Jerry's, which for many years limited the salary ratio between top-level executives and entry level employees to a 5-to-1 (and later 7-to-1) ratio.[12] Although few companies have set up such explicit egalitarian structures, a significant number of companies have followed some type of egalitarian strategy in an attempt to increase corporate loyalty and identification (e.g., Gallup, Mars Candy, A.G. Edwards, Chick-Filet; see Olian & Rynes, 1991; Reichheld, 1996).

Business Strategy

Another reason that employers may distribute the same overall pay level differentially across job levels or job types is that some jobs may be more important than others for executing the organization's strategy (Gerhart & Milkovich, 1992). For example, to the extent that, say, Web designers are more important to e-commerce firms than to mortar-and-brick companies, e-commerce employers are more dependent than other employers on successful attraction and retention of high-quality Web developers. The idea of paying more to attract and retain high-quality employees in critical positions, known as *resource dependence theory* (see Pfeffer & Davis-Blake, 1992), is similar in some respects to the premises of efficiency wage theory, except that in this case the strategy is followed selectively for only those jobs that are particularly important to an organization's strategic execution (Carpenter & Wade, 2002).

Measurement: What Do We Mean by Pay Level?

Finally, we need to recognize that organizations having the same pay level may appear to differ if our definitions and measures of pay level are deficient. For example, an organization such as Lincoln Electric may pay below-average base pay, but it would be erroneous to conclude that Lincoln has a below-market pay level, because most of its compensation comes in the form of performance-contingent pay. This includes programs such as profit sharing, stock, and individual incentive plans that when properly accounted for, usually far exceed average market compensation. As another example, SAS is also not known for its high salaries, but it does have a very lucrative benefits package.

Yet as we review empirical research, we will see that pay level is typically defined as *wage rate.* This may not be a major problem in some studies in which it can be assumed that benefits and performance-contingent pay are similar across employers. However, empirical evidence suggests that there is in fact great variance in how employers allocate given sums of money to managers and executives (e.g., Gerhart, 2000), and there is also increasing variance in pay form between employers for all types of employees (R. Heneman, Ledford, & Gresham, 2000).

Research on Pay Level Decision Making

Given the clear evidence of large differences in pay levels across employers and various theories as to why this is the case, one would expect to find a considerable amount of research devoted to testing these theories and explaining observed differentials. Surprisingly, however, few studies have directly attempted to investigate how managers make decisions about pay levels. Rather, for the most part we are left to *infer* pay level decision processes on the basis of observed pay levels (e.g., Rynes & Bono, 2000). As such, we do not really know whether most managers think like efficiency wage theorists in setting pay levels (although anecdotal evidence from the post-institutional economics era suggests that they might) or how they make trade-offs between higher pay levels and other forms of pay such as benefits or profit sharing.

Still, public statements by corporations suggest that there are indeed differences in pay level (and basis) across organizations and that these differences are designed to achieve particular objectives. For example, of the three companies represented in Exhibit 2.1, Coca-Cola appears to be the most aggressive in terms of pay for performance (heavy emphasis on stock price and pay at risk); selection of benchmark companies (highest performers on long-term profits and return on equity among large public companies, including those outside the food-and-beverage industry); and target pay level (top quartile on total compensation). In contrast, Ford appears to benchmark relatively more on company size and reputation, and aims to meet rather than exceed the market on executive pay.

The processes by which such decisions are actually made (as opposed to how they are explained to the public *after* they are made) are typically clothed in secrecy, although occasionally a former executive or compensation consultant decides to lift the veil and reveal the inner workings of compensation committees (e.g., Crystal, 1991). In contrast, academic research on the subject has been much more prosaic.

For example, Viswesvaran and Barrick (1992) examined the criteria used by human resource managers in choosing which companies to include in a pay survey. This is a potentially important decision, since the set of companies chosen for benchmarking could have a fairly dramatic impact on ultimate pay levels (Rynes & Milkovich, 1986). To examine the selection process, Viswesvaran and Barrick collected data on pay survey choices from 35 compensation specialists holding positions such as vice president of human resources and compensation manager. Respondents were given a brief description of a hypothetical firm that wished to establish the market wage for the job of "secretary." They were then given information on other hypothetical firms and asked to rate how likely they would be to include data from these firms in establishing a market rate.

Actually, respondents made two decisions: whether to include the firm in an initial survey and then whether to retain the firm in the subset of firms used in the actual data analysis. This second step is necessary because data quality cannot be evaluated until after survey data are

Exhibit 2.1 Examples of Executive Compensation Strategies at Various Companies

Coca-Cola

The Company emphasizes total compensation opportunities and focuses less attention on the competitive posture of each component of compensation. The development of at-risk pay policies is driven more by Company strategy than by competitive practice. Over time, the level of the Company's competitiveness in compensation opportunities is based heavily on the Company's stock price performance relative to other large companies. In line with this principle, current total compensation competitiveness is targeted in the top quartile of the range of total compensation of a comparator group of companies described in the next section of this report. . . . The Company seeks talent from a broader group of companies than the Food, Beverage and Tobacco Groups against which performance is compared.

Total compensation comparators are selected by screening large public companies for such performance characteristics as profit growth and return on equity. Those companies exhibiting leadership in the performance measures over sustained periods are selected as benchmarks for the Company's total compensation standards.

Ford

The Compensation Committee wants the compensation of Ford executives to be competitive in the worldwide auto industry and with major U.S. companies. Each year, the Committee reviews a report from an outside consultant on Ford's compensation program for executives. The report discusses all aspects of compensation as well as how Ford's program compares with those of other large companies. Based on this report, its own review of various parts of the program, and its assessment of the skills, experience, and achievements of individual executives, the Committee decides the compensation of executives.

(Continued)

Exhibit 2.1 (Continued)

The consultant develops compensation data using a survey of several leading companies picked by the consultant and Ford. General Motors and Chrysler were included in the survey. Eighteen leading companies in other industries also were included because the job market for executives goes beyond the auto industry. Companies were picked based on size, reputation, and business complexity.

The Committee looks at the size and success of the companies and the types of jobs covered by the survey in determining executive compensation. One goal of Ford's compensation program is to approximate the survey group's average compensation, adjusted for company size and performance.

Procter & Gamble

When the Company achieves solid earnings growth and stock price appreciation, executive compensation levels will be expected to equal or exceed the middle compensation range for a comparative group of companies. This group includes a combination of leading consumer products companies and other corporations of size and reputation comparable to Procter & Gamble (and with which Procter & Gamble must compete in hiring and retaining the employees it needs). The composition of this group is updated periodically in order to assure its continued relevance.

The Committee believes the compensation levels of the Company's executive officers are competitive and in line with those of comparable companies. This conclusion is derived in part from consultations with independent outside compensation consultants.

SOURCE: Excerpts from Coca-Cola, Ford, and Procter & Gamble Proxy Statements, 1998 (available at www.sec.gov).

collected; thus, firms that are initially chosen might later be rejected for problems with data quality or poor job matching. Respondents were asked to judge 50 descriptions of firms for the first decision and 45 firms for the second decision.

Viswesvaran and Barrick (1992) manipulated the characteristics of the potential benchmark firms as follows. In the first decision step, firm descriptions varied by union status (yes/no), industry similarity (4 levels), geographic location (4 levels, ranging from "nearby" to "100 miles away in a medium-sized city"), organization size (5 levels), and hiring practices of the firm (5 levels, from "seldom hires" to "frequently hires secretaries"). For the second decision step, potential benchmark firms varied according to the method used to collect information (phone interview, mailed survey, personal interview), source of data (clerk, human resources generalist, compensation specialist), degree of job match (5 levels), completeness of reported data (3 levels: base pay only; base pay plus incentives and overtime; and base pay, incentives, overtime, and benefits), and completeness of data describing the benchmark firm (5 levels).

Importance weights of these factors were derived in two ways: policy-capturing and self-reported weights, with the latter being based on respondents allocating 100 points to the factors based on their importance in each of the two steps. The self-reported weights were provided after respondents had worked through the 50 scenarios for the first decision and the 45 scenarios for the second decision.

A key finding was that the importance of factors differed, depending on the method. For example, for the decision about which firms to include in the initial survey, union status was the most important factor based on self-reported weights, but geographic location was most important based on policy-capturing decisions. For the second decision (which data to use in the final analysis), the self-report method indicated that method of gathering data was most important, whereas quality of job match was far and away the most important criterion based on the policy-capturing results. These discrepancies between self-reported and policy-capturing weights raise the intriguing possibility that differences in pay level might occur through unintentional decision processes rather than through differences in strategic intent.

A more recent policy-capturing study on pay survey use was conducted by Trevor and Graham (2000). They were interested in the amount of weight given to product market (concern for controlling costs) versus labor market (concern for being able to attract and retain employees) considerations in pay setting as a function of job pay level (above or below $40,000), labor-to-total-cost ratio, attraction and retention difficulty, and job type. Among the jobs Trevor and Graham asked about were core jobs (defined as nonmanagerial jobs directly involved in providing the primary product or service, such as lawyer in a law firm or driver at a delivery service), noncore jobs (e.g., a lawyer at a software firm) and managerial jobs (jobs with managerial but not executive level responsibility). Each of 17 compensation professionals evaluated 16 pay scenarios, for a total of 272 observations.

Trevor and Graham (2000) found that core jobs and higher pay levels were associated with greater reliance on product market (presumably reflecting ability-to-pay concerns) as opposed to labor market comparisons.[13] These findings are consistent with earlier field evidence, which suggested that product market considerations generally outweighed labor markets in pay setting (e.g., Reynolds, 1951; Slichter, 1950) at least among blue-collar workers. Surprisingly, however, Trevor and Graham (2000) found that neither labor-cost-to-total-cost ratio nor attraction and retention difficulty predicted degree of emphasis on product market competitors. Why? As always, it is possible that the findings are sample specific.[14] Or it may be that the respondents simply made decisions based on something other than current market conditions, consistent with the argument of post-institutionalists. In any case, little work has been done on the relative importance of product market and labor market factors in influencing pay decisions. There are, however, some interesting related studies that have been conducted in the area of executive pay. Although we recognize that this is a small and unique group in many ways, we nevertheless discuss these studies for their insights into pay decision processes.

Porac, Wade, and Pollock (1999) sought to examine the factors that determined the choice of benchmark firms by boards of directors in setting the pay of chief executive officers (CEOs) in S&P 500 firms. The main source of information was the proxy report that these firms are required to file annually with the Securities and Exchange Commission (SEC). A key aspect of this report is a description by the compensation committee of the board of directors regarding its description and rationale for executive pay at the firm. A key dependent variable was the number of firms selected as benchmarks that were from within the same industry relative to the number selected from outside the industry. Industry was measured at the 2-digit level of the SIC, which ranges from 1-digit (broadest grouping) to 4-digit (narrowest grouping, most similar firms). Forty-eight different SIC codes were used.

Similar to versions of efficiency wage theory that emphasize social considerations in pay setting, Porac et al. (1999) investigated the extent to which executive pay-setting processes appeared to be influenced by political and social (as well as efficiency) objectives. Like Crystal (1991), they highlight the effects of power and politics and the interests of organizational actors in rationalizing decisions that while being in their self-interests, are subsequently communicated to shareholders as having an efficiency basis: "Organizations have been shown to be quite ingenious in packaging their accounts and rationalizations for delivery to external constituencies. Explanations for corporate performance are worded quite carefully to deflect blame from management" (Porac et al., 1999, p. 116). Thus, Porac et al. expected that while the primary source of benchmark companies should come from within a firm's industry (reflecting efficiency considerations), compensation committees may also be tempted to look outside the industry for benchmark firms that will make the subject firm look better. That is, if a company has had a worse year than the rest of its industry, its performance can be made to look better by adding firms from outside industries that also underperformed the market.

Thus, a key dependent variable in the Porac et al. (1999) study was the relative number of benchmark firms chosen from within—as opposed to outside—the industry. Samplewide, Porac et al. reported that 69% of benchmark firms were from within the industry and 31% outside. The average number of firms in a benchmark group was 19.55, with 12% of firms using more than one benchmark group.

One interesting hypothesis was that firms using more benchmark firms from outside the industry would provide more explanatory text (measured as number of sentences) in the compensation committee report to justify this choice. This hypothesis was supported, although interpreting the regression coefficient of .04 indicates that for each firm chosen outside of the industry, there was only an additional .04 of a sentence. Given a mean of 4.05 sentences, this would reflect only 1% more explanatory text for each benchmark firm chosen from outside of the industry.

Another key hypothesis was that choosing benchmark firms from outside the industry would be associated with lower overall performance of the benchmark firms (thus making the performance of the subject firm look better). This hypothesis, too, was supported. The coefficient was –.74, suggesting that for each additional benchmark firm chosen from outside of the industry, 5-year cumulative market returns of the benchmark group were lower by –.74. This effect size implies that at the mean return of 189.20, the addition of each nonindustry firm lowered the 5-year performance of the set of benchmark firms from 189.20 to 188.46, or 0.4%. Consequently, adding nonindustry firms may not have a large impact on how a firm's relative performance looks.

The Porac et al. study is unique in its insights into the way that boards choose data on benchmark firms to use in evaluating the performance of the firms and CEOs they oversee. Although its findings do raise the possibility that boards operate to make the firm and the CEO look better through their choice of benchmark firms, interesting questions remain for future research.

For example, it is not clear that the industry or product market is the only relevant type of comparison. (Our examination of relative performance evaluation in Chapter 5 suggests that evaluation of executive performance is not confined to industry comparisons.) To the extent that executives move between industries, lower-paying industries will not be able to compete with higher-paying ones if their compensation packages are based solely on what other industry competitors are paying.[15] Thus, the question of within- versus between-industry movement of executives is an important one for researchers to examine. To the degree that there is movement in and out of industries, it may be rational to focus more on labor market comparisons by using benchmark firms selected across industries.

In addition, it should be noted that the main justification for product market comparisons is to ensure that one's labor costs do not exceed those of product market competitors. This suggests that one issue to be considered is the portion of total labor cost represented by the CEO's pay. To the extent that this proportion is very small, product market considerations would be expected to be less relevant. Finally, knowing whether the firm competes on the basis of cost (versus differentiation) might also be relevant for explaining when firms will look more, or less, to product market comparisons. In summary, although Porac et al. have raised interesting issues, we encourage future researchers to also include labor market and strategy variables in examining these issues.[16]

A final and very interesting question is whether managers actually employ efficiency wage concepts—and if so, which version—in their decisions about pay level. Unfortunately, there is surprisingly little research that directly examines this question. However, a small 1990 study by economists Blinder and Choi (which the authors themselves describe as a "shred of evidence") suggests that concerns about equity and fairness may be more important than efficiency in setting pay levels (see also Levine, 1993a).

Specifically, Blinder and Choi (1990) asked managers whether they agreed or disagreed with several statements designed to uncover their implicit theories of the relationship between pay level, motivation, and worker ability and effort. Interestingly, the answers they got varied with the wording of the question, a finding that has long been established in psychological research on pay (e.g., Lawler, 1971; Opsahl & Dunnette, 1966). For example, 13 of 19 managers agreed that if they lowered wages, their employees would work less hard. Open-ended comments referred to beliefs that "Money is status," "We keep score by how much people make," and "Wage cuts are ego demeaning." On the other hand, only 2 of 19 managers mentioned pay as one of the most important factors in causing employees to work hard.

Managers were also asked, "You interview two workers who appear equally qualified. One is willing to work for the offered wage, but the other is not. Is the latter likely to be more productive?" None of the managers answered in the affirmative, a finding that Blinder and Choi (1990) interpreted as lack of support for the adverse selection version of efficiency wage models.

Although Blinder and Choi's findings are rather limited by small sample size and a restricted range and number of questions, their evidence tends to suggest that when managers describe how they make decisions, their responses focus less on shirking and adverse selection versions of efficiency wage theory and more on psychologically based explanations. These types of explanations play a greater role in gift exchange versions of efficiency wage theory and are also more consistent with (post-)institutional approaches.[17]

As the preceding review indicates, only a few studies have looked directly at how pay level decisions are made in organizations or at how much discretion employers actually have in setting pay levels. Understanding the degree of discretion available to managers is important because differences in pay by themselves do not necessarily imply either discretion or strategic intent. We return to this issue in Chapter 7.

Summary

Although most theories about pay levels originate from a relatively simple model, the material in this chapter suggests that the realities of pay level are actually quite complex. For example, theories of how pay levels are determined have been extended to incorporate notions such as efficiency wages, compensating differentials, pay structure, pay strategy, and pay form. In addition, our understanding of pay levels has gradually moved from a state in which pay levels were believed to be largely equal for the same type of work to one in which some employers—particularly the most profitable ones—are believed to have a fair amount of discretion in setting pay.

All this suggests that studying both the determinants and the effects of pay level is a very complex enterprise. When one sees a pay level that appears to be higher than the market average, one does not know whether that result is intentional or unintentional, or strategic or not. Furthermore, because pay levels are typically studied separately from pay form (e.g., benefits) and basis (e.g., incentives, merit increases, stock options), it is not clear whether a high pay level actually reflects higher-than-average *total compensation.* Finally, it is very difficult to know whether the precise combination of pay level, pay structure, pay basis, and pay form attracts employees who are more, or less, loyal; more, or less, intelligent; or who devote more, or less, energy to their task. As will be seen throughout the remainder of this book, these complexities make it very difficult to disentangle "What leads to what."

In summary, despite a slow start in neoclassical economics, the importance of organizational differences in compensation practices has emerged as a central focus of current economics and strategy research. As such, the field has shifted quite a bit since Milkovich's (1988) review, a time when there was still some question about whether organizational differences in compensation were really strategic. In the next chapter, we move from our discussion of pay level determinants to a discussion of their effects on outcomes such as attraction, retention, satisfaction, performance, and overall utility.

Resource 2.1

Additional Notes on Deviations From the Neoclassical Model

In addition to the failure of markets to produce the predicted "market rate," post-institutionalists also made a number of other discoveries that did not accord with neoclassical theory. These are described as follows.

Imperfect Mobility of Labor. Economists who studied local labor markets in considerable detail observed that workers generally developed close attachments both to their employers and their communities and were loathe to search far afield for better opportunities (e.g., Myers & Schultz, 1951; Reynolds, 1951). Observing this, Kerr (1954) concluded that "The labor market is like the marriage market, and separation is for cause only" (p. 95). Similarly, Arthur Ross (1957) spoke of a new "industrial feudalism," while Kerr (1954) referred to the "enclosure movement" (p. 552). Of course, both marriage and labor markets have changed somewhat during the last 50 years (Cappelli, 1999). However, in both cases, many long-term relationships continue (Reichheld, 1996), giving Kerr's observation continued relevance.

Internal Labor Markets and Other Rule-Based Constraints to Mobility. In addition to the limits on mobility that workers imposed on themselves, employers further constrained mobility by restricting access to the most prized jobs to individuals who were already employed inside the firm. In other words, employers created internal labor markets in which jobs were effectively off-limits to those outside the firm (Doeringer & Piore, 1971; Thurow, 1975). In addition, unions restricted mobility by creating rules about who could or could not become members and by negotiating terms with employers that reserved the best jobs for union members with the highest seniority.

Imperfect Information. Post-institutional economists who studied job search and choice processes observed that workers fell far short of having "perfect information" about employment opportunities. Specifically, most workers had only a vague idea of which firms might be hiring (subsequently called *extensive information;* Rees, 1973) and even less information about the specific terms of employment in various organizations *(intensive information).* Later, Stigler (1962) argued that exhaustively researching the range of jobs available and acquiring accurate information about their attributes is time-intensive work that has opportunity costs. Thus, for workers to behave rationally, they must balance the potential benefits of investing additional resources in search against the costs. For these reasons, job seekers are rational only within bounds, thus leaving room for modest wage differences to exist across employers.

Apparent Lack of Utility-Maximizing Behavior by Workers. Contrary to theoretical assumptions, workers did not appear to seek to maximize utility in their job searches. Rather, they often accepted the first job that met minimally acceptable standards with respect to wages (i.e., reservation wage) and other attributes, such as location (Reynolds, 1951). Once again, this did not mean that job seekers were irrational in their decisions, but rather that they were "boundedly rational," that is, rational only within the limits of the information, time, and financial resources available to them (Simon, 1979).

Pay Setting Based on Relative Rather Than Absolute Rates. Dunlop (1957) and Slichter (1950) found that rather than modifying wages to meet the market, employers instead made wage decisions in ways that preserved their *relative* position among employers. For any given occupation in a local labor market, some employers were routinely found to be wage leaders, whereas others consistently lagged the market. When one employer (usually a wage leader) increased wages, others eventually followed suit in order to retain their relative rankings.[18]

Weak Links Between Labor Supply and Rates of Pay. According to neoclassical theory, wages increased to attract additional workers in times of low unemployment and decreased in times of high unemployment. However, this was not what post-institutional economists observed in actual labor markets. Rather, post-institutionalists concluded that "The level of unemployment has nothing directly to do with the time at which wage increases begin or with the speed of the advance. Rather, this is determined mainly by the commodity pricing mechanism" (Reynolds, 1951, p. 231), with agricultural price increases being particularly good predictors of subsequent wage increases.

Pay levels tend to correlate highly with employer profitability. Slichter (1950) found a correlation of .70 between profitability and the average hourly earnings of unskilled labor, concluding that "Wages, within a considerable range, reflect managerial discretion, that where managements can easily pay high wages they tend to do so, and that where managements are barely breaking even they tend to keep wages down" (p. 88).

Employers did not attempt to get by with the lowest possible rate necessary to attract labor. In contrast to theoretical predictions, employers with high ability to pay (usually due to favorable product market conditions) *preferred* to pay more than necessary to attract workers. In fact, high-wage employers often would have preferred to pay even more than they did but were restrained from doing so by pressure from other employers. According to Reynolds (1951):

> One finds in any area, then, a range or band of feasible wage levels at which a firm may operate. . . . Under nonunion conditions the top of the band appears to be defined, not by the highest wage which the most prosperous firm in the area could

afford to pay, but by the maximum which it can pay without being considered "unethical" by other employers. The lower limit of the band is partly a function of the upper limit. . . . It is also importantly influenced by minimum wage legislation and the level of unemployment compensation benefits. (pp. 233–234)

Wages are "sticky." In contrast to economic theory, employers almost never cut nominal pay rates, regardless of unemployment rates or decreases in profits. Rather, wages are elastic in an upward direction, but inelastic downward (Blinder & Choi, 1990; Klaas & Ullman, 1995).

Actual wage patterns cast severe doubt on the assumption of compensating wage differentials. Observers of wage patterns frequently noted that the highest wages generally tended to correspond with the "best" jobs. The only undesirable job attribute that was consistently rewarded with a wage premium appeared to be the risk of injury or death (Ehrenberg & Smith, 1988).

Taken together, observations of the actual operation of labor markets suggested that the "weakness" of market factors on the supply (i.e., employee) side provided firms "with a degree of discretion in their compensation policies that would not exist if workers had the kind of market information and mobility in response to wage differences that is visualized by the competitive model" (Segal, 1986, p. 390). Indeed, large interfirm disparities in wages were so much the rule rather than the exception that they caused Ross (1957) to observe the following:

It is generally recognized that competitive forces in the labor market are not sufficiently strong to produce a single rate even for a single "grade" of labor. It is true that a few employments are so rudimentary and unstructured that a single rate prevails even though no one has decreed that this must be so . . . [e.g.] cotton pickers in a particular county at a particular stage of the harvest. . . . Such groups are the salvation of the economics instructor who wishes to demonstrate the mechanics of a competitive labor market, but are impressive chiefly for their quaintness and singularity. Generally the single rate is a reliable token of *combination rather than competition* at work. (p. 189; emphasis added)[19]

The obvious gaps between theory and reality with respect to wage determination led Paul Samuelson, a future Economics Nobel Prize winner, to acknowledge the following (as quoted in Lester, 1952):

When the economic theorist turns to the general problem of wage determination and labor economics, his voice becomes muted and his speech halting. If he is honest with himself, he must confess to a tremendous amount of uncertainty and self-doubt concerning even the most basic and elementary parts of the subject. (p. 483)

Still, Samuelson did not see any great need for economic theory to modify itself to accommodate empirical realities, because "In economics it takes a theory to kill a theory; facts can only dent the theorist's hide" (as quoted in Boyer & Smith, 2001, p. 207).[20] Thus, although Samuelson (1951) acknowledged that "The fact that a firm of any size must have a wage policy is additional evidence of labor market imperfections," he also emphasized that "Just because competition is not 100% perfect does not mean that it must be zero" (as quoted in Boyer & Smith, 2001, p. 213).

Thus, in Samuelson's view, neoclassical theory explained a large percentage of what was observed in labor markets. It was not perfect, but in his opinion, it was better than what other schools, including the post-institutionalists, had to offer. Coase (1998) expressed a similar opinion about the institutional school that had preceded them:

> John R. Commons . . . and those associated . . . were men of great intellectual stature, but they were anti-theoretical, and without a theory to bind together their collection of facts, they had very little they were able to pass on.[21] Certain it is that mainstream economics proceeded on its way without any significant change. . . . Mainstream economics . . . has become more and more abstract over time, and although it purports otherwise, it is in fact little concerned with what happens in the real world. . . . The success of mainstream economics in spite of its defects is a tribute to the staying power of a theoretical underpinning, since mainstream economics is certainly strong on theory if weak on facts. (p. 72)

Notes

1. The bivariate correlation between pay and other desirable job attributes is typically positive. Although this seems to be inconsistent with the compensating wage differential approach, it ignores the fact that higher ability or higher market value workers command higher total compensation, meaning that both pecuniary and nonpecuniary aspects will be higher. Within ability levels or total compensation levels, however, compensating wage differentials should exist.

2. This entire section draws heavily on Ehrenberg and Smith (1988, Chapter 2).

3. The importance of the ratio of labor cost to total cost is one of Alfred Marshall's four laws of derived demand, which were later amended by John Hicks (see Rees, 1979).

Survey data from the Saratoga Institute, for example, show that labor costs as a percentage of revenues in health care are more than twice the corresponding percentage in manufacturing, which, in turn, is twice as high as the percentage in the insurance industry. Industry differences are also apparent using comprehensive economy-wide data on national income and product accounts provided by the Bureau of Economic Analysis, which show that compensation cost as a percentage of gross domestic product is 64% in manufacturing, but 25% in finance, insurance, and real estate (Lum, Moyer, & Yuskavage, 2000).

4. If a firm faces an artificially higher labor cost, the firm may also reduce employment as it seeks to substitute less expensive production inputs (e.g., new technology) for the costly labor input.

5. Note that the detrimental effects of higher wages depend on the existence of a competitive market. One violation of this assumption may occur when a union has organized the entire product market, thereby taking wages out of competition. The U.S. automobile industry (before the advent of international competition) provides such an example (Kochan & Capelli, 1984).

6. In this, they drew on the early institutional economics approach of Richard Ely, John Commons, and others at the University of Wisconsin and its emphasis on describing how the labor market "really worked." However, the post-institutional approach is seen as having given greater weight to market forces than did the earlier institutional school (McNulty, 1966; Segal, 1986).

7. Brown and Medoff (1989) use several data sets and controls for factors such as human capital. They report that establishments 1 standard deviation above the mean on *ln* (employment) pay 6% to 15% more than establishments 1 standard deviation below the mean.

8. This, of course, fits nicely with Marxist discussions of the role of the "reserve army." Furthermore, Weisskopf, Bowles, and Gordon (as cited in Yellen, 1984) have argued that such things as unemployment benefits have contributed to the slowdown in U.S. productivity growth because of the consequent "loss of employer control due to a reduction in the cost of job loss" (Yellen, 1984, p. 202).

9. A *quasi-rent* is the excess return beyond what it would take to keep (versus attract) the resources to that activity (Milgrom & Roberts, 1992).

10. van Ark and McGuckin (1999) also present data on GDP per hour worked. Countries where workers work many hours fare worse on this measure. For example, Japan drops to 82% of the OECD average, and the United States drops to 120% of the OECD average. Germany, in contrast, because of its lower average hours worked per year, moves up to 105% of the OECD average. van Ark and McGuckin note that there were two different estimates of hours worked for the United States: 1,628 or 1,966. They decided to use 1,628. Obviously, the GDP per hours worked for the United States would have been much lower had the higher estimate of hours worked been used. Recall from our discussion of the neoclassical economics model that workers are assumed to place a positive utility on leisure. It may be that U.S. workers fall short of their European counterparts on this measure.

11. As Alfred Marshall noted, additional factors such as the elasticity of demand for the product would also play a role in determining the importance of controlling labor costs.

12. This ratio or cap was later eliminated. The company reported that the cap did not allow them to pay a competitive salary, which was needed to attract and retain executives of sufficient quality.

13. Trevor and Graham (2000) also provided descriptive data on survey practices. Respondents reported that they acquired approximately three surveys per job per year for use in pay-setting decisions of the core and managerial jobs and closer to two surveys per year for the noncore jobs. Thus, more investment was made in pay setting for the core and managerial positions. The primary source of surveys was purchase (e.g., from a consulting firm), followed at some distance by conducting their own survey, and lastly the use of publicly available surveys (e.g., from the Bureau of Labor Statistics).

14. Another possibility is that the labor market and product market competition manipulations in the scenarios were not strong enough to generate meaningful effects. As will be seen in the next chapter, the observed "importance" of a variable in policy-capturing studies depends on the degree to which variance is built into the "high" versus "low" conditions.

15. Although a single example is limited in its value, it is interesting to us that Lincoln Electric, a company famous for being cost-conscious and having little in the way of corporate largess with respect to its executives (no corporate jets, no executive dining room, pay based on performance), uses no industry comparisons in its executive pay setting.

16. There is also an issue with coding information on pay comparisons from proxy statements. Our reading of proxy statements suggests that the performance graph that compares 5-year return of the subject company with one or more peer groups often includes different benchmark companies than those described in the compensation committee report on benchmark companies. It

strikes us that the graph tends to focus to a greater degree on product market comparisons, whereas the compensation committee report often moves more toward a focus on labor market competitors in recruiting top executive talent.

17. The veracity of Blinder and Choi's findings depends on the dual assumptions that managers have self-insight into their own decision processes and are not affected by social desirability, assumptions that often do not appear to hold in survey research (e.g., Rynes, Schwab, & Heneman, 1983; Slovic & Lichtenstein, 1971). In addition, Blinder and Choi's findings suggest that responses may differ depending on whether one is contemplating pay cuts, or pay increases. This latter result may not be due to lack of self-insight, but rather to differences in the framing of pay changes as either losses or gains (Tversky & Kahneman, 1981). In addition, as we shall soon see in Chapter 3, at least two psychological theories suggest that the motivational effects of pay may genuinely depend on the level of pay in conjunction with factors such as workers' present circumstances, expectations, and how pay is communicated (e.g., Herzberg, 1987; Maslow, 1943).

18. Similar results have been found more recently by Groshen (1988) and Gerhart and Milkovich (1990), although Leonard (1989) has argued that relative hierarchies are quite unstable.

19. A single rate might suggest either the presence of a labor union (which typically seeks the same pay rate for its members in a particular job, within and across companies) or that employers are colluding to fix wages at a particular level (to control costs). The latter is illegal under antitrust law.

20. For another evaluation of challenges to standard economic theory, see Cain (1976).

21. Coase has also described the consequence of a lack of theoretical framework in the instititionalist school as follows: "Without a theory they had nothing to pass on except a mass of descriptive material waiting for a theory, or a fire" (as quoted in Boyer & Smith, 2001, p. 200).

3 Effects of Pay Level

WHAT DO EMPLOYERS GET IN RETURN FOR HIGHER PAY?

If you focus solely on compensation and change compensation only, you will get two results: nothing will happen, and you will spend a lot of money getting there.

—Director of Compensation at Xerox Customer Operations (as quoted in Pfeffer, 1998a)

The committee considered it appropriate, and in the best interest of the share owners, to set the overall level of the company's salary, bonus and other incentive compensation awards above the average of companies in the comparison group in order to enable the company to continue to attract, retain and motivate the highest level of executive talent possible.

—2001 Proxy Statement Report of the Compensation Committee of the Board of Directors, General Electric, the company having the highest market value in the world at the end of the year 2000

In the previous chapter, we saw that pay for the same nominal job can vary widely across organizations, industries, and geographic areas. We also saw that there are many different reasons why this might be so. For example, by paying more, employers may be able to attract and retain higher-quality, more productive employees than organizations that pay less. On the other hand, employers may pay too much (or too little) because of poor information on what competitors pay or because of institutional factors (e.g., "downward stickiness" in pay, labor unions).

In this chapter, we examine evidence on the question "What do employers get in return for higher pay?" We begin by briefly reviewing theories about the relative importance of pay to individuals, followed by empirical evidence concerning this issue. We then review empirical evidence regarding the relationships between pay level and outcomes such as employee satisfaction, attraction, retention, and productivity. Evidence as to how other aspects of pay systems (e.g., pay structure, pay basis, or pay form) affect individual and organizational outcomes will be presented in subsequent chapters.

Theories of the Importance of Pay to Individuals

> *Money is the crucial incentive because, as a medium of exchange, it is the most instrumental. . . . No other incentive or motivational technique comes even close to money with respect to its instrumental value*
>
> —Locke, Feren, McCaleb, Shaw, and Denny (1980)

> *Literally hundreds of studies and scores of systematic reviews of incentive studies consistently document the ineffectiveness of external rewards.*
>
> —Pfeffer (1998a)

General Theories

Both economists and psychologists have speculated about the importance of pay in motivating employee behavior, particularly in relation to the motivating potential of other job and organizational characteristics, such as autonomy, praise, or the work itself. Although there are exceptions (e.g., see the Locke et al., 1980, quotation above), economists have generally tended to assume that pay is a stronger motivator than have psychologists, as reflected in economists' tendency to create models depicting pay as the *only* incentive, assuming everything else is equal.

Rottenberg (1956) explained that economists have several good reasons for assuming the primacy of pay as a motivator. First, unlike attributes such as job security or quality of supervision, money is continuously quantifiable on a common scale and highly visible to both job seekers and current employees. Second, unlike some other job attributes (such as travel or responsibility), virtually all people can be assumed to have uniformly positive preferences for money (i.e., to always prefer more money to less). Third, although economists do not strictly believe that money is the only motivator, models based on pay alone persist because they "give tolerably good results. . . . Everywhere there is massive aggregate evidence that people move from low-income areas to high . . . not in the opposite direction" (Rottenberg, 1956, p. 188). In addition to these economic justifications, a number of psychologists have also argued that pay is the preeminent motivator because it is instrumental for meeting so many other kinds of needs (e.g., security, status, esteem, and feedback about achievement; Lawler, 1971; Locke et al., 1980).

Still, at least three well-known psychological theories question the efficacy of compensation as a motivator: Maslow's (1943) need hierarchy, Herzberg's (1987) two-factor theory, and Deci and Ryan's cognitive evaluation theory (Deci, 1975; Deci & Ryan, 1985). The implication of these three theories is that monetary rewards are not a major determinant of work motivation. If that is correct, then why write a book on compensation? The answer, as we show in this and later chapters, is that pay *is* a major determinant of work motivation, work behaviors, and labor cost, and plays a primary role in an organization's success. As we also now describe, support for the validity of the Maslow, Herzberg, and Deci and Ryan perspectives on monetary rewards is lacking.

Maslow's (1943) need hierarchy theory posits that human needs are arranged in a hierarchy of prepotency that is biological or instinctive in nature (Miner, 1980). According to the theory, a need that is deprived acts as a primary motivator (i.e., "monopolizes consciousness"), while a need that is satisfied has less motivational impact.

At the bottom of Maslow's (1943) hierarchy are physiological (food, sleep) and safety (e.g., housing) needs—precisely those needs posited to be most effectively satisfied by money. However, once these more basic needs are satisfied, individuals are hypothesized to focus on "higher" needs, such as love (e.g., affiliation, belongingness), esteem (e.g., achievement, independence, confidence), and self-actualization ("to become everything that one is capable of becoming," p. 382), which Maslow hypothesized are more likely to be met through engagement in meaningful work. Although Maslow did not view need satisfaction as an all-or-nothing process (i.e., a person could simultaneously be motivated to varying degrees by needs at different levels), the expectation was that on average, all people progress through the hierarchy in roughly the same manner.

A second psychological theory, Herzberg's (1987) motivation-hygiene theory, focuses on identifying factors that contribute to satisfaction or dissatisfaction at work. Herzberg viewed satisfaction and dissatisfaction not as opposite ends of the same continuum, but rather as two distinct constructs: "The factors involved in producing job satisfaction (and motivation) are separate and distinct from the factors that lead to job *dis*satisfaction" (p. 9). Like Maslow, Herzberg saw hygienic needs as being driven by the "animal nature" of people (p. 9). In contrast, motivational factors or factors associated with the work itself were posited to "relate to that unique human characteristic, the ability to achieve and, through achievement, to experience psychological growth" (p. 9). Most important for present purposes, Herzberg posited that money is more likely to be a "hygienic" factor, that is, one capable of causing or reducing *dis*satisfaction, than to be a satisfying or motivating one. Thus, Herzberg believed that money plays a role in creating or reducing dissatisfaction but not in contributing to satisfaction or motivation.

Although Maslow's and Herzberg's theories were intuitively appealing to many people, research has not supported either theory to any great extent (e.g., Kanfer, 1990; Miner, 1980). For example, both theories have been criticized on the basis of the methods by which they were developed, extensive interviews with highly creative individuals in Maslow's case and a storytelling, critical incidents method in Herzberg's. Unfortunately, when other methods are used to elicit motivational factors, there is little support for a clear dichotomy between Herzberg's hygienics and motivators or across Maslow's hypothesized levels of motivation (e.g., Campbell & Pritchard, 1976; Hall & Nougaim, 1968; House & Wigdor, 1967; Steers & Porter, 1975).

In fact, in the case of Herzberg's theory, there is considerable attribute overlap between the motivator and dissatisfier categories even when using his own methodology. For example, although achievement is more often mentioned as a motivator ($n = 440$) than a dissatisfier ($n = 122$) in Herzberg's (1966) study of 1,220 people in 6 studies, in terms of raw frequencies, achievement is also the 3rd most frequently mentioned dissatisfier according to his data (House & Wigdor, 1967). Similarly, a later summary of his own research (12 studies, 1,685 subjects; Herzberg, 1987) showed that pay was mentioned as a motivator nearly as often as it was listed as a dissatisfier. Finally, there are good reasons to question Herzberg's equation of "satisfiers" with "motivators," since these two constructs represent quite different phenomena (Schwab & Cummings, 1970). Indeed, it is a fundamental premise of several psychological models of motivation that a satisfied need is *not* a motivator (e.g., Adams's equity theory, 1963; Maslow, 1943).

Subsequent observers have suggested that many of the early empirical studies that challenged these two theories had methodological problems of their own that may have prevented the authors from finding supportive results. These problems include the use of small samples, difference scores (which tend to be highly unreliable), and questionnaires with questionable construct validity (e.g., Hall & Nougaim, 1968; Lawler & Suttle, 1972; for more on the construct validity issue, see Schwab, 1980a). Nevertheless, the result of the nonsupportive findings has been to reduce recent interest in trying to either validate or invalidate the basis tenets of Maslow's and Herzberg's theses (Ambrose & Kulik, 1999; Kanfer, 1990; Pinder, 1998).[1]

More recently, a third psychological theory has been developed that similarly questions the efficacy of compensation as a motivator: Deci and Ryan's (1985) cognitive evaluation theory (CET). One fundamental principle of CET is the so-called *overjustification* effect (Lepper, Greene, & Nisbett, 1973), which proposes that people who receive extrinsic rewards for performing an interesting activity will attribute the cause of their behavior to the extrinsic reward, thus discounting their interest in the activity per se (intrinsic interest) as the cause of their behavior. Deci and Ryan (1985) describe intrinsic motivation as "based in the innate, organismic needs for competence and self-determination" (p. 33) and argue that it occurs in its purest form when "A person does an activity in the absence of a reward contingency or control" (p. 35).

Although the theory is somewhat more complicated than described here, in general, CET argues that placing strong emphasis on monetary rewards is likely to decrease people's interest in the work itself, thus dampening a potentially powerful alternative source of motivation. Deci and Ryan (1985) argue that this is because when effort is exerted in exchange for pay, pay takes on a controlling aspect that threatens the individual's need for self-determination. For example, according to Ryan, Mims, and Koestner (1983), if one must perform a task "in some particular way, at some particular time, or in some particular place . . . to receive the reward, the reward tends to be experienced as controlling" (p. 738).

In addition, however, Ryan et al. (1983) propose that the effects of pay on intrinsic interest depend on the information embedded in pay outcomes. Specifically, they argue that intrinsic interest is likely to be impaired to the extent that information about rewards is seen to be controlling. However, to the extent that pay provides meaningful information regarding self-competence in a context where a person has discretion in choosing how to perform a task, then monetary rewards can *increase* intrinsic outcomes. Thus, the net effect of rewards on intrinsic interest depends on the relative impact of monetary rewards on perceived control versus perceived self-competence. In general, however, Deci and his colleagues have tended to argue that the net effect of monetary rewards on intrinsic interest is usually negative.

Because most of the research testing this theory has focused on pay-for-performance systems rather than pay levels per se, we do not review the evidence in great detail here. However, we feel it is important to address the evidence at this early stage of our book because it has been interpreted incorrectly, in our view. For example, Pfeffer (1998b, p. 112) labels the idea that people work for money as a "myth" and claims that "A substantial body of research has demonstrated, both in experimental and field settings, that large external rewards can actually undermine intrinsic motivation" (p. 216). Kohn (1993) has made similar claims.

Nevertheless, evidence on CET does not justify such claims, particularly as applied to workplace settings. For example, a comprehensive meta-analyis (Eisenberger & Cameron, 1996) examined 83 studies that compared a rewarded group (verbal or tangible rewards) with a no-reward control group on two traditional measures of intrinsic outcomes: free time (44 effect sizes)[2] or attitude toward the task (e.g., interest, enjoyment, or satisfaction, 39 effect sizes). Across studies, the mean correlation between reward condition and free time was –.04, and between reward condition and task-related attitude it was .14. Therefore, the detrimental effects of rewards were generally not supported in their meta-analysis, even using the free-time measure.

Subsequently, Deci, Koestner, and Ryan (1999) conducted a meta-analysis on the same issues addressed by Eisenberger and Cameron (1996). Although Deci et al. concluded that more overall support existed for the detrimental effects of extrinsic rewards than did Eisenberger and Cameron, Deci et al. found "no effect for performance-contingent rewards" on the attitude measure of intrinsic interest (p. 644). However, in considering how CET might operate in workplace settings, perhaps most noteworthy is the finding of Deci et al. that extrinsic rewards "are more detrimental for children than for college students" (p. 656). This is important because the vast majority of research on this theory has been performed in school rather than work settings, often with elementary school-aged children. As a partial explanation, Deci et al. suggested that college students (and presumably adults) can better separate informational and controlling aspects of rewards and thus may be more likely to interpret extrinsic rewards as indicative of their own competence.

Fang and Gerhart (2002) suggest that Deci and Ryan (1985) may have focused too much on the potentially controlling aspects of rewards and not enough on the informational aspect, particularly in employment settings. For example, employment relationships typically last more than a few hours (the duration of most laboratory studies), and the norms for payment are quite different (e.g., unlike in schools, monetary payments are expected in the workplace; Staw, 1977). Accordingly, Kanfer (1990) hypothesized that performance-contingent rewards are likely to have a more positive influence on task interest in work settings than in non-work settings. Consistent with this hypothesis, Fang and Gerhart (2002) reported that employees covered by pay-for-performance plans reported higher intrinsic motivation than employees not covered by such plans.

In summary, although the ideas developed by Maslow, Herzberg, and Deci have had considerable appeal to many people, the prevailing view in the academic literature is that the specific predictions of these theories are not supported by empirical evidence. On the other hand, it would be a mistake to underestimate the influence that these theories have had on research and practice. Pfeffer, Kohn, and others continue to base their argument regarding the ineffectiveness of money as a motivator on such theories.

On a more positive note, Herzberg's hygiene-motivator theory was a major impetus for the growth of the job enrichment movement (Hackman & Oldham, 1976), which provided a clear counterpoint to scientific management by emphasizing the motivating potential of aspects of work such as autonomy, variety, task significance, task identity, and feedback. Indeed, *high-performance work systems* (HPWS; e.g., MacDuffie, 1995), which have been found to have substantial positive effects on organizational performance, typically follow a work design strategy that is high in these dimensions. Thus, the broad ideas proposed by Maslow and Herzberg (and also McGregor, 1960) for giving workers more responsibility and taking greater advantage of their capabilities are being put to good use in many organizations. As Dunham (1984) notes, "Herzberg is living proof that a theory need not be perfect to make valuable contributions" (p. 123).[3]

In summary, while recognizing that a range of rewards can be motivational, it is nevertheless important to question the minor role sometimes accorded to money by psychologists, particularly in motivation-hygiene theory. One reason to question this secondary role is the overall lack of support for the specific predictions of these theories. A second reason is the ample evidence from several types of studies showing that monetary rewards have a substantial impact on observable behaviors. Before reviewing this evidence, however, we briefly discuss situational (rather than general) theories of pay importance.

Contingency Theories of Pay Importance

In contrast to Maslow and Herzberg's general theories of motivation, economists and psychologists have tended to argue that the importance of an attribute such as pay cannot be determined in the abstract. The types of contingency factors emphasized by economists and psychologists tend to differ, however.

Market-Based Contingencies

Economists have emphasized that attribute importance can be determined only in concrete choice situations, "in a framework in which other job properties are given" (Rottenberg, 1956, p. 190). For example, consider a nurse with school-aged children who must choose between two jobs, one of which offers Monday through Friday daytime working hours and another that pays 10¢ an hour more but requires weekend and evening work, with variable scheduling from week to week. In this case, money is not likely to be an important factor in the job choice, both because it does not vary much across the two jobs and because another valued attribute, work schedule, varies considerably.

Economists, then, talk about the importance of pay and other attributes in terms of *marginal rates of substitution:* for example, how much more pay it would take to induce a potential applicant to take one job over another, given existing levels of other job and organizational characteristics. The main implication of this model for our purposes is that the importance of pay in motivating behavior is likely to vary across different market conditions.

Individual Differences

Both psychologists and economists have also noted that different types of people place different degrees of emphasis on compensation as well as on other attributes. However, while the two disciplines agree on the importance of individual differences in *ability* (e.g., cognitive ability), economists see less value in studying other individual differences, such as tastes or preferences. These are viewed as too difficult to measure and as not especially relevant because their effects are expected to average to zero across individuals (Brickley, Smith, & Zimmerman, 1997, pp. 27–28), thus not affecting the aggregate impact of a pay level policy. In contrast, psychologists have been considerably more interested in trying to find reliable patterns associated with differences in pay importance and other preferences (e.g., Lawler, 1971), with the underlying idea that a better match between pay level and individual preferences will contribute to better effectiveness. For example, a variety of reasons have been proposed for expecting pay to be of lower importance to women than to men: that women are often (though increasingly less so) the "secondary" wage earner in families (e.g., Mincer & Polachek, 1974); that work is less central to women because of differential child-rearing responsibilities; or that other job attributes (e.g., pleasant coworkers, useful product or service) are more highly valued by women than by men. If these observations proved to be correct, than attracting, motivating, and retaining employees in organizations where most employees are women might rely less on pay level and more on other job attributes that women value more.

In 1971, Lawler summarized the existing literature on individual differences in pay importance in this way:

> The employee who is likely to value pay highly is a male, young (probably in his twenties); he has low self-assurance and high neuroticism; he belongs to few clubs and social groups; he owns his own home or aspires to own one and probably is a Republican and a Protestant. (p. 51)

More recent research suggests that valuing high pay is associated with materialism and risk seeking (Cable & Judge, 1994) and with a lower tendency to be committed to any particular employer (Trank, Rynes, & Bretz, 2001). Clearly, additional research would be useful. For the moment, however, available evidence suggests that some of the characteristics of individuals who are highly attracted by pay are not characteristics that would necessarily be preferred by employers. As such, results suggest caution against placing too much emphasis on up-front, *noncontingent high-pay levels* in attracting and retaining employees.

Another source of individual differences in reactions to pay is the individual's current level of pay. For example, the widely accepted economics principle of declining marginal utility suggests that all else being equal, the higher an individual's current pay, the more additional pay it will take to motivate job changes or additional effort. In this sense, the *declining marginal utility principle* makes a point similar to that of Maslow's hierarchy: Once monetary needs are substantially satisfied, obtaining additional money can take on lesser importance relative to other factors. Indeed, development economists have sometimes talked about the phenomenon of a "backward-bending labor supply curve," whereby once people hit a certain target level of income, it becomes very difficult to entice them to do additional work for pay alone.[4]

Economists (from the post-institutional school) have also discussed another way in which the importance or motivational value of a given increment of pay might depend on the actual level of pay. Reynolds (1951) observed that unemployed workers or workers seeking to change jobs often set a "reservation wage," or minimally acceptable pay level, below which they would not accept jobs. This threshold was often determined on the basis of prior compensation history or assessments of how much money it would take to produce a target lifestyle. However, once the reservation threshold was met or exceeded, Reynolds observed that workers became more flexible about trading money for other desired attributes. Thus, additional increments in money might be seen as crucial at some points in a range of possible pay alternatives, but far less important in other parts of the range. As such, the relationship between pay level and pay importance may be nonlinear in a number of respects.

In summary, there is good reason to believe that pay importance depends on a variety of contingency factors, including those that are market based (e.g., other job attributes) and those that stem from individual differences (e.g., preferences).

Empirical Evidence Regarding Pay Importance

Although it may seem rather straightforward to measure the importance of pay relative to other attributes, early researchers soon realized that it was not such an easy task. In particular, early reviewers of the "pay importance" literature discovered that findings regarding the importance of pay were likely to vary to a considerable degree merely as a function of the methodology employed (Lawler, 1971; Opsahl & Dunnette, 1966).

For example, the earliest studies of pay importance tended to use either rating (e.g., measuring the importance of various attributes on 5-point scales) or ranking methodologies (ranking pay against other attributes, such as working conditions, type of work, etc.). As both Opsahl and Dunnette (1966) and Lawler (1971) observed, the resulting rank of pay in these hierarchies depended on things such as terminology used to define the factors (e.g., *high pay* versus *fair pay* versus *enough pay to live on*), the nature and number of other attributes included, and the extent to which pay was broken down into component parts (e.g., pay level, pay form, pay structure). These considerations—which have nothing to do with true differences in pay importance—led Lawler to argue that it was inappropriate to infer individual or group differences in pay importance unless standardized methods and instruments were employed across all samples.

In addition, however, rating and ranking methodologies suffered from a number of other disadvantages that could not be remedied via mere standardization. For example, these methods asked people about attribute importance in the abstract and as such did not address the contention of economists that importance could be determined only in a specific choice or decision context. For similar reasons, rating and ranking studies did not address the concerns of decision scientists that people seem to have limited self-insight into their decision processes and therefore are likely to misrepresent the ways they actually make decisions. For example, a common early finding was that when asked to rate or rank attributes in the abstract, people routinely overreported the importance of minor factors and underreported the importance of major ones (Slovic & Lichtenstein, 1971). Related to this, it appeared that people tended to underreport the importance of factors that were regarded as socially less acceptable than others. Thus, all else being equal, individuals were probably likely to overreport the (socially desirable) importance of job challenge or opportunities for learning, while underreporting the importance of "low-level" motivators, such as pay.

Evidence that such concerns were justified emerged from studies that compared direct self-reports of pay importance with other, less direct ways of capturing preferences. For example, in policy-capturing studies, individuals are asked to evaluate the attractiveness of holistic job descriptions comprising multiple attributes such as pay, type of work, location, and promotion patterns. The importance of each underlying attribute is then inferred by regressing subjects' overall evaluations of attractiveness on measures of each underlying characteristic (e.g., pay level, location). In this way, the importance of each underlying job characteristic to overall assessments can be inferred without asking direct questions about relative importance. In such studies, pay has generally been found to be a substantially more important factor when inferred from participants' overall evaluations of job attractiveness than from their direct reports of pay importance (Feldman & Arnold, 1978; Rynes, Schwab, & Heneman, 1983).

Findings by Jurgensen (1978) are also consistent with the notion that pay importance might be underreported due to social desirability considerations. In his study, Jurgensen assessed the relative importance of 10 job characteristics (including pay) to 50,000 applicants over a 30-year period. Based on applicants' self-reports, pay appeared to be the fifth most important characteristic to men and the seventh most important to women. However, when asked to rate the importance of those same 10 attributes to "someone just like yourself—same age, education, gender, and so on," pay jumped to being *the* most important among both men and women. In other words, people seemed to believe that pay was the most important motivator to everyone except themselves.

Another important finding from the policy-capturing literature is that economists' predictions about the dependence of pay importance on factor variability seem to be accurate. For example, in an experimental policy-capturing study, Rynes et al. (1983) showed that pay explained an average of 65% of the variance in subjects' overall evaluations of job attractiveness when presented with jobs having a wide range of salary alternatives, compared with only 40% when presented with a pay range that was half as great. Similarly, in the wider pay variability condition, subjects were far more likely to display choices consistent with reservation-wage behavior, that is, rejecting all job alternatives in which pay fell below a certain level, regardless of the levels of other attributes.

An alternative way to examine the importance of money is to examine what, in fact, happens to people's compensation when they change jobs: Does it stay the same (as might be expected if other factors are more important in driving decisions to quit), or does compensation tend to increase? Keith and McWilliams (1999), using a national sample of young adults, found that relative to "stayers," those voluntarily quitting their jobs for non-family-related reasons received wage increases of 8% to 11%. Furthermore, of this group, those who had actively searched for new jobs while still employed realized wage gains of 14% to 18% at their new jobs, relative to stayers. Given that their sample was composed largely of people in jobs paying below the national average, one might expect that the salary growth resulting from changing jobs at higher job levels would be even larger.

Consistent with this hypothesis, Gomez-Mejia and Balkin (1992b) studied a sample of approximately 350 college and university faculty and found that each change of employer was associated with a 9-month salary increase of $10,520. Given that the average salary in the sample (pooling those who had changed jobs and those who had not) was $48,380 and that the average number of moves was .66, this implies that faculty with no employer changes earned $41,436, compared with $51,956 for a faculty member with one employer change—a difference of 25.4%. Gomez-Mejia and Balkin also make the point that this salary advantage continues into future years, meaning that the payoff from mobility over the course of a career is much higher. One might also add that summer research support and any benefits that depend on salary (e.g., retirement benefits) would likewise be higher in future years.

Another study, this time using a sample of MBAs who had graduated several years earlier, found that those who had changed employers at least once had salaries that averaged $15,020 higher than those who had not (Dreher & Cox, 2000). Given a mean salary of $84,880 and with 59% of the sample having changed employers at least once, this implies a mean salary for stayers of $76,018 versus a mean salary for leavers of $91,038, or a 20% difference.

Thus, a wide variety of evidence seems to suggest that pay is relatively important to individuals. (Consistent with this point, evidence reviewed in Chapter 5 shows that monetary incentive plans have a major impact on behavior.) However, the fact that the measurement of pay importance appears to be so methodologically sensitive suggests that the importance of pay is best determined by examining the effects that differences in pay have on actual behaviors in real labor markets. We turn now to the existing evidence on the relationships between pay level and various outcomes: pay satisfaction, applicant attraction, employee retention, employee quality and effort, and overall utility.

What Do Employers Get in Return for Higher Pay Levels?

Higher pay levels result in higher labor costs per worker, which by itself reduces the ability of a firm to compete on product or service price.[5] Nevertheless (as Exhibit 3.1 indicates), higher pay has the potential to enhance effectiveness by influencing the work attitudes, effort, and performance of employees (via the incentive and sorting effects discussed in Chapter 2). We review the evidence on effects of pay level on these outcomes and then show how utility theory can be used to understand the net impact of using different pay level policies.

Exhibit 3.1 Possible Consequences of High Pay Levels

Costs	
Labor Cost	Higher
Benefits	
Satisfaction	Higher
Attraction	Higher
Retention	Higher
Effort	Higher
Performance	Higher
Overall Utility	
Higher or Lower, depending on context and basis for pay	

Pay Satisfaction

One potentially important attitudinal outcome of pay level is pay satisfaction. Although organizations might not be terribly concerned with employees' pay satisfaction per se, most psychological theories specify that pay influences behavior only through its effects on employee attitudes and perceptions. As such, relationships between pay level and, say, applicant attraction or employee turnover are assumed to be primarily indirect rather than direct (for an empirical example, see Motowidlo, 1983).

In 1985, H. Heneman concluded that "The consistency of the pay level-pay satisfaction relationship is probably the most robust (though hardly surprising) finding regarding the causes of pay satisfaction" (p. 131). Nevertheless, 15 years later, H. Heneman and Judge (2000) concluded that "The simple pay level-pay satisfaction correlation is quite weak—typically, $r = .15$" (p. 71). In other words, the relationship is consistently positive, but not large. Furthermore, Heneman and Judge admitted to being "puzzled by the apparent weak empirical link between objective pay and pay satisfaction" (p. 84).

To some extent, the relatively weak (although consistent) relationship between pay level and pay satisfaction is predicted by several psychological theories. For example, both theories (e.g., H. Heneman, 1985; Lawler, 1971; Locke, 1976) and research (Dyer & Theriault, 1976; H. Heneman & Judge, 2000; Rice, Phillips, & McFarlin, 1990) on pay satisfaction suggest that it is a function of the *discrepancy* between perceived pay level and what an employee believes his or her pay "should" be (Berger, Olson, & Boudreau, 1983). The finding that employees evaluate pay in relation to some notion of what they ought to be paid introduces considerable complexity into the translation from pay level to pay satisfaction.

The problem as described by equity theorists (e.g., Adams, 1963) is that a great variety of comparisons can be called on in deciding whether a particular pay level is "fair" or "satisfying," or not. According to equity theory, a person *(P)* evaluates the fairness of his or her situation relative to a comparison other *(CO)*, which can be another person or a situation that *P* has experienced in the past or anticipates in the future. *P* compares his or her own ratio of perceived outcomes *(O)* (e.g., pay, benefits, working conditions) to perceived inputs *(I)* (e.g., effort, ability, and experience), with the *O/I* ratio of the *CO*.

$$O_P/I_P <, >, \text{ or } = O_{CO}/I_{CO}?$$

If *P*'s ratio (O_P/I_P) is smaller than the *CO*'s ratio (O_{CO}/I_{CO}), *P* will feel underrewarded; if it is larger, *P* will feel overrewarded. (Note: Equity theory diverges from discrepancy theory on this latter point.)

The important point for present purposes is that individuals can consider a wide range of factors in assessing relevant inputs and outcomes. For example, they can look at their personal pay histories, the pay of those in other occupations in the same organization, pay of others in the same job in the same organization, pay of others in the same job in other organizations, pay of others with lower or higher seniority or performance, and so on. Moreover, Lawler (1990) argues that most people have a propensity to seek comparisons that will make them look disadvantaged in pay, thus leading to a perpetual tendency toward pay dissatisfaction for most individuals. (We return to this issue in our discussion of equity theory in Chapter 5.)

For these reasons, there can be considerable "slippage" between objective pay levels and subjective pay satisfaction. To take a very simple example, the much higher pay levels of managers compared with secretaries may not result in higher managerial pay satisfaction because managers "expect" their pay to be higher (due to higher inputs) and thus do not consider secretaries to be a relevant comparison group. Rather, managers are more likely to pay attention to what other managers are paid in similar firms or what other managers at the same level are paid within their own firms. These types of comparisons are most likely to produce mixed equity judgments (some favorable, some not), thus dampening the effects of objective pay level on pay satisfaction.

Another major psychological theory also suggests that other factors intervene between objective pay levels and pay satisfaction. Specifically, justice theory proposes that pay satisfaction is determined not only by the amount of money received (distributive justice) but also by the processes through which pay is distributed and the ways in which pay decisions are communicated. In other words, employee attitudes are hypothesized to be affected by *procedural* as well as distributive justice (e.g., Greenberg, 1987, 1990). Dyer and Theriault's (1976) research provided an early indication of the incremental importance of procedural justice (over distributive justice alone) in explaining pay satisfaction, a finding that has subsequently been replicated by additional work by Greenberg (1987, 1990) and Folger and Konovsky (1989).

To this point, we have discussed the relationship between objective pay level and pay satisfaction, treating pay satisfaction as the implied dependent variable. However, employers are also concerned about pay satisfaction as an *independent* variable, that is, as an affective reaction that can lead to productivity-related behaviors such as effort expenditure, turnover, or absenteeism. In 1985, H. Heneman concluded that the amount of research on behavioral consequences of pay satisfaction was "underwhelming." However, 15 years later, H. Heneman and Judge (2000) noted substantial progress on this front: "Research has unequivocally shown that pay dissatisfaction can have important and undesirable impacts on numerous employee outcomes" (p. 85).

For example, Bretz and Thomas (1992) showed that baseball players who lost salary arbitration cases (and hence were assumed to feel less equitably paid) were more likely to have decreased subsequent performance relative to those who won in arbitration and were also more likely to move to other teams or to leave baseball altogether. Koslowsky, Sagie, Krausz, and Singer (1997) reported a corrected correlation coefficient of .22 between pay satisfaction and employee lateness, while Davy and Shipper (1993) reported a significant relationship between pay dissatisfaction and voting for union representation.

In a striking display of the importance of procedural (and distributive) justice for pay satisfaction and of pay satisfaction for the absence of negative outcomes, Greenberg (1990) examined the experience of three matched plants in the same company. Plants A and B both subsequently received 15% pay cuts, but Plant C received no such cut. Employees in Plant A received an adequate explanation concerning the reasons behind the pay cuts in addition to a statement of serious remorse by the company. In contrast, workers in Plant B received no such communication. Although the control group (Plant C) and the two pay cut groups began with the same theft rates and pay equity perceptions, theft rates differed dramatically after the cut. Specifically, theft rates stayed the same in the control (no pay cut) plant, while rising 54% in the "adequate explanation" group (Plant A) and a whopping 141% in the "inadequate explanation" group. In this case, both pay level and pay communication had large, independent effects on employees' attitudes and behaviors. Similarly, in a lab study, Greenberg (1993) showed that subjects who were inequitably paid (i.e., using a different pay rule than the one stated at the beginning of the experiment) sought to restore their sense of equity by stealing money when the experimenter left the room.

At present, we can conclude that pay level is modestly but consistently related to pay satisfaction. In addition, we know that pay dissatisfaction can be associated with a number of undesirable outcomes (e.g., turnover, absenteeism, reduced performance, theft). However, there is still a good deal to be learned.

For example, H. Heneman and Judge (2000) suggest that future researchers move beyond examining static pay level-pay satisfaction linkages in favor of studies that look at before-and-after pay satisfaction in relation to changes in pay policies. Several good examples of this approach already exist in areas other than pay level (e.g., with respect to pay basis, Brown & Huber, 1992; with respect to pay raises, Trevor, Gerhart, & Boudreau, 1997).

One curious feature of the pay level-pay satisfaction literature is that there are virtually no studies that correlate pay level with *general* job satisfaction or that look at the effects of pay satisfaction vis-à-vis satisfaction with other attributes (e.g., supervision) in determining behaviors and more general attitudes. As Gerhart and Milkovich (1992) noted, employers have many choices about how and where to invest their resources. Even if the decision is made to invest in improving employee attitudes, there is little work to tell us whether overall attitudes are most efficiently increased by increasing pay satisfaction or some other aspect of employee attitudes. In addition, as H. Heneman and colleagues (e.g., Heneman & Judge, 2000; Heneman & Schwab, 1985; Judge, 1993) have shown, pay satisfaction is itself a multidimensional construct, with pay *level* satisfaction being only one of four components (the others being satisfaction with *benefits, raises,* and *structure/administration*). It may well be that once an individual has been hired, other forms of pay satisfaction (such as pay raise satisfaction) become much more salient than pay level. Thus, there is little guidance for employers as to where they are most likely to get the biggest behavioral "bang for the buck" as a result of improving satisfaction.

Finally, H. Heneman and Judge (2000) have raised concerns about the prominent role of equity theory in the literature on compensation attitudes. As we note in our discussion in Chapter 5, equity theory is ambiguous in at least two important ways: choice of comparison standard (a key determinant of equity perceptions) and choice of specific "action" (cognitive or behavioral) that will be taken to restore perceived equity. Heneman and Judge's concern echoes Gerhart and Milkovich's (1992) point regarding organization differences in pay level:

> Surprisingly little is known about the factors governing applicant and employee choices among the various comparison standards (e.g., organizations in the same product market, organizations in the same labor market) that could be used in evaluating their pay and what the consequences of choosing different standards are. (p. 494)

Attraction and Retention

Applicant attraction and employee retention are different constructs. *Applicants,* by definition, are actively engaged in search and may or may not be currently employed. In contrast, the individuals that organizations seek to *retain* are currently employed but may or may not be actively seeking alternative employment. Nevertheless, both theory and research suggest that pay level influences both decisions in a somewhat similar manner. For example, Barber and Bretz (2000) argue that regardless of whether a current employee is being "pulled" by the attraction of other opportunities or "pushed" by dissatisfaction with the present one, the "decision to leave an employer (turnover) is tightly coupled with evaluation of potential new employers (attraction)" (p. 33). As such, they argue that there is substantial overlap in the psychological processes underlying attraction and retention.

Theory suggests that pay level may be a relatively important factor in attraction and retention decisions for a variety of reasons. First, pay level is one of the most easily observable attributes for comparing competing offers. In contrast, attributes such as quality of supervision or even the basis for pay raises must often be inferred or taken on trust from the employer's word. Second, pay level and benefits are the two aspects of pay that are most directly connected with the decision to join or leave an organization. In contrast, other aspects of pay (e.g., pay raises and increases associated with promotions) are more likely to be contingent on effort and other inputs and outcomes once inside the organization. In their 1992 review, Gerhart and Milkovich stated that "There is ample evidence that pay level can increase the size of the applicant pool, the likelihood of job acceptance, and the quality of job applicants" (p. 491). Similar conclusions have been reached by Barber (1998) and Barber and Bretz (2000). This evidence has been obtained from both laboratory and field research.

Turning first to experimental research, several policy-capturing studies have suggested that pay is a rather important factor (relative to other attributes) in the job application decision (e.g., Feldman & Arnold, 1978; Zedeck, 1977). However, some of the earliest policy-capturing studies took little care to define attribute levels in ways that closely corresponded with real-market alternatives (e.g., Feldman & Arnold, 1978, used the "presence" and "absence" of various attributes). Defining attributes to reflect real markets is important because as Rynes et al. (1983) demonstrated, both pay *importance* (percentage of variance explained in overall decisions) and whether pay is evaluated in compensatory or noncompensatory fashion both depend on the range of pay alternatives (and presumably the range of other attributes as well; Rottenberg, 1956). In any event, using attribute levels that were carefully pegged to the college level sales and management trainee markets, Rynes et al. found that pay level swamped location, type of work, and opportunities for promotion.

In a different type of experimental study, Barber and Roehling (1993) used verbal protocols to determine how college students processed decisions about whether or not to interview for positions. As in Rynes et al. (1983), descriptions were constructed to bear a reasonable resemblance to real-market alternatives. They found that pay level and benefits were the second and third (of 10) most often mentioned attributes in the protocols, with location being the first. Consistent with Rynes et al., Barber and Roehling also found that subjects paid more attention to attributes that were extreme or unusual in some way (e.g., more-than-typical amounts of vacation).

Turning to evidence from the field, Krueger (1988) found that both the application rate and applicant quality increased for government jobs as the ratio of government-to-private sector wages increased. Similarly, Holzer (1990) found that higher wages reduced vacancy rates, increased the perceived ease of hiring, and resulted in less time spent on informal training (see also Barron, Bishop, & Dunkelberg, 1985).

In the only study with mixed or contrary findings, Williams and Dreher (1992) examined a variety of relationships between the compensation practices of 352 banks and their relative success in attracting applicants. As expected, pay levels were positively related to job acceptance rates. However, contrary to expectations, higher pay levels were associated with *longer* times to fill vacancies and not at all associated with applicant pool size. Post hoc investigation of these surprising results suggested that the banks tended to modify pay in reactive fashion, such that increases in pay or benefits were often implemented in *response* to difficulty in attracting workers.

Turning to retention, Ehrenberg and Smith's (1988, p. 368) analysis of the evidence led them to conclude that the relation between pay levels and quit rates is "strong." For example, Raff and Summers (1987) examined the impact of a pay increase at the Ford Motor Company in 1914. Prior to 1914, introduction of assembly line production and scientific management greatly increased productivity, but annual turnover rates reached 370%, and absenteeism averaged 10% per day. Although the wage rate of $2.50 per day provided plenty of replacement workers (there were apparently long queues of applicants), Ford decided to double wages to $5.00 per day in hopes of reducing turnover and absenteeism (and also perhaps because of his paternalistic management style). The 100% pay increase reduced quits by 87% and absenteeism by 75%.

Lakhani (1988) studied the effects of salary increases and retention bonuses on the reenlistment behaviors of soldiers the U.S. Army wished to retain. Although both forms of compensation were found to increase retention, bonuses were more effective than equivalent increases in salaries. This is a potentially important finding for employers, because bonuses are not "rolled into" base pay and hence may be a more cost-effective means of retaining employees.

According to Klaas and McClendon (1996), Freeman and Medoff (1984) estimated that a 20% increase in organizational pay level was associated with a 10% reduction in turnover at the individual level of analysis.[6] Unfortunately, there is little research on pay and turnover at the organizational level of analysis to either confirm or disconfirm this estimate (Barber, 1998; Powell, Montgomery, & Cosgrove, 1994).[7] Among existing research, three other studies that have looked at this issue do not provide any stronger relationships than that suggested by Freeman (Leonard, 1987; Powell et al., 1994; Wilson & Peel, 1991). However, a recent study by Shaw, Delery, Jenkins, and Gupta (1998) suggests a much stronger relationship between pay level and voluntary turnover ($\beta = -.31$). In their sample of 227 trucking companies, the mean wage was $34,912 (standard deviation = $6,289), and the mean turnover was 25.6% (standard deviation = 32.4%). Based on these results, the best estimate of the change in turnover to be expected from a 20% pay increase (at the mean) is 44%, a reduction from the current mean turnover of 25.6% to only 14.4%.

Although they did not study turnover per se, Bretz, Boudreau, and Judge (1994) found that compensation had a substantial effect on the extent to which 1,021 executives searched for alternative jobs while employed. Compensation had the largest zero-order correlation (−.42) with job search activity of any predictor. Moreover, after controlling for job satisfaction, current job level, perceived organization success, and several other motivation-to-search variables, compensation continued to have a substantial relationship with the extent of job search.

In sum, we know that higher pay levels are associated with better attraction and retention, but further work is needed to determine the precise size of these relationships and the degree to which they are affected by moderators. The nature of these relationships is central to predicting whether the benefits of high pay levels are likely to exceed the additional costs. In the case of the 1914 Ford increase, Raff and Summers (1987) were not able to provide a definitive answer to this question (partly due to the number of years that had elapsed) but suggested that the benefits probably did not completely offset the higher wage costs. Holzer (1990) estimated that although some of the pay increase in his study was offset by lower recruitment and training costs, approximately half the increase was not.

Employee Effort and Performance

In addition to the effects on acceptance and turnover rates, the overall utility of pay increases can also be dramatically affected by differences in the quality or effort levels of those who are attracted or retained by higher pay rates. As indicated in the previous chapter, economists have offered several hypotheses as to why paying higher wages than average may be efficient. For example, highly paid employees may work harder and with less supervision because there is more to lose from being fired than in a comparable but low-wage job.

Groshen and Krueger (1990) tested one version of efficiency wage theory in a study of pay and supervision in hospitals. They hypothesized that high pay levels would reduce shirking by increasing the penalty of job loss, thus reducing the need for supervision. In other words, Groshen and Krueger proposed that supervision and wage premia are substitutes for one another.[8] Thus, they expected to find fewer supervisors (i.e., a broader span of control) in high-paying hospitals.

To test their hypothesis, Groshen and Krueger (1990) examined the relationships between pay and supervisor-to-staff ratios in four occupations: registered nurse, food service, radiography, and physical therapy. Support for the hypothesis was found in only one of the four occupations (nursing). In that occupation, results suggested that doubling the supervisor-to-staff ratio from its average of 6.5 nurses per supervisor to 3.25 nurses per supervisor was associated with a 13.3% decrease from the average hourly pay of $12.18. Thus, the total savings would be $.133 \times 12.18 \times 6.5 = \$10.53$ per hour. Groshen and Krueger note that the $10.53 is less than the hourly wage, $15.39, of the new supervisor, suggesting that adding a supervisor would not be efficient. However, they also note that regulations in the hospital industry may require more supervisors than hospitals would hire if left to make the choice freely based on efficiency.

A second test of the trade-off between pay and supervision was conducted by Neal (1993) at the level of the individual worker (rather than the firm). Like Groshen and Krueger, Neal reasoned that workers would report less intense supervision in high-wage industries if industry wage differentials were the result of efficiency wage policies. Controlling for demographics (but not cognitive ability) and a coarse (1-digit) measure of occupation, he found the reverse to be true: Workers in high-wage industries reported closer supervision. Neal suggested that "Firms with high shirking costs maximize profits by using a combination of supernormal wages and increased monitoring to deter shirking" (p. 414). However, Neal later concluded that "Results presented here do not constitute direct evidence that wage premia are not substitutes for monitors because the analysis does not address the simultaneous determination of both wages and monitoring intensity" (p. 416).

Cappelli and Chauvin (1991) provide a test of the hypothesis that shirking decreases as the wage premium becomes larger and as the likelihood of unemployment after job loss increases (proxied by the area unemployment rate and the percentage of workers on layoff at each plant). They used rates of worker dismissal as an indicator of shirking. Their sample consisted of manufacturing plants within a single company, with all plants having the same wage rate. However, variance in relative pay was achieved by measuring the degree to which the wage rate differed from the prevailing rate in each area. Cappelli and Chauvin found that facilities with higher relative wage rates had lower worker dismissal rates, consistent with the efficiency wage (shirking) model. Evidence on the other key variables was mixed, with percentage of workers on layoff having the expected effect of reducing dismissal rates, but no relationship between dismissal rates and area unemployment rates.

Although their findings provide some support for one aspect of efficiency wage models (i.e., that higher wages may decrease shirking), Cappelli and Chauvin (1991) acknowledged that "The more difficult question is whether the wage premium is in fact a cost-effective way of reducing shirking" (p. 783). Although they made a gallant attempt to tackle this more difficult (and central) question, they ultimately concluded that no clear answer was possible.

Related research examines whether or not the higher wages paid to unionized employees "pay for themselves" via higher productivity. Here, the answer seems to be "no." Although productivity is often higher with unions, it does not appear to be enough higher to offset the increased labor costs. Thus, higher union wages come partly at the expense of lower profits and shareholder returns (Abowd, 1989; Becker & Olson, 1992; Hirsch & Morgan, 1994). Historically, economists have viewed unions as a market imperfection that exists for the most part in industries protected from competition. As competition has increased (e.g., because of deregulation and international competition), union coverage has decreased in the United States.

Perhaps the most direct test of how effort responds to pay level is a study by Levine (1993b). He estimated a *(log)* wage equation for individual workers using demographic, human capital, and job characteristics as predictors, then used the wage residual as a proxy for inequity. Positive residuals would be overreward inequity; negative residuals underreward inequity. He then used the wage residual to predict self-reports of various types, including the item, "I'm willing to work harder than I have to for this company." The coefficient on the wage residual in the equation for this *work harder* item was .25 in his sample of U.S. workers (.13 for Japanese workers). The .25 coefficient seems to indicate that a wage residual of .10 (i.e., a wage 10% higher than predicted) would be associated with a .025-point higher response on the *work harder* scale, which has a mean of 3.90, standard deviation of .86, and a range of 1 to 5. In other words, the practical significance of the relationship seems to be quite small, suggesting that "overpayment" has essentially no meaningful effect on self-reports of effort. In contrast, the coefficient on the wage residual was 1.58 for pay satisfaction, or about 6 times the magnitude of the coefficient for *work harder.* This disparate impact of the wage residual on pay satisfaction versus self-reported effort might suggest that people are quite pleased to be overpaid, but it does not have any discernible effect on their effort levels.

While the preceding studies are intended to address the question of whether worker effort responds to wage level (i.e., an incentive effect), we observe that none of them permits one to disentangle incentive effects from sorting effects. The latter effect describes a situation in which pay level influences the ability-related characteristics of those who apply for jobs (or leave them). Unfortunately, there appears to be a surprising lack of direct research on this question as well. However, the well-known positive relationships between education and earnings found in the human capital literature and between ability and success in the status attainment literature suggest that such sorting effects do exist. In the specific case of applicant attraction, one study (Tannen, 1987) showed that increasing the amount of educational benefits provided to army enlistees increased both applicant pool size and applicants' ability test scores. Of course, educational benefits are not direct pay, but this relationship is consistent with the human capital literature.

With respect to employee retention, theoretical models of turnover suggest a number of reasons to expect a positive relationship between worker productivity and turnover. For example, turnover theories specify that workers can either be "pushed" from the current employer via dissatisfaction or "pulled" by the lure of competing offers (e.g., Hulin, 1991; March & Simon, 1958). Clearly, the likelihood of being explicitly "pulled" by a competing offer increases for high-performing individuals (e.g., Schwab, 1991), particularly in occupations in which output is highly visible even to those outside the organization (e.g., academics, sports, computer programming). Moreover, Frank and Cook's (1995) work on winner-take-all markets suggests that the ability to monitor worker quality from outside an organization has increased dramatically with improvements in technology (witness, for example, the ease of conducting citation counts in academic research relative to just a few years ago). Thus, if anything, we can expect attempts to lure top workers away from other employers to escalate in the future.

In addition, consistent with the hypothesized sorting effects of pay, high-performing employees may also be more likely to be "pushed" by dissatisfaction, particularly if an organization does not have a strong pay-for-performance system to supplement its general pay level. This is because workers compare inputs to outcomes in assessing whether or not their current employment is satisfying (Adams, 1963; March & Simon, 1958). Thus, unless outcomes are correspondingly higher for high performers, they are likely to be at greater risk of being pushed toward other employers through job dissatisfaction.

Supportive of these predictions, Trevor et al. (1997) found that employees with the highest performance levels were especially sensitive to how closely their performance was recognized by pay growth over time. Where pay growth did not keep up with performance, high performers were at increased risk of leaving. In other words, better performers may be less likely to stay, at least when there is a weak pay-for-performance relationship inside the organization.

Pay Level and Overall Utility

> Do enterprises that pay more-than-average wages usually get a bargain? Are hourly earnings above the average so effective in attracting superior workers and in inducing men to do their best in order to hold desirable high-paying jobs that the price of labor is lowest where wage rates are highest? Are [these high-wage firms] really smart buyers of labor? (Slichter, 1950, p. 90)

As several researchers have noted, estimating the total utility to be gained by increases in pay is a complex exercise. That an increase in pay will have a direct and short-term impact on labor cost is clear. By contrast, quantifying the long-term effects on labor cost and effectiveness is more difficult. Fortunately, considerable work has been done since 1950 to develop utility models that can address Slichter's question. At this point in time, utility models are most helpful in understanding how changes in composition of the workforce (i.e., the sorting effect) can influence performance levels. Recognition of incentive effects is perhaps less straightforward, although we will suggest below that this is also possible. Utility models were originally developed to evaluate the utility of alternative selection (as opposed to compensation) practices. Thus, we begin by presenting a basic selection utility model and then discuss briefly how this model can be used to examine the effects of compensation decisions.

The basic model specifies that the utility (dollar value) per hire per year of a selection predictor (or set of predictors) is (Boudreau, 1991):

$$u = r_{yx} \times SD_y \times Z - C/SR$$

where:

u = Utility per hire per year in dollars

r_{yx} = Correlation between performance criterion, y, and the predictor(s), X

SD_y = Standard deviation of the dollar value of performance increments

Z = Mean standard score (z) on predictor, X, of those hired/selected

C = Cost per applicant

SR = Selection ratio, defined as hires/applicants

It represents the value created by using one or more selection predictors minus their cost. Higher and more positive values are better, implying higher profit. The predictor or set of predictors having the highest *u* represents the best selection strategy. This parameter is higher for more complex and demanding jobs. Thus, good selection decisions have the highest payoff in jobs where performance differences have a large impact on firm performance.

The more selective an organization is in its hiring process (hiring only the best, low selection ratio), the more likely its hires are to be above the mean and to have positive *z* scores. *Z* is the mean of these *z* scores. Note that *Z* is a function of *SR:* the more selective, the higher the average *Z* score. Some values of *Z* at various levels of *SR* are as follows:

SR	*Z*
.2	1.40
.5	0.80
.8	0.35

Utility models suggest that increases in pay level may affect overall utility in two contradictory ways. First, pay increases may *decrease* utility by increasing the post-hire cost per selected employee. Alternatively, they may *increase* utility by attracting more and higher-quality applicants, thus (a) decreasing costs of attraction per applicant and (b) decreasing *SR* and increasing *Z*, the average score on the predictor of those hired (or retained). Thus, the overall impact of an increase in pay depends heavily on whether or not the decrease in hiring costs and selection ratio, as well as the increase in *Z*, outweigh the larger post-hire compensation costs.

Earlier, we said that utility theory's primary focus seems to be on sorting effects, the change in the composition of the workforce.

However, one might extend utility theory by broadening the definition of Z to include a worker's responsiveness to pay level (i.e., the probability of an incentive effect) once employed. Thus, valid selection decisions combined with a higher pay level could affect both worker quality and their responsiveness to pay level. By the same token, however, note that if the employer relies on selection devices with close to zero validity (such as handwriting analysis, where $r_{yx} = 0$; Schmidt & Hunter, 1998), the increase in applicant pool size and decrease in the selection ratio will have no impact on performance, because selectivity in hiring will have no impact on job performance.

Although utility theory lends itself nicely to the analysis of compensation decisions (Gerhart & Milkovich, 1992), we are aware of only two such applications, both of which are based on simulations. In the first, Klaas and McClendon (1996) used the Boudreau and Berger (1985) utility model, which simultaneously illustrates the utility consequences of both selection and retention patterns. Specifically, the Boudreau and Berger model describes utility as a function of the quantity and quality of the workforce at the end of Period 1, the quality and quantity of those who entered and those who left in Period 2, and the transaction costs associated with entry and exit.[9] Klaas and McClendon note that wage level is a factor in entry and exit decisions and suggest that the transaction costs portion of the Boudreau and Berger model can be modified to include wage costs.

Klaas and McClendon (1996) then develop their simulation using pay level as the compensation policy in question. Three pay levels—20% below market (lag), at the market (match), and 20% above the market (lead)—were studied in the context of bank teller jobs, using parameters estimated in previous studies. For example, based on empirical work by Williams and Dreher (1992), they assumed an average teller turnover rate of 32%. Based on Freeman (1980), they assumed that paying 20% above market will be associated with 10% less turnover. Thus, a bank leading the market by 20% would be assumed to have a turnover rate of 29%, while a bank lagging the market by 20% would be assumed to have a turnover rate of 35%.

Furthermore, it is necessary to estimate the correlation between performance and turnover and how that might vary under the three different pay policies. Consistent with efficiency wage theory, Klaas and McClendon (1996) assumed a positive ($r = .20$) relationship between performance and retention, which translates into a .13 standard deviation difference ($d = .13$) between those staying and those leaving, using a match pay policy. Using a lag policy would mean greater loss of high performers, leading Klaas and McClendon to set $d = .11$ in this case. With a lead policy, high performers would be more likely to be retained, so $d = .16$ was assumed.

Among the other parameters in their model, a particularly important one is SD_y, for which Klaas and McClendon (1996) used three different values: 20%, 30%, and 40% of the mean salary, which was $14,350.[10] Another parameter of interest is Z, the mean standard score on the predictor. As we have pointed out, Z is a function of the selection ratio. Thus, all else being equal, a smaller selection ratio is good because it increases Z, given a nonzero validity. In this particular case, Klaas and McClendon used validity values of .1, .35, and .6.

However, as Murphy (1986) has shown, it is also necessary to factor in the acceptance rate of applicants and whether or not those rates are related to ability. For example, it may be that high-ability workers are less likely to accept any particular job offer because they have many alternatives. To address this issue, Klaas and McClendon (1996) assumed a correlation between acceptance and ability of –.5 under a lag policy versus –.3 under a match policy and –.1 under a lead policy. Note that much the same issue arises with turnover, where they also assumed a nonzero correlation—although in this case, a positive one—between retention and performance. Thus, the impact of pay level policy (lag, match, or lead) on both job acceptance rates and turnover decisions is recognized in the Klaas and McClendon simulation.

The results of the simulation were very clear. Across all combinations of assumed SD_y and validity, the lead pay policy yielded the *lowest* utility. In other words, the gains realized from making better quality hires and retaining more high-performing employees were smaller than the additional wage costs. As such, Klaas and McClendon's (1996) findings stand in contrast to predictions of efficiency wage theory, which tends to equate high pay with "efficient" pay.

The Klaas and McClendon paper makes a very important contribution by demonstrating how utility theory can be applied to compensation decisions and by carefully describing the choices to be made in estimating the many complex parameters in any such application. Still, as with any simulation, one can raise questions about the assumptions and choices of parameter values. One important issue in this case is the fact that the job of bank teller is a relatively low-wage, low-complexity job. Thus, it is quite possible that lead pay policies would return positive utility in jobs where SD_y, the dollar value of performance differences, is higher. In such a setting, SD_y would be higher not only because salary would be higher but also because in more complex jobs, SD_y may far exceed 40% of salary (see Boudreau, 1991, Appendix B), the largest value used by Klaas and McClendon.

Another issue with the Klaas and McClendon (1996) research is that although they assumed that high-ability applicants were less likely than lower-ability applicants to accept job offers, they contrarily assumed that high-performance employees were more likely than low performers to stay with the company. However, as indicated earlier, there are good reasons to believe that high-performing workers will be more, rather than less, prone to turnover (e.g., March & Simon, 1958; Schwab, 1991; Trevor et al., 1997). The implication of a positive relationship between performance and turnover is that there may be larger gains to be realized from a lead pay policy than is implied by the Klaas and McClendon article.

In fact, in a utility-based extension of the Trevor et al. (1997) findings, Boudreau, Sturman, Trevor, and Gerhart (1999) examined the utility consequences of different pay-for-performance schemes. They examined three alternative policies: the current policy (a moderate link between pay and performance, where pay growth tailed off at very high performance levels); a policy where high performers received larger pay increases than under the current policy; and finally, a policy where high performers not only received larger increases, but low performers received smaller pay increases than previously. Another important difference from the Klaas and McClendon study is that Boudreau et al. used data on exempt employees with a mean salary of approximately $55,000 (in 2001 dollars), considerably higher than the average salary for the tellers (approximately $19,500 in 2001 dollars) studied by Klaas and McClendon. This difference alone would serve to make the SD_y parameter nearly 3 times larger in the Boudreau et al. study. In addition, Boudreau et al. argued that for their sample of exempt employees, one might wish to assume that SD_y was as high as 100% of salary (rather than the maximum of 40% that Klaas and McClendon used for the job of teller). Thus, Boudreau et al. conducted their evaluation using three SD_y values: 20%, 40%, and 100%.

Boudreau et al. (1999) found that while the cost for each of the two more aggressive pay-for-performance policies would be higher than for the current policy, the net benefit of the more aggressive policies would also be higher so long as one could justify the assumption that SD_y was 40% of salary or higher. Only under an assumption of $SD_y = 20\%$ was the current pay policy found to yield a higher net benefit.

It is worth noting that Boudreau et al.'s (1999) utility estimates reflect only what Gerhart and Milkovich (1992) described as the "workforce composition effect" (changes in who stays and who leaves); the effect of a more aggressive pay-for-performance system on the behaviors of current employees is not captured. In this sense, the utility estimate is likely to be biased downward. In addition, based on Rosenbaum's (1984) work on mobility within corporations, Boudreau et al. argue that those who are the top performers early in their careers are more likely to advance to higher-level positions where SD_y will be much larger. To the degree that a more aggressive pay-for-performance policy results in more of these future high-impact employees staying with a company, the utility estimate based only on the SD_y in the current job will again yield an underestimate, this time because it does not recognize the value of performance differences over the course of a career. Finally, we note that the Boudreau et al. study is useful in that it helps to illustrate the sensitivity of these models to differing assumptions and parameter estimates. We hope that it fosters additional research that will permit assumptions to be made with greater confidence.

Pay: How Much? (But Also, How?)

Although our focus in this chapter has been on pay level, or how much organizations pay, we will see that the influence of pay level is likely a function of how strongly the pay level depends on performance. For example, in the Boudreau et al. (1999) research described above, the three pay policies had essentially the same pay level (and cost), but the more aggressive pay-for-performance policies resulted in higher anticipated performance levels. In other cases, we will see that pay level is often higher in organizations that closely link pay to performance.

A well-known example of a company that pays what might be described as an efficiency wage is the previously discussed Lincoln Electric Company. In 1996, the average production worker annual earnings were reported to be $55,000, or $60,254 in 2000 dollars (Hodgetts, 1997). Table 2.1 (in our Chapter 2) indicates that the average hourly wage in the goods-producing sector of the economy was $16.25 in 2000, which implies annual earnings of $33,800. Thus, earnings at Lincoln Electric are 78% higher than the average. An examination of its recent financial statements reveals that a major portion of earnings at Lincoln Electric come from the bonus pool, which is tied to profitability. In a typical year, the bonus pool at Lincoln is nearly as large as its net income. Lincoln Electric also has very few supervisors, one per 100 workers (Hodgetts, 1997). This suggests that workers at Lincoln are given more responsibility and expected to be more entrepreneurial and productive than production workers at most other companies. A company that paid 78% above some market benchmark without the type of strong pay-performance link found at Lincoln would probably not find that its pay level had the same effects.

Future Research

One of the surprising discoveries we made while researching this chapter concerns the relative paucity of field studies examining relationships between pay level and important outcomes such as attraction, turnover, and employee productivity. As we have just seen, the scarcity of such studies makes it almost impossible to estimate with any precision the likely effects of changes in pay level on either attraction or retention at the level of the work unit or firm. In addition, even fewer studies examine relationships between pay level and direct measures of employee effort or quality using the firm or work unit as the level of analysis. As such, all three topics—the effects of pay level on applicant attraction, turnover, and employee effort and quality—are desperately in need of greater research attention.

Research on the relationship between pay level and employee quality is particularly needed because economists and psychologists tend to make different assumptions about the type of person most attracted by high pay levels. Specifically, while several economic theories assume that higher wages attract higher-quality applicants and harder-working employees, psychologists tend to see money as a lower-order inducement that may attract individuals with low commitment to any given employer and lower interest in the work itself. Indeed, because empirical research has supported some of the psychologists' concerns (e.g., Lawler, 1971; Trank et al., 2001), it seems likely that high pay levels must be buttressed with a number of other supportive human resource (HR) practices for maximal effectiveness.

As a practical matter, this means that future research on pay levels should ideally measure several other HR practices at the same time, so that joint and interactive effects can be determined. Three other HR practices that would seem to be particularly important for explaining differences in the returns to higher pay levels are the validity of selection procedures, the extent of pay for promotion (pay structure; see

Chapter 4), and the nature and extent of performance-contingent pay (pay basis). For example, combined use of high pay levels with valid selection devices and strong pay-for-performance contingencies may eliminate many of the overpayment risks inherent in high pay level strategies. In any event, focusing only on pay level and average rates of attraction and turnover is bound to miss a good deal of information that is critical to employers.

As researchers attempt to examine these questions, a number of challenges must be addressed. One such challenge (noted earlier) is that pay levels may not be a good reflection of total compensation, particularly when some employers use high benefits rather than high wages to attract and retain employees (e.g., Dreher, Ash, & Bretz, 1988, found benefits to be negatively correlated with direct pay). Similarly, if employers actually set pay in such a way as to compensate for undesirable features of the work, then the effects of pay level will again be underestimated unless other attributes are also measured.

In addition, there is the problem of determining causality in cross-sectional field research, as demonstrated in the findings of Williams and Dreher (1992). If higher pay rates are partly endogenous (i.e., being used mostly in situations where turnover or attraction are problems), the influence of pay rate will be underestimated unless this endogeneity is addressed.

Given these difficulties with cross-sectional research, we urge researchers to investigate the changes in outcomes from natural experiments that arise when organizations decide to raise or lower pay levels for strategic purposes. Although quasi-experiments are likely to deviate somewhat from perfect experimental conditions (e.g., Cook & Campbell, 1979), one advantage is that one can observe how contextual factors not observable in more controlled conditions may affect the results. Second, the long-term effects (and survival) of programs can be assessed.

Finally, as indicated in the previous chapter, there is also a surprising lack of both laboratory and field research pertaining to how pay level decisions are actually made in organizations. We believe that this research could be greatly enhanced by studies designed to uncover the mental models of motivation used by real executives and compensation specialists in designing pay programs. A related topic would be to determine whether organizations are more effective when the beliefs and mental models of their executives are closely aligned with their actual pay practices. Some examples that come to mind are General Electric under CEO Jack Welch, or Southwest Airlines under CEO Herb Kelleher.

Notes

1. Although neither theory has received much support, reviewers of the literature have been reluctant to completely invalidate their propositions. For example, Miner (1980) concluded that although "the available research does not support the Maslow theory to any significant degree. . . . This does not imply that the theory is wrong, merely that it has not yet been supported" (p. 41). Similarly, Kanfer (1990) speculated that Maslow's hierarchy "can potentially explain similarities across individuals in their needs and interests over a lifetime," although she also noted such observations might be of limited use since "Motivational theories are often judged in terms of their power to explain and predict differences in behavior between individuals over relatively brief time spans" (p. 85).

2. Intrinsic interest has been measured in two ways: via direct self-reports and as amount of free time devoted to a task when the monetary (or verbal) reward is subsequently withdrawn.

3. Indeed, one continues to see the influence of Herzberg, Maslow, and Deci's beliefs, both in the popular business press and among academics. For example, in a recent *Fortune* cover story on "God and Business: The Surprising Quest for Spiritual Renewal in the American Workplace," Nobel-prize-winning economist Robert Fogel argues that post–World War II prosperity has created enough wealth that many Americans' primary desires are not for material goods, but rather for spiritual and intellectual assets:

> In a world in which all but a small percentage are lacking in adequate nutrition and other necessities, self-realization may indeed seem like a mere ornament, but not in a country where even the poor are rich by past or Third World standards. (As quoted in Gunther, 2001, p. 66)

4. We shall see in the next chapter, however, that this prediction might not hold to the extent that people evaluate their own compensation relative to the compensation of others, or when compensation is used as a signal of rank-ordered competence or achievement. In these situations, there may not be much (if any) fall-off in pay importance.

5. In the case of a not-for-profit organization, it means less money available for delivering its product or service.

6. An examination of Table 6–1 of Freeman and Medoff (1984) shows that this estimate is based on seven different national samples. All results are based on using the individual worker, not the firm, as the unit of analysis.

7. For an early review of turnover research at the individual level of analysis, see Parsons (1977).

8. Groshen and Krueger (1990) also recognized the possibility that the sorting version of efficiency wage theory could explain a trade-off between wages and supervision by implying that lower-ability workers need closer supervision.

9. The Boudreau and Berger model also recognizes the importance of employee tenure with the firm as a determinant of utility, as well as financial (present value) and tax considerations that influence utility estimates.

10. A review of models for estimating SD_y and findings can be found in Boudreau (1991).

4 Pay Structure

RELATIVE PAY WITHIN ORGANIZATIONS

There is a fundamental ideological tension between the egalitarian premises that underlie participative management and the existence of large interclass reward differentials.

—Cowherd and Levine (1992)

Competition encourages increased effort. . . . But competition also discourages cooperation. . . . The larger is the spread between the compensation that the winner and loser receive, the more important is each of these effects.

—Lazear (1989)

In the previous two chapters, we concentrated on differences in pay level *across* employers, where pay level is the "average" of rates paid by an employer across different jobs or skill groups (Milkovich & Newman, 1999, p. 185).[1] In the present chapter, we shift our focus to pay structure, which refers to differences in pay *within* employers based on different types or levels of work or skill (Milkovich & Newman, 1999, p. 53).

To illustrate the difference between pay level and pay structure concepts, consider two jobs, marketing manager and financial manager, in two different companies, but having the same job content. In Company 1, annual pay for both jobs is $85,000. However, in Company 2, the marketing manager receives $80,000, and the financial manager is paid $90,000. Under our definitions, the two organizations have the same pay level (average pay = $85,000 in both) but different pay structures, because the relative pay of the two jobs differs within the two organizations.

Table 4.1 Pilot Compensation at Southwest Airlines Versus Three Major Carriers

	First Officer Year 1	*First Officer, Medium-Sized Aircraft Year 5*	*Captain, Smallest Aircraft Year 10*	*Captain, Largest Aircraft Maximum*
Southwest	$36,132	$82,068	$140,412	$143,508
American (A)	$25,524	$67,092	$132,276	$185,004
Delta (D)	$33,396	$95,040	$112,308	$209,388
United (U)	$29,808	$95,100	$128,124	$200,796
Avg. (A,D,U)	$29,576	$85,744	$124,236	$198,396

SOURCE: Adapted from Proctor (1999).

As another example, consider how the pay structure for pilots differs across airlines. As Table 4.1 demonstrates, there are smaller differentials based on pilot rank (i.e., job level) at Southwest Airlines than at United, American, or Delta. Specifically, Southwest offers comparable or slightly higher cash compensation for pilots early in their careers, but considerably less at the highest ranks.

Why does Southwest do this? Such a structure is consistent with the egalitarian philosophy of Southwest's founders, which includes profit sharing for all and following the same compensation "rules" for executives as for employees. However, this more egalitarian structure also supports Southwest's business strategy, which is based on very high productivity and customer satisfaction. One key to high productivity is keeping planes fully utilized (i.e., in the air). To this end, Southwest leads the industry in minimizing on-the-ground turnaround time, which saves it millions of dollars per year by being able to service the same number of customers with fewer planes. One of the main tactics it uses to get fast turnaround is to involve everyone (even pilots) in doing whatever it takes to get planes back in the air as quickly as possible. Southwest believes that this kind of camaraderie is more likely to take place in a context of egalitarianism.

Southwest also uses other aspects of its compensation strategy to reinforce its focus on the importance of cooperative action in achieving success. For example, Southwest recently contributed 14% of employee pay into a deferred profit-sharing plan, in which employees can invest in a variety of ways. A popular investment is Southwest stock, 10% of which is owned by employees (Rosen, 2002). Southwest also pays employees in part

Table 4.2 Revenues, Capacity, and Costs: US Airways Versus Southwest Airlines, 2000

	US Airways	*Southwest Airlines*
Revenues	$8,341,000,000	$5,649,560,000
Operating Costs	$9,322,000,000	$4,628,415,000
Labor Costs	$3,637,000,000	$1,683,470,017
Available Seat Miles (ASMs)	66,506,000,000	59,909,965,000
Labor Cost/Revenue	43.6%	29.8%
Labor Cost/Employees	$83,672	$57,507
Operating Costs/ASM	$0.140	$0.077
Labor Costs/ASM	$.055	$.028

SOURCE: Southwest Airlines (2001); US Airways (2001).

on the basis of the number of trips they make on the job, an incentive to keep planes moving on time (Freiberg & Freiberg, 1996).

Why are Southwest pilots willing to work for less cash compensation (compared with other airlines) at higher seniority levels? First, because the company has performed well, stock ownership has created a great deal of wealth for the pilots. Second, the fact that Southwest pilots fly more trips, combined with pay by the trip, also leads to higher total compensation. (Flying more trips does not necessarily mean more time away from home, because Southwest's point-to-point flights result in less time at airports than spent by pilots flying under competitors' hub-and-spoke systems; McCartney, 2002.) Finally, unlike some other airlines, Southwest has not laid off pilots because of economic downturns.

Southwest's compensation strategy, including its unique pay structure, appears to achieve the desired results. The productivity and financial effects of Southwest's human resource (HR) practices can be seen in Table 4.2, which compares Southwest's performance with that of US Airways, an airline with similar capacity (available seat miles, or ASMs). Note that ASMs, a measure of capacity (seats available times miles flown), is similar between the two airlines. US Airways has generated more revenue than Southwest with a similar level of capacity, which might be expected given that Southwest competes via a cost leadership strategy, whereas for the most part, US Airways does not.

The problem for US Airways is its cost, which exceeds its revenues. One area of substantial cost advantage for Southwest is labor, which represents 29.8% of revenue, compared with 43.6% of revenue at US

Airways. In the airline industry, cost per ASM is a widely used measure of efficiency. Southwest's operating cost per ASM is nearly 50% lower (7.7¢ versus 14¢) than at US Airways. Labor cost per ASM is 2.8¢ at Southwest, compared with 5.4¢ at US Airways. How important is this difference? If US Airways were somehow able to bring its ratio of labor cost per ASM down to the Southwest level of 2.8¢, US Airways would save $1.8 billion per year in labor costs. Clearly, how much an organization pays is not the only aspect of compensation that can have important consequences. Labor cost per employee at US Airways is 45% higher than that of Southwest, yet Southwest is more efficient. And Southwest has been the mostly consistently profitable company in the U.S. airline industry.

In Chapter 2, we briefly discussed several reasons why an employer might want to exercise discretion (i.e., deviate from the market) in setting pay rates. In this chapter, we examine such reasons in greater detail. Before doing so, however, we make a brief digression to explain the primary mechanism (job evaluation) for creating unique internal pay structures.

The Role of Jobs and Job Evaluation in Pay Structure

A fundamental premise of discussions of pay structure is that pay rates are linked to *jobs.* Although the job has long been a fundamental unit of analysis in post-institutional economics and HR management, until recently, it was largely ignored in neoclassical economics. Indeed, it was not so very long ago that Lazear (1995a) observed that "The entire notion of a 'job' . . . is virtually absent from most labor-market analyses" (p. 260).

Instead, neoclassical economists tended to emphasize supply-side factors (i.e., worker characteristics) as the main sources of differential pay. As mentioned briefly in Chapter 2, human capital theorists such as Becker (1975), Mincer and Polachek (1974), and Schultz (1963) proposed that workers invest in their own productive capacity (via formal education, on-the-job training, and improvements in health) as a means of enhancing future rates of return to their employment. Human capital theory conceptualizes workers as "embodying a set of skills that can be 'rented' out to employers," with the "knowledge and skills a worker has . . . generating a certain stock of productive capital" (Ehrenberg & Smith, 1982, p. 229).

Human capital theory was quickly embraced by neoclassicists because it provided a basis for responding to post-institutionalist critiques of the neoclassical model. For example, it provided a rationale for arguing that differences in wage levels across employers were probably more illusory than real, as a result of having workforces with differing levels of productivity-enhancing productivity (e.g., efficiency wage theory). Also, the theory received considerable empirical support in that higher levels of investment in health and education tended to correlate with higher productivity and income at both the individual and national levels of analysis (Becker, 1975).

Still, human capital theory could not explain many other observations of the post-institutionalists, such as the existence of elaborate social norms and rules for hiring and promotion inside firms; the existence of barriers to mobility based on factors other than human capital (such as race and sex); the existence of "kinks" in age-earnings profiles due to changes in position held (as opposed to the smooth progression implied by a human capital perspective); and the administrative reality that wages in most organizations were attached to *jobs* rather than to individuals. (For example, a welder with a Ph.D. was likely to be paid much the same as other welders.)

In response to these anomalies, neoclassical economists began to provide a more central role for jobs in their models and analyses (Lazear, 1999; Lazear & Rosen, 1981; Williamson, 1996). Theoretical developments such as transaction cost economics (TCE), tournament theory, and personnel economics (all of which will be reviewed shortly) all created a central role for jobs in their models of labor mobility and pay.

Turning from theory to application, the main administrative tool for establishing pay rates that deviate from those based on the external market is *job evaluation* (Dunlop, 1957; Livernash, 1957; Schwab, 1980b). In job evaluation, a committee of raters typically assigns a score that is intended to reflect the relative value of each job to the firm. Because of unique factors such as business strategy or organizational structure, this relative value may differ across employers. For example, a firm that has a very flat structure or highly interdependent jobs may choose to pay smaller differentials between jobs than would be suggested by pay surveys of other firms having similar jobs.

This is not to say that job evaluation replaces the impact of the external market, however. Although job evaluation information can be used to deviate from the market, as we discussed in Chapter 2, there is a limit to how much a firm can deviate before it faces difficulties in either product or labor markets. Indeed, the primary use of job evaluation is probably to help efficiently capture the market pay policy and apply it

Table 4.3 Compensable Factors Used in U.S. Bureau of Labor Statistics National Compensation Survey

Compensable Factor	*Maximum Points Available*
Knowledge	1,850
Supervision received	650
Guidelines	650
Complexity	450
Scope and effect	450
Personal contacts	110
Purpose of contacts	220
Physical demands	50
Work environment	50

SOURCE: U.S. Bureau of Labor Statistics (2002).

to the internal pay structure (Dunlop, 1957; Livernash, 1957; Schwab, 1980b). Job evaluation scores can then be used to equate jobs across firms, which is essential for interpreting pay survey data. (Table 4.3 provides the factors used by the U.S. Bureau of Labor Statistics National Compensation Survey to equate jobs across employers.) Some subset of jobs, referred to as *key jobs,* are typically used for this purpose, partly to reduce the complexity of the task and partly because "The exterior cannot operate directly on a thousand slightly differentiated jobs" (Dunlop, 1957, p. 130). Indeed, job evaluation "must produce acceptable results," which are judged to a considerable extent "by the degree of correlation achieved between points for key jobs and accepted wage relationships among the jobs" (p. 163). (For more information on different job evaluation systems and research, see Gerhart & Milkovich, 1992; Milkovich & Newman, 2002.)

In the only known study that directly examined how compensation decision makers simultaneously use market surveys and job evaluation points to determine job pay, Weber and Rynes (1991) found that external equity (market rates) weighed much more heavily than internal equity (job evaluation points) in final pay decisions. In an extensive examination of pay-setting influences, they obtained approximately 400 responses from members of the American Compensation Association (ACA) who had completed an ACA course on creating pay structures. Respondents were asked to recommend pay changes in nine scenarios that manipulated market survey pay (either 6% above, equal to, or 6% below current job pay) and job evaluation points (either 6% above, equal to, or 6% below the number of job evaluation points that equated to current job pay). In addition, variance in current job pay was achieved by using nine different job titles having different current pay rates. Finally, in addition to these manipulations, Weber and Rynes obtained between-subjects measures of two pay strategy variables: market position (i.e., lead, lag, or meet the market) and internal/external equity orientation of their firms.

Results suggested that current job pay had a coefficient of approximately 1.0 (i.e., a dollar-for-dollar effect) in predicting the recommended new pay rate. Both the market survey and job evaluation manipulations also influenced recommended pay, although the market pay manipulation had approximately twice as large a coefficient as the job evaluation manipulation. With respect to pay strategy, respondents from firms with pay-leader strategies recommended pay rates that were 4% higher on average, whereas respondents from market-lagging firms recommended rates that were 1% lower. In addition, those with a stronger internal equity focus gave greater relative weight to the job evaluation manipulation than did other respondents.

These findings suggest that market comparisons are especially important in pay setting.[2] At the same time, strategy has an important effect on how organizations respond to market comparisons. In other words, consistent with our earlier arguments, organizations seem to have at least some flexibility to set unique internal pay rates, and in fact they often exercise this flexibility. We turn now to a more extensive discussion of why employers might choose to deviate from market rates.

Theories of Differences in Pay Structure

Internal Labor Markets

The internal labor markets (ILM) perspective (Doeringer & Piore, 1971) offered the first systematic explanation for why an employer might choose to have an internal pay structure that differs from that implied by the external market. The ILM approach builds heavily on the earlier work by post-institutional economists that we discussed in previous chapters, but it provides a more systematic explanation for why ILMs may be efficient for employers. The key feature of an ILM is that "The pricing and allocation of labor is governed by a set of administrative rules and procedures" (Doeringer & Piore, 1971, p. 2). This internal "market" is distinguished from the external labor market, which operates more in accordance with conventional neoclassical theory. The employee-employer relationship is long-term under an ILM. Indeed, "Stability of employment is the most salient feature of the internal labor market" (Doeringer & Piore, 1971, p. 40).

However, the internal and external labor markets are connected at certain key jobs that serve as "ports of entry" from the external labor market to the ILM. Thus, supply and demand play key roles in determining wages for these ports of entry jobs. However, once workers enter the ILM, rules largely supplant external market forces.[3] The central focus of these rules is on lines of progression, or promotion ladders. Movement up these ladders "is associated with a progressive development of knowledge or skill" (Althauser & Kalleberg, 1981, p. 130). ILM rules determine how many steps are in these ladders, the rate of progression, and the criteria used for deciding who progresses.[4] For example, ability often comes into play (particularly for professional and staff positions), although typically in conjunction with some emphasis on seniority (Mills, 1985). Well-specified rules also govern layoff decisions, in which seniority is generally given much higher priority than in the case of advancement. In fact, Kerr (1954) observed that "The man on the job (given good behavior) is the only man eligible for it, and when he leaves the next man on the seniority list (given minimum ability to perform the task) is the only eligible candidate" (p. 533).

Like the post-institutionalists, ILM theorists recognized not only institutional forces but also market and efficiency considerations. In fact, at one point, Doeringer and Piore (1971) state that "It is assumed that ILMs are initiated solely at the discretion of management . . . to minimize their labor costs" (p. 28). This is hypothesized to occur in three ways.

First, skill specificity leads to a greater proportion of training costs being borne by the employer because employees are less willing to invest in skills that do not transfer across employers (Becker, 1975). From the employer's point of view, specific skills preclude economies of scale in training (for example, using an outside organization). Thus, to recoup its investment, the employer will want to set up a system that encourages worker tenure (Oi, 1962).

Second, skill specificity makes informal on-the-job training more prevalent, presumably because it is often more efficient. A key concern here is whether more senior employees, the holders of critical on-the-job knowledge, will be willing to transfer this knowledge to trainees. If senior workers fear that they will be replaced by younger (and cheaper) workers once they transfer their knowledge, on-the-job training will break down. Thus, seniority provisions that protect senior workers from arbitrary discharge play a key role here (Thurow, 1975).

A third factor in Doeringer and Piore's model (1971) is custom. When employment is stable, workers come into regular and repeated contact with one another. This regularity often leads to the development of a set of unwritten rules that govern the employment relationship, including accepted pay differentials between jobs. These rules may eventually become formally institutionalized.

Although the efficiency consequences of decisions based on seniority and custom may be debated, Doeringer and Piore's (1971) general view is that ILMs exist because they are efficient. First, turnover may be lower because workers tend to like the job security, advancement opportunities, and due process inherent in ILM firms. This is advantageous because when a firm invests in its workers, it needs an adequate amount of time to recoup that investment (Oi, 1962). Otherwise, the effect is similar to purchasing a piece of capital equipment with a life span that is too short to justify its price. Second, there may be technical efficiencies in (internal) recruitment, screening, and training due to the greater availability of information regarding the ability, motivation, and interests of current employees. Thus, ILMs should permit better and less costly decisions in these areas.[5]

Although empirical interest in ILMs has tapered off since the 1970s, Baker, Gibbs, and Holmstrom (1994a, 1994b) reported on a large archival data set including all management employees in a medium-sized U.S. service firm from 1969 to 1988. Based on this sample (which included 62,957 person-years of data), the authors concluded that an ILM indeed existed in the firm but that there was "mixed evidence on the underlying conditions that the theory suggests are necessary to support an ILM" (1994a, p. 883). For example, they found considerable support for the existence of administrative rules, a job-based pay structure, and "large numbers of lengthy careers characterized by movement through numerous jobs" (1994a, p. 883). On the other hand, they found mixed evidence regarding the importance of firm-specific human capital and little evidence of restricted ports of entry and exit (indeed, they reported "significant" movement in and out at all job levels). In their second article based on this data set, Baker et al. (1994b) report the existence of a clear "cohort effect," such that "Much of the variation between cohort wages seems to come from the starting wages and to persist from that point

Exhibit 4.1 IBM's Move to Emphasize External Competitiveness in Its Pay Strategy

Historically, IBM was an excellent example of a firm run largely by ILM principles. Employees were hired through entry level positions and typically stayed with IBM for life. Because of IBM's strong emphasis on marketing and sales, even technical employees with engineering or programming backgrounds often found it beneficial for their careers to rotate through sales and marketing functions. Consistent with these career patterns, IBM emphasized internal rather than external equity in its pay structure: "In any given salary grade, accountants, development engineers, HR professionals, programmers, and manufacturing managers would be paid comparably off the same salary structure, irrespective of what market data said about . . . each job family" (Richter, 1998, p. 53). Not surprisingly, this policy led to some job families being overpaid, on average, relative to the external market, and others being underpaid.

Although this policy worked well for IBM under so-called lifetime employment, problems developed in the 1990s as IBM laid off some employees and was abandoned by others. In short, less positive business conditions at IBM led it to loosen its ILM and compete more directly with other employers at all levels of the labor market. Not surprisingly, by the mid-1990s, IBM changed from a single salary structure (for nonsales job families) to different salary structures (and merit budgets) for different job families (Richter, 1998). This corresponds to the type of policy one would expect to be associated with an organization that was no longer able to buffer itself from the external market.

on" (p. 935). The existence of a cohort effect is consistent with similar within-firm evidence reported earlier by Gerhart (1990).

IBM is an example of a company that traditionally had an ILM but eventually modified its system. Exhibit 4.1 provides a description. More broadly, the argument has been made that there has been a shift away from ILMs to different types of employment relationships (e.g., Cappelli, 1999, 2000).

Transaction Cost Economics (TCE)

In their development of ILM theory, Doeringer and Piore (1971) stressed that both efficiency and institutional forces (such as social custom) led to the development of ILMs. In contrast, TCE focuses entirely on economic or efficiency explanations. This approach grew out of the work of Coase (1937), who focused on the deceptively simple question of why firms exist (McKenzie & Lee, 1998). Later, Williamson (1975) sought to explain the existence of ILMs, in which direct market forces are often supplanted by rules.

Williamson (1975) hypothesized that firms exist because the market mechanism has a variety of "transaction costs" associated with it. Broadly speaking, these refer to the costs of "discovering the best deals in terms of prices and attributes of products, negotiating contracts, and ensuring that the resulting terms of the contract are followed" (McKenzie & Lee, p. 25). According to Williamson, Wachter, and Harris (1975), there are ordinarily several types of contracts that can be used to control transaction costs. However, the problem faced in economic production can be traced to what Williamson et al. refer to as "small-numbers bargaining."

To describe this problem, Williamson et al. (1975) begin with Kenneth Arrow's lighthouse example. There is only one lighthouse and (in the simplest case) only one ship. Thus, a trading problem arises because there is only one seller (the lighthouse) and one buyer of the service (the ship). This means that competitive forces cannot operate to establish an equilibrium price that clears the market, because there is no market. Similarly, the lack of a market means that the lighthouse can act opportunistically and engage in monopoly pricing.[6]

A firm similarly finds itself confronted with a small-numbers bargaining problem, causing it to supplant spot contracts with ILMs governed by rules. The primary cause of this problem is job idiosyncrasy, which requires training to take place in an on-the-job context (Williamson et al., 1975, p. 257). Based on Doeringer and Piore's work, Williamson et al. identify four sources of job idiosyncrasy that typically make classroom or general training unsuitable: equipment, processes, informal team accommodations, and communications. However, like Doeringer and Piore before them, Williamson et al. (1975) recognize the following:

> Success of on-the-job training is plainly conditional on the information-disclosure attitudes of incumbent employees. . . . The danger is that incumbent employees

will hoard this information to their personal advantage and engage in a series of bilateral monopolistic exchanges with the management—to the detriment of both the firm and other employees as well. (p. 257)

To make things even more complex, the tasks that comprise idiosyncratic jobs are subject to "periodic disturbance by environmental changes" such as shifts in demand, changes in relative factor prices, and technological change. Efficient production requires that workers continually adapt to these changes. Thus, transaction costs arise from the fact that employers and employees make decisions in uncertain and complex environments, where either side might be tempted to behave in opportunistic ways to exploit the other. This would not be so important if there were large numbers of employers and workers for each job, but because job idiosyncrasy creates a small-numbers exchange condition, market forces are unable to operate in a manner to discipline both parties and ensure efficient contracts.

In addition, these problems are exacerbated by bounded rationality, which makes it less likely that all possible outcomes can be foreseen and explicitly included in an *ex ante* contract. Consequently, a firm must rely on developing an understanding with its workers (or an informal organization to supplement the formal organization) that within their "zone of indifference" (Barnard, 1951), they will cooperate with management in ways that are not explicitly laid out in a formal contract.

Thus, as Herbert Simon (1957a) observed, it is often more efficient to establish longer-term contracts or relationships in which workers agree to accept direction from managers (within broad limits) in return for certain obligations on the part of the employer. In the case of an internal labor market, such obligations would typically include promotion from within, seniority as an important factor in job allocation, protection from arbitrary discipline, and long-term careers with pay increasing with years of service. Note that seniority plays an especially important role in encouraging senior workers to share idiosyncratic knowledge with junior workers without fear of competition (Thurow, 1975). In return, the organization hopes to obtain the "consummate cooperation" of employees, "an affirmative job attitude [that] includes the use of judgment, filling gaps, and taking initiative" (Williamson et al., 1975, p. 266).

In summary, the TCE framework provides an efficiency-based explanation for the existence of ILMs and long-term employment relationships. This is not to say that all employment relationships are long-term or that all workers are employees. The contract, implicit or explicit, between workers and organizations varies across and within organizations according to its length, amount of investment made in human capital, and whether it is an employment relationship or some alternative arrangement (e.g., independent contractor; e.g., Cappelli, 1999; Rousseau & Ho, 2000; Tsui, Pearce, Porter, & Tripoli, 1997). Nevertheless, the concepts described in the ILM and TCE models remain widespread today, even as the diversity of relationship types has grown.

Tournament Theory

While ILM and TCE theories tend to focus on specific skills and on-the-job training as motivations for steeper pay in internal labor markets, tournament theory focuses more on the fact that movement up the job hierarchy (promotion) plays a key incentive role in organizations. The tournament model has several key features (Lazear, 1995b, 1999; Lazear & Rosen, 1981). First, it recognizes that pay growth over time is not smooth; rather, there are "kinks" from promotion effects on pay. This emphasis on the *job* (and job changes) as a driver of pay contrasts in part with human capital theory, where emphasis is on the return to investment in one's own *individual* human capital, which suggests smooth pay growth (Lazear, 1999).

Second, the incentive effects of tournaments are tied directly to the size of the prize differentials between ranks or levels, with effort being predicted to increase directly with increases in the differentials. Third, pay growth is larger at higher job levels than at lower ones because the number of levels available for future promotions becomes smaller, and thus promotion is less likely. To maintain the expected value of a promotion at sufficiently high levels, there must be an increase in the payoff to offset the decline in the promotion probabilities (i.e., the relationship between job level and pay is convex). Thus, there must be a very large prize at the highest level (i.e., chief executive officer, or CEO) because there are no further levels to which one might progress.

It should be noted that in contrast to the predictions of marginal productivity theory, tournament theory does not require the pay and the marginal product of an individual to be equal at any given point in time. Indeed, people in the very highest levels (e.g., top executives) do not need to be worth the amount of the prize for the scheme to be efficient. This is because the efficiency properties come largely from the incentive effects that these large prizes have on employees lower in the hierarchy. Another feature of tournaments is that those who "lose" in early rounds of the tournament (i.e., do not get early promotions) may find that they cannot compete in later rounds (for empirical evidence of this phenomenon, see Kanter, 1977; Rosenbaum, 1984). Thus, performance in the early rounds has long-term consequences. Moreover, promotion (or pay) decisions are based on relative, not absolute, evaluations of performance. Since each vacancy or prize can be allocated to only one person, it does not matter whether the best person is only slightly better or a great deal better than the next-best person; the decision is the same. Finally, to the degree that relative performance is measured with error, tournament prizes need to be even larger to compensate for this increased risk to contestants.

Why would an organization find it efficient to use a tournament structure? According to Lazear and Rosen (1981), tournaments are most likely to be found in situations where the costs of monitoring behavior are highest. By implication, this suggests that tournament structures are more likely where performance is most critical. We have also seen that tournaments are used to offset diminished opportunities for promotions. Thus, tournament structures may be especially relevant for executive level jobs, where performance is critical and promotion opportunities are increasingly limited with upward progression.

We also observe, building on generalizability theory (Cronbach, Gleser, Nanda, & Rajaratnam, 1972), that the *relative* nature of tournament competition is particularly important if monitoring costs need to be minimized, because relative judgments require less information than do absolute judgments.[7] Although supervisors may agonize over whether employees deserve a *3* or a *4* on their performance ratings, it is usually a simpler matter to decide whether one employee or executive is more productive than another. (The caveat is that there may be efficiency losses due to increased competition.[8]) In other words, monitoring costs should be lower under a relative performance system than under an absolute performance system. Thus, given the reduced need for monitoring combined with the potential for substantial incentive effects, a tournament structure may prove to be very efficient for some organizations, particularly for some jobs.

What does empirical evidence say about the predictions of tournament theory? For the moment, we confine ourselves to observations about whether or not tournament structures appear to exist. Effects of such structures on individual or organizational performance are considered later in the chapter.

One question relating to tournament theory is whether the relationship between job level and pay is actually convex. Here, there is fairly long-standing evidence of the predicted convex relationship, particularly at the managerial and executive levels. For example, Elliott Jaques (1961) and others (e.g., Kuethe & Levenson, 1964; Mahoney & Weitzel, 1978) found remarkable consistency in the estimates of various samples of people regarding what constitutes fair pay for positions at various levels. Interestingly, this result was obtained even in samples of people who were largely ignorant of actual pay levels, even though their estimates were highly consistent with actual pay.

In general, differentials of 30% to 40% appeared to be regarded as fair across most managerial levels, while differentials of only 15% were perceived as fair between supervisory and managerial levels, and larger differentials (approximately 55%) were regarded as fair as one moved to the very top of the hierarchy (i.e., CEO). Moreover, these relative valuations were rather successfully modeled by Herbert Simon (1957b) in his theory of executive compensation.

Thus, Jaques (1961) and others found that from a psychological perspective, people with varying knowledge of actual pay patterns nevertheless produced the convex pattern of relationships between job level and pay that is predicted by tournament theory differentials. As summarized by Mahoney (1979b):

> The relative consistency of the evidence is particularly striking in view of the variety of sources and is suggestive of a general phenomenon relating distinctions in organizational rank or level with equivalent distances on a continuous scale of compensation. (p. 199)

However, Mahoney (1979a) went on to say that there were notable "breaks in the general distance relationship at both ends of the managerial hierarchy" (pp. 735–736) that were consistent with tournament theory's predicted convex relationship (i.e., smaller differentials at the lowest levels and larger ones at the highest).

More recent empirical studies have also shown convex job level-pay relationships, although they tend to be steeper than the ones observed in earlier years. For example, in a study of over 20,000 managers within seven levels of the board of directors, Gerhart and Milkovich (1990) found that job level increases at the bottom levels yielded average increases in base salaries of just over 10%, whereas movement into one of the top two job levels yielded base pay increases of 86%. Using the same data set, Lambert, Larcker, and Weigelt (1993) reported that the total compensation (base, bonus, long-term incentives) of group

CEOs was 70% larger than that of divisional CEOs and that the total compensation of corporate CEOs was 182% larger than that of the group CEOs.[9] Similarly, Main, O'Reilly, and Wade (1993) reported that in a 1984 sample, base plus bonus increased 29% from Job Level 5 to Job Level 4; 43% from Job Level 4 to Job Level 3; 83% from Job Level 3 to Job Level 2; and 142% from Job Level 2 to Job Level 1.[10]

Main et al. (1993), however, make two important observations. First, pay differentials between job levels do not directly estimate the payoff to promotion because some percentage of people in those levels probably came from outside the organization. By examining pay growth only of those promoted from inside, they found that the estimated payoff to promotion to corporate CEO was substantially diminished.

Second, Main et al. (1993) note that whereas the above adjustment diminished the estimated payoff to promotion, another adjustment—recognizing that the value of the promotion prize carries over into future years—raises the promotion payoff by a substantial amount. By making assumptions regarding the average tenure as CEO and using a discount rate of 3%, Main et al. estimate the present value of promotion to CEO to be $4.6 million. By also adding data on the value of long-term incentives, the estimate increases to $6.2 million.

Another piece of evidence concerning the existence of tournament models concerns the importance of jobs (and thus promotions) in mediating the relationship between performance and pay. (Recall Lazear's observation that the notion of a job had been mostly ignored by mainstream economic theory.) For example, Gerhart and Milkovich (1989) examined the relationship between performance, promotion, and pay in a longitudinal study of over 6,000 exempt employees in job levels 1 through 7 (of a 15-level structure) of a large, diversified firm. They found that each 1-point increase in average performance rating (on a 4-point scale) over a 6-year period was associated with about 0.4 additional promotions. Thus, an employee receiving an average rating of *3* over the period would have received 1.8 promotions on average, while an employee averaging a *4* rating would have received 2.6 promotions. In addition, promotions had a substantial payoff: On average, there was an 11% increase for each increment to job level. Similarly, Lazear (1999), using data from a large financial services company, found that promotions were associated with a 14% increase in pay, as well as with the hypothesized job-related "kinks" in age-earnings profiles. Therefore, these findings support the tournament theory's emphasis on the job as a driver of pay at least partly independent of individuals' human capital.

One other partial test of tournament theory has evaluated the hypothesis that larger prize differentials will be required to offset the decreased probability of winning when there are more contestants in the tournament. Two studies have provided supportive evidence, while one has not. On the nonsupportive side, O'Reilly, Main, and Crystal (1988), using firms included in a 1985 *Business Week* cover story on executive compensation, tested the hypothesis that the more vice presidents (i.e., more contestants) in a firm, the greater the differential between average vice president pay and CEO pay. Contrary to expectations, their results showed that the differential was smaller in firms having more vice presidents, which they interpreted as being inconsistent with tournament theory.

In contrast, Main et al. (1993), using the consulting-firm data described above, reported that the number of vice presidents was positively related to the payoff to CEO promotion, consistent with tournament theory. Each additional vice president increased the size of the payoff by 3%. Given that there were an average of 16 vice presidents in each firm, their estimates imply that doubling the number of them would increase the promotion payoff by 48% while simultaneously decreasing the probability of promotion by one half.

Another supportive study was recently conducted in the United Kingdom, using data on 500 executives from the top three levels of 100 U.K. firms (Conyon, Peck, & Sadler, 2001). They found not only the predicted convex relationship between job level and pay but also, like Main et al., found that higher CEO pay differentials were associated with larger numbers of executives in the levels just below the CEO. Specifically, for each added executive in the two job levels below the CEO, the differential between CEO pay and the median pay of the rest of the executive team increased by 3.5%.

In summary, although the evidence is mixed on some of the specifics, the bulk of the evidence seems largely consistent with the existence of tournaments at top levels of organizations. In particular, the existence of convex relationships between job level and pay seems to be widely supported.

Work-Life Incentives

Human capital and tournament models both recognize the importance of lifetime earnings in influencing worker decisions. Lazear (1979) suggests that better incentive properties will be generated by paying workers less than they are worth early in their careers and more than they are worth later in their careers (Lazear, 1995b). As long as this steeper age-earnings path has a present value that is equal to alternative (less steep) profiles, workers and employers should have no preference between the alternatives, all else being equal. However, Lazear (1979) argues that "Other things are not equal" (p. 1266), in that a steeper path "may yield the worker a higher lifetime wealth" because "the steeper path reduces the worker's incentive to cheat, shirk, and engage in malfeasant behavior" (p. 1266). This expected greater wealth means that workers, particularly those who expect to stay with the firm, will prefer the steeper path (Salop & Salop, 1976). Employers, too, will prefer the steeper path because greater wealth stems from greater output. However, the main challenge for employers is to limit the length of employees' careers so that overpayments do not continue so long as to offset the favorable incentive properties of the steeper age-earnings profile.

The logic of work-life incentives relates to the ideas of both tournament theory and efficiency wages. As with tournament theory, one's current marginal product and current wage are not necessarily equal at any given point in time. However, Lazear differentiates the two by noting that tournament theory describes between-job pay growth, whereas the work-life incentives model pertains to within-job pay growth. In that sense, the theories complement one another. (Although tournament theory has received more empirical attention.) As with efficiency wage theory, during the portion of the career when one is overpaid, there is an incentive not to shirk, because job loss would mean giving up a high wage premium to work in a lower-paying job (Lazear, 1999). In the inimitable language of economists, Lazear (1979) explains,

> A worker will cheat when the present value of cheating exceeds the cost of cheating. The major cost of cheating is the loss of the current job which carries with it earnings greater than the individual's reservation wage. . . . Stated otherwise, a firm which withholds payment until the end of individual's work life is less likely to experience worker cheating than one that pays workers more at the beginning and less at the end of the worker's career. (p. 1267)

Winner-Take-All Models

Reminiscent of tournament theory, Frank and Cook (1995) begin with the observation that performance differences between the very best and next best in many occupations (entertainment, sports, executives) appear to be small, yet the differences in pay are often large and have become larger in recent years: "Olympic gold medalists go on to receive millions in endorsements while the runners-up are quickly forgotten—even when the performance gap is almost too small to measure" (p. 17). Thus, relative performance is the key. Why should this be the case?

According to Frank and Cook (1995), the most important factor is that small differences in ability can indeed be worth a great deal to employers or product endorsers. The value of these small differences is large, and competitive market forces reward these small differences accordingly. In the case of executives, for example, one can envision that a small number of decisions, if better made than those that would have been made by the next-best person, could have tremendous repercussions for the value of the firm.

As a dramatic example of how much "the best" employee can be worth, in 1998, *Fortune* magazine estimated the overall value that Michael Jordan had contributed to the U.S. economy since the start of his NBA career (Estrine, 1998). Their estimate included Jordan "brand" products (e.g., sports videos, Jordan biographies, cologne, underwear, and the movie *Space Jam*), ticket sales, merchandising, television revenues, Nike products, and Jordan's value as an endorser. Their estimate? An astonishing $10 billion,[11] which compares rather favorably with Jordan's (then) $32 million salary!

A second factor driving large pay differences based on relative performance is that advances in technology have made it easier to observe and share the "best performances" more widely. For example, tennis fans can now watch matches on television between the first- and second-ranked players in the world (Frank & Cook, 1995). Before this was technologically feasible, the only option would have been to physically attend a tennis match, the vast majority of which involve much lower-ranked individuals. Now, however, the very best players can be watched in real time by millions around the world, yielding the networks millions in advertising and the players millions in endorsements.

A third factor that contributes to winner-take-all markets is the drive for accountability of managers for their decisions. For example, in making a decision about which attorney to hire in a high-stakes case, it is very important that the person making that decision be able to demonstrate that no corners were cut in giving the firm the best chance to win. If the firm were to lose the case, there would certainly be questions regarding the quality of the lawyer that had been hired. Thus, it is much better to be able to say, "I hired the best" than to say, "I hired the second best." The same can be said of boards of directors being accountable to shareholders regarding the hiring of a top executive or the university athletic director being accountable to fans in hiring a coach.

There are obvious similarities between winner-take-all and tournament models, with each emphasizing the central role of relative performance and the large "prizes" for winning. However, Frank and Cook (1995) argue that the tournament model reflects a decision by the firm to consciously structure its compensation in that manner (e.g., to control monitoring costs and to provide strong incentive properties), whereas the winner-take-all phenomenon is a "natural feature of the competitive environment."

Our own view is that the key difference between the models is that the tournament model does not require that performance and pay be equal for a particular person at every point in time. Thus, an executive may in fact be paid more than his or her performance is worth. However, this "overpayment" may still be efficient because of the incentive effects on those lower in the tournament hierarchy. In contrast, Frank and Cook's model (1995) seems to imply that the executive is worth the very high pay because even small differences in performance are of great value. (They do, however, argue that winner-take-all pay structures lead to inefficient allocation of labor in that too many people are induced to pursue large prizes in fields that are already oversupplied and for which they may have little talent.) In any event, relative standing matters a great deal in determining compensation in both winner-take-all and tournament markets. We are unaware of any research that has compared the validity of the winner-take-all with tournament explanations.

Resource-Dependence

One of the earliest papers to explore the possible link between business strategy and unique internal job value used a resource-dependence model to examine the relative pay of academic staff positions at private versus public universities (Pfeffer & Davis-Blake, 1987). The authors reasoned that private and public universities compete for resources in different ways, thus making some jobs more critical to private universities and others more critical to public ones. For example, public universities derive a significant (although shrinking) proportion of their financial support from the state budget process, whereas private universities tend to be more dependent on private gifts and endowments.

Similarly, public universities may find that the success of their athletic teams contributes to the support they receive from citizens and their representatives in state government, whereas some private schools appear to "wear" their less successful athletic programs as something of a badge of honor (e.g., Columbia).

If one accepts these arguments, the implication is that certain positions are more central to the successful acquisition of resources in private schools than in public ones. In turn, whatever positions are most critical will have higher pay relative to other positions in the university. Thus, private and public universities would have an array of pay rates that differ from the market average, even though they compete in generally the same product market. For example, Pfeffer and Davis-Blake (1987) hypothesized that the chief development officer would be more critical to private universities where there is heavier reliance on private giving. On the other hand, the director of athletics was predicted to be more central to strategy at public universities, as was the director of community services.

To test these propositions, Pfeffer and Davis-Blake (1987) defined their dependent variable as the ratio of the wage paid to a position divided by the mean wage for all administrative positions reported by the universities. Consistent with their hypotheses, the relative wage for the chief development officer was .18 percentage points higher at private universities, while the relative wages for directors of athletics and community services were .04 and .17 percentage points higher, respectively, at public universities. Thus, the results were generally supportive of the notion that organizations having different business strategies would also have different pay structures.[12]

More recently, Carpenter and Wade (2002) showed that the resource-dependence framework also applies to executive compensation in private sector companies. Using cash compensation data from 1981 to 1985, they proposed that (a) the finance function is more critical in capital intensive and highly diversified firms; (b) the marketing function is more critical in firms having large expenditures on marketing and advertising; (c) research and development (R&D) executives are more critical in firms that focus on product innovation; and (d) international positions are more critical in firms having a significant portion of their sales from overseas markets. Carpenter and Wade found general support for these predictions with the exception of the international hypothesis (international positions actually received slightly lower pay in international firms). The magnitudes of the effects were also substantial. For example, research and development executives in firms having R&D expenditures at the 75th percentile were paid 12% more than those in firms with median levels of R&D expenditure.

Fairness: Equity and Relative Deprivation Perspectives

To this point, all the theories presented have focused primarily on why internal pay structures might be steeper than those suggested by external market surveys or why certain jobs might be paid relatively more than similar jobs in other firms. However, some theorists have posed arguments in the opposite direction: specifically, that there may sometimes be good reasons to dampen the size of differentials or "prizes" between high-level and low-level employees.

Indeed, even some theorists whose main contributions have been to identify the potential advantages of steep pay structures have also acknowledged some of their disadvantages (e.g., Frank & Cook, 1995; Lazear, 1989). For example, Lazear (1989) suggests that despite the potential benefits of tournament models, their emphasis on relative performance may also cause corresponding difficulties: "Competition encourages effort, which has a positive effect on output. . . . But competition also discourages cooperation among contestants and can lead to outright sabotage" (p. 562). These considerations led Lazear to suggest that pay differentials should be smaller when "workers have the ability to affect each other's output" (p. 563).

Even for employees who are not effectively in competition with each other (e.g., production workers and executives), there can be a downside to large pay differentials across levels. According to equity and relative deprivation theories (Martin, 1981, 1982), lower-paid employees may still make comparisons between their own pay and that of higher-level executives. One need only go the AFL-CIO Web site (http://www.afl-cio.org/) for an illustration of how such comparisons can be used. The Web site invites the user to enter the name of his or her company and rate of pay. The site then reports the chief executive's pay at that company, as well as how many years it would take for the employee to earn as much as the CEO makes in one year, the clear implication being that executive's pay is both too high and unfair.

Although on average, the ratio of executive- to lower-level pay has increased dramatically over the past 20 years (Colvin, 2001; Crystal, 1991; Frank & Cook, 1995), there are nevertheless a number of companies that feel very strongly about creating solidarity among all levels of employees through a more egalitarian pay system (e.g., Southwest Airlines, Springfield Remanufacturing, Ben & Jerry's, A.G. Edwards). Although this is partially a strategic decision, it also seems to arise partly from the values and philosophy of the organizational founders. For example, after asking Southwest's pilots to freeze their base pay over a multiyear contract in return for additional variable pay incentives, then-CEO Herb Kelleher also froze his own base pay for the same period of time. Similarly, the founders of Ben & Jerry's ice cream for many years put a cap of 7:1 on the ratio of executive salary to hourly pay, although they eventually dropped the policy as they encountered difficulty in recruiting and retaining chief financial officers and CEOs.

The SAS Institute is another example of a company that uses an egalitarian pay structure to support its business strategy, which is to lease rather than sell its software (Pfeffer, 1998c). To support this strategy, SAS seeks to maintain long-term relationships with its customers and to solicit detailed customer input regarding desired changes and improvements. Because constant innovation is required in the fast-changing world of software development, SAS believes its strategy is best supported by a long-term relationship with its employees, which in turn facilitates the desired long-term relationship with its customers.

To facilitate these long-term relationships, SAS provides an extensive benefits package to increase employee retention. Making all employees eligible for the same extensive benefits creates a form of pay compression that reduces distinctions among ranks and individuals. In addition, SAS has only four organization levels, thus deemphasizing promotion as a reward strategy. Although there is a great deal of internal mobility, much of it is horizontal, involving working on different projects or in different areas of the business. SAS consciously avoids differentiation because of its belief that innovation is more successful when people have less incentive to take individual credit for ideas rather than sharing and developing them in cooperation with others.

Summary

Each of the preceding theories offers a slightly different explanation as to why pay structures may differ across employers. These include differences in monitoring costs, skill specificity, and need for cooperation and teamwork. Some of the theories imply definite strategic intent on the part of employers, while others view structures as phenomena that largely emerge from market or institutional forces.

Most of the models emphasize the potential advantages of pay differentials, although for slightly different reasons. For example, the tournament model seems to focus mainly on promotion incentive effects. In contrast, the winner-take-all and resource dependence models have more of an efficiency wage flavor in that they emphasize the value of pay for attracting and retaining the best people in the most critical positions. The ILM, transaction costs, and work-life models emphasize still other types of incentive concerns—in this case, the incentive for senior workers to share knowledge with others and for employees to stay long enough to recoup the firm's investments in specific training. As such, these models place relatively less emphasis on competition and more emphasis on cooperation over an extended period.

Finally, the equity and relative deprivation approaches most explicitly highlight the potential downside for cooperation of large differentials in pay, particularly those based on job level. Companies that base their systems on these approaches often reveal deliberate intentions to use pay egalitarianism to support their business philosophies and strategies.

Although norms of fair payment have almost certainly changed over the past 40 years, it is clear that the actual gap between executive pay and the pay of most other workers is far larger than it was in earlier years (Bok, 1993; Frank & Cook, 1995). For example, in 1974, the typical CEO of a large American company earned approximately 35 times what an average factory worker earned (Crystal, 1991). By 1990, that figure had increased to 120 times (Crystal, 1991) and by 1998, to 326 (Reingold, Melcher, & McWilliams, 1998). In 2000, *Business Week's* annual executive salary survey (Lavelle, 2001) showed that the average total compensation for top executives of large U.S. companies was approximately $13 million. In contrast, the average annual compensation for all workers in that same year was around $30,000. In other words, top executives now earn approximately 400 times as much as the average worker.

Surprisingly, there is little hard research evidence concerning the causes—or especially the consequences—of rising pay inequality across levels. Thus, we cannot definitively say whether, when, or why these new differentials are, on balance, positive or negative. Also, as we shall see in Chapters 5 and 6, questions about the optimal size of pay differentials also extend to comparisons of individuals holding the same job (e.g., Bloom, 1999), as well as to questions of differentials in alternative forms of pay (e.g., benefits and stock options). However, the limited evidence that does exist concerning the effects of wide-versus-narrow differentials across job levels is explored in the following section.

Empirical Research on the Effects of Pay Structure

Earlier, we showed that research evidence supports the existence of tournament-like pay structures in organizations. Perhaps a more important question, however, is whether pay structures such as tournaments actually increase effort and performance. A small number of field studies have attempted to answer this question, most often focusing on tournament theory.

Two studies have used performance in sports events to test tournament theory. Ehrenberg and Bognanno (1990) examined the effect of different prize levels (holding differentials between finishing levels mostly constant) on scores in golf tournaments on the 1984 PGA tour. These prize structures appear to fit a tournament model, with the first-place finisher receiving 18% of the prize money, second place receiving 10.8%, and third place receiving 6.8%. By contrast, the 22nd and 23rd finishers receive 1.1% and 1.0%, respectively. Controlling for player ability and course difficulty, they found that an increase of $100,000 in prize money was associated with scoring 1.1 strokes lower (better) for the event.

The magnitude of this association does not appear to be large. Although the mean score across tournaments was not reported, one assumes that it was in the neighborhood of 280. If so, a 1-stroke differential seems small, given a 25% increase in prize money at the mean (which was $400,000). However, this may be a rather stringent comparison. Perhaps one should select a range in which most players fall (e.g., 270–290, or 20 strokes) and use that range as the base.

A second study examined tournament models in auto racing. Becker and Huselid (1992) used data from races held by both the National Association for Stock Car Auto Racing (NASCAR) and the International Motor Sports Association (IMSA). The results based on the two data sets were mostly similar. We focus on the NASCAR results, which are based on 44 drivers in 28 different races. To measure driver performance, Becker and Huselid used a combination of finish position and average speed of the race. This variable, *adjusted finish,* was defined as the finishing position of each of the 44 drivers in each race multiplied by the ratio of the winning speed in that particular race to the winning speed of the fastest race in the sample of 28 races. (Thus, the lowest score on the dependent variable would be for the driver winning the fastest race. The next-lowest score could be either the second-place finisher in the fastest race or the winner of the next-fastest race.) The mean score was 28 with a standard deviation of 18. The key independent variable was the "spread" (or difference) between the prize money available for top finishers versus lower finishers.

Based on initial analyses, Becker and Huselid (1992) settled on measuring spread as the difference between the prize money available for the top 20 finishers versus that available for the remaining drivers. This spread variable had a mean (in 1990) of $11,400 (standard deviation = $2,800; minimum = $8,300; maximum = $22,000). Thus, there was variance in tournament structures across the 28 races (cf. Ehrenberg & Bognanno, 1990).

Becker and Huselid (1992) found that spread had a substantial relationship with adjusted finish. Specifically, a race that had a payoff structure 1 standard deviation above the mean had a predicted adjusted finish of 24.9, versus 31.1 in a race having a spread 1 standard deviation below the mean, a 25% difference. Becker and Huselid also used spline functions to determine whether the effect of spread on adjusted finish was linear. Their findings suggested it was not, with diminishing returns to bigger spreads, particularly using the NASCAR data.

One comment on the Becker and Huselid study is that their measure of spread (top 20 versus remaining 28 drivers) does not really seem to reflect the focus of tournament theory, which emphasizes that incentive effects depend on ever-increasing differentials (a convex relationship) between pay and job levels (or finishers in auto racing), especially near the first-place spot. This might suggest focusing on the difference between first and second place or between first place and everyone else, rather than the top 20 and everyone else. A second comment is that their study, as well as Ehrenberg and Bognanno's, used only one job level, whereas tournament models emphasize the relative pay of different job levels and promotions.

Moving from the individual level of analysis (and sports as the setting), three studies have used field data to examine the relationship between tournament structure and firm performance. Main et al. (1993) used the coefficient of variation in cash plus bonus among members of the executive team as a measure of pay dispersion (i.e., incentive strength) and found that it was positively related to both stock market returns and return on assets, although only the coefficient in the latter equation was statistically significant.

Main et al. (1993) also provided an interesting test of the Lazear (1989) hypothesis that incentive strength will be most effective in situations where there is low interdependence between "contestants." Interdependence was measured as the proportion of executives holding some type of profit center head title. Organizations having a large proportion of executives holding these titles were classified as having low-interdependence executive teams. However, results suggested no significant interaction between pay dispersion and executive interdependence with respect to firm performance.

Eriksson (1999) used two variables to measure tournament structure in Danish firms: the coefficient of variation of pay (cash plus bonus plus pension contributions) within a firm and the differential between the CEO and others in the firm. He found that both variables were positively related to (the *log* of) profits/sales. Specifically, a 1 standard error increase in these pay dispersion variables was associated with 4% to 5% higher firm performance. Also, like Main et al., Eriksson also tested the hypothesis that this positive effect of pay dispersion would depend on the degree to which cooperation was required of executives. Using the same operationalization as Main and colleagues, Eriksson also did not find a significant interaction between interdependence and pay dispersion in predicting firm performance.

Finally, the previously mentioned U.K. study by Conyon et al. (2001) also estimated the relationship between pay dispersion in the top executive team and two measures of firm performance—shareholder return and return on assets. The coefficient of dispersion failed to reach statistical significance in either equation.

Although the studies reviewed to this point hypothesized a positive relationship between pay differentials and either individual or firm performance, Cowherd and Levine (1992) hypothesized the opposite. Using equity theory and relative deprivation theories (Adams, 1965; Martin, 1981) as a base, they hypothesized that larger pay differentials between top executives and lower-level employees would be associated with lower product quality. Their hypothesis was supported, using a sample of 102 business units from 41 corporations in North America and Europe.

There were a number of limitations of the study. First, although Cowherd and Levine (1992) assumed that the causal mechanism for lower quality was perceived inequity, the authors did not actually measure such perceptions. Second, the quality data were based on executives' perceptions of product quality,[13] which, combined with the cross-sectional nature of the data set, raises serious questions about causality. For example, executives in firms that pay relatively lower wages to low-level employees may have more negative impressions of the ability or motivation of those employees, absent any actual quality data. Finally, the study actually focused on *equality* rather than equity, since the only measure of inputs used in the study was a control variable for organizational size (which they treated as a proxy for executive "responsibility," p. 312). Despite these limitations, future research that builds on the work of Cowherd and Levine would be of great interest, as questions about the impact of large versus small differentials are among the major issues in compensation research and practice today (e.g., Bok, 1993; Colvin, 2001; Frank & Cook, 1995).

In summary, although the size of pay differentials has received a good deal of theoretical attention, empirical research lags behind. We provide suggestions for future research on pay structures in the following section.

Future Research

There are several very interesting substantive areas for future research on pay structures. There are also some basic methodological issues that need to be considered that span a variety of substantive areas. We turn first to these.

One of the most pressing needs for future pay structure research is to develop alternative ways of measuring structure and to determine the likely implications of using each measure. Several types of measures are possible, including the number of job levels, pay differentials between job levels, overall variation in pay within an organization (e.g., using a gini coefficient), or number of separate structures (Gerhart & Milkovich, 1992). Cowherd and Levine (1992), for example, focused on pay differentials between different levels in organizations, including those between the lowest and highest levels. Other work has looked exclusively at pay differentials between the top two executive levels (Main et al., 1993; O'Reilly et al., 1988). These different measures may be useful for assessing different kinds of phenomena. For example, differentials between adjacent levels may be most appropriate for assessing incentive effects, while relative deprivation issues may come more into play when differentials between distant levels are examined.

Another general measurement approach is to determine the degree to which an organization's pay structure deviates from that implied by the external market (Gerhart, Milkovich, & Murray, 1992; Murray, 1993). This can be done by using regression analysis to estimate a marketwide pay policy and then using this policy equation to predict pay in each firm. Firms for which the overall R^2 is lower might be said to focus more on internal equity in their pay structures or perhaps, consistent with the resource-based view, to follow a strategy of differentiation. Whereas the first measurement approach (assessing differentials) is more relevant to pay differentials based on rank, the second approach (assessing fit with the market) is probably more relevant to differentials based on job family, skill group, or business unit.

A second key methodological issue follows from the fact that the most important questions about pay structure—namely, questions about their effects—can probably no longer be answered by looking at base pay levels only. Given the dramatic escalation in use of various pay forms (particularly stock options) and the tremendous effect that these noncash forms have had on the "winnings" of top executives, studies that look only at cash compensation to determine the effects of structure on worker behavior are likely to be seriously deficient.

A third methodological issue concerns the difficulty of determining *why* various structures are associated with particular outcomes. For the most part, studies of structure-outcome relationships have been based entirely on archival data, meaning that the underlying incentive and motivational processes can only be hypothesized. Of course, as Cowherd and Levine (1992) point out, it can be difficult to get perceptual data concerning pay equity from multiple employees (executives and nonexecutives) in multiple firms. Data from nonexecutives would be of interest in part because one of the most intriguing questions concerns the motivational effects of executive compensation on those lower down in the organization.

In this vein, it may be useful to consider the effects of both distributive justice and procedural justice perceptions of nonexecutives. For example, it may well be that workers do not begrudge their CEOs high pay if all employees are playing by roughly the same rules and if employees are given adequate information about the business and sufficient input into company decisions. Given what we know about the considerable importance to employees of relative pay and changes in compensation (as opposed to absolute, static levels of pay), the most basic rule of structural fairness may be that employee and executive compensation levels move in the same direction and in roughly the same proportions. Although this principle is clearly followed by companies such as Southwest Airlines and A.G. Edwards, executives in other companies are rewarded largely on the basis of cutting costs (including labor) to boost short-term share prices, in which case the interests of executives and their employees may diverge considerably (O'Shea & Madigan, 1997). In addition, we know that employee behaviors and attitudes can be significantly affected by the way changes in pay are communicated (e.g., Greenberg, 1990; Klein, 1987). Thus, studies that look only at differences in relative levels of pay at one point in time will miss all these very important underlying dynamics.

Turning to substantive issues, the most central questions concern whether (and why) different structures yield different performance consequences. In terms of the "whether" question, the sparse results to date are mixed. For example, both Main and colleagues (1993) and Eriksson (1999) found that higher differentials—at least within the executive levels—were associated with higher firm financial performance. However, Conyon et al. (2001) did not find a similar effect in their U.K. sample, and Cowherd and Levine (1992) found that *smaller* differentials between executives and lower-level employees were associated with higher perceived product quality. In addition, there are also several examples of highly successful organizations with very egalitarian pay structures (e.g., SAS, Southwest, A.G. Edwards) as well as very highly differentiated ones (e.g., General Electric).

Although far more (and far more detailed) research will be necessary to provide a definitive answer to whether high (or low) differentials result in "better" performance overall, it may well be that the answer to this question depends on a variety of factors. Indeed, an "It depends" answer would be consistent with a resource-dependence view of the firm, as well as with the notion of firm performance resulting from an appropriate degree of fit and attraction-selection-attrition between organizations and employees (e.g., Schneider, 1987).

Likely moderators discussed in this chapter include firm skill specificity, which is an important reason for using an ILM structure. A related moderator might be product market strategy. In paper mills, for example, the product market is relatively stable, and innovation is less important than in some other types of firms. Here, an ILM might be more effective than in information technology, where technologies and products, and thus needed skills, change rapidly and may be more general. Job level is another potential moderator. The discretion and complexity of top executive jobs suggest more difficulty in monitoring performance. Relative performance is easier to monitor, pointing to the use of a tournament structure. Limited opportunities for promotion at high levels also point to tournament structures. However, tournament structures also foster competition. The relative importance of cooperation and competition will also drive the structure, with smaller prizes for promotion being possible where more cooperation is desired.

To the extent that the effects of particular pay distributions depend on other factors, the most critical question changes from *which is best* to *when* and *why.* As indicated earlier, an adequate answer to this latter question will require more sophisticated research than has been conducted to date. For example, pay differentials will have to be studied in relation to potential moderator (e.g., business strategy) and mediator variables (e.g., perceived inequity, employee quality, differential turnover or motivation; see also Becker & Gerhart, 1996; Gerhart, 2000). In addition, it would be nice to see more frequent tests of "strong inference" (Platt, 1964)—that is, where one model (e.g., tournament theory) is pitted against a conflicting model (e.g., relative deprivation)—rather than the more usual case where data sets are tested only for consistency with a single model (for an example of testing competing theories, see O'Reilly et al., 1988). Such studies have the potential to provide stronger causal inferences than those that have been performed to date.

Realistically, it is likely that researchers will need to call on multiple methodologies to answer such questions. Although ideally it would be nice to rely mainly on "real" data from "real" organizations, some of the mediator or process variables (e.g., perceived pay fairness or motivation) will be very difficult to obtain in field settings, particularly across multiple firms. The best chance of obtaining such data sets will be to work in conjunction with consultants who routinely monitor the motivational and behavioral characteristics of employees (e.g., Gallup, Hewitt) or with benchmarking groups that agree to share such data privately among each other (e.g., the Mayflower Group). Absent such data sets, answers to questions of *when* and *why* will have to be pieced together from a variety of other methods, including laboratory and field experiments (Greenberg's 1987, 1990, research program on behavioral responses to perceived pay inequity presents an excellent example of such an approach).

A final important question for future research involves possible shifts in the relative importance of jobs versus individual characteristics for determining pay structures. Ironically, just as economists have begun to accept jobs as an important aspect of pay determination, there is evidence that they are becoming *less* important as a source of pay variation in some organizations (e.g., R. Heneman, Ledford, & Gresham, 2000).

This appears to be happening for several reasons. One is that traditional ILMs and the job-focused pay structures on which they are based may have become too inflexible and costly in the present highly competitive economic environment. For example, as organizations "de-layer," implement teams, and hire employees from the outside at virtually all levels, the traditional practice of basing pay on where one fits in a hierarchy of narrowly defined job levels may cause a variety of problems (e.g., inability to attract employees from the external labor market or, if structures are violated, serious inequities between long-service employees and new hires from the outside). In addition, narrowly defined job categories and pay structures may make workers reluctant to transfer to other positions unless they receive promotional increases of at least 10% to 15%, which may become prohibitively expensive in a world of rapidly changing jobs and organizational structures.

In response to these sorts of rigidities, two important trends have emerged with respect to developing pay structures. The first, de-layering or *broadbanding,* collapses numerous grades and jobs into a smaller number of categories (e.g., Gerhart & Milkovich, 1992; R. Heneman et al., 2000). For example, Pratt and Whitney recently consolidated 11 pay grades and 3,000 job descriptions into 6 pay grades (bands) and only several hundred job descriptions. One consequence is that the spread between the minimum and maximum rate of pay within a job band has changed from as little as 35% to 50% in the grade system to as high as 300% in the broadband system (R. Heneman et al., 2000). A second innovation, often implemented in conjunction with broadbanding, is to pay workers for increases in skill or knowledge, regardless of whether or not they actually change their formal positions. In addition to increasing worker productivity, this innovation is believed to increase flexibility in worker assignments and hence to permit lower levels of overall staffing due to greater flexibility in employee assignments. In addition, it is designed to provide additional compensation to employees who continue to learn, regardless of their formal positions. For example, desk clerks at Marriott can earn more by learning to be waiters and maids, regardless of their formal classification, because this aids the hotel when maids or waiters are absent or in short supply.

Relative to highly structured, job-based ILMs, broadband systems also increase managerial flexibility with respect to *what* is rewarded by organizations (e.g., job level versus individual productivity, or knowledge or skills versus ability to attract or retain). Although in theory, broadbanding permits greater flexibility and the possibility of greater cost-effectiveness (by applying pay exactly how and where it is needed), it also opens up the possibility of decreased understanding regarding pay "rules" among employees, charges of supervisory favoritism, and the potential for increased overall labor costs. Indeed, it is this type of discretion in pay setting that labor unions, for example, have always opposed. Thus, with greater discretion comes a greater challenge to demonstrate that larger pay differentials have a legitimate basis. As such, there is a big need for future research on shifts from job bases to individual bases for pay (for an example of such research, see Murray & Gerhart, 1998.)

To recap, to this point, we have reviewed theories and evidence relating to similarities (and differences) in pay levels across employers, as well as unique decisions by employers to deviate from market averages with respect to job pay levels. In Chapter 5, we describe a variety of theories designed to explain how organizations use various forms of compensation (e.g., profit sharing, gainsharing, stock grants, stock options, merit pay) to reward inputs or contributions in an effective manner. In Chapter 6, we turn to empirical evidence regarding the correlates and effects of such programs.

Notes

1. Our use of the terms *pay structure* and *pay level* is different from that of Milkovich and Newman. Our term, job structure, is similar to their use of pay structure.

2. As with any policy-capturing study, the relative magnitude of (standardized) effect sizes also depends on the relative strength with which the variables are manipulated.

3. In an ILM, workers do not "bid" for promotions by offering to take the job for less money than their competitors. Likewise, the pay rate for the job vacancy does not decline as the supply of those competing for the promotion increases (see Thurow, 1975).

4. Our discussion is most relevant to what Doeringer and Piore (1971) describe as "enterprise markets" (as opposed to craft markets).

5. A rather similar theoretical model was recently offered by Gibbons and Waldman (1999), who, like Doeringer and Piore (1971), observe that wage rates are more directly linked to job classifications than to human capital. Under the "job assignment" portion of their model, they argue that ILMs allow employers to obtain full information on workers' productive capabilities, such that employees can be efficiently assigned to jobs in which the best workers will have the highest impact. Consistent with predictions of utility (e.g., Boudreau & Berger, 1985) and information-processing theories (Henderson & Fredrickson, 1996), Gibbons and Waldman suggest that high-ability workers will be most valuable where they have responsibility for larger-scale operations. However, one empirical observation that is inconsistent with the job assignment hypothesis is the existence of demotions and wage decreases, which clearly suggest mistakes in hiring or promotion (i.e., less-than-perfect information). Thus, they supplement the job assignment model with a learning model wherein firms are assumed to be uncertain about a worker's productive capability when first hired, but become less and less uncertain over time. Finally, they concur with Doeringer and Piore and others (e.g., Williamson et al., 1975) that internal wage rates are not directly linked to the external market, because firm-specific skills are not readily transferable.

6. Williamson et al. (1975) argue that indivisibility of production, a factor emphasized by others as the root cause of market failure, is not of central importance. In the lighthouse example, Williamson et al. assume that the light is either on or off.

7. Cronbach et al. (1972) show that generalizability coefficients for relative decisions are always as high or higher than those for absolute decisions because the error term for the latter is always as large or larger than the error term for relative decisions.

8. Thus, a company like General Electric, with its independent business units, might have less concern for cooperation between business unit heads but be more concerned about cooperation among executives within business units.

9. Lambert et al. also included a fourth job, plant manager. However, based on our knowledge of this particular data set, we believe that there are other jobs between the plant manager and divisional CEO position, so the differential between the latter two jobs may not be informative with respect to tournament theory.

10. Eriksson (1999), using data on Danish firms, also reports a convex relationship between job level and pay, with the largest-percentage increase coming with a promotion to the CEO level.

11. Subcategories included a $4.33 billion effect on NBA merchandise, $165 million on box office receipts, and a $5.2 billion effect on Nike.

12. The finding that pay rates differ between organizations within the same industry is consistent with both the post-institutional and pay strategy literatures discussed earlier. The variation in rates of pay also calls into question the assumption that there is a single going rate of pay. Instead, the variation in rates indicates that even if an employer were to ignore its own strategy in choosing a pay level, it would nevertheless find that there was no single going rate of pay to imitate. Not only will there be a range of rates in any particular set of employers, but the question of how to choose the relevant employers also has no clear-cut answer (Rynes & Milkovich, 1986).

13. Although Cowherd and Levine (1992) indicated that the executives "typically based their quality ratings on previously conducted market research," the fact remains that quality was measured perceptually rather than objectively.

5 Pay Basis

THEORIES OF MOTIVATION AND PAY FOR PERFORMANCE

Probably the one issue that should be considered by all organization theories is the relationship between pay and performance.

—Lawler (1971)

It [is] clear that a variety of psychologically meaningful parameters of pay can be varied by a company without increasing the total salary expense over time, yet the motivational leverage of alternative forms at constant cost has had remarkably little empirical investigation.

—Haire, Ghiselli, and Gordon (1967)

In the previous three chapters, we focused on differences in how much organizations pay (pay level) and differences in relative pay for jobs within the same organization (structure). However, as Haire and his colleagues point out, the same pay level can be achieved or distributed in different ways. For example, some organizations may aim to pay 10% above market for all jobs, regardless of performance, while others pay 10% below market when performance is low but considerably above market when performance is high. Similarly, organizations may pay *all* employees at the market average for their jobs, or they can pay the market rate "on average," while giving above-market pay to high performers and below-market pay to the poorest performers.

We use the term pay *basis* to refer to these decisions regarding how to pay. There are several reasons to believe that the decisions of organizations regarding *how* to pay are in some sense more strategic and more important to performance outcomes than decisions about *how much* to pay. One basic principle, alluded to above, is that organizations are more constrained in pay level decisions (because of the need to attain rough parity with product and labor markets) than they are in decisions about how to "divide up" a given desired level. Indeed, empirical evidence supports the view that organizations differ more in terms of how they pay than how much and also that differences in type of pay (e.g., contingent versus noncontingent on performance) bear a stronger relationship with organizational performance than pay levels per se (e.g., Gerhart & Milkovich, 1990).

In this chapter, we consider general theories from psychology and economics regarding the linkages between pay and performance. In Chapter 6, we describe how specific pay-for-performance programs operate and provide a review of empirical evidence regarding the effectiveness of each type of program.

Before turning to our theoretical review, we briefly present evidence from several meta-analytic reviews that have examined the overall effect sizes associated with various types of motivational programs, both pecuniary (e.g., individual and group incentive systems) and nonpecuniary (e.g., goal setting, employee participation). In general, these studies suggest that the incentive effects of pay-for-performance schemes can be substantial, perhaps larger than the effects of any other single type of motivational system.

Effects of Pay and Motivational Programs on Performance: Meta-Analytic Results

In Chapter 3, we reviewed empirical evidence demonstrating that pay level plays an important role in influencing job choice, job search (by employed workers), and retention. However, we also noted that the impact of pay level is likely to depend on what is expected of employees in return for high pay. Here, we review empirical evidence regarding the general incentive effects of pay-for-performance plans. (Effects of specific types of programs, such as merit pay plans versus stock ownership, are discussed in the next chapter.) In evaluating these results, the reader should bear in mind that most of the research included in these meta-analyses pertains to relatively simple work tasks and that most studies have been conducted at the individual rather than organizational level of analysis. Although these characteristics limit its external validity, this work is nevertheless helpful for establishing the general motivational potential of monetary incentives.

Locke, Feren, McCaleb, Shaw, and Denny (1980) reviewed the impact of four motivational techniques: monetary incentives, goal setting, participation, and job enrichment. Their sample included only studies that were conducted in the field, used either control groups or before-and-after designs, and used hard performance criteria (e.g., physical output). They found that monetary incentives resulted in the largest median performance improvement (30%), followed by goal setting (16%), job enrichment (8.75%-17%), and participation (0.5%). As indicated in Chapter 2, Locke et al. concluded that "Money is the crucial incentive. . . . No other incentive or motivational technique comes even close to money with respect to its instrumental value" (p. 379).

Another meta-analysis by Guzzo, Jette, and Katzell (1985) examined the average effects of several types of human resource (HR) interventions, including financial incentives, work redesign, and other policy changes that had been previously described in books by Katzell, Bienstock, and Faerstein (1977) and Guzzo and Bondy (1983). They included studies based on criteria similar to those of Locke et al. (1980) but also looked at two additional productivity criteria (besides physical output): withdrawal (turnover and absenteeism) and disruption (e.g., accidents, strikes). They found that financial incentives had a substantial mean effect across 13 studies of $d = .57$, meaning that the experimental groups receiving incentives were on average .57 standard deviation units higher on the three productivity criteria than the control groups not receiving incentives. However, the variability of effects was also large, with the 95% confidence interval ranging from –.10 to 1.24.

Limiting the analysis to the eight studies that used the physical output criterion, Guzzo et al. (1985) found that financial incentives had by far the largest mean effect ($d = 2.12$), a finding that was not only statistically significant but was also obviously quite large in practical terms. As such, their results are very similar to those of Locke and colleagues (1980). By way of comparison, Guzzo et al. also examined the effects of job enrichment. Across 18 studies, the mean effect size was .42, with a 95% confidence interval of .28 to .56. Then, narrowing the focus again to studies that used the physical output criterion, a still higher (and statistically significant) mean effect of .52 was obtained. This effect size is also substantial, although much smaller than that associated with financial incentives.

Stajkovic and Luthans (1997) estimated meta-analytic effect sizes on task performance of the following organization behavior modification interventions: monetary rewards, feedback, and social rewards (e.g., recognition). They, too, found substantial effect sizes for pay, ranging from $d = 1.36$ in manufacturing organizations (based on 12 effect sizes, 523 people) to $d = .42$ in service sector organizations (67 effect sizes, 2,063 people). Feedback and social rewards were found to have effect sizes comparable to those of monetary rewards.[1]

Jenkins, Mitra, Gupta, and Shaw (1998) conducted a meta-analysis of the relationship between financial incentives and performance quantity and quality in studies in which "hard" performance measures were used and the incentives were at the individual (as opposed to group) level. In addition, only studies using adult samples were examined. Examples of performance measures included number of IBM cards punched (Yukl, Wexley, & Seymore, 1972); number of rats trapped per hour (Saari & Latham, 1982); number of Tinkertoys assembled (Terborg & Miller, 1978); and number of trees planted (Yukl, Latham, & Pursell, 1976). Jenkins et al. (1998) reported an average correlation of .32 between financial incentives and quantity and no reliable correlation between financial incentives and quality. In addition, the average correlation was larger in field studies than in laboratory studies.

Similarly, Judiesch (1994) reported the following increases in productivity following incentive implementation: 48.8% for eight survey studies, 40.7% for 22 case studies, 50.3% for four experimental field studies, and 43.7% across all types of field studies. These results are even stronger in percentage terms than those previously reported by Locke et al. (1980), which averaged 30%. Also, like Jenkins et al., Judiesch found smaller effects for laboratory studies: an average of 26.8% higher than control groups (18 studies) and 9.5% higher in three lab studies that switched from fixed rate to piece rates. Judiesch attributes these weaker results to the much smaller monetary amounts and shorter time durations of the laboratory studies.

In summary, several meta-analyses have documented that monetary incentives have a substantial impact on performance. Two of the three studies (Guzzo et al., 1985; Locke et al., 1980) that compared financial and nonfinancial incentives additionally demonstrated that the effect size for monetary incentives was substantially larger than the effect size for nonmonetary rewards. These findings are rather compelling in terms of the substantial effect sizes. We should note, however, that most jobs do not lend themselves to objective measurement of performance (e.g., number of trees planted) and that subjective and objective measures of performance are not interchangeable (R. Heneman, 1986). As such, the underlying studies examine only a subset of all jobs, particularly in today's increasingly skilled and knowledge-based economy.

Given that the motivational impacts of pay can apparently be quite substantial, we turn now to a discussion of theories that help understand the potential incentive effects of pay-for-performance plans.

Theories of Pay-Performance Relationships

As indicated earlier in Chapters 2 and 3, *how* an organization decides to pay can influence ultimate performance in two distinct ways (Gerhart & Milkovich, 1992; Lazear, 1999; Rynes, 1987). First, there can be a direct incentive effect on those who are currently employed by the organization, with different pay systems influencing both the amount of money that can be attained as well as the estimated likelihood of its attainment. These characteristics, in turn, are believed to influence how hard, smart, and persistently people work toward obtaining such rewards.

In addition, however, different bases for pay (e.g., individual merit pay versus group gainsharing) can also have important indirect effects on performance through their influence on who applies for positions (Cable & Judge, 1994) and who stays with the organization (e.g., Harrison, Virick, & William, 1996; Trevor, Gerhart, & Boudreau, 1997). The idea that pay practices might affect the characteristics of job applicants and employees (i.e., through *sorting* effects) has previously been recognized in the case of pay *level*, in that efficiency wage, human capital, and utility theories (via the *Z* parameter described in Chapter 3) all assume that higher pay levels are capable of attracting and retaining individuals of higher ability levels.

More recently, however, the notion of a relationship between pay practices and characteristics of applicants and employees has been extended to the case of pay basis, or how one pays. For example, Schneider's (1987) attraction-selection-attrition (ASA) model has been adopted by others (e.g., Bretz, Ash, & Dreher, 1989; Cable & Judge, 1994) to predict individual differences in attraction to firms that, for example, have individual versus group incentive systems or that offer high levels of across-the-board benefits (such as SAS), versus those with high levels of contingent pay for performance (such as Lincoln Electric).

In Chapters 2 and 3, we distinguished between incentive effects (how compensation influences attitudes and behaviors of the current workforce) and sorting effects (how compensation influences the ability and personality characteristics of the current workforce via attraction, selection, and attrition). To date, most of the empirical research on relationships between pay basis and performance has focused on incentive effects rather than sorting effects. As such, we segment our theoretical review in much the same way, distinguishing between theories of incentives (or motivation) and theories of sorting or fit.

Psychological Versus Economic Perspectives

In the following sections, we focus on four psychological theories that relate pay to motivation and performance: expectancy, goal setting, social cognition, and equity theories. In addition, we discuss one major economic theory, agency theory, that has had a considerable effect on thinking in both academic and management circles about how to design pay-for-performance schemes. Although the current chapter includes only one economics-based theory (agency theory), recall that our earlier chapters had a large economics component. This probably reflects the fact that economists have been more interested in firm level policies, such as pay level and pay structure, and corresponding aggregate behaviors (e.g., average firm level turnover), whereas those with a more psychological orientation have been more interested in individual level processes, such as motivation and related cognitive processes (e.g., goal commitment, self-efficacy), a primary focus of the present chapter.

Before discussing the specific theories, we make some additional observations on how the approaches of psychologists and economists tend to differ. One difference that will become very clear as we examine psychological and economic theories of motivation was also apparent in our earlier discussion of pay level. Specifically, psychologists tend more often to focus on sources of motivation *other than* compensation, whereas economists, at least in empirical practice, tend to focus almost exclusively on money as *the* motivator. Thus, as we review theories such as social cognition theory (SCT), we will see that much psychological speculation revolves around ways to obtain higher motivation through practices other than pay (e.g., selection or training), even when it might seem equally reasonable to think about monetary mechanisms. The source of this difference may go back to the value system of many psychologists, who tend to see money as a "lower-order" motivator (e.g., Maslow, 1943) or not even as a motivator at all (e.g. Herzberg, 1987; Kohn, 1993).

In particular, psychological theories of motivation accord an important role to intrinsic aspects of motivation, most notably, interesting work. Although the economics perspective can incorporate intrinsic factors into utility functions of individuals, in practice, these factors have received little attention from economists. In fact, the idea that meaningful work might increase motivation or utility seems to be largely inconsistent with another assumption of the economic model—that effort is aversive. Thus, as incomes rise, economists speculate that people are more likely to maximize utility by purchasing increased amounts of leisure. Given this presumed preference, either monetary payments or very close supervision are necessary to encourage people to keep working and to avoid *shirking,* a concept we encountered earlier in our discussion of efficiency wage theories. These assumptions again come to the fore in our discussion of agency theory, which focuses on the use of monetary incentives, monitoring, or other forms of control (i.e., bonding) to combat this assumed tendency to shirk and seek leisure.

A second obvious difference is that psychologists spend a great deal of time thinking about and measuring the underlying cognitive processes that "translate" rewards or punishments (such as pay, praise, or disciplinary actions) into subsequent behaviors. Thus, for example, as we review goal-setting theory, we will note how goal-setting theorists have devoted considerable attention to measuring goal choice and goal commitment as possible mediators between monetary incentives and subsequent performance. Similarly, we will see that social cognition theorists accord a prominent role to self-mastery (roughly, learning by doing) and observational learning (i.e., through role modeling) as partial explanations for observed performance, and we discuss several (mostly nonpecuniary) ways to encourage such mastery and learning.

Is there practical value to studying mediating cognitive processes? If evidence shows that monetary incentives influence performance, do we really need to know why such an effect exists? Yes, and here is why: Factors other than monetary incentives may influence goals and intentions and thus, performance. As Locke has noted, long-standing evidence indicates that workers' output norms (i.e., goals) are the key determinant of their production level (e.g., Roethlisberger & Dickson, 1939; Whyte, 1955). What this suggests is that workers under the same incentive system may choose very different goals, resulting in very different effort and performance levels. However, if researchers had observed only the existence or strength of monetary incentives and worker output without measuring intervening cognitive processes (e.g., goals, trust in management), there would have been no explanation for why incentives sometimes worked and sometimes did not. Thus, the psychological approach sees these intervening variables as crucial to any real understanding of motivation and to drawing strong inferences regarding causal processes that are likely to ensue from exogenous changes in pay policies. This fuller understanding, in turn, helps to inform policy.

Indeed, as we review meta-analytical evidence concerning each of these theories, we will show that the relationships between incentives and performance seem to depend on many moderators, such as goal difficulty, task complexity, work interdependence, and individual self-efficacy. As such, it is quite useful to know about the types of nonpecuniary variables that are likely to influence the success or failure of a monetary intervention. Similarly, from a strategic perspective, it is desirable to think about types of interventions (such as feedback or selection) that might cost less than pay increases and yet might independently improve performance and/or bolster the effects of existing pay practices.

Another clear difference between psychological and economic theories is that psychologists place much more emphasis on the importance of individual differences in efforts to explain performance. Although economists devote some attention to individual differences (e.g., the role of ability in efficiency wage theory), psychologists have found many more variables (e.g., personality, need for achievement, self-esteem) to be important in determining individuals' responses to workplace incentives. We return to this point later in the present chapter.

Although economists do not reject the importance of such variables out of hand, they nevertheless choose not to emphasize them. Brickley, Smith, and Zimmerman (1997) explain it this way:

> As a management tool, the usefulness of focusing on personal preferences is often limited. Preferences are generally not observable, and virtually anything can be explained as simply a matter of tastes.... The focus (instead) is on aggregate behavior or what the typical person tends to do.... Managers are typically interested in structuring an organizational architecture that will work well and does not depend on specific people filling particular jobs. Individuals come and go, and the manager wants an organization that will work well as these changes occur. (pp. 27–28)

Brickley et al. (1997) go on to say that "In this context, the economic framework will be very useful," although they acknowledge that in other contexts, "Other frameworks may be more valuable" (p. 28).

Of course, the psychological (and sociological) view would be that by failing to take account of both individual and contextual differences, managers are likely to find it impossible to truly optimize performance.

This is also the perspective taken more recently by strategy theorists, including contingency theorists (e.g., Miles & Snow, 1978), as well as the resource-based view of the firm (Barney, 1991).

Finally, psychological theories tend to focus more on the *meaning* that money has to people and the role it plays in their lives (e.g., Barber & Bretz, 2000). One particularly important role of money is in providing information about how one's efforts and outcomes are viewed in relation to the efforts and outcomes of others (Frank & Cook, 1995; Lawler, 1971). Thus, in contrast to economists who tend to look at money in terms of its absolute value, psychologists and sociologists tend to look at it more in terms of its signaling value and achievement (What does this amount of money say about my performance relative to others?; Frank, 1985). These are important questions because some behavioral phenomena are difficult to explain as a simple function of absolute amounts of money, which will become clear as we reexamine equity theory and related evidence.

Expectancy Theory

Expectancy theory (Vroom, 1964) has been widely used over the past three decades in attempting to understand and predict the motivational and behavioral consequences of different pay plans. Our discussion here is relatively brief, because there are several good in-depth reviews available (e.g., Campbell & Pritchard, 1976; Kanfer, 1990; Mitchell, 1974) and because relatively little empirical work has been done in recent years (Ambrose & Kulik, 1999).

Although direct tests of expectancy theory are rarely performed anymore, its basic concepts continue to be incorporated into empirical work on motivation and performance. For example, as we shall see in a few pages, Wood, Atkins, and Bright (1999) used the expectancy theory concept of instrumentality to explain why goal commitment did not lead to performance in quite the way predicted by goal-setting theory. Thus, although expectancy theory is rarely tested as a stand-alone theory these days, its core components have become part of the standard language of motivational psychology and a common component of empirical studies based primarily on other theories. As such, it is important to briefly review its major features.

Expectancy theory is a within-person theory of motivation that views performance as a joint function of a person's *ability* and *motivational force* to engage in one level of behavior rather than another (Vroom, 1964).

Motivational force, in turn, is hypothesized to be a multiplicative function of three factors: expectancy (the perceived link between effort and behaviors), instrumentality (the perceived link between behaviors and outcomes, such as higher pay or greater fatigue), and valence (the value the person expects to derive from those outcomes). Thus, a pay-for-performance plan might not be motivational if (a) a person believes that no matter how hard he or she tries, performance will not improve (e.g., the second author's experience with golf); (b) the person does not believe that higher levels of performance will be sufficiently rewarded with higher levels of pay; or (c) the person places a low value on pay, particularly in relation to other outcomes that might also result from higher effort and performance (e.g., fatigue, stress, insufficient family time).

Expectancy theory can be a useful vehicle for thinking about the likely consequences of moving from one type of pay system to another. For example, consider the case of changing from a subjectively determined merit pay system to a formula-driven incentive system. The most predictable effect associated with this change would be to boost the instrumentality of the pay system: If the individual attains the target, he or she knows precisely how much money will be awarded. In addition, there are also likely to be effects on expectancy. For example, by having a very explicit production target, employees may focus much more directly on how to accomplish it and, in the process, increase their beliefs that the goal can be achieved (e.g., Locke, 1968; Whyte, 1955).

As another example, expectancy theory can be used to think about the effects of changing from an individual to a group incentive system. Although instrumentality should still be high (if the goal is achieved, the money is rewarded), expectancies would generally be expected to decrease, because whether or not the target is reached depends on people other than oneself. Indeed, this is what Schwab (1973) found. In addition, movement to a group system may also make some other outcomes besides pay more salient. For example, relations with coworkers may either become more harmonious, or more strained, with introduction of a group system (e.g., Slichter, Healy, & Livernash, 1960). (Interestingly, Whyte, 1955, showed that the implementation of *individual* incentive systems can also have profound effects on coworker relations.)

Turning to empirical evidence about the theory, there is little question that performance levels are correlated with each of the major components of the expectancy model. For example, a meta-analysis by Van Eerde and Thierry (1996) reported that the mean correlations with performance were .21 for valence, .16 for instrumentality, and .22 for expectancy.

However, the details of expectancy theory—in particular, the hypothesized multiplicative form of the relationship—have not received strong support. In part, Van Eerde and Thierry (1996) speculate that this may be due to the fact that many expectancy studies (like most studies performed several decades ago) employed suboptimal data analysis techniques. Even more important, however, is the fact that most studies were "performed incorrectly from the original theoretical point of view" (Van Eerde & Thierry, 1996, p. 581). Specifically, most expectancy studies were performed at the between-subjects level of analysis, whereas the theory is specified at the within-person level (see also Mitchell, 1974; Zedeck, 1977).

Still, it should be noted that studies using within-subjects analysis have not necessarily been supportive of the multiplicative model, either (e.g., Rynes & Lawler, 1983). In addition, other theories of motivation make predictions that would seem to be inconsistent with the multiplicative model suggested by expectancy theory. For example, goal-setting theory (discussed shortly) predicts that performance increases as goal difficulty increases, at least so long as the goal is regarded as attainable. If so, then very high levels of expectancy (as would be associated with very easy goals) may not be particularly motivating or lead to very high levels of performance.

Despite the lack of support for the precise mathematical formulation of the theory, its basic components are widely accepted, and the general ideas behind the theory are often used to explain findings in empirical studies. And given the basic support for each of the three components as correlates of performance, we feel safe in concluding that pay is likely to be a stronger motivator to the extent that (a) people believe they have control over their performance levels, (b) pay is clearly linked to performance, and (c) money is highly valued by those who are doing the "performing."

Goal-Setting Theory

Goal-setting theory (GST) places central importance on cognitive processes such as goal setting, intentions, and commitment as determinants of motivation (Locke, 1968; Ryan, 1958). In particular, the theory predicts that higher effort and performance results when people commit to difficult and specific goals rather than to vague commitments to

"Do your best," a notion that has been well supported by subsequent research (Locke & Latham, 1984).

In addition, GST predicts that monetary incentives will affect performance only to the extent that such incentives influence the choice of goals and the extent of goal commitment. This is because monetary incentives alone generally do not convey to workers what particular goal should be pursued (Locke, 1968). For example, employees may know that rewards will be distributed on the basis of merit, but this vague piece of information does not tell them which aspects of the job are most important in terms of assessing merit or the precise level of performance to be achieved on each aspect. Similarly, a manager might know that there is a very large prize associated with "winning" the tournament for CEO, but that tells him or her very little about the performance required to get there.

Despite the lack of explicit goals in most (though not all) nonexecutive pay programs, monetary incentives can nevertheless facilitate goal setting in two ways: by getting a person to set (or accept) particular goals and by retaining his or her goal commitment over time (see also Hollenbeck & Klein, 1987; Klein, 1989). However, Locke and Latham (1984) have cautioned that the relationships between incentives, goal setting, goal commitment, and task performance are likely to be rather complex. For example, although it is generally believed that employee participation in goal setting is useful for facilitating goal commitment, participation can also have negative effects on the level of goal difficulty, which would in turn be expected to decrease task performance.

A third prediction of GST is that goal commitment will interact with goal difficulty to determine performance (Klein, Wesson, Hollenbeck, & Alge, 1999). With easy goals, there typically is not much problem obtaining goal commitment, because there is little cost to doing so. However, when ambitious goals are set (e.g., to double sales over a 12-month period), individuals may be reluctant to commit because of the extra effort involved and/or the increased probability of failure and its attendant consequences. Thus, for a difficult goal to have the intended effect of increasing performance, it is both more important (and more challenging) to gain goal commitment.

In sum, goal-setting theory predicts that (a) monetary incentives predict performance only to the extent that they are mediated by goal choice and goal commitment and (b) there is an interaction between goal difficulty and goal commitment with respect to performance. What does the evidence say?

Research as to whether or not the effects of monetary incentives are mediated by goal choice and commitment has been equivocal. Early studies seemed to support this notion, although Locke cautioned in 1968 that "The issue of goal commitment has not been dealt with" (pp. 185). Nearly 20 years later, Hollenbeck and Klein (1987) concluded that much of the goal-setting literature still assessed commitment only in post hoc fashion, usually in terms of offering a possible explanation as to why the hypothesized effects of goal difficulty on performance had not been as large as expected. Thus, Hollenbeck and Klein recommended that researchers measure and study goal commitment in a more systematic fashion. Another 13 years later, Bartol and Locke (2000) still concluded that "Evidence for mediation of pay effects by goals (and commitment) is inconsistent" (p. 115).

In contrast, research examining the predicted interaction of goal difficulty and commitment with respect to performance has been largely supportive. Based on a meta-analysis of 66 effect sizes, Klein et al. (1999) found that the sample-weighted average correlation between goal commitment and task performance (corrected for unreliability in commitment) was .35 under high goal difficulty versus .20 and .18 under moderate and low levels of difficulty, respectively.

While these estimates of the main effects of commitment are useful, Locke (1968) and his colleagues (Locke & Latham, 1984) have also suggested that there may be complex interactions with other variables. For example, in a well-designed study consisting of three separate experiments, Wood et al. (1999) found very complex patterns of interactions between goal condition, difficulty of self-set goals, goal commitment, persistence, and task performance.

A major feature of their experiment (Wood et al., 1999) was to compare self-set goals and subsequent performance under control conditions (where subjects were assured of payment for goal attainment) with an experimental condition where payment was based on whether or not subjects performed in the top half or top quarter of all participants, an outcome that could be known only at the end of the experiment. Given this incentive structure, subjects in the control condition had an incentive to set easy goals, while those in the experimental condition were more likely to set difficult goals as a way of boosting performance. This expectation was confirmed.

However, despite setting higher goals in the uncertain payoff condition, subjects attained lower, rather than higher, overall performance. This was particularly surprising in light of the fact that experimental subjects reported the same levels of goal commitment as control subjects and actually exhibited higher persistence toward attaining their goals (i.e., participated in more trials). Wood et al. (1999) reported that the lower performance in the experimental condition was almost entirely explained by lower instrumentality perceptions of the experimental subjects, who could never know whether their performance level was going to be "good enough." This is a very interesting condition to study, since it pretty much captures the situation of all employees who operate under merit or forced-distribution pay systems, as well as all those who compete for promotions with other employees.

Turning now to potential antecedents of goal commitment, Klein et al. (1999) found that three components of expectancy theory were all correlated with goal commitment: expectancy perceptions, outcome attractiveness, and motivational force (.36, .29, and .33, respectively). In addition, goal commitment correlated .37 with participation in goal setting and .16 with ability or past performance. Interestingly, goal level (i.e., difficulty) was almost completely uncorrelated with goal commitment (.03), suggesting that commitment can often be obtained even for difficult goals. Finally, and most directly relevant to compensation, goal commitment correlated .20 with the use of incentives, although this finding was based on the cumulation of only three studies.

GST in Field Settings

One potential limitation of GST research (and the meta-analytic summaries) is that much of it has been conducted in laboratory settings. Relative to actual work situations, laboratory studies tend to use simple tasks, to be of short duration, and to use very small incentives (usually only a few dollars). These characteristics may have rather serious implications for attempts to generalize laboratory findings to ongoing work relationships in real organizations. The laboratory-versus-field question has been addressed head-on in the GST field, with evidence suggesting that laboratory findings hold up well in the field (Locke, 1986). We observe, however, that studies cited to show GST's application to field settings have often used very structured and simple tasks (e.g., number of trees cut by loggers, number of logs loaded on trucks, words processed; see, for example, Locke & Latham, 2002).

In contrast, employees in field settings typically may have less structured jobs and multiple potential goals to pursue. As such, they must make decisions about how to allocate scarce resources of time, energy, and attention (Kanfer & Ackerman, 1989). For example, due to the massive reorganization of health care facilities, physicians and nurses often have to serve large numbers of patients but must do so in ways that do not jeopardize patient health. Similarly, manufacturing employees are often under substantial pressure to attain production targets, even though pursuit of those goals may jeopardize employee safety or product quality.

Thus, one important concern with the combined use of goal setting and incentives in field settings is that employees may focus their attention only on goals that are explicitly measured and rewarded and not improve their *overall* performance (see similar discussions of the *equal compensation principle* in economics; Milgrom & Roberts, 1992). Rather, the main effect may be to redistribute effort and performance away from implied goals toward explicit goals.

An interesting demonstration of this effect was obtained in a laboratory study by Wright, George, Farnsworth, and McMahan (1993), who found that the provision of individual incentives inhibited prosocial helping behaviors toward other participants. The authors concluded that "When individuals are committed to difficult goals, they may strive to achieve these goals at the expense of the performance of other behaviors that are necessary for organizational effectiveness, yet not directly associated with individual goal attainment" (p. 378).

One way of attempting to circumvent such problems is to put other control systems in place to support the goals that are not rewarded by monetary incentives. For example, both Southwest Air and Akibia (which advertises "No Jerks!" on its Web site) place a strong emphasis on cooperative values and behaviors in their selection systems. The potential effectiveness of this strategy was suggested by Deckop, Mangel, and Cirka (1999), who studied the joint relationships of incentive use, values alignment, and performance in eight energy and utility companies. The found that when values alignment was high, incentive use did not produce any decrease in prosocial behaviors.

Another way of dealing with potential conflicts between explicit and implicit goals is to set multiple goals or goals at multiple levels of analysis (e.g., individual, group, and organization as a whole). As an example of the first strategy, despite its heavy emphasis on individual incentives, Lincoln Electric also allocates 25% of its annual bonus award on the basis of supervisory ratings of employee cooperativeness (e.g., idea generation, information sharing, and other forms of cooperation that benefit Lincoln as a whole; Jasinowksi & Hamrin, 1995). With respect to the second strategy, General Electric (GE) and Amoco Canada make bonuses at the business unit level contingent on first meeting targets at the corporate level. Other companies (such as Donnelly) similarly reward at multiple levels but do so in a compensatory rather than "gated" fashion (e.g., 50% of the bonus is based on corporate performance and 50% on unit performance; Case, 1998). Because the psychological processes underlying employee responses to these systems remain almost completely unexamined from a GST perspective, there are some exciting opportunities to collect field data on attentional allocation across goals, as well as goal commitment and persistence in multigoal programs.

A second issue that cannot be optimally studied in the laboratory is that of persistence toward goal attainment over time. According to Locke (1968),

> The subject's degree of commitment to his goal may play an important role in determining how easily he will give up in the face of difficulty, how likely he will be to "goof off" when not being pressured from the outside, how likely he will be to abandon hard goals, and how prone he will be to "leave the field'" (i.e., job) in the face of stress. (p. 186)

One suspects that in field settings, where it may take months or even years to first achieve a goal, persistence and enduring commitment may take on greater importance than in lab settings.

Although we know of no field studies that directly assess the role of incentives in enhancing persistence of commitment to difficult goals, several studies seem to address it at least indirectly. For example, in a well-designed longitudinal study with both experimental and control groups, Pritchard, Jones, Roth, Stuebing, and Ekeberg (1988) examined the combined roles of goal setting, feedback, and an incentive program (where up to one day off per month could be earned) on unit performance in a military setting. Goal setting and feedback interventions were implemented first, resulting in a substantial performance gain of 75%. Although the subsequent addition of the incentive program did not contribute to any further performance gains, performance was nevertheless sustained over an extended time period. It is quite possible that while the incentives were not necessary to obtain initial commitment to the high performance goals, persistence or ongoing commitment to achieving these goals may have been considerably less without the eventual use of incentives. It is also possible that the results would have been different were overall pay to have increased under the incentive program.

Another field study that indirectly suggests the helpfulness of incentives for persistence in pursuing difficult goals was performed by Wagner, Rubin, and Callahan (1988). They used archival data to measure foundry productivity over a 114-month period, in which an incentive system was implemented in the 41st month. At the end of 83 months under incentives, productivity was 103.7% higher than when the study began. In addition, productivity continued to increase throughout the entire incentive period rather than leveling off after an initial burst of improvement.

Management by Objectives Research

One body of goal-setting research that has been pursued almost exclusively in field settings is management by objectives (MBO), a goal-setting and feedback program that was particularly popular in managerial and professional settings during the 1970s and 1980s. Ironically, the move toward MBO was facilitated in part by a seminal article in the *Harvard Business Review* arguing that discussions of pay should be kept separate from discussions about performance (Meyer, Kay, & French, 1965).[2] This recommendation was based on the supposedly distracting and "demoralizing" aspects of discussions about pay in performance appraisal, a notion that recalls Herzberg's notion of pay as a demotivator.

Another major impetus for MBO was GST itself. The basic features of GST can be seen in the core features of MBO (Carroll, 1986; Noe, Hollenbeck, Gerhart, & Wright, 2000). For example, MBO requires the setting of specific difficult goals as well as the development of plans to achieve them. Second, goals are not set unilaterally by supervisors, but rather in conjunction with subordinates. Third, managers are expected to monitor goal attainment and give feedback throughout the performance period.

A 1991 review of 70 MBO programs found that 68 appeared to demonstrate performance gains (Rodgers & Hunter, 1991). Yet despite these apparent gains, many MBO programs have now been abandoned (Bartol & Locke, 2000; Carroll, 1986). One of the biggest difficulties was that managers tended to set low, easily attainable goals rather than the difficult goals envisioned by the theory, thus confirming the warnings of Locke and Latham (1984) about using incentives in connection with self-set goals. According to Bartol and Locke (2000), MBO systems became "very unpopular" because, as one CEO put it, "It was a system whereby smart managers tried to convince their bosses that their easy goals were hard" (p. 116). Similarly, Jensen (2001) describes paying people for "target" attainment as "paying people to lie." Another source of difficulty appeared to be that the goal-setting and planning process took a considerable amount of time and was often disliked by managers and their employees.

Although MBO per se appears to have fallen into decline, the practice of basing managerial pay on numerical goals clearly has not. Indeed, more than ever before, managerial pay depends on whether or not particular operational or financial goals are met (R. Heneman et al., 2000). However, relative to MBO programs, the goals are now more often likely to be set nonparticipatively, to "cascade down" from corporate goals, and to focus mainly on goals for unit (rather than individual) performance. These changes in the nature of managerial goal-setting processes present fascinating opportunities for renewed research in field settings on topics such as goal commitment and the extent to which performance effects of goal setting are mediated by goal commitment.

In summary, there is strong support for GST both in laboratory and field settings. However, we feel it would be useful to have research that more directly addresses how GST works in field settings where there are multiple goals or where goals are somewhat ill defined, especially given the greater emphasis on knowledge-based work in today's economy. The problems encountered using MBO in the workplace (Bartol & Locke, 2000) provide an example of the challenges that arise in field settings.

Social Cognition Theory

SCT (Bandura, 1986) also gives a central role to cognitive factors in motivation. According to SCT, three sets of factors—cognitive and other personal factors, behavior, and the external environment—influence one another in "triadic reciprocal causation" (Wood & Bandura, 1989). As such, SCT argues that people "make their environments," rather than being "shaped and controlled by environmental influences or by internal dispositions" (Wood & Bandura, 1989, p. 361). In an organizational context, SCT focuses on increasing motivation through three processes: (a) the development of people's competencies through mastery modeling, (b) the cultivation of people's beliefs in their capabilities so that they will use their talents effectively, and (c) the enhancement of people's motivation through goal systems.

A key (cognitive) self-regulatory mechanism in SCT is self-efficacy, which refers to "people's beliefs in their capabilities to mobilize the motivation, cognitive resources, and courses of action needed to exercise control over events in their lives" (Wood & Bandura, 1989, p. 364). Self-efficacy is a task-specific construct, meaning that it differs from concepts that focus on generalized confidence across tasks, such as general self-efficacy or self-esteem (Stajkovic & Luthans, 1998b). According to Bandura (1986), general self-efficacy (like self-esteem) behaves like a trait, whereas self-efficacy, although related to self-esteem, varies as a function of specific situations.

Empirical evidence shows that self-efficacy is clearly related to performance. For example, a meta-analysis of the relationship between self-efficacy and performance at the individual level of analysis yielded a weighted average correlation of .38 (Stajkovic & Luthans, 1998a), while a similar meta-analysis at the group level reported a weighted average of .44 (Stajkovic & Lee, 2001). Because this is clearly a rather robust relationship, SCT theorists have devoted considerable attention to ways of increasing self-efficacy.

Wood and Bandura (1989) suggest four possible paths. The first is through (direct) mastery experiences; that is, success breeds confidence. Put another way, successful performance increases self-efficacy (just as self-efficacy increases performance) in the sort of mutual causation proposed by the theory. A second route is through modeling or observational learning, that is, by watching how other successful people perform. Although direct mastery experience is seen as the most effective path to self-efficacy, Bandura (1986) argued that learning through direct experience is often very inefficient, thus leading him to focus much of his own work on the way people infer behavioral consequences by observing the behavior, attributes, and outcomes of others in specific situations. Third, social persuasion in the form of realistic encouragement can also build confidence. Fourth, Wood and Bandura (1989) suggest that it may be helpful to decrease stress or improve a person's physical condition, because people may interpret their own emotional arousal and tension as signs of vulnerability to poor performance.

In many ways, discussions about how to increase self-efficacy are similar to discussions about how to raise expectancy perceptions under expectancy theory. For example, Stajkovic and Luthans (1998b) conclude that managers can improve workers' self-efficacy through provision of clear task expectations and performance measures, training, and removal of task environment constraints, recommendations that are all consistent with expectancy theory. Yet motivation theorists also see some differences between the two constructs (e.g., Bandura, 1986).

For example, Locke and Latham (1990) believe that self-efficacy and expectancy are clearly related, but that self-efficacy "is broader in meaning" (p. 256) and "plays a ubiquitous role" (p. 255) in goal-setting theory, such as affecting goal choice, goal commitment, and reactions to feedback, as well as having direct effects on performance. Similarly, Kanfer (1990) notes that self-efficacy and expectancy "are often positively associated, . . . but discrepancies between the two may arise and have motivational implications" (p. 133).

From our own perspective, SCT and the self-efficacy approach appear to place less emphasis on "uncontrollable" factors (e.g., ability or situation) as determinants of the link between effort and behavior/performance. For example, a worker may already have the skills to be successful but need help in seeing that success is possible. By comparison, expectancy theory tends to focus on "real" changes in the person's likelihood of being able to accomplish a task, brought about through changes in selection, training, and job design. These factors are also important in the self-efficacy literature but are not its exclusive focus. The second difference follows directly from the first: The self-efficacy perspective sees a greater possibility that performance improvements can be obtained without significant investments in HR programs such as selection, training, or compensation. This, of course, is a very attractive idea to managers wishing to maximize payoffs while holding down costs.

Although we believe that the nonpecuniary recommendations that flow from SCT are important and of practical value in many cases, we also believe it is useful to keep in mind the challenges of obtaining long-term commitment and goal persistence in real organizations. As such, we suggest that future SCT researchers pay more explicit attention to the potential value of incentives for increasing self-efficacy. Indeed, some prominent observers of pay-performance relationships (e.g., Crystal, 1991; Frank & Cook, 1995) have noted that pay is one of the most salient signals to individuals of "how they are doing." Given the powerful effect of money as a feedback device, its potential for increasing self-efficacy should not be ignored.

In addition, we suspect that reward systems also have a powerful (albeit vicarious) effect on the *direction,* as well as the level, of effort exerted by employees. As SCT suggests, employees are often keen observers of what successful people do and what kinds of behaviors tend to be rewarded via promotions and pay increases. This is an important observation, because an organization's tangible reward systems (e.g., pay, promotions, and dismissals) can sometimes run counter to verbal reinforcement systems (praise, feedback, and publicity statements). For example, CEOs can say, "People are our most important asset" but then lay off employees at the first sign of an economic downturn (e.g., T. Stewart, 1996; Swoboda, 1995). Similarly, companies tend to emphasize the primacy of "people skills" for employees (especially managers), and yet Luthans, Hodgetts, and Rosenkrantz (1988) found that managers who receive the most promotions (and hence the most pay) actually spend the least time dealing with people. For these reasons, it seems important to explicitly consider the role of money—in conjunction with other reinforcement systems—in shaping both employee self-efficacy and direction of effort.

Equity Theory

As discussed earlier in Chapter 3, equity theory proposes that people make judgments about the fairness of their pay on the basis of assessments of their perceived outcomes/inputs ratio relative to the ratio of some salient comparison other. We reintroduce equity theory here because we believe that pay basis decisions (such as merit increases or bonuses) are more likely than other pay decisions to evoke equity comparisons.

There are a variety of reasons for this prediction. First, as we indicated earlier, people often judge the "goodness" of their pay in relative rather than absolute terms, just as employers evaluate the reasonableness of their pay level in relation to what others are paying. Second, pay basis decisions often involve comparisons among people doing exactly the same kind of work in the same organization, whereas pay level decisions involve comparisons across organizations, and pay structure decisions involve comparisons across jobs. In contrast, comparisons of the merit increases of people in the same job and organization are likely to be particularly salient. Related to this, pay basis decisions are often explicitly personal (e.g., merit-increase decisions), while decisions about pay level or pay structure generally involve decisions about large groups of people. Finally, pay basis decisions often involve *changes* in compensation, which also tend to be more salient than steady-state pay practices (e.g., Brown & Huber, 1992; Reynolds, 1951; Slichter, 1950). For these reasons, we expect pay basis decisions to be the source of considerable employee monitoring and reactivity. Exhibit 5.1 provides an example of the importance of pay comparisons.

Exhibit 5.1 Pay and Social Comparisons: Baseball Players and Executives

To illustrate the importance of relative comparisons in annual pay increases, consider the contract that shortstop Alex Rodriquez signed in 2000 with the Texas Rangers baseball team. According to the contract, Rodriguez is guaranteed a minimum of $21 to $27 million per year (plus incentives) during the 10-year span of his contract. However, two key provisions could result in him earning substantially more than that. One provision states that during the 2001 to 2004 seasons, his base compensation must be at least $2 million higher than that of any other shortstop in major league baseball. A second provision permits Rodriquez to void seasons after 2008 unless his 2009 and 2010 base compensation is at least $1 million higher than any position player in major league baseball. Otherwise, Rodriguez is free to leave the Rangers. These provisions, which explicitly peg Rodriguez's pay to that of other players, is a compelling example of the importance of how people evaluate pay in relative terms.

Moreover, as might be expected, the story does not end here. According to Daley (2001), an immediate effect of Rodriguez's contract was to cause other baseball players to seek to renegotiate their own contracts. Frank Thomas of the Chicago White Sox (who made $9.93 million per season at the time of the article) explained his negotiations this way:

> The pay scale is getting out of whack. You can't have A-Rod making $25 million [per year] and we're coming in at $7 million, $8 million, $9 million. It's just like Hollywood. You can't have the top actor making $25 million and the rest making $10 million. (Daley, 2001, p. 12B)

As we saw in our company examples from Chapter 2 (Coca-Cola, Ford, and Procter & Gamble; see Exhibit 2.1), relative comparisons are key compensation drivers not only in sports but also in business organizations. Recall that at each of these three companies, the compensation committee was careful to specify that executive compensation levels were chosen with an eye toward being competitive with a particular set of companies. This is because executives are keenly aware of what their peers receive and, like Frank Thomas, are very interested in being paid "equitably" by comparison. What differs, however, is that executives, unlike baseball players, may be able to exert direct influence (independent of their performance) on their own compensation levels (Crystal, 1991), a topic we return to in our discussion of agency theory.

Although equity theory has served to highlight the importance of fairness perceptions and social comparisons in understanding people's attitudes and behaviors, its limitations have also been noted many times (Campbell & Pritchard, 1976; Miner, 1980; Mowday, 1996). First, recall that the theory suggests that people seek to restore equity not only when they feel underrewarded but also when they feel overrewarded. While the theory's predictions regarding reaction to underpayment are generally supported, as we noted in Chapter 2, there is little evidence that people react in any practically significant way to overreward, particularly in field settings (Campbell & Pritchard, 1976; Lawler, 1968; Locke, 1976; Mowday, 1996; but for a less pessimistic view, see Miner, 1980).

A second broad concern with equity theory is its inability to specify a priori predictions (Miner, 1980; Mowday, 1996). One ambiguity concerns which comparison standard will be chosen (Goodman, 1974). Another ambiguity is that the theory does not identify what input and outcome factors will be identified by people nor which will take on the greatest importance to different individuals in influencing equity perceptions. The empirical research typically includes effort and performance, but the theory recognizes a broader set of inputs and outcomes that may be perceived as important to some people some of the time. Finally, if inequity is perceived, the theory is ambiguous as to what course of "action" the person will take to restore equity (Opsahl & Dunnette, 1966). Will it be behavioral or cognitive? Will it entail changing a persons's own inputs or outcomes, or those of the comparison standard? Will it lead to a change in a person's choice of comparison standards, or will it lead to that person leaving the situation? The theory provides no a priori prediction.

Because of these ambiguities, it is difficult to use equity theory to make the kinds of direct predictions about performance that tend to be made by the other theories discussed in this chapter. However, simply because the model is not easy to use operationally does not necessarily invalidate its premises or reduce its usefulness as a heuristic device. Moreover, because equity theory assumes that in-balance *I/O* ratios are not motivators, it may be that equity theory is more likely to be more useful for understanding pay *dissatisfaction* (i.e., underreward inequity), as well as some of the less "desirable" employee reactions to pay (from the employer's perspective). In other words, we suspect that equity theory may be most useful for examining behaviors that may be costly to an employer: effort withholding, turnover, collective action, legal action, and renegotiation behaviors—in short, the "dark side" of reactions to compensation decisions.

Agency Theory

Agency theory is the major economic theory of relevance to decisions about pay basis. As such, the reader will probably notice some differences in assumptions relative to the psychological theories reviewed to this point. For example, agency theory takes a less sanguine view of the motivational makeup of employees than do most psychological theories (particularly those of Herzberg, Maslow, and Deci). Specifically, workers are assumed to find work aversive and hence to choose leisure or shirking whenever possible. To avoid these outcomes, the proper incentives must be provided to align interests between owners and employees (or, put more positively, to achieve the cooperation emphasized by Barnard, 1951, and Simon, 1957a). Alternatively, employers can purchase information about worker actions and performance, which can then be used to monitor contract compliance.

In general, agency theory attempts to specify when it will be most effective to use subjective evaluations (based on monitoring) to motivate and reward performance, versus formula-driven evaluations based on prespecified financial or operational targets. Agency theory starts from the observation that separation of ownership from control is an important feature of the modern corporation. Although this separation has important advantages for owners (such as allowing them to diversify their investment portfolios to reduce risk), it also tends to remove them from knowledge of day-to-day operations of the firm. As such, it creates the need for an agency relationship, under which one or more principals (e.g., owners) contract with one or more agents (e.g., managers) "to perform some service on their behalf which involves delegating some decision making authority to the agent" (Jensen & Meckling, 1976, p. 308).

Although agency theory has most often been applied to executive compensation, it can actually be applied to any case in which delegation occurs. This includes not only owners delegating to executives but also executives delegating to their subordinates. Even more broadly, Jensen and Meckling (1976) argue that "Agency costs arise in any situation involving cooperative effort . . . by two or more people even though there is no clear-cut principal-agent relationship" (p. 309). For example, the theory may also be used to analyze the case of a team member with an interest in seeing that other team members produce their fair share of output.

The problem with agency relationships is that agents do not always act in the best interests of the principal. There are two reasons for this. First, *goal incongruence* refers to the fact that the interests of principals and agents are not identical. Therefore, in the absence of an effective contracting scheme, agents may exert less effort than desired (i.e., shirking) or allocate their efforts in different directions than the principal would prefer. One possible source of goal incongruence is a presumed difference in risk preferences between principals and agents. Specifically, as an owner, the principal is likely to be able to diversify risk by investing in multiple companies. In contrast, the agent/employee may rely entirely on his or her earnings for income. Therefore, the agent is likely to be more risk averse as a manager than the principal might desire, for fear that risky projects (if unsuccessful) could greatly reduce the agent's future compensation.

Second, principals suffer from *information asymmetry* relative to agents. This means that principals have less information than agents about both (a) characteristics of the agent (e.g., ability) and (b) decisions made and actions taken by the agent. In combination with goal incongruence, information asymmetry contributes to two types of possible opportunistic behaviors: adverse selection and moral hazard (Zajac, 1995). When either or both exist, contract enforcement by the principal is made more difficult.

Adverse selection results from opportunistic behaviors that occur prior to the setting of a contract. As an example, a top manager applying for an executive position may create a resumé that overstates his or her past accomplishments or that fails to disclose the true reasons for leaving a previous company. As another example, suppose an executive is negotiating his or her starting compensation package. Adverse selection might occur if, for example, an executive has inside information (unavailable to owners) that the company will beat profit targets in the next few quarters, which in turn will drive up the stock price. Given this information, the executive may push for a compensation arrangement that links pay more strongly to stock price than the owner might wish.

In contrast to adverse selection, *moral hazard* occurs after a contract has been put into place (Milgrom & Roberts, 1992). For example, once an executive has accepted the contract, he or she may be tempted to manipulate accounting ratios (e.g., profitability) as a way to influence the stock price. Because the owner is likely to be at an informational disadvantage relative to the executive (because owners are typically not actively involved inside the firm), the only way owners would be able to detect this manipulation would be to invest resources in gathering independent information. If as a result of these informational advantages, an executive manages to manipulate the stock price, it is an example of moral hazard.

Of course, the notion of a single owner is increasingly outdated as companies become larger and larger. As ownership becomes more dispersed, owners increasingly rely on a set of representatives (board of directors) to monitor the actions of executives. As a result, there is even greater potential for information asymmetry. Indirect evidence of the relative informational disadvantage of outside representatives comes from studies that have compared the nature of compensation at owner-controlled firms (where one owner controls 5% or more of the company's shares) with manager-controlled firms (where there is no such large shareholder). As would be predicted, evidence suggests that in owner-controlled rather than manager-controlled firms, monitoring of top executives is greater and executive pay more closely tied to performance (e.g., Gomez-Mejia, Tosi, & Hinkin, 1987; Tosi & Gomez-Mejia, 1989). Exhibit 5.2 illustrates one manner in which managerial control might affect managerial pay.

The costs that arise from the principal's efforts to reduce goal incongruence, information asymmetry, and the resulting problems of moral hazard and adverse selection are referred to as *agency costs*. Agency theory examines how agency costs can be minimized by choosing the most efficient contracting scheme. Two general types of contracts are possible: outcome based or behavior based.

An outcome-based contract links agents' pay to outcomes on measures such as total shareholder return or productivity. Because these measures have a direct impact on the wealth of the principal, they provide an appropriate incentive for the agent to act in the best interests of the principal. Thus, although executives may continue to seek ways to

Exhibit 5.2 Managerial Control and Pay

As an example of how managerial control might be exploited by an executive to maximize his or her pay at the expense of shareholders, consider the argument made by former executive compensation consultant Graef "Bud" Crystal that there is a comparative ratcheting process that routinely occurs at the executive level in U.S. corporations. This can be done in subtle fashion by manipulating the companies included in the executive compensation survey to incorporate the new big winners in the annual contract "sweepstakes." A compensation consultant who serves at the pleasure of the chief executive (i.e., his or her customer) may be quite receptive to the chief executive's thoughts on this matter. According to Crystal (1991):

> Which companies should we survey? . . . An objective observer ought to be able to look over the list of potential survey companies and comprehend almost instantly why each company is on the list. So, if the company commissioning the survey is an oil company, the objective observer will easily understand why Mobil Oil and Exxon are on the list. But Walt Disney? You may sheepishly reply: "Well, they use oil, don't they?" Or: "Well, they're headquartered in Los Angeles and so are we." Of course, an equally plausible reason for including Walt Disney is that Michael Eisner, Disney's CEO, earns a ton of money. When Eisner jumps into a swimming pool of compensation data, half the water flies out; he is single-handedly capable of raising the survey average by $1 million per year. (p. 44)

appropriate wealth, if the bulk of their upside earnings potential depends on total shareholder return, shareholders may be better off than in the absence of such a contract. In addition, results-based contracts of this sort have two additional potential advantages: They permit the principal to shift risk to the agent, and they do not require the principal to be able to monitor the behaviors used to achieve the results. This feature is especially important in cases where monitoring costs would be particularly high, for example, when the owner does not have the necessary expertise (e.g., in complex technical fields) or in cases of wide geographic dispersion.

However, a difficulty arises because contracts that have desirable incentive properties from the principal's point of view tend to have unfavorable risk properties from the agent's point of view. This is because results-based measures are less controllable by the agent than behavior-based measures. So, for an agent to be willing to accept a results-based contract, a compensating differential for risk (or risk premium) must be paid. Thus, results-based contracts are expected to be more costly than behavior-based contracts. Nonetheless, a results-based contract will be efficient if the positive incentive effects more than offset the costs of risk bearing by the agent.

In contrast, behavior-based contracts link the pay of the agent to the effectiveness of the specific behaviors or actions undertaken by the agent. Effectiveness in this case is more subjectively determined. Moreover, this effectiveness measure may or may not be closely related to the effectiveness measure that is of most importance to the owner (i.e., owner wealth creation). Thus, the owner bears the entire cost of risk as well as the cost of information to monitor the agent's behaviors.

Monitoring costs include the costs of both observing and evaluating behaviors. Growth, decentralization, and globalization of operations are some of the factors that make observation of behaviors costly or impossible. The ability to accurately evaluate behaviors is limited by the monitor's own knowledge and abilities, which may fall short in areas where complex science and technology are central. For example, a principal may be able to observe the behaviors of a scientist mapping a human gene but may find it rather difficult to judge whether the behaviors are sensible and likely to succeed.

Empirical Tests: Data on Executives

Tests of agency theory have used a range of methodologies and data and focused on different theoretical implications. Much of the earliest work focused on identifying the most important determinants of executive pay, with the idea being that if agency theory is correct, executives should be rewarded primarily for performance, as indicated by measures such as profitability and shareholder returns (Hallock & Murphy, 1999).

Pay for Performance. One of the most frequently cited studies examining this issue was conducted by Jensen and Murphy (1990). They found that for every additional $1,000 in shareholder wealth, the average CEO received "only" an additional $3.25 in compensation. They (like many subsequent writers) interpreted the $3.25 as evidence that there was not a sufficiently strong link between pay and performance in CEO compensation, thus casting some doubt on the descriptive power (if not the prescriptive power) of agency theory.

Of course, a moment's reflection raises some concerns about the interpretation and implications of the Jensen and Murphy (1990) study. For example, their sample consisted of CEOs at the 430 largest publicly traded U.S. companies. To see what their $3.25 finding implies for executive pay, consider how CEO compensation would change given a modest change (10%) in the market value of companies this size. For example, GE had a market value of approximately $296 billion early in 1998. A 10% increase in market value (a modest increase in that year's stock market) would have implied an additional $96 million in compensation for (then) CEO Jack Welch. Is the argument that $96 million is not sufficiently large to provide Welch with the necessary incentive effect? Or consider a much smaller company such as Health South, which was Number 471 on the *Fortune 500* list that year, with a market value of approximately $11.4 billion. A 10% increase in market value, using the Jensen and Murphy estimate, would imply an increase in CEO compensation of $2.8 million. How does one decide whether that increase is too small, too large, or just right?

In any event, other researchers have also sought to identify the main determinants of executive compensation and concluded that pay-for-performance relationships are insufficiently strong. For example, Tosi, Werner, Katz, and Gomez-Mejia (2000) compared the relative ability of firm size and firm performance to predict executive compensation. They found that firm size "explained almost nine times the amount of variance in total CEO pay than the most highly correlated [accounting] performance measure" (p. 329). They interpreted this finding as supporting the existence of agency problems and managerialism, that is, that CEOs seek to increase firm size as a means of justifying higher compensation for themselves.

Although this is an important issue, we suggest that a strong relationship between firm size and CEO compensation cannot be interpreted in such a straightforward fashion. First, growth is a desired objective of most owners, not just CEOs. It would not make much sense to say that shareholders were hurt by growth at Microsoft, Intel, and Medtronics, for example. Second, there is actually little reason to expect accounting measures of performance to strongly predict total CEO pay, since typically, only annual bonuses depend on accounting performance. Third, the more relevant basis for examining CEO pay from an agency perspective is total shareholder return (rather than accounting profits), something that was not linked to CEO pay in the Tosi et al. (2000) study.

Risk and Pay for Performance. Aggarwal and Samwick (1999) make the important argument that "The *average* level of pay-performance sensitivity cannot be used to judge the validity of the principal-agent model" (p. 67), regardless of the performance measure used. Rather, they propose that a more direct test of agency theory focuses on what they refer to as its "comparative static predictions." By this, they refer to agency theory's central focus on the trade-off between risk and incentives. A key implication of the theory is that "Pay-performance sensitivity of a manager's compensation is decreasing in the variance of her firm's returns" (p. 67). In other words, variance in firm performance increases the risk borne by the agent (manager), requiring a larger risk premium, thus making stronger incentives more costly to use as variance in firm performance increases.

Using a broader sample (1,500 of the largest U.S. publicly traded companies) and a more recent time period (1993–1996) than Jensen and Murphy (1990), Aggarwal and Samwick (1999) estimated the pay-performance sensitivity of executive compensation (for CEOs and the next four highest-paid executives) as a function of the riskiness (variance) of stock returns at each company (see Table 5.1). As the table indicates, among CEOs, the pay-performance sensitivity was approximately 19 times greater at the firm with the lowest variance in stock returns than at the firm with the highest variance. A similar pattern emerged among the remaining executives, although the difference was closer to a factor of 10. Aggarwal and Samwick concluded that their findings "strongly support the principal-agent model" (p. 67). In addition, they noted that the $14.52 pay-for-performance sensitivity for CEOs at the sample median for risk was substantially larger than the corresponding figure, $3.25, from the Jensen and Murphy study.

One possible concern with the Aggarwal and Samwick (1999) study is that the authors may have exaggerated the importance of differences in pay-for-performance sensitivities by using extreme values of risk (the minimum and maximum values in the sample). This concern is alleviated by the fact that Aggarwal and Samwick also examined pay-for-performance sensitivity as a function of variance in stock return quintiles and found similar results. For example, pay-for-performance sensitivity at the lowest-variance quintile was 30.5 versus 2.4 in the highest-variance quintile. However, one limitation that was not

Table 5.1 Pay-Performance Sensitivity (Change in Compensation for each $1,000 Increase in Shareholder Wealth)

Variance of Stock Returns	*CEO*	*Next Four Highest-Paid Executives*
At sample maximum	$1.45	$0.22
At sample median	$14.52	$1.18
At sample minimum	$27.60	$2.15

SOURCE: Aggarwal and Samwick (1999).

addressed was that the authors did not provide an index of goodness of fit to indicate how precise the relationship was between risk and pay for performance. Thus, it may be that much of the variance in pay-performance sensitivity is unexplained by risk differences, leaving open the possibility that other factors (e.g., power) also play an important role.

Other studies have also documented the negative relationship between company risk and pay-for-performance sensitivity among top executives, both in the economics (e.g., Garen, 1994) and management literatures (Beatty & Zajac, 1994; Bloom & Milkovich, 1998). The Bloom and Milkovich study (1998) is of particular note because it examined more executive levels (150,000 executives in 700 firms) and because it examined the consequences for firm performance of following what agency theory suggests is an optimal strategy, namely, having less performance-sensitive pay (cash plus bonus only) in riskier companies. Bloom and Milkovich did indeed find that performance (measured as total shareholder return) was substantially higher when companies with high performance variability had lower pay-performance sensitivity.

Relative Performance Evaluation

One way to lessen the trade-off between risk and incentives (and thus allow greater incentive intensity) is to pay on the basis of relative performance evaluation (RPE; Aggarwal & Samwick, 1999; Antle & Smith, 1986; Gibbons & Murphy, 1990; Miller, 1995; Murphy, 1999), which seeks to adjust measured performance for external shocks that influence raw performance but are not under the control of the executive. By making such adjustments, a pay-for-performance contract will carry less risk for executives, reducing agency costs due to risk aversion and allowing the use of more powerful incentive contracts that better align the interests of the executive with those of owners (Holmstrom, 1982).

How do we determine whether RPE describes the pay practices of firms? Typically, executive compensation is regressed on firm performance and the performance of the benchmark group. Under RPE, the expectation is that the firm performance coefficient will be positive and the benchmark performance group coefficient will be negative. In other words, compensation will be high only if firm performance exceeds benchmark performance. On the other hand, compensation may also be high even with poor firm performance if the performance of the benchmark group is significantly worse.

The most thorough empirical examination of whether RPE is used in American industry was conducted by Gibbons and Murphy (1990), who compared the predictive power of firm performance and two potential measures of benchmark group performance: industry versus broad market performance, using longitudinal data on 1,668 CEOs in 1,049 firms over the 1974 to 1986 time period. First, they estimated an equation for cash compensation (salary plus bonus) using only total shareholder return of the firm as a predictor and obtained a positive coefficient of .16, indicating that CEO cash compensation increases 1.6% for each 10% increase in total shareholder return. The R^2 for this equation was .047. Next, Gibbons and Murphy added the total shareholder return for the 2-digit Standard Industrial Classification (SIC) industry code for each firm. The coefficient on this variable was −.075, and the R^2 increased to .050. Removing 2-digit industry total shareholder return and replacing it with broad market shareholder return yielded a coefficient of −.149 and an R^2 of .054. In subsequent regressions, Gibbons and Murphy further demonstrated that the explanatory power of industry performance declined as industry was defined more narrowly (i.e., at the 3-digit and 4-digit levels). These results led Gibbons and Murphy to conclude that "CEO performance is more likely to be evaluated relative to aggregate market movements than relative to industry movements" (p. 39-S). This is consistent with the point we made in Chapter 2 that both product market and (broader) labor market comparisons are important in pay setting.[3]

We make the following observations on the Gibbons and Murphy (1990) results. First, we note that the increment to R^2 (from .047 to .054 in their Table 5.1) obtained by adding a benchmark performance measure was small, calling into question the importance of RPE in typical executive compensation contracts.[4] However, an analysis of more recent data (from the 1990s) by Murphy (1999) yielded somewhat stronger support (an increase in R^2 from .057 to .078 from adding a broad market return benchmark). So, perhaps RPE has become more important in recent years. On the other hand, a second observation is that the Gibbons and Murphy (1990) results and those of Murphy (1999) are based almost exclusively on using cash compensation as a dependent variable,[5] which excludes stock-related components. As we know, these components have come to make up an increasingly large portion of executives' total compensation. Unless these stock-related components are more strongly tied to RPE, it seems unlikely that the overall impact of RPE on total compensation would be very important in the typical executive compensation contract. Indeed, Murphy (1999) observes that "Although stock options could theoretically be indexed to industry or market movements, indexed options are virtually nonexistent in practice" (p. 39). Although Murphy does not cite any data to support his statement, if he is correct, the role of RPE in executive total compensation seems to be small.

Although Murphy is probably correct, it is possible that RPE may play more of role in stock plans in the near future, which would increase the RPE nature of executive pay. Rappaport (1999) has made the argument that boards of directors should use stock option plans that tie the exercise price to a benchmark index. For example, if the index increases by 15%, then the exercise price of the CEO's options would likewise rise 15%. Thus, the CEO can make money on the options only if the firm's stock returns exceed those of the firms included in the index. What companies should be included in the index? According to Rappaport, "Companies can choose either an index of their competitors or a broader market index such as the Standard & Poor's 500" (p. 93). His preference is for an industry-based competitor group, because industries have differed in their performances even when the S&P 500 was doing well overall. On the other hand, he notes that "Because many companies have diversified into a wide range of products and markets, it is sometimes difficult to identify a set of peers" (p. 94).

We note that Rappaport gives no examples of firms that have implemented indexed stock option plans of this sort, supporting Murphy's claim that RPE "never" exists in such plans. However, even though explicit RPE of this sort in stock plans is rare, it may be that in practice, there is an element of RPE in such plans. Thus, there may be an opportunity to reexamine the RPE hypothesis using total compensation as the dependent variable and using the most recent data available.

According to a more formal model of RPE, the ideal benchmark group would be determined on the basis of the correlation between the performance of the firm and the performance of the benchmark group. Whatever benchmark group has the highest correlation is the optimal benchmark group to use. Gibbons and Murphy (1990) examined this hypothesis as well, by computing the correlation between market stock return and firm stock return over each preceding 2-year period. They then divided the sample into two groups: (a) firms having a correlation between their stock return and the market stock return that exceeded the median correlation and (b) firms where the correlation was smaller than the median correlation. They found that CEO compensation was more responsive to market stock return in the former group ($b = -.1775$) than in the latter group ($b = -.0916$), consistent with the RPE hypothesis. (The variance explained by this interaction was not reported.)

In summary, even though RPE is hypothesized to have the important advantage of allowing stronger pay-for-performance linkages by reducing the risk borne by agents, the evidence suggests that RPE does not describe executive pay setting to the degree that would be expected given this theorized advantage. It would be useful to further explore this disconnect between theory and practice. One simple explanation is that executives would probably not earn as much under RPE when the broad (stock) market is doing well, as had been the case in the 1990s. So, while reducing downside risk is attractive to executives, the reduction in their upside earnings potential that also follows with RPE may mean, on balance, that executives are "RPE averse," raising the cost to organizations that use such plans.

Empirical Tests: Data on Nonexecutives

Like much of the economics literature, the management literature has also focused on tests of pay-for-performance relationships as tests of agency theory. Although Aggarwal and Samwick's point is well-taken (i.e., that this is perhaps not the purest test of agency theory), the question is still an interesting one.

One of the earliest and best studies in this vein was conducted by Gomez-Mejia and Balkin (1992b), who applied agency theory to specify and test a model of faculty pay. They argued that "In a university setting, principals face a classical agency problem with respect to faculty" because "information asymmetries between faculty and administrators create steep agency costs for the latter if they attempt to directly monitor faculty behavior" due to the fact that "areas of expertise and research tend to be idiosyncratic to individuals" (p. 923). They further note that "Except for student contact time in the classroom, which seldom exceeds 12 hours a week, faculty members are subject to very few structured constraints on their time" (pp. 923–924). Thus, the challenge for administrators is to figure out "how to prevent faculty members (agents) from taking advantage of their privileged and nonprogrammable position" (p. 924), which might occur, for example, by putting minimal effort into teaching or research.

According to Gomez-Mejia and Balkin (1992b), the most efficient way for administrators to address the agency problems of information asymmetry and possible goal incongruence is via outcome-based contracts. Specifically, research output (in high-quality outlets) and teaching performance ratings are two key outcomes that are hypothesized to influence faculty pay. This model received strong support, particularly with respect to the role of high-quality research. (The findings on teaching performance were more mixed, although that may have been partly due to the positive colinearity between publication and teaching performance.) Specifically, those with the strongest publication records had 37% higher salaries than those with the weakest records, even controlling for faculty rank. Clearly, rank (promotion) and tenure also depend on publication success and thus would be further expected to increase the rewards for higher performance. Finally, as Gomez-Mejia and Balkin also observed, this salary difference continues to accumulate over the course of an entire career. As faculty, we are gratified that administrators have figured out such a clever way to keep us from shirking!

Research from management literature has extended tests of agency theory beyond executives. For example, Eisenhardt (1988) studied retail sales clerks and found, as did Aggarwal and Samwick, that contingent (i.e., high pay-performance sensitivity) pay systems were more likely to be used in stores where risk or outcome uncertainty was low. (Risk was measured on the basis of two dimensions: failure rate for the type of store and number of competitors in the standard metropolitan statistical area.) The marketing literature has also used agency theory to understand how salespeople can be directed toward particular objectives (e.g., generating new sales, maintaining current customers) and the degree to which trade-offs may exist with such compensation schemes (Anderson & Oliver, 1987; Oliver & Anderson, 1994).

In addition to extending agency theory to nonmanagerial realms, management literature has also recognized the potential importance of institutional factors in influencing pay-performance sensitivity.

Eisenhardt (1988) provides indirect evidence on this point by observing that the type of merchandise and the age of the chain (proxies for the history of traditional pay systems) explained variance in pay-performance sensitivity beyond that explained by agency theory variables.

Conlon and Parks (1990) took the importance of tradition a step farther, finding that agency theory predictions (e.g., that the inability of a principal to monitor agent behaviors would result in greater use of results-based contracts) applied only in the absence of a strong tradition of payment norms in the simulated industry and company in which subjects operated. So, institutional factors were an important moderator (or boundary condition) here.

In a second simulation, Parks and Conlon (1995) introduced another potential moderator variable, environmental munificence. This time, they found that agency theory predictions regarding contract choice held only under munificence, which was basically operationalized as the size of the economic pie available to be shared between the principal and agent. In contrast, they found that as the pie became smaller, the principal's ability to monitor was actually associated with greater use of contingent pay. Parks and Conlon interpreted this finding to mean that scarcity and information (from monitoring) combine to create more collaboration, leading to greater sharing of both information and profits.

The idea of collaboration between principal and agent is one that perhaps receives too little attention in applications of agency theory to work organizations. Many organizations seek to establish collaborative employment relationships that are oriented toward achieving mutual gains by both employees and owners (Kochan & Osterman, 1994). Indeed, this is a core principle of much of management and industrial relations theory. To be sure, goals do not converge completely, but neither do they diverge completely. Therefore, while it is important to address how divergent goals can be aligned through compensation contracts, it is also important to recognize that attraction-selection-attrition processes can result in substantial alignment of goals and that HR practices can further build goal alignment.

The literature on organizational commitment, for example, distinguishes between commitment based on economic considerations (e.g., the need to receive a salary) and commitment based on noneconomic factors (e.g., values or affective commitment; for a review, see Takao, 1998). For example, O'Reilly and Chatman (1986) conceptualize organizational commitment as comprising three dimensions: *internalization* (attachment to an organization based on congruence of values between the individual and the organization), *identification* (attachment based on desire for affiliation), and *compliance* (attachment based on achieving rewards). Their internalization dimension is consistent with our point regarding value congruence, while the compliance dimension corresponds most closely with the agency theory emphasis on compensation contracts. A model by Allen and Meyer (1990) similarly highlights the importance of both economic and noneconomic commitment, such as employees' "emotional attachment to, identification with, and involvement in, the organization" (p. 1).

The key point is that agency theory, at least as it is typically interpreted and studied, emphasizes goal divergence rather than goal congruence as the starting point for making decisions regarding compensation contracts. However, where there is significant congruence in values or goals, the types of problems that arise with results-based contracts may be mitigated because these other drivers of behavior help assure that employees do not focus solely on goals that are explicitly rewarded by incentives (see Deckop et al., 1999).

We return to the choice between behavior-based and results-based contracts (in conjunction with their results) in the next chapter. For now, we turn to theories about the other major process (besides incentive effects) through which pay basis decisions can affect individual and organizational performance, namely, through their effects on sorting and workforce composition.

Workforce Composition, Sorting, and Personality-Based Theories

Building on earlier work by Rynes (1987), Gerhart and Milkovich (1992) emphasized that compensation decisions can influence employee behaviors in two ways. First, and most obviously, compensation has an effect on the motivation and behavior of an organization's current workforce. We have referred to this as an incentive effect (Lazear, 1986, 1999). Most of the theories we have discussed (e.g., goal setting, expectancy, tournament, agency) focus primarily on incentive effects. In addition, however, compensation decisions also have an effect on the composition (e.g., in terms of ability, personality) of an organization's workforce via attraction, selection, and attrition processes (Schneider, 1987). We have referred to this as a sorting effect (Lazear, 1986, 1999). The fact that compensation influences workforce characteristics suggests that some organizations will have more productive workforces on average and that some organizations will have workforces that are better matched (i.e., more responsive) to their compensation strategies.

Sorting effects occur in any organization but are perhaps most visible when an organization changes its compensation system. In this situation, the incentive effect would be estimated by the average change in performance of employees present both before and after the change. The sorting effect would be estimated by the degree to which employees present before the change decide to leave and are replaced by employees who have different performance levels. Thus, an organization changing its compensation system might observe two different mechanisms by which overall workforce performance changes.

In the following sections, we review psychological and economic theory and research on the sorting effect of compensation.

Applied-Psychology Models

Although pay level has traditionally been emphasized as the key determinant of applicant or employee quality in organizations (see our earlier discussions of utility and efficiency wage theories), the implications of pay decisions for workforce composition are broader than that. Specifically, it appears that *how* employers pay (e.g., how strongly pay and individual performance are linked) may influence who enters and stays with the organization. Consequently, different pay strategies may attract and retain different employee profiles, which in turn can have important implications for workforce attitudes and behaviors.

In discussing individual differences in attraction and retention, it may be helpful to think of two different categories of personal attributes. One category consists of personal characteristics for which "more" is almost always to be preferred over "less." Perhaps the clearest example of this type of attribute is general mental ability *(g)*, which has been shown to correlate positively with performance in all types of jobs (but especially higher-complexity jobs; Schmidt & Hunter, 1998). The other category consists of individual differences that may be useful in some situations but are less relevant (or even dysfunctional) in others. Examples include personality traits such as agreeableness and openness to experience, or values such as individualism versus collectivism or competitiveness versus cooperativeness. The distinguishing feature of this latter category of traits is that their value depends on their fit, or match, with job and/or organizational attributes.

This idea of fit between the person and the organization dates back at least to the Minnesota model of work adjustment (Dawis, 1991; Dawis,

Lofquist, & Weiss, 1968). This model hypothesizes that fit between the needs of the person and the rewards of the job results in *satisfaction,* while fit between the abilities of the person and ability requirements of the job results in *satisfactoriness* (i.e., performance). Expectancy theory clearly incorporates the person-job fit notion with respect to ability (e.g., via expectancy) and also with respect to needs (via valence).

However, until recently, personal characteristics have been the "poor cousin" to environmental factors in the compensation literature (Mitchell, 1997). Two major developments in the broader field of applied psychology are changing that status. First, there has been a dramatic resurgence of interest in personality resulting from the development of the "Big Five" personality classification (extraversion, emotional stability, agreeableness, conscientiousness, and openness to experience; Digman, 1990). Previously, the primary focus of individual differences in applied psychology had been on cognitive ability. However, the discovery of reliable relationships between personality characteristics and job performance—some of which appeared to be general and others, specific to particular job types (see Barrick & Mount, 1991)—brought a renewed interest in individual differences and fit. In addition, recent years have also seen development of scales designed to identify workers' relative preferences for extrinsic (e.g., money) and intrinsic (e.g., challenging work) rewards (Amabile, Hill, Hennessey, & Tighe, 1994).

The other major impetus to research on individual differences and fit has been the growing influence of Schneider's ASA model (Schneider, 1987). The ASA model hypothesizes that both organizations and workers seek to achieve a fit between their own characteristics and characteristics of the other. This fit process unfolds via both selection (by organizations) and self-selection (by applicants and employees). That is, in cases of good fit, the organization and the worker make a joint selection decision to enter into a relationship and then make subsequent joint decisions about whether or not to continue it. In sum, ASA processes are hypothesized to result in a degree of homogeneity within organizations such that people are more similar within organizations than across them (Schneider, 1987).

To date, most empirical work based on ASA has used policy-capturing designs and focused on applicant decisions (real or hypothetical) to pursue or accept different job opportunities. However, Schneider, Smith, Taylor, and Fleenor's (1998) study is unique in that they examined personality homogeneity across 142 organizations. They found that 24% of the variance in organization membership was explained by the Myers-Briggs Type Indicator, providing the strongest evidence yet of ASA processes.

Although Schneider et al.'s (1998) study provides solid evidence of the relative homogeneity predicted by ASA, they did not examine any specific ASA processes (e.g., selection) that might cause this homogeneity. Therefore, the sources of the homogeneity remain unclear.

Recent empirical evidence generally supports the importance of pay in ASA processes on the attraction side (Bretz et al., 1989; Bretz & Judge, 1994; Cable & Judge, 1994). In the first empirical study on this question, Bretz et al. (1989) showed respondents two videotaped segments of an applicant in two simulated interviews with two different companies. In both segments, the applicant asks questions about the company. The video segments differ in that in one segment, the interviewer describes an organization having an individually oriented reward system, whereas in the other, rewards are linked more to organizational results and cooperation. Bretz et al. found "marginal support" for the hypothesis that respondents choosing the individually oriented reward system had a higher need for achievement than did those choosing the other system.

Turban and Keon (1993) asked respondents (management students) to rate their attraction toward working for an organization that had either merit-based or seniority-based pay systems. Reward system was manipulated as merit versus seniority based. Two personality variables, self-esteem and need for achievement, were proposed as moderators of the effects of reward systems on attraction. As hypothesized, "need for achievement" was found to moderate the relationship, such that respondents with high need for achievement were much more attracted to the organization when the pay system was merit based. However, no support was found for the moderating effect of self-esteem.

Cable and Judge (1994) examined the job search behaviors of engineering and hotel administration students approaching graduation at a large northeastern university. In the policy-capturing portion of their study, subjects evaluated 36 job scenarios that varied, among other things, on whether pay was fixed versus contingent on performance, or individually versus group based. Preferences were estimated by using the beta weights on the compensation variables from each person's regression equation, based on their 36 evaluations. Among the individual differences they studied were collectivism, risk aversion, and (general) self-efficacy.

The findings of Cable and Judge (1994) largely supported their hypotheses. For example, preferences for contingent pay were higher among job seekers with low risk aversion. In addition, preferences for individual-based pay were higher among respondents having high self-efficacy but lower among collectivists. In fact, the largest regression weight of any personality variable in predicting pay preference was for collectivism in predicting a preference against individual-based pay. A policy-capturing study by Bretz and Judge (1994) similarly demonstrated that individuals having a preference for equal rewards were more attracted to organizations having group-based (versus individual-based) rewards.

G. Stewart (1996) examined the roles of conscientiousness and extraversion as well as the nature of the compensation system in predicting two dimensions of salesperson performance: obtaining new sales and retaining current customers. This study took place in an organization where some divisions (and subjects) worked under a plan that rewarded new sales, while others worked in a division that based rewards on both new sales and customer retention.

Based on previous personality research using the Big Five traits, G. Stewart (1996) hypothesized that conscientiousness would have a main effect on both types of job performance (new sales and customer retention) under both plans (Barrick & Mount, 1991). Specifically, Costa and McCrae (1992) have argued that conscientious individuals "have a strong will to achieve that is largely independent of external rewards" (as quoted in G. Stewart, 1996, p. 622). In contrast, Stewart argued that extraversion is an important indicator of a person's susceptibility to external rewards (Gray, 1973), with extraverts being very responsive to such rewards. As such, Stewart expected that extraverts would respond more strongly to whatever the reward system emphasizes and that they would actually deemphasize whatever was not rewarded.

G. Stewart's (1996) results supported his hypotheses. Specifically, conscientiousness was found to have a positive relationship with both types of performance. In contrast, the regression coefficient for extraversion was negative ($b = -.32$) for new sales when customer retention was rewarded and positive for new sales ($b = .36$) when new sales were rewarded. Similarly, the coefficient for extraversion was negative ($b = -.06$) for customer renewals when new sales were rewarded but positive ($b = .15$) when renewals were rewarded.

As noted above, collectivism has been found to be related to pay preferences of applicants (Cable & Judge, 1994). Given this important role of collectivism, we describe a study by Wagner (1995) that did not examine compensation directly but that nevertheless seems relevant to our discussion of the impact of personality in the context of group-based pay plans. In contrast to the Cable and Judge study, Wagner focused on respondents already in a "work" setting. He used a sample of 492 undergraduate students enrolled in an introductory management course, who worked in groups to prepare an oral case presentation that typically required 18 to 20 hours of working together. He found, as predicted, that both group size and perceived feeling of diffused responsibility were negatively related to (peer-rated) individual cooperation. However, Wagner also hypothesized an important role for personality on the logic that collectivists "favor the pursuit of group interests" and "seek out and contribute to cooperative endeavors that benefit their groups, irrespective of the immediate personal implications of these endeavors" (p. 155).

In support of his hypothesis, Wagner (1995) found that collectivists indeed received higher peer ratings on cooperation. In addition, he found that collectivism was an important moderator variable. In fact, the moderating effect of one dimension of collectivism was so substantial that the typical overall relationship between group size and cooperation did not exist in the high-collectivism group. That personality can completely blunt the effect of a powerful situational factor such as group size is striking and suggests that "free-rider" or "social-loafing" problems can be substantially mitigated, at least in groups of the (small) size studied by Wagner.

Several issues may affect how one interprets Wagner's (1995) results. First of all, the unit of analysis was the individual. Cooperation, for example, was measured by asking students to divide 100 points among group members. To offset the fact that larger groups would have lower cooperation scores for individual members, Wagner reported that he standardized these scores using a *z*-transformation "to compensate for the effects of different group sizes" (p. 9). Assuming that this was done within groups, it would then represent a measure of the relative degree of cooperation of each individual within a group, but the average *z* score within and across groups would need to sum to zero. In other words, his cooperation measure appears to constrain the average level of cooperation at the group level to be equal across groups. Although knowing who was most cooperative within groups is interesting, it would also be useful to have research that examines when total group cooperation will be highest.

In addition, the maximum group size in Wagner's study was 8 participants. As such, it is not known whether the moderating effect of collectivism would hold at larger group sizes, which are often the focus from a compensation perspective. Finally, it appears that Wagner may have measured collectivism after measuring cooperation. If so, collectivism self-reports may have been influenced by respondents observing their own recent behavior in the group context studied by Wagner.

In any case, Wagner's study is interesting and certainly raises the possibility that personality can play a large role in determining behavior within groups.

A different way to think of personality in groups is in terms of the optimal mix of personality types. Whereas Wagner's findings suggest that more collectivism is always better for cooperation, one might ask whether too many collectivists could be too much of a good thing. Although no study has addressed the specific issue of collectivism in group composition, a related study by Barry and Stewart (1997) did examine the influence of extraversion on group performance. They found a curvilinear relationship, such that having a greater percentage of extraverts enhanced group performance, but only to a point. After that, having an increased percentage of extraverts was associated with lower group performance. Barry and Stewart suggested that extraversion was generally helpful in that it helped group members interact to improve performance. However, after a point, extraversion may have hindered task focus, perhaps due to increased social interaction, only some of which was task related.

Compatible findings were recently obtained by Kristof-Brown, Barrick, and Stevens (2001), who examined the role of extraversion/introversion of individual team members on overall assessments of team cohesion. Based on two independent samples (56 teams of 293 MBA students and 24 teams of 184 production workers), they found that in general, extraversion and perceived cohesion were positively related ($r = .24$ for the MBAs, and $r = .19$ for the production teams). However, perceived cohesion was actually highest in the teams with a mix of extraverts and introverts, thus supporting a complementary fit (versus supplementary fit) model of personality and team cohesiveness.

Taken together, Barry and Stewart's (1997) and Kristof-Brown et al.'s (2001) results seem to suggest that "too-high" proportions of extraverts may indeed have negative influences on team performance. However, the two studies offer somewhat different speculations as to why this might be the case. Specifically, Barry and Stewart (who studied team *performance*) speculated that teams composed almost exclusively of extraverts might become too socially (rather than task-) oriented. However, the findings of Kristof-Brown et al. (who studied team *cohesiveness*) suggest that social cohesion may actually be lower in teams of all extraverts, relative to more personality-diverse teams. Still, both Kristof-Brown et al. and Barrick, Stewart, Neubert, and Mount (1998) found that teams comprised solely of extraverts were nevertheless more cohesive than teams comprised solely of introverts, suggesting that if one must have personality-homogeneous teams, extraversion may be more desirable than introversion.

One important implication of these studies is that sorting or ASA processes might work "too well" in some cases if these processes lead to too much homogeneity of certain individual characteristics. Even where homogeneity positively influences current effectiveness, its long-run effects may be negative if it constrains an organization's ability to adapt to changes in its environment (Schneider, 1987). Thus, an organization that hopes to benefit from the sorting effects of its compensation system must also recognize that there may be potential costs as well.

The sorting and ASA effects of compensation systems can, however, be very helpful in shaping a workforce that is well aligned with the HR and business strategies. Firms that compete by differentiating their business strategies often require different workforces and cultures as well. For example, well-known strong-culture companies such as SAS, Lincoln Electric, and Southwest Airlines are unique in their industries with respect to their HR strategies and cultures. If the ASA model is correct, this implies that they are also unique with respect to the attributes of their employees. Thus, the way that pay contributes to ASA dynamics is likely an important mechanism by which pay influences organization performance.

In summary, compensation can have a major influence on organizational effectiveness via its effect on workforce composition. Although there can be drawbacks to too much workforce homogeneity, many organizations appear to experience substantial benefits from an alignment between their workforces and HR and business strategies.

Economic Models: Personnel and Organizational Economics

As noted earlier in this chapter, there are fundamental differences between economic and psychological perspectives on motivation and performance. One goal of our book is to identify the ways that these perspectives are similar and how they differ. One key distinction is in their treatment of individual differences. Although the attention to person and environment factors in psychological models of pay and motivation may ebb and flow, both are explicitly recognized as important. In contrast, in economic models, attention to person factors is limited in theory (although occasional reference is made to the influence of "tastes") and essentially nonexistent in empirical research (Kaufman, 1999). Although economists have increasingly discovered the importance of theory and research that opens the proverbial "black box" of the firm and establishment, person factors in recent organizational economics models (e.g., Brickley et al., 1997; Milgrom & Roberts, 1992) continue to be conspicuous by their absence. For example, Brickley et al. (1997) include three factors in their "three-legged-stool" approach to organizational architecture: decision rights assignment, performance evaluation, and rewards. There is no explicit recognition of person factors, such as ability, personality, or preferences.

Indeed, as noted earlier, Brickley et al. (1997) explicitly exclude individual differences in their approach, noting that "Managers are typically interested in structuring an organizational architecture that will work well and does not depend on specific people filling particular jobs" (p. 28). Obviously, this is quite different from the oft-cited psychologists' belief that "People make the place" (Schneider, 1987). Of course, interest in individual differences can be carried too far as well, such that average tendencies or situational influences are underemphasized (Gerhart, 1987; O'Reilly & Pfeffer, 2000). Still, if policies have different effects on different people, that can be valuable information.

Lazear's treatment of "personnel economics" models (e.g., Lazear, 1995b, 1998) is somewhat more complete in this respect. Lazear (1986) recognized early on that the type of payment scheme could influence performance by attracting and retaining different sets of workers. In 1999, he provided empirical evidence of the importance of this sorting effect on workforce composition as well as the more widely discussed incentive effect, defined as the change in productivity of the same workers. Specifically, Lazear studied 1-year productivity data from more than 2,000 workers at multiple sites of an auto glass installation chain as it switched from hourly wages to piece rates.

Lazear (1999) reported a 44% increase in overall productivity as a result of the change to piece rates. In addition, he attempted to quantify which portion of this improvement was due to sorting (quits and new hires) and which was due to incentive effects among those who stayed with the firm over the entire year. Results showed that 22% (or half) of the increase was attributable to higher productivity among those who had been with the firm over the entire period (i.e., the incentive effect). However, the other 22% was due to sorting or changes in workforce composition. Specifically, high-output individuals showed a decline in separation rates from 3.5% to 2.9% per month (a reduction of approximately 16%), while separation rates for "normal-output" workers increased from 4.6% to 5.3% per month. Thus, Lazear inferred that half the productivity increase was due to incentive effects and half to sorting.

While Lazear and other economists thus recognize sorting effects, the general point made above—that the economics literature does not focus to any significant degree on person characteristics—remains generally accurate. For example, even in Lazear's work, the conceptualization of personality does not receive a great deal of attention. Consistent with game theory terminology, Lazear (1995b) talks about "hawks and doves" as personality types but does not present any theory or evidence for the importance of such a typology. Not surprisingly, the psychological literature is more advanced in this area and could contribute better-grounded personality frameworks and measures.

As indicated throughout, to the extent that economists attend at all to individual differences, it is most often with respect to ability. However, as with personality, ability is often not measured, but rather inferred (e.g., by education level or quality). Again, there would be much to gain in this regard from the psychology literature, given that the definition and measurement of cognitive and other abilities (through instruments such as the Wonderlic Personnel Inventory and the General Aptitude Test Battery) is well advanced there. Second, the psychology literature makes a critical distinction between traits that are almost always beneficial (e.g., ability and conscientiousness) and those whose usefulness depends on context (e.g., individualism, extraversion). This latter notion of fit is central to the applied-psychology literature (e.g., Dawis's model of work adjustment and Schneider's ASA model) but marginal in economics.

Future Research

We have covered several theories that differ in their disciplinary background (psychology versus economics), their focus (incentive versus sorting effects), and their emphasis on psychological mechanisms or mediators (e.g., goal setting versus self-efficacy). All the theories (except for SCT) we have reviewed agree that pay is an important motivator, and the empirical evidence supports this as well. As we have already reviewed the theories in some detail, we focus our comments here on two broad and related issues in studying pay: disciplinary differences and the level-of-analysis issue.

Perhaps the most important step for future theorizing would be to blend the economic and psychological approaches to the greatest extent possible. Each of these two disciplines has strengths and weaknesses from the perspective of understanding pay basis and its effects. For example, economic approaches are parsimonious and straightforward in their distinctions between incentives and sorting, as well as between behavior- and outcomes-based contracts. In addition, economists tend to place a high priority on the valuable practice of measuring and comparing average effect sizes, as was seen in their measurement of pay-performance sensitivities. However, they have not capitalized on the considerable progress that has been made regarding the psychological processes that mediate pay policy-outcome relationships. In addition, the major economic theory regarding incentives (agency theory) has been applied almost exclusively to executive compensation and has had little to say about the potentially perverse effects on overall or long-term performance that may result from attaching pay exclusively to stock price or accounting profits. Finally, by undergirding all motivational theories with an underlying assumption that people are "born to shirk," economists may be missing a significant part of the motivation equation.

Psychologists, in contrast, have paid considerable attention to mediating cognitive processes. They have also focused on the fact that not all individuals are alike and that the extent of person-organization fit can be an important determinant of both individual satisfaction and organizational performance. In addition, they have made considerable progress toward identifying which individual characteristics are almost always an asset to organizations and which depend on the job, the organization, or other particularistic circumstances.

At the same time, because psychologists have studied phenomena mostly at the individual level of analysis, they have tended to assume (at least implicitly) that organizational performance is merely the aggregation of individual effects (Schneider, Smith, & Sipe, 2000). For example, to overstate the case a bit, one sometimes gets the impression from reading the industrial-organizational psychology literature that all it takes to have a successful organization is to hire intelligent, conscientious people, and the rest will take care of itself (e.g., Behling, 1998; see also O'Reilly & Pfeffer, 2000; Schneider et al., 2000). If managing organizations were this simple, it would be extremely difficult to explain the large number of recent "dot-com" crashes.

Although research at individual or dyadic levels can provide clues about possible higher-level processes and outcomes, it cannot be assumed that phenomena at the microlevel translate directly into similar effects at the organizational level (e.g., Bryk & Raudenbush, 1992; Klein, Dansereau, & Hall, 1994; Ostroff, 1993; Rousseau, 1985). Similarly, it is not always straightforward as to how a complicated psychological theory such as goal setting can actually be implemented into policies that will work well (witness the experience of MBO; Bartol &

Locke, 2000). Thus, it is important that psychologists move more actively to examine psychological concepts and HR practices at the policy or practice level of analysis (e.g., Rynes & Barber, 1991; Taylor & Collins, 2000), something that is slowly but surely beginning to happen (see Becker & Gerhart, 1996; Klein & Kozlowski, 2000).

In recommending that economists and psychologists build on each other's work, we are not suggesting that each discipline abandon its own unique competencies and source of competitive advantage. Indeed, we expect that economists will always have more to say about the economy as a whole and large subsets of it (e.g., industries), while psychologists will have more to say about microphenomena and underlying psychological processes. But each field could surely provide more useful, satisfying explanations of phenomena if they were to incorporate wisdom from each other as well as from disciplines at intermediate levels of analysis, such as sociology or cultural anthropology.

Although there are exciting opportunities for theoretical development at multiple levels of analysis (Klein & Kozlowski, 2000; Rousseau, 2000), further theoretical advances will almost certainly develop in conjunction with multilevel empirical findings. In the next chapter, we move from theories about the effects of differences in pay basis to an examination of how differences in practice actually affect important individual and organizational outcomes.

Notes

1. That feedback and social rewards had comparable effect sizes (to monetary rewards) is interesting. The question would be whether these effects would be sustainable over time if they do not lead to higher pay either via merit (or incentive) pay or promotion. In this vein, Stajkovic and Luthans (1997) make the following observation regarding social rewards:

> According to Bandura (1986), several factors contribute to the effectiveness of social reinforcement. First, the approval or disapproval of those who have the authority and resources to administer rewarding or punishing consequences produces stronger effects than the approval or disapproval of those who have no power to subsequently provide any tangible rewards. Second, indiscriminate approval that does not eventually result in material benefits becomes an empty reward, disapproval that is never followed by aversive consequences becomes an empty threat, and both lack the potential to control human behavior. (p. 1134)

2. A rare direct study of the Meyer et al. "split roles" hypothesis found no support (Prince & Lawler, 1986).

3. Executives do not necessarily stay within a single industry when they change jobs (Fulmer, 2003). Cross-industry mobility suggests that the labor market for executives is only partly defined by industry.

4. One potential problem with the Gibbons and Murphy specification is that it used stock market returns in its performance measures, yet the bonus (annual incentive) portion of cash compensation is typically linked explicitly to accounting-based measures (e.g., return on assets) of firm performance rather than to stock-based measures. The latter have their primary influence on long-term (i.e., stock-based) plans (see evidence from Janakiraman, Lambert, & Larcker, 1992, and comments by Murphy, 1999, and Aggarwal & Samwick, 1999).

5. Gibbons and Murphy did perform one set of analyses in which executive compensation included the value of restricted stock but not the value of unexercised stock options or the value realized from exercised stock options. Another analysis did include these stock option components, but the sample was limited to 73 manufacturing firms, and only the performance of the 1-digit industry group, a very broad industry grouping, was analyzed.

6 Pay-for-Performance Programs

EMPIRICAL EVIDENCE

> *Bribes in the workplace simply can't work.*
>
> —Kohn (1993)

> *Overall, this study underscores the generalizable positive relationship between financial incentives and performance.*
>
> —Jenkins, Mitra, Gupta, and Shaw (1998)

In previous chapters, we showed how decisions about pay level and structure signal the value that organizations assign to different job or skill groups, based on both external market considerations and internal assessments of job or skill criticality. Last chapter, we shifted our focus from how *much* to pay to the question of *how* to pay, describing relevant theories. In this chapter, we continue our treatment of the how-to-pay question. We examine the ways in which organizations differentially compensate individuals and groups based on their contributions to an organization's success. Whereas the previous chapter focused exclusively on theories, we now take a somewhat more applied perspective, describing key pay basis policy decisions and using both theory and empirical evidence to analyze their strengths and weaknesses.

As we have indicated, different companies in the same industry often use dramatically different pay policies. For example, consider Microsoft and SAS, both of which operate successfully in the software industry. Microsoft tends to pay below-market base salaries but heavily supplements base pay with stock incentives. (Indeed, Microsoft is said to have created over 10,000 millionaires via stock options by the late 1990s; National Center for Employee Ownership, 1999.) The amount of stock received by an individual is determined subjectively (as in merit pay decisions) and is highly variable across employees, both within and across organizational levels. Thus, although Microsoft employees are rewarded primarily as individuals and are not paid directly on the basis of results, the actual value of their pay is determined heavily by Microsoft's collective performance as evaluated by the stock market.

In contrast, SAS offers no stock incentives to its employees. Instead, it has an extensive benefits program (e.g., on-site daycare, a school, recreation facilities), and employees are encouraged to work only 35 hours per week—a policy almost unheard of in the software industry. Furthermore, there are few distinctions by organizational rank, and pay and benefits are distributed in a much more egalitarian fashion than at Microsoft.

What accounts for these differences, and what are their effects? In this chapter, we discuss the latter of these questions. We begin by discussing three fundamental decisions related to pay basis, followed by a discussion of empirical evidence concerning the effectiveness of various pay programs such as merit pay, gainsharing, profit sharing, and stock awards and options.

Broad Policy Decisions

In recognizing contributions to organizational performance, there are three broad strategic choices that we feel are most critical. First, how much emphasis should be placed on results-oriented performance measures relative to behavior-based measures? Second, how strong (or intensive) should incentives be? In practice, the first and second questions are closely related in that results-based plans tend to have much higher incentive intensity than behavior-based plans and to place considerably higher risk (but also potential rewards) on employees. Third, how much emphasis should be placed on individual contributions relative to collective contributions?

Behavior- Versus Results-Based Pay

Most organizations continue to use traditional merit increase programs to recognize employee contributions, especially among exempt employees. Merit increases are based on subjective assessments (usually by an employee's supervisor) of the effectiveness of employee behaviors.

In agency theory terms, merit pay is a behavior-based contract. Accordingly, merit pay requires that the rater (i.e., the principal) have an adequate opportunity to monitor the actions of the agent and that the principal be sufficiently knowledgeable to judge the effectiveness of the agent's actions. Furthermore, the principal's interests must be sufficiently aligned with those of the organization so that he or she rates employees in accordance with the organization's best interests rather than his or her own personal interests. For example, supervisors must not underrate performance in order to hoard good employees (by making it difficult for them to get promoted) or underevaluate effective employees due to personal dislike. Moreover, the cost of this monitoring must be considered in light of the alternative approach: less intense supervision and greater use of outcome-based compensation.

Increasingly, organizations have moved toward greater use of results-based plans (or *contracts,* in agency theory terms). Examples of results-based plans include stock options, profit sharing, gainsharing, and individual incentives. In part, the greater use of results-based pay has come from the extension of pay programs once reserved for executives to individuals at lower levels of the organization. Another boost to results-based pay has come from the growth of new high-technology organizations (where stock options are often used to supplement below-market base pay levels; e.g., Bunnell, 2000) as well as growth in alternative forms of employment relationships such as outsourcing, temporary employment, and individual contracting (Pink, 1998).

Interestingly, the decision to pay on the basis of outcomes rather than behaviors can have a fairly substantial impact on the rank ordering of employees for pay purposes (Bommer, Johnson, Rich, Podsakoff, & MacKenzie, 1995; R. Heneman, 1986). For example, Bommer et al. (1995) reported a corrected mean correlation of only .39 between behavior-based and results-based performance measures. In other words, only about 16% of the variance in one type of measure can be explained by variance in the other type. Thus, behavior- and results-based effectiveness measures provide different and sometimes conflicting information. For this reason, striking the right balance is a critical design issue. In the following sections, we describe the advantages and disadvantages of each type of program.

Behavior-Oriented Performance Measures

Behavior-oriented measures such as the traditional performance appraisal rating offer a number of potential advantages (Gerhart, 2000). First, they can be used for any type of job. Second, they permit the rater to factor in variables that are not under the ratee's control but that nevertheless influence performance. Third, they permit a focus on how results are achieved, thus helping to control agency costs (e.g., achieving results in a way that is unethical or harmful in the long run to the organization).

Despite these potential advantages, behavior-oriented measures have always raised concerns regarding potential subjectivity and inaccuracy. In their extensive review of performance appraisal, Murphy and Cleveland (1995) concluded that "It is surprisingly difficult to determine whether or not performance ratings provide valid and accurate indications of individuals' performance" and that "Raters' tendency to distort their evaluations when filling out performance appraisal forms may continue to be the most difficult issue in evaluating the validity and accuracy of ratings" (p. 298). These are certainly not ringing endorsements of the accuracy of performance appraisals.

These problems suggest that it can be very difficult to link pay to behavior-oriented performance in a credible way. For example, a survey by the Hay Group (1994) found that only 22% of hourly employees believed that better performers received higher merit increases than those having lower performance. These percentages were higher among middle managers and professional/technical employees (45% and 32%, respectively) but still indicated that most employees see no significant link between pay and performance.

One explanation for the weak pay-performance relationship is that managers tend to avoid making distinctions among employees, particularly by avoiding low ratings (Longenecker, Sims, & Gioia, 1987). From one perspective, managerial tendencies toward leniency and lack of differentiation may be caused by an agency problem, that is, supervisors giving inflated ratings because they want to be personally popular. However, from another perspective, it may be that managers accurately anticipate negative fallout from lower or more differentiated ratings in terms of workgroup cohesion, prosocial behaviors, and management-employee relations (H. Heneman & Judge, 2000; Lazear, 1989). If so, managers might actually be operating effectively on the organization's behalf by giving relatively undifferentiated (though technically "inaccurate") ratings. In any case, the net result is a weakened link between pay and individual performance in many organizations.

In addition, the use of merit-increase grids—which "translate" performance appraisal ratings into actual pay increases—also serves to reduce the pay-for-performance link. This is because merit-increase grids typically provide smaller pay increases to those near the top of a pay range (i.e., those who have consistently performed at a high level) for purposes of controlling costs. As such, merit grids inherently have a built-in "antimerit" feature, aside from whatever problems might exist with supervisory ratings.

Small merit increases can also be explained by what Milgrom and Roberts (1992) describe as the "informativeness principle," which says that the cost of providing incentives increases as the error in measuring performance increases. In discussing behavior-based measures in pay-for-performance plans, Lawler (1971) stated that employees "often see them as arbitrary, based upon inadequate information, and simply unfair" (p. 168). To the extent this is true, the informativeness principle would apply, and one would expect supervisors to be cautious about making high pay differentiations on the basis of subjective ratings.

A recent research review provides evidence to support the concerns regarding accuracy (or validity) of performance appraisals. Specifically, Viswesvaran, Ones, and Schmidt (1996) reported that the mean interrater reliability of supervisory ratings of overall job performance is only .52, with interrater reliability among peers being even lower (.42). These modest levels of reliability indicate that ratings have a large idiosyncratic factor to them.

Consider the implications of a .52 level of reliability in terms of the standard error of measurement and the resulting confidence interval for ratings on, say, a 7-point scale. Assume that the mean rating is 5 and the standard deviation is 1.8. The standard error of measurement, defined as *standard deviation x (1-reliability),*$^{1/2}$ would then be 1.25. To construct a confidence interval, we first compute the true score, defined as the *mean + reliability x (score-mean).* For a score of 4, the true score would be 4.48. The 95% confidence interval is 4.48 +/− 1.96 (1.04), or 2.03 < true score < 6.93. This is an uncomfortably wide confidence interval when we are making decisions about how much to pay an employee. Even with a 75% confidence interval, the range would still be wider than desirable when making important pay decisions (3.04 < true score < 5.92). Imagine as a manager the prospect of paying employees significantly different rates on the basis of such error-laden performance measures and then having to explain the decision to employees.

We know that validity and accuracy are not possible without reliability. Unless this lack of reliability in single-rater ratings can be overcome, it is quite difficult to justify to employees the use of such performance measures to pay strongly differing amounts to employees doing the same job. This, in turn, limits the use of pay as an incentive and helps to explain survey results showing that many employees do not believe that merit pay exists.

In summary, that behavior-based performance ratings are subjective (i.e., require judgment) is both their strength and weakness. If the goal is to make meaningful pay distinctions between employees, ratings must have adequate precision and credibility. One concrete step in this direction is to use multiple raters.

Results-Oriented Performance Measures

Results-oriented measures of performance, such as productivity, sales volume, shareholder return, and profitability, would seem to provide an obvious antidote to the subjectivity and inaccuracy of behavior-based performance ratings. Lawler (1971), for example, concluded that "In general, objective measures enjoy higher credibility; that is, employees will often grant the validity of an objective measure . . . when they will not accept a superior's rating" (p. 166).

As noted previously, one can think in terms of a choice between monitoring and results-based contracts. Under a behavior-based system, work must be more closely monitored, meaning that more managers are needed. Because managers are expensive, the use of behavior-based contracts can also be expensive. In contrast, with results-based measures, there may be more self-monitoring and mutual monitoring by coworkers, thus permitting organizations to have larger spans of managerial control.

In addition, there is also ample evidence that results-oriented measures can have substantial incentive effects, especially for plans that emphasize individual performance (Guzzo, Jette, & Katzell, 1985; Jenkins et al., 1998; Judiesch, 1994; Locke, Feren, McCaleb, Shaw, & Denny, 1980; Stajkovic & Luthans, 1997). Case studies such as those involving Lincoln Electric, Whirlpool, Springfield Remanufacturing, and Oregon Steel Mills also provide compelling examples of the effectiveness of results-oriented plans (Case, 1997; Jasinowski & Hamrin, 1995). For example, at Lincoln Electric, a major part of production workers' pay is based on individual incentives tied to the volume of high-quality physical output. A second major part of their income comes from individual bonuses, which are drawn from an overall bonus pool that depends on Lincoln's profitability. For example, the 1999 bonus pool was $60.1 million, or $9,500 per employee, with some employees earning much more and some much less. Lincoln executives claim that their incentive system is responsible for fostering the most productive employees in the industry.

Thus, there is ample evidence that results-based incentive plans can greatly increase performance. Yet with the possible exception of sales employees, such plans are quite rare, particularly at the individual level. Why is this the case? One reason is that individual incentive plans like the one found at Lincoln require a situation where physical output can be both accurately measured and attributed to the efforts of a single employee. This type of situation was already uncommon 30 years ago (Cummings & Schwab, 1973, p. 98) and is increasingly uncommon today (e.g., Pfeffer, 1998a). Instead, today's work outputs are often collaboratively produced, difficult to quantify, and uncertain with respect to their long-term outcomes.

As such, results-based incentive plans, especially at the individual level, face their own set of problems. Although these problems have long been recognized in the psychology literature, economists have tended to assume that output can be "easily measured" (Gibbons, 1998, p. 118). As such, economists have tended to place "excessive focus on the contracts of workers for whom output measures are easily observed" despite the fact that "most people don't work in jobs like these" (Prendergast, 1999, p. 57). Over time, however, economists and agency theorists have gradually begun to reject the assumption that output can be easily measured and have thus incorporated measurement issues into some of their models (e.g., Baker, 1992; Holmstrom & Milgrom, 1991).

For example, Prendergast's (1999) review highlights the fact that because contracts cannot completely specify all relevant aspects of worker behavior, "Contracts offering incentives can give rise to *dysfunctional behavioral responses,* whereby agents emphasize only those aspects of performance that are rewarded" (p. 8). In the economics literature, this problem is referred to as *multitasking* and refers to cases where "Compensation on any subset of tasks will result in reallocation of activities toward those that are directly compensated and away from the uncompensated activities" (p. 8).

For instance, in a production setting, productivity may be achieved at the expense of product quality, equipment maintenance, or employee willingness to forego current earnings to learn new skills. Thirty years ago, Lawler (1971) warned that "It is quite difficult to establish criteria that are both measurable quantitatively and inclusive of all the important job behaviors" and that "If an employee is not evaluated in terms of an activity, he will not be motivated to perform it" (p. 171). Likewise, the *equal compensation principle* (which is closely linked to the multitasking problem noted above) states that "If an employee's allocation of time or attention between two different activities cannot be monitored by the employer, then either the marginal rates of return to the employee must be equal, or the activity with the lower marginal rate of return receives no time or attention" (Milgrom & Roberts, 1992, p. 228).

An example of these challenges can be seen in the experience of Sears auto repair centers, where employee compensation was tied to the value of repairs sold. The incentive to sell repairs seemed to be working well—too well, it appears. Sears ran into legal problems when customers claimed to have been overcharged and sold unnecessary repairs. The company subsequently modified the incentive plan to include other measures of effectiveness, such as customer satisfaction.

Another problem is that although results-based measures appear to be objective, they can still be manipulated because of information asymmetry. For example, some hospitals associated with Columbia/HCA were alleged to have misclassified patients' medical conditions in order to maximize reimbursement from government programs, such as Medicare. In turn, higher reimbursements were alleged to have resulted in larger bonuses for administrators.[1] As another example, accounting improprieties at companies such as Enron, Sunbeam, Cendant, and Global Crossing show how executives can manipulate (reported) profits as a means of driving up the stock price, an increasingly important determinant of executive pay. What this all suggests is that results-based measures do not necessarily solve information asymmetry problems or the moral hazard problems that follow. Although there may be less monitoring (and monitoring cost) than under behavior-based plans, there are still risks that stem from measurement problems, and these, too, require an expenditure of resources. For example, it may be necessary to allocate more resources to auditing (e.g., of profit reports) to ensure that results are not being manipulated. However, the auditors themselves need to audited, as recent events at Andersen Accounting suggest. In the case of piece rate plans, standards must be set by time-study methods, and quantity and quality of output measured on an ongoing basis. If production processes change, rates will often need to be restudied. In the case of Lincoln Electric, for example, there are more than 70,000 piece rates (Wiley, 1993). Thus, Lincoln's system could easily become prohibitively expensive if these rates were subjected to wholesale changes or frequent disputes. In fact, however, only 0.2% of incentive rate changes are challenged at Lincoln, due to the close cooperation between management and employees.

According to Prendergast (1999), one of the most striking aspects of observed contracts is that "The Informativeness Principle—i.e., that all factors correlated with performance should be included in a compensation contract—seems to be *violated* in many occupations" (p. 2), giving rise to the types of dysfunctional behaviors observed at Sears and Columbia. Indeed, Prendergast (2000) goes so far as to say that the trade-off between risk and incentives, which she describes as a "mantra among economists" (p. 424), is less important in practice than would be implied by its central role in agency theory. Her argument is that although weaker-than-expected incentive contracts do result in part from risk-bearing concerns, weak incentives are primarily a consequence of measurement and information issues that constrain the ability to adequately specify and measure the full spectrum of performance (i.e., bounded rationality).

Nevertheless, the reactions of employees to risk bearing do pose a challenge to the use of outcomes-based incentive plans (Gibbons, 1998). Although a results-based contract may have the advantage of better incentive properties from the principal's point of view, the agent's need for insurance (insulation from risk) means that the strongest possible incentive is not necessarily optimal. In any event, agency theory predicts that agents will require a pay premium to bear increased risk. The size of this premium will depend on both the amount of risk and on the risk aversion of the individual agents. For example, previous research has shown that high levels of outcome variability (i.e., firm performance) are associated with low levels of compensation risk (Aggarwal & Samwick, 1999; Bloom & Milkovich, 1998; Conlon & Parks, 1990; Eisenhardt, 1989).[2]

The consequences of risk bearing may go unnoticed when a plan is paying out, but can quickly become a major employee relations issue when results decline and payoffs go down. Where results are perceived as being strongly influenced by factors beyond employees' control (e.g., poor decisions by top executives), feelings of inequity can be strong. To restore equity, employees are likely to pressure management to change the plan in some way.

One example is the evolution of the collective-bargaining agreement between Saturn and the United Auto Workers (UAW) over time. The variable component of worker pay at Saturn was well received by workers when Saturn sales were high, but became a major employee relations issue when sales (and thus bonuses) declined. Consequently, the UAW negotiated changes to the compensation plan that reduced the variable-pay component in favor of greater base pay.[3]

A similar fate befell the incentive program at DuPont Fibers Division, which set base pay approximately 4% lower than that of similar employees in other divisions, but with substantial upside opportunity. Initially, the profit goal was exceeded, the plan worked fine, and the division received considerable attention as the developer of a "best practice" compensation system. However, when profits decreased considerably the following year, employee relations concerns caused Du Pont to eliminate the plan and return to a system of fixed base salaries with no variable component.

As we will see later, similar phenomena apply at executive levels as well (e.g., when underwater stock options are repriced to keep executives whole). As a result, one of the purported advantages of variable-pay plans—that they make labor costs variable rather than fixed—may be more illusory than real.

Another employee relations issue that can undermine results-based plans is a lack of trust between employees and managers. Much of the research on this issue has been in the context of individual incentive plans. Based on a careful sociological study of piece rates and worker productivity in the early 1950s, Whyte (1955) concluded that only about one third of piece rate incentives were set at the appropriate level. The rest were either set too high or too low, both situations that Whyte claimed resulted in employees holding back from their true production capabilities. In cases where targets were set too high (or incentives too low), workers withheld their effort, accepted the base pay rate, and pressured employers for a relaxation of standards. Alternatively, in cases where targets were set too low and incentives were very easy to attain, workers *goldbricked* (i.e., did not work as hard as they could) so that employers would not discover their mistake and "ratchet up" standards (see Milgrom & Roberts, 1992). Thus, in either case, employees withheld their best efforts, and employers ran the joint risks of paying too much money and/or receiving too little output. (We return to this issue in our section on individual incentive plans.)

The natural inclination of management is to renegotiate targets and rates under these circumstances. However, this is a tricky process, and if renegotiation is not handled in a way that is seen as credible by employees, trust in management will be eroded and employees will be less likely to embrace any future "innovations." In agency terms, attempts to increase targets might be described as *postcontractual opportunism* (a form of moral hazard) that lowers workers' future instrumentality perceptions and hence, motivation. However, the fast-paced nature of global competition means that in many industries, standards and rates must be renegotiated with ever-increasing frequency to insure the continuous improvement necessary to survive.

To sum up, while using results-oriented performance measures may, at first blush, seem to solve the problem of subjectivity in performance measurement, other problems, perhaps even more serious, can arise. These include dysfunctional actions aimed at gaming the incentive plan as well as employee relations problems. Companies that can avoid or minimize such problems can benefit greatly from using results-oriented plans, but the downside risks cannot be ignored.

Incentive Intensity

In our preceding discussion, we noted two reasons why incentives are often not as strong as theory would predict. First, measuring performance fully and accurately has proved to be much more difficult than originally envisioned by agency theory. Although measurement deficiencies are generally less of a problem at higher levels of aggregation, expectancy theory leads us to question whether incentive effects will be strong enough if the results-based measures are perceived to be too far removed for individual employees to influence. Moreover, even when measurement is straightforward (as in the case of stock prices), there is still the possibility of manipulation (e.g., through manipulation of accounting results, as is believed to have occurred at Sunbeam, Cendant, Global Crossing, and Enron). Unfortunately, behavior-based measures do not necessarily provide a solution, because it is difficult to use strong incentives when there is the kind of measurement error typically found in performance appraisals.

Second, using strong incentives can be costly to employers because of employee reactions to the transfer of risk. This may take the form of renegotiation of the amount of risk or of the size of the compensating differential required to accept it (the Saturn and DuPont experiences are relevant here). Third, as we discuss later in this chapter, if incentives are both strong and linked exclusively to individual performance, still other problems may arise, such as lack of cooperation or cutthroat competition (Deming, 1986; Lazear, 1989; Pfeffer & Langton, 1993).

At the same time, we have seen that strong incentive intensity can sometimes lead to tremendous gains in performance (Jenkins et al., 1998; Locke et al., 1980; Stajkovic & Luthans, 1997). What this discussion suggests is that there can be substantial variance in the effects of high incentive intensity across situations. In the financial literature, variance in investment returns is interpreted as a measure of risk. This same perspective can be applied to compensation investment decisions. "In looking at any investment in compensation, what do we know about the risk associated with that investment? . . . We think risk warrants significant attention because outcomes from the same pay plan vary across firms" (Gerhart, Trevor, & Graham, 1996, p. 170). Using strong incentives opens up the possibility of obtaining substantial performance gains but it also increases the possibility of something going terribly wrong. Thus, a strategy of using strong incentives might be described as a high-risk, high-return strategy (Gerhart et al., 1996, p. 145). This is due in part to the informativeness principle (as emphasized by Prendergast) and to the other potential problems discussed previously under results-oriented plans.

Which incentive intensity level is optimal? One answer is given by Milgrom and Roberts (1992), who introduce the following incentive intensity principle: "The optimal intensity of incentives depends on four factors: the incremental profits created by the additional effort, the precision with which the desired activities can be assessed, the agent's risk tolerance, and the agent's responsiveness to incentives" (p. 221).

The last two factors, agent's risk tolerance and responsiveness to incentives, are quite interesting, as they would seem to open the door to individual differences: "An employee with wide discretion facing strong wage incentives may find innovative ways to increase his or her performance, resulting in significant increases in profits" (Milgrom & Roberts, 1992, p. 222). Thus, although Milgrom and Roberts focus more on the characteristics of the situation (work discretion) than the person (innovativeness), a psychological approach would also introduce the very real possibility that different employees may respond differently to strong wage incentives (e.g., Cable & Judge, 1994; Trank, Rynes, & Bretz, 2001).

To summarize, our discussion of incentive intensity is closely related to our discussion of results-oriented performance measures. The main conclusion is that high incentive intensity can have substantial effects on employee behaviors but not all such effects are necessarily positive. We have also introduced the idea that there are individual differences in employee responsiveness to incentives.

Individual or Group Performance?

> It is often taken for granted, at least where economic objectives are involved, that groups of individuals with common interests usually attempt to further those common interests. . . . But it is *not* in fact true that the idea that groups will act in

> their self-interest follows logically from the premise of rational and self-interested behavior. . . . Indeed, unless the number of individuals in a group is quite small, or unless there is coercion or some other special device to make individuals act in their common interest, *rational self-interested individuals will not act to achieve their common or group interests.* (Olson, 1965, pp. 1-2; emphasis in original)

As an example of Olson's point, Garret Hardin's (1968) "The Tragedy of the Commons" describes how a common pasture becomes damaged from overgrazing if each shepherd pursues narrow self-interest by maximizing herd size. Similarly, if large numbers of individuals have the right to fish in an area with no effective limits, there is a danger that the fish population will be diminished to a point where it cannot recover.

To characterize such problems, Dawes (1975, 1980, as cited in Schroeder, 1995) developed the concept of a *social dilemma,* which has two characteristics.[4] First, "Each individual receives a higher payoff for a socially defecting choice (e.g., having additional children, using all the energy available, polluting his or her neighbors)," and second, "All individuals are better off if they cooperate rather than if all defect" (Dawes, 1980, p. 169). Milgrom and Roberts (1992) describe this as "one of the saddest incentive problems," which also goes by a number of other labels (i.e., the *common-resource problem,* the *public-goods problem,* and the *free-rider problem*). The basic theme is that when people share the obligation to provide a resource, it will be undersupplied, because the residual returns to the resource are shared, even by those who do nothing to increase or maintain its value.

This problem is very relevant to the design of compensation systems that link pay to group rather than individual performance. When individual members of a group seek to maximize their own utility, each may be able to do so (particularly in the short run) by reducing their own effort while still receiving a payout if others in the group exert sufficient effort.

Kidwell and Bennett (1993) have identified three strands of literature that address the propensity for individuals to withhold effort when working in groups. Although the three literatures have tended to stay somewhat separate from one another, they rely on quite similar explanatory variables. The first, *shirking* (Alchian & Demsetz, 1972), suggests that a person may withhold effort because of monitoring difficulties, self-interest, or opportunism. In other words, shirking mirrors the agency theory approach in its emphasis on concepts such as information asymmetry, monitoring costs, and moral hazard.

Second, *free riding* (Olson, 1965) refers to individuals who receive the benefits of being a group member but do not bear a proportional share of the cost of achieving such benefits (Albanese & Van Fleet, 1985). In a slight variation, Stigler (1974) refers to such individuals as "cheap riders" because their effort level is not zero, just less than that of others in the group. Olson's work, for example, addressed problems such as free riding in labor unions. In American labor law, the duty of fair representation means that a labor union must represent the interests of all members of a bargaining unit, regardless of whether or not they are dues-paying members. Olson noted that in the absence of a strong mechanism for compelling individuals to join (e.g., a union shop contract clause), unions face potentially serious free-rider problems, whereby individuals receive union-negotiated benefits without making any contribution to defray their costs. In support of this notion, union membership is typically lower in states with right-to-work laws (i.e., where compulsory union membership or dues are illegal).

Third, *social loafing,* a concept from the social psychology literature, similarly describes the tendency for individuals to exert less effort when their outputs are combined with those of others (Latané, Williams, & Harkins, 1979; Shepperd, 1993). However, social loafing extends Olson's (1965) focus on mostly large collectives (e.g., labor unions) to a focus on smaller groups. Moreover, the empirical research on social loafing has typically been conducted in laboratory settings under controlled conditions. The classic paradigm is to instruct subjects to perform various tasks (such as shouting or clapping as loud as they can) either alone, or with others. The general finding is that subjects exert more effort when alone than when performing with others. Shepperd's review finds that similar results have been obtained for a wide variety of tasks, both physical (e.g., pulling a tug-of-war rope or swimming in a relay race) and cognitive (solving mazes or evaluating poems).

Shepperd (1993) suggests that because most tasks are tiring, there is a cost to performing them and that in addition, "Particularly in larger collectives, [subjects] are likely to believe that their individual contributions will have little effect on the collective's overall performance" (p. 68). A final part of the explanation is the concern that by working hard, others will free ride on one's efforts. This has been described as the "sucker effect," which occurs when individuals reduce their effort in response to the belief that their efforts are subsidizing others who are giving less effort (Orbell & Dawes, 1981). In all three cases, the result is the same: a partial defection from the group and consequent suboptimal group performance.

Although there is compelling evidence of efficiency losses in groups, this concern needs to be placed in context. Consider, for example, that a great deal of economic activity continues to take place in groups. Although sole proprietorships are the most common business form in the U.S. economy, the majority of the nation's output is produced in partnerships and corporations, that is, in "group" production (McKenzie & Lee, 1998). Therefore, in many cases, the potential drawbacks of groups are apparently more than offset by their advantages.

Indeed, criticisms have sometimes been leveled at organizations for focusing too much on individual performance and rewards. Deming (1986), for example, was a strong opponent of measuring and rewarding individual performance because "Apparent differences between people arise almost entirely from the system that they work in, not from the people themselves" (p. 110). System factors include coworkers, supervision, work design and layout, materials, customers, technology, and the environment, all of which Deming viewed as being more under management's control than the worker's. Thus, to Deming, any performance assessment of individual workers is essentially "a lottery," implying that it does not make sense to reward or penalize individuals. Deming also argued that focusing on individual performance discouraged teamwork: "Everyone propels himself forward, or tries to, for his own good. . . . The organization is the loser" (p. 110).

Pfeffer (1998a, 1998b) likewise advocates the need for U.S. organizations to move away from such a strong focus on the individual. He has argued that group-based pay plans are generally preferable to individual-based plans, based on his belief that the "so-called free-riding problem" is "surprisingly meager" (1998a, p. 219). As such, Pfeffer admonishes readers "not to be reluctant to implement collective bases of rewards because of the fear of free-riding" (p. 219).

Although the potential pitfalls of individual-based pay for performance raised by Pfeffer and Deming are important to consider, the literature is quite clear that group-based plans have their own drawbacks that should not be underestimated.[5] Major reviews (e.g., Albanese & Van Fleet, 1985; Cooper, Dyck, & Frohlich, 1992; Shepperd, 1993) are in agreement that the free-rider problem is important.[6] Indeed, their reviews typically devote considerable attention to how free-rider effects might be mitigated.

In summary, both individual-based and group-based pay plans have their own potential limitations. Individual-based plans may generate too little cooperation and are of limited value in cases where system factors, rather than individual effort and ability, drive performance. Group-based plans can weaken incentive effects via free-rider problems, which generally increase with group size. Group-based plans can also result in detrimental sorting effects if high achievers go elsewhere to have their individual contributions recognized and rewarded.

Although we believe that the potential for efficiency losses in groups does not necessarily mean that rewards should be entirely individually based, neither do we believe that efficiency losses in groups should be ignored.

Pay Dispersion Within Groups

The preceding discussion addressed the fundamental problem of motivating people in group settings where they have the option of obtaining rewards—not through effort, but rather via free riding, especially as group size increases. However, a different sort of motivation problem may arise in groups through a rather different mechanism. Specifically, to the extent that there are substantial pay differentials among members of the same group, some theories suggest that group cohesion, individual perceptions of equity, and group performance may suffer.

Perhaps the most influential research on this issue is Pfeffer and Langton's (1993) work on the consequences of pay dispersion. Pfeffer and Langton provide a useful examination of the potential advantages and disadvantages of pay dispersion in group settings. At the outset, they emphasize that the *basis* for dispersion is a key issue. If pay dispersion has its basis in a pay-for-performance policy, there are two potential benefits. First, pay for performance can have powerful incentive effects on current workers (as we demonstrated earlier). Second, consistent with our discussion of the attraction-selection-attrition framework, pay for performance may attract and retain high performers and discourage poorer performers from joining or staying with the organization (Bishop, 1984). On the other hand, to the extent that dispersion is not accepted as being based on performance differences or other acceptable equity considerations, dispersion may have detrimental effects. From our discussion of equity theory, we know that underrewarding inequity perceptions may lead to adverse reactions, including lower effort.

Pfeffer and Langton's (1993) empirical work focused on the satisfaction, collaboration, and productivity of college and university faculty as a function of pay dispersion within academic departments. Controlling for several other key determinants, including the correlation between salary and productivity within departments, they found a statistically significant regression coefficient of –.378 for salary dispersion in the research productivity equation, indicating that research productivity was lower in departments having greater salary dispersion, net of other factors in the productivity equation. To interpret the regression coefficient, we make use of the fact that the mean productivity (an index formed by standardizing and summing 3 items) in the sample was .444. The standard deviation of salary dispersion was .113, which implies that a 1-standard deviation increase in salary dispersion from its mean was associated with a change in productivity from .444 to .401, a change of approximately 10%, which may or may not strike one as being of practical significance.

However, the interpretation of this coefficient requires additional information. First, the zero-order correlation between productivity and salary dispersion was only –.0123, suggesting that productivity and overall salary dispersion were essentially unrelated. Second, the regression coefficient of –.378 is the partial effect that remains after controlling for other factors thought to influence productivity, including the correlation between pay and productivity within the department. In other words, the –.378 regression coefficient indicates the relationship between productivity and *unexplained* salary dispersion, that is, salary dispersion that is not related to differences in pay based on differences in individual productivity. Therefore, we interpret Pfeffer and Langton's (1993) study as suggesting that only unexplained salary dispersion has detrimental consequences for productivity.

In addition, it is important to note that in departments with higher correlations between pay and productivity, productivity was substantially higher than in departments where productivity was not rewarded with pay (Pfeffer and Langton, 1993). Moreover, this relationship was considerably stronger than the relationship between productivity and unexplained salary dispersion. Specifically, the regression coefficient (.843) implies that a 1-standard deviation (.199) increase in the correlation between pay and productivity was associated with a change in productivity from a mean of .444 to .612, a 38% increase. In other words, salary dispersion that depended on performance had a substantial positive relationship with productivity.

So, although Pfeffer and Langton (1993) conclude that their findings "are quite consistent" with the view that "There are important efficiency properties that emerge from more compressed pay distributions" (p. 403), we argue that what their findings show instead is that lower *unexplained* pay dispersion is associated with higher productivity. However, we are not aware that anyone has ever recommended having unexplained pay dispersion, which would imply a policy of paying equally qualified and productive people in a group differently. To the contrary, a well-designed pay for individual performance component can generate effective incentive and sorting effects.

A more recent study sought to examine the relationship between pay dispersion in major league baseball teams and team performance. Specifically, Bloom (1999) reported that teams having less pay dispersion had better performance (operationalized in multiple ways). However, there are some issues that need to be considered in interpreting his results.

One issue is that in specifying his model of team performance, Bloom (1999) controlled for both team talent and team pay in estimating the coefficient on pay dispersion. His rationale was that he wanted to assess the influence of pay dispersion, net of any efficiency wage effect. (As noted earlier, the adverse-selection version of efficiency wage theory suggests that higher pay levels permit employers to be more selective, thus resulting in higher ability/talent levels.) Our concern would be that team talent and team pay should not be treated as control variables, because to do so parcels out the positive effects of pay dispersion: attraction and retention of star players who are paid a great deal, thus resulting in better team performance, higher team pay, and greater dispersion. By controlling team pay and team ability, these advantages of pay dispersion are omitted from the dispersion coefficient.

A second issue relates to the degree of teamwork that takes place in baseball relative to other sports or other employment settings. Admittedly, there are team aspects to baseball, such as advancing a runner or playing while hurt. Yet most of what happens on the baseball diamond is separable, additive individual action. Even where teamwork is involved, it is often straightforward to identify and evaluate individual contributions. For example, a double play that requires teamwork among the shortstop, second baseman, and first baseman requires that each player do his part. If the shortstop makes a bad throw to first, it is clear why the double play was not turned successfully. Moreover, it is difficult to conceive of the shortstop intentionally making a bad throw, for example, because the second baseman earns much more money than he does. This, again, is due to the fact that individual contributions can be separated. No team will want to give a lucrative contract to a shortstop who makes bad throws.

We suggest that a better test of the effects of pay dispersion (using a sports setting) would be to use hockey or soccer teams. In hockey, a player has the choice of whether to pass the puck or shoot, so incentive effects may come into play. A player could conceivably decide not to pass to a highly paid teammate. He or she may instead take the shot in an attempt to increase his or her own goal total (and eventual pay). Or, if there is a team spirit (resulting from low pay dispersion), the player may pass the puck if the other player has a better shot. But even in hockey, it is not clear that players see high salaries for star players as some sort of problem. In fact, a major achievement of the National Hockey League Players Association (NHLPA) was to obtain free agency for players so that players could make themselves available to the highest-bidding team. This bidding has "driven up salaries league-wide," which is exactly what the NHLPA wanted to achieve (Warren, 2000). Thus, when one player pushes salaries higher, that increases the probability that other players will also receive higher salaries.

Indeed, some players (e.g., defenseman Raymond Bourque) have been criticized in the past because they did not test the free-agent market and instead, out of loyalty to their teams, signed contracts for less money than they would have received if they had made themselves available to the highest bidder. When a premiere player behaves in this fashion, the concern is that salaries for other players don't go up as quickly as they otherwise might. Indeed, it has been said that "Top level players certainly feel some sort of 'obligation' to assist the growth of salaries" (Morganti, 2001).

Recently, Shaw, Gupta, and Delery (2002) explicitly tested the joint effects of worker interdependence, use of performance-based pay, and extent of horizontal pay differentiation (across workers holding the same types of jobs) on company performance. In their first study, they examined an industry (long-distance trucking) where performance is highly individualistic. Consistent with predictions, they found that objective measures of organization level performance (accident rates and time spent out of service) were highest where there was strong use of pay incentives combined with high pay dispersion. In contrast, organizational performance was lowest where pay dispersion was high but not linked to performance or where actual pay dispersion was low despite the ostensible use of performance-based pay.

In a second study, Shaw et al. (2002) studied 141 concrete-pipe plants to examine the joint effects of pay dispersion, pay for performance, and amount of work interdependence (proxied by the use of self-managing teams) on two measures of objective organizational performance (labor hours per ton and lost-time accidents). Similar to results from the first study, the poorest levels of organizational performance were found when pay dispersion was high but use of pay for performance was low (i.e., pay dispersion was not performance based). Predicted interactions were also found with respect to the extent of worker interdependence: Organizational performance was poorest when pay dispersion was high in combination with high worker interdependence.

As a final comment, we note that many successful companies are very diligent in making distinctions among employees, both in performance assessments and in compensation awards. This "uncompressing" is accomplished by ranking or forced distribution ("grading on a curve") at a variety of companies, including Microsoft, Ford, Cisco Systems, and perhaps most famously, General Electric (GE) (Abelson, 2001). There, the top 20% and the bottom 10% of managerial and professional employees are identified each year, with the bottom 10% finding that they must leave GE. In 2001, CEO Jack Welch provided the rationale for this policy in a letter to shareholders: "A company that bets its future on its people must remove the lower 10%, and keep removing it every year—always raising the bar of performance and increasing the quality of its leadership" (Abelson, 2001, p. A1). The top 20%, however, are well rewarded and received a great deal of personal attention from Welch, who groomed them for key positions at GE (Strauss, 2001).

In summary, balancing individual and group performance objectives is a key consideration in designing pay-for-performance plans. All organizations require some combination of individual excellence and cooperative effort. The incentive and sorting implications of these programs must be given careful consideration in designing a strategy.

Putting It All Together: Empirical Evidence on Pay Programs

In our preceding discussion, we examined broad policy issues in the design of pay programs that seek to reward contributions to organizational performance. Here, our discussion turns more specific, focusing on the description and analysis of specific pay programs such as merit pay, individual incentives, profit sharing, stock plans, and gainsharing. Although we describe these programs separately, it should be kept in mind that people are often paid using a combination of these programs. We believe that it makes sense to begin by understanding the strengths and weaknesses of each program. Then, as a next step, one may wish to consider how a combination of programs might leverage the

Table 6.1 Pay-for-Performance Programs, by Performance Measure Attributes

	Type of Performance Measure	
Level of Aggregation	*Results*	*Behaviors*
Individual	Individual incentives Sales commissions	Merit pay Merit bonuses Skill-based/ Competency-based
Collective	Group incentives Gainsharing Business unit plans Profit sharing Stock plans	Merit pay for groups

strengths and minimize the weaknesses of each program, consistent with a balanced-scorecard type of approach.

We rely primarily on two of the strategic dimensions introduced earlier in this chapter, results- versus behavior-based performance and group-versus-individual performance, to classify the various programs (see Table 6.1), several of which we discuss in this chapter. For example, merit pay relies on a behavior-based measure of performance (e.g., supervisory ratings) and focuses on the performance of an individual. In contrast, profit sharing relies on some type of profit measure, a results-based performance measure at the firm level of aggregation. It would be possible to introduce other dimensions as well. For instance, under some programs, changes to pay become a permanent part of base pay (e.g., merit pay), whereas in other programs (e.g., bonuses or profit sharing) the pay must be re-earned during each time period (Milkovich & Wigdor, 1991).[7] Another dimension is whether pay is based on absolute or relative performance. This has implications for the degree of focus on individual versus group goals because a relative performance measure encourages competition rather than cooperation (only a fixed number of high-performance ratings are permitted). Finally, incentive intensity is a key policy choice for any pay-for-performance program.

Merit Pay

Merit pay continues to be a widely used pay program, especially among exempt employees. As noted previously, behavior-based programs such as merit pay offer a variety of advantages. Perhaps the most important of these is that they give managers the opportunity to exercise judgment about important factors such as the influence of idiosyncratic events on performance, the means used to achieve results, and whether any important aspects of performance have been sacrificed to "make the numbers." In other words, merit pay systems run less of a risk than output-based systems that the criteria for pay increases will be *deficient* in some major way. In addition, although impression management may exert some influence over performance ratings, such ratings cannot be directly manipulated or distorted by ratees in the same way many results-based measures can.

However, merit pay programs are also characterized by substantial weaknesses. Perhaps the most important of these is the previously mentioned fact that employees often do not perceive a strong link between performance and the size of merit increases (Hay Group, 1994). According to expectancy theory, a weak instrumentality perception of this sort reduces motivation. Several phenomena contribute to this perception. First, managers are often reluctant to differentiate among employees and in particular worry about the consequences of giving low ratings (e.g., Longenecker et al., 1987). As a result, performance ratings are often bunched together at the top of the rating scale.

To compound the lack of differentiation in ratings, managers are similarly reluctant to differentiate employees with respect to pay. As with performance ratings, managers fear demotivating or angering people on whom they depend for future productivity. In addition, however, merit guidelines typically put a limit on the raises that can be given to high performers who are already near the top of their pay ranges and thus put employees directly in competition with one another. These constraints have been found to result in merit increases that are more compressed than merit-based bonuses, which are not subject to the same administrative rules (e.g., Kahn & Sherer, 1990).

These features of merit pay programs create a situation where managers often agonize over relatively small distinctions in performance ratings and pay. For example, consider the case of two employees, each earning \$50,000 per year. Suppose that the first receives an *excellent* performance rating and a 6% merit increase, while second receives a *very good* rating and a 5% increase. On an annual basis, the differential is only 1%, or \$500. On a weekly basis, the differential is \$500/52 = \$9.62. With a marginal tax rate of, say, 40%, the after-tax weekly differential is \$5.77. Is this performance payoff sufficient to motivate Employee A to maintain the same level of high performance or to motivate Employee

B to aspire to higher performance? Many people would say "no." Furthermore, given the imprecision of performance ratings, there is no assurance that better performance by Employee B would actually result in a higher rating and the modestly higher take-home pay. Thus, it is easy to understand why employees often report that merit pay policies are rather ineffective (Eskew & Heneman, 1994).

Despite employee skepticism about the link between merit ratings and pay, a literature review by R. Heneman (1990) found the relationship between performance ratings and pay increases to be statistically significant in the vast majority (28 of 30) of studies. Thus, although the linkages may be modest, they do appear to exist in most cases. Moreover, the strength of actual merit pay links in organizations has been found to be positively related to average levels of job satisfaction and employee motivation (Kopelman, 1976).

A major limitation of the merit pay literature, however, is that there is surprisingly little evidence about the *performance* implications of adopting or not adopting merit pay programs. R. Heneman (1992, pp. 247-252) listed 10 studies that purported to address the relationship between merit pay and performance. Five of the reported relationships were positive (using statistical significance as the criterion), while the rest of the relationships were nonsignificant. No statistically significant negative relationships between merit pay and performance were reported. It is important to note, however, that Heneman's review was narrative rather than meta-analytic. As such, the conclusions are limited by small sample sizes, sampling error, and other weaknesses associated with single-study results. Moreover, very few studies used control groups, longitudinal designs, or objective measures of performance.

One of the biggest weaknesses of the merit pay literature is the scarcity of studies that assess performance at supra-individual (i.e., unit or organizational) levels. Of these, the most well-known study is by Pearce, Stevenson, and Perry (1985), which is widely cited as suggesting that merit pay programs are not effective. Although Pearce et al. represents a laudable attempt to tackle a difficult issue, for reasons outlined below, we believe that it is inappropriate to draw such negative conclusions from their study.

Pearce and her colleagues (1985) collected organization level performance data (three measures of claims-processing speed and one of accuracy) from 20 Social Security district and branch offices over a 48-month period. Data collection began prior to implementation of a merit pay system for managers and ended in two thirds of the cases after the merit pay program had been implemented and initial training begun, and in one third of the cases after one round of increases had actually been distributed. Results suggested that unit performance climbed during the entire 48-month period, including the period after the introduction of the merit pay plan. However, because the rate of postimplementation improvement was not statistically significantly higher than the rate of preimplementation improvement (there was no control group), the authors concluded that "The positive effects of the implementation of merit pay . . . were not supported by the data" (p. 271).

However, just two paragraphs later, Pearce et al. (1985) suggested that there were "limitations to this study that prevent drawing definitive conclusions about the effect of merit pay on organizational performance" (p. 271). For example, they acknowledged that "8 of our 12 tests assess the effect of *training and the start of the program* on organizational performance, an emphasis somewhat different from testing changes in organizational performance *after merit pay rewards were distributed*" (p. 271; emphases ours). In addition, the authors cautioned that there was "evidence that the implementation of this federal merit pay program was flawed in several ways" (p. 271), in part because there were court challenges and disputes among federal agencies that caused some managers to believe "that this program was intended by the political leadership to communicate its dissatisfaction with bureaucratic inefficiency to the electorate rather than to actually reward high performance" (p. 274). Third, there was no control group, thus raising the possibility that performance might have been stagnant, or even declined, in the absence of the merit system.

Fourth, as Gerhart and Milkovich (1992) noted, "To study the impact of a pay-for-performance system, one must first establish that there is indeed pay for performance" (p. 524). They pointed out that only one half of the annual pay increase of the plan was tied to merit (the other half was an across-the-board increase) and that only 40% of the merit increase portion was based on the performance measures studied by Pearce et al. In other words, incentive intensity appears to have been weak, in turn contributing to weak instrumentality perceptions and motivation. Finally, the merit pay program was intended to apply to supervisors but not to the workers they supervised. This combination of factors, particularly the apparent lack of any strong merit pay system and the fact that most of their tests were conducted *before* merit raises had even been awarded, suggest that this is a very problematic study for supporting the claim that merit pay is not effective.

The problems with drawing conclusions based only on stated (as opposed to actual) merit pay policies are clearly illustrated in a 3-year study of 10 branch offices of a large financial services organization. Kopelman and Reinharth (1982) examined the average size of the performance rating/merit pay increase relationship in each branch over a 3-year period and then correlated the size of these average instrumentality relationships with average performance appraisals in each unit. Moreover, they conducted these tests not only within a given year but also lagged across 1- and 2-year time periods (e.g., they examined the effects of performance-pay relationships in Year 1 on average performance in Year 2 or 3). Their key finding was that "The stronger the performance-reward tie, the higher the level of *subsequent* performance" (p. 34). This suggests that the timing of Pearce et al.'s study (i.e., two thirds of the tests were not even concurrent, but rather occurred *before* increases were awarded) provides an extremely weak test of the possible effects of changes to a merit pay system.[8]

In a *reverse-direction* type of field experiment, Greene and Podsakoff (1978) examined changes in production workers' individual performance ratings and their satisfaction after *removal* of a merit pay system from a unionized paper plant.[9] Results suggested that relative to the control plant, average performance ratings dropped dramatically after the removal of merit pay. Furthermore, subgroup analyses showed that satisfaction with pay and supervision increased for those who had been rated as poor or average performers but declined for those who had been rated as high performers. Greene and Podsakoff cautioned that the drops in performance ratings combined with the increasing dissatisfaction of workers that management most wanted to keep (the high performers) raised serious concerns about the wisdom of merit pay removal.

Overall, despite considerable skepticism about merit pay, the actual evidence on merit pay is primarily positive. First, there appear to be statistically significant links between performance ratings and pay increases in the vast majority of merit systems. Second, the higher the actual links between performance and pay, the higher the average job satisfaction and motivation of employees (e.g., Kopelman, 1976), particularly among the highest-performing employees (Greene & Podsakoff, 1978). Third, reported relationships between merit pay and performance are almost exclusively positive, although not always statistically significant.[10] However, these studies are limited by the scarcity of control groups, longitudinal assessment, objective measures of performance, and unit measures of performance.

Thus, one very important priority for future research is to conduct more studies that examine the link between merit pay programs and unit or organization level performance. The most fruitful sites for such studies will probably be in multiple units of the same organization, the strategy used by Pearce et al. (1985) and Kopelman and Reinharth (1982). In addition, it would be helpful to have studies that use objective rather than subjective performance criteria at the individual level. However, we realize that merit pay systems are often adopted precisely because objective measures of individual performance are difficult to create for many jobs.

In the meantime, on the basis of existing evidence, we are left with cautiously positive conclusions about merit pay. In addition, we believe that three other potentially important effects of merit pay have been largely ignored in the research literature. Specifically, prior research has generally ignored the cumulative (i.e., year-after-year) effects of merit pay, as well as the indirect (but substantial) effects of performance on pay via its influence on promotion, and the probable sorting effects of merit pay on employee quality. Viewed from this broader perspective, the evidence is bound to look considerably more positive.

To illustrate the cumulative effects of merit increases over time, let us return to our scenario involving the two $50,000 employees. Table 6.2 depicts the impact over a 20-year period of a 1%-higher merit increase each year. After 20 years, Employee A is earning $121,024, while Employee B is earning $101,078. Moreover, during that 20-year period, Employee A has earned $148,785 more than Employee B, which is a substantial amount, even if adjusted to its present value ($76,690).[11] If employees were informed that performing at a level consistently above average during the first half of their careers would yield this amount of extra cash, perhaps their instrumentality perceptions would be stronger and they would react differently to merit pay, even at modest levels (Gerhart, Minkoff, & Olsen, 1995). However, this hypothesis remains untested to date.

In addition, it may not make sense to interpret merit pay as including only annual merit increases, because we know that merit ratings also influence promotions (Gerhart & Milkovich, 1989). Promotions, in turn, generally have a twofold effect on career earnings (Gerhart & Milkovich, 1992; Trevor, Gerhart, & Boudreau, 1997). First, there is typically a pay increase that goes along with the promotion, which may be considerably larger than the typical annual merit increase. In 1990, for example, the average promotional increase was about 12%, compared

Table 6.2 Pay for Performance: Accumulation Over Time

	Employee 1 *Performance Rating = Average* *Annual Pay Growth = 5%*		*Employee 2* *Performance Rating = 1 point above average* *Annual Pay Growth = 6%*	
Year	*Nominal*	*Real*[a]	*Nominal*	*Real*[a]
1	$40,000		$40,000	
2	$42,000	$40,000	$42,400	$40,381
3	$44,100	$40,000	$44,944	$40,766
4	$46,305	$40,000	$47,641	$41,154
5	$48,620	$40,000	$50,499	$41,546
.				
.				
.				
20	$101,078	$40,000	$121,024	$47,893
Total	$1,322,638	$760,000	$1,471,424	$836,690
Difference			$148,785	$76,690

[a] Using 5% discount rate.

with approximately 4.5% for within-grade merit increases (Hay Group, 1994). More recently, Lazear (1999) reported an average 14% promotional increase. Moreover, this increase is considerably larger at top management levels, often more than 70% (see earlier discussion of Gerhart & Milkovich, 1990, in Chapter 4's discussion of tournament theory).

Second, a promotion usually moves the employee to a new pay grade where he or she will have a lower compa-ratio. Merit-increase grids typically provide larger percentage increases to those with lower compa-ratios in the interest of moving their pay toward the target level for that position. Thus, the impact of performance on promotions can have significant consequences for the strength of pay-performance relationships, but these will be revealed only with longitudinal data (e.g., Gerhart & Milkovich, 1989; Trevor et al., 1997).

Not surprisingly, studies that ignore the importance of promotions are less likely to find a strong link between pay and performance. For example, in a widely cited study of professional and managerial pay plans, Medoff and Abraham (1981) focused exclusively on within-grade analyses, thereby ignoring the large indirect effect of merit ratings on pay via promotion. Likewise, although Konrad and Pfeffer's (1990) study of college and university faculty concluded that the effect of productivity on pay was "small" (p. 270), they focused exclusively on the within-rank relationship (by including rank in their equation).

However, controlling for rank ignores the fact that the main influence of individual performance on pay occurs via rank. Productivity is a determinant of rank, and rank is a determinant of pay. Indeed, based on Appendix A.2 in Konrad and Pfeffer (1990), productivity correlated .37 with full-professor rank, and full-professor rank, in turn, correlated .61 with salary. The correlation between productivity and salary was .49. In other words, more productive faculty were promoted to higher ranks, and higher ranks were paid more. If merit pay is defined in this broad fashion, it becomes clear that even in contexts where there are no so-called merit pay increases (e.g., a unionized workforce), there may still be sizable relationships between performance and pay over time if performance plays any role in promotions.

The third important, but largely ignored, effect of merit pay is the sorting effect that we have discussed previously (Gerhart & Milkovich, 1992; Lazear, 1999; Rynes, 1987; Trevor et al., 1997). Organizations using merit pay (actual, not just stated) are likely to attract and retain workforces who find merit pay to be attractive. Presumably, this would tend to be people high in ability, achievement motivation, or both (Trank et al., 2001). In addition to this self-selection process, organizations as disparate as universities, consulting firms, and multinational corporations (e.g., GE) may choose to aggressively "manage out" those who do not meet their high-performance standards. If this performance management process leaves only high performers who are well paid, there may not appear to be a strong link between pay and performance within the organization, but there clearly is such a link across organizations.

Individual Incentives

We have noted previously that there is very strong evidence that individual incentive plans can generate substantial increases in performance (Guzzo et al., 1985; Jenkins et al., 1998; Judiesch, 1994; Locke et al., 1980; Stajkovic & Luthans, 1997). At the same, we have also pointed out that such plans have limited applicability because it is rare that performance can be defined objectively and in a way that separates the unique contributions of individual employees.

Our main focus here will be to explore an issue that helps explain why more incentive plans (of any type) do not exist and why those that are implemented can easily end up being terminated after a short period of

Table 6.3 Piece Rate Example

Production Level	*Hourly Rate*
10 units produced (or less)	$10.00 per hour (guaranteed)
12 units produced	$12.00
14 units produced	$14.00
16 units produced	$16.00
18 units produced	$18.00
20 units produced	$20.00

NOTE: Piece Rate = $1.00/unit produced; Standard = 10 units/hour

application. The issue is the difficulty in designing an incentive plan that is acceptable to both management and employees because of the temptation on both sides to "game" the system.

An example of a very simple individual incentive plan is provided in Table 6.3. Note that in this example, a minimum of $10 per hour is paid even if production is below 10 units. In addition, there is no cap on potential earnings. In this situation, what output level would we expect workers to choose? As noted earlier, that depends on worker trust in management as well as management's ability to get the incentive standards right in the first place (sometimes in consultation with workers or their unions).

The lack of trust between employees and managers and the subjectivity inherent in standard setting are illustrated in the following passage from Whyte (1955). This exchange records the comments made by an experienced worker advising an inexperienced worker about how to deal with the time-study engineer:

> If you expect to get any kind of price, you got to outwit that son-of-a-bitch! . . . You got to add in movements you know you ain't going to make when you're running the job! Remember, if you don't screw them, they're going to screw you! . . . You were running that job too damn fast before they timed you on it! I was watching you yesterday. If you don't run a job slow before you get timed, you won't get a good price. They'll look at the record of what you do before they come around and compare it with the timing speed. Those time-study men are sharp! . . . Remember those bastards are paid to screw you. . . . They'll stay up half the night figuring out how to beat you out of a dime. (p. 15)

Suppose that the workers have been successful in fooling the time-study engineer, with the result that a standard of 10 units per hour is actually very easy to attain. Under these circumstances, would we expect workers to produce just as much as they possibly can? According to Whyte (1955), probably not, because workers soon learn that "too-high" productivity is likely to cause management to increase the difficulty of the standards:

> A couple of operators (first and second shift on the same drill) got to competing with one each other to see how much they could turn in. They got up to $1.65 an hour, and the price was cut in half. And from then on they had to run the job themselves, as none of the other operators would accept the job. (p. 22)

Thus, Whyte (1955) suggested that employees working under standards that were too easy would withhold effort, an effect he referred to as "quota restriction." In addition, they would pressure other workers to do the same so that "rate busters" would not cause the time-study engineer to reset rates: "Don't let it go over $1.25 an hour, or the time-study man will be right down here! And they don't waste time either! They watch the records like a hawk! I got ahead, so I took it easy for a few hours."

Lest the reader think that such phenomena are a thing of the past, consider this much more recent description by a worker on a General Motors (GM) assembly line. Here, he describes a situation in which his job standard had become sufficiently easy that he and a coworker were able to cover for each other for up to half of each work shift (in the meantime, the other one either slept, read, or left the plant entirely):

> Doubling up was one thing. But to double up while working and still have time to browse the paper or kibitz with fellow linemates just didn't wash. We were being watched. We knew it and we should have slowed down to make it appear more difficult than it really was. But we didn't. We'd simply become too damn cocky. Not surprisingly, Dale and I arrived at our jobs one afternoon to find a swarm of bossmen grouped around our bench. . . . The picture was dreadfully clear. The bastards were adding work to our jobs! (Hamper, 1991, p. 63)

Alternatively, consider the situation where standards are set too high, in our simple example, and it would take tremendous effort even to produce 11 pieces per hour. In this case, workers would be expected to produce less than 10 pieces per hour because they can still earn $10 while exerting less effort. In addition, by holding back on their output, employees send a message to management that the standard needs to be reduced. Whyte (1955) called this type of output restriction "goldbricking."

Eventually, the dual games of quota restriction and goldbricking may cause the system to break down as the conflict between employees and management begins to loom larger than any incentive effects that might have been achieved. Indeed, the recent growth of group incentive plans (e.g., gainsharing or profit sharing) can be seen in part as a response to the dysfunction of individual incentive systems and merit pay programs (Case, 1998; R. Heneman et al., 2000; Schuster, 1990).

In sum, research suggests that individual incentive programs *can* produce substantial increases in productivity (e.g., Lincoln Electric). Moreover, the stronger the individual incentives, the greater their (sorting) effects in getting rid of poor performers through turnover (Harrison, Virick, & William, 1996). However, actually achieving these outcomes at reasonable cost and without dysfunctional spillover (e.g., poor employee relations or negative effects on prosocial behaviors or unmeasured work outcomes) appears to be very difficult. Indeed, as noted earlier, Whyte (1955) estimated that it happened only about one third of the time with individual incentive rates.[12]

This suggests that a comprehensive examination of the usefulness of individual incentive systems also requires a close look at the *survival* of such programs, but little of this type of work has appeared (for an early effort in this regard, see Gerhart et al., 1996; for an analysis of gainsharing rather than individual incentive plans, see White, 1979).[13] Our sense is that both the applied-psychology and economics literature tend to emphasize the best-case scenarios of incentive plans, particularly in top-tier research journals.[14] However, if research on the effectiveness of plans fails to include terminated plans and only reports on successful ones, the average effect sizes reported in such studies will be overly optimistic from the perspective of a manager trying to decide the expected value and risk of implementing an individual (or other) incentive plan. We turn now to one form of group incentive plan that may alleviate (although not entirely eliminate) these concerns.

Gainsharing

As suggested in Table 6.1, gainsharing is a results-based program that links pay to performance at a collective (usually, facility) level. Thus, although expectancy and instrumentality perceptions are typically reduced relative to the case of individual incentives, they are still likely to be higher than in collective plans where results are based on the performance of an entire organization (e.g., profit sharing, stock plans). A second feature of gainsharing plans is that they often target multiple objectives other than productivity, such as schedule attainment, safety, customer returns, customer satisfaction with quality, and number and value of employee suggestions. Thus, gainsharing plans can be customized to desired objectives and also provide an opportunity to ensure that objectives such as productivity do not come at the expense of other key goals, such as quality. A third potential advantage of gainsharing relative to individual incentives is that targets are generally based on historical standards rather than on time-study methods (Case, 1998). As such, many of the gaming aspects associated with individual incentives are reduced, although as we shall see, negotiation and conflicts of interest between management and employees are not entirely eliminated in gainsharing programs, either.

The potential advantages of gainsharing led Milkovich and Wigdor (1991) to suggest the following:

> Group incentive plans may provide a way to accommodate the complexity and interdependence of jobs, the need for work group cooperation, and the existence of work group performance norms and still offer the motivational potential of clear goals, clear pay-to-performance links, and relatively large pay increases. (p. 86)

And indeed, the empirical evidence on gainsharing appears to be quite favorable (Gerhart & Milkovich, 1992; Welbourne & Gomez-Mejia, 1995). For example, one 5-year study of 28 sites found positive effects of a variety of gainsharing plans on productivity (Schuster, 1984a). Another study (Hatcher & Ross, 1991) found that changing from individual incentives to gainsharing resulted in a decrease in grievances and a fairly dramatic increase in product quality (defects per 1,000 products shipped declined from 20.93 to 2.31).

Arthur and Jelf (1999) examined approximately 7 years of monthly data (2 years before and 5 years after gainsharing implementation) on outcomes of a new gainsharing plan at an automobile parts manufacturing plant employing 1,600 people. Outcomes measured were labor costs, costs of maintenance materials, perishable tools, scrap, rework, and supplies. Savings were measured relative to the first 2 years of the period, before the gainsharing plan was implemented. Arthur and Jelf report that during the 5-year period, the facility realized a total of $15 million in savings. In addition, after gainsharing was implemented, they observed decreases of 20% in absenteeism and 50% in grievances.

Finally, using the same data base, Arthur and Aiman-Smith (2001) reported an increase in the ratio of "double-loop" to "single-loop" suggestions received by workers over time, a phenomenon they interpret as evidence of increased organizational learning. Single-loop suggestions are those that do not question fundamental procedures or assumptions (such as suggesting the purchase of less expensive supplies), whereas double-loop solutions are those that reexamine fundamental processes and ways of doing things. Over the first 4 years of the gainsharing plan, double-loop suggestions increased from 40% to 60% as a proportion of all suggestions received.

Petty, Singleton, and Connell (1992) compared one division of an electric utility company that implemented a gainsharing plan with another division that did not. The gainsharing division performed better on 11 of 12 objective performance measures, providing an estimated savings of somewhere between $857,000 and $2 million. Moreover, favorable interpretations of the Petty et al. results are bolstered by the fact that they also measured employee perceptions of teamwork and other factors designed to be influenced by the plan, and generally observed positive changes on these factors.

In addition, a study by Wagner, Rubin, and Callahan (1988) examined the effects on productivity of a nonmanagement group incentive pay plan. One of the interesting features of this plan is that in contrast to most gainsharing plans (McAdams, 1995), this plan apparently did not have a strong worker participation feature. Rather, work tasks were assigned a standard number of hours for completion; if a task was completed in a shorter amount of time, employees shared in the savings. Wagner et al. found a substantial increase in productivity under the plan (103.7), as well as statistically significant decreases in labor costs and grievances.

In addition, Wagner and colleagues (1988) made some interesting observations about the context of the plan's implementation and the effects of the plan on specific behaviors. For example, the company had already gained experience with incentive plans in other plants, which may have reduced worker concerns about rate cutting and managerial trustworthiness. Wagner et al. also observed greater employee concern for cooperative behaviors (e.g., helping coworkers with temporary work overloads) as well as coworker "policing" of quantity and quality to assure equitable contributions.

Banker, Lee, Potter, and Srinivasan (1996) examined 34 stores of a major retailer, 15 of which implemented a store level incentive plan. Time-series data were used, resulting in a range of total observations from 238 to 2,618, depending on the analysis. They reported that stores with the incentive plan had 4.9% higher sales, 3.4% higher customer satisfaction, and 4.4% higher profit than stores without the incentive plan. In addition, there were three contextual variables that proved to be important moderators. Specifically, the largest impact of the incentive program was in stores facing the toughest competition, having the most upscale customer profiles, and having the least monitoring (defined as a low ratio of supervisors to sales associates). When these three variables were each 1 standard deviation above (or below, in the case of monitoring), their respective means were 18.7% higher for sales, 7.0% higher for customer satisfaction, and 16% higher for profit. This study provides a nice framework for understanding where incentive plans may be most valuable. In addition, the finding regarding monitoring supports the agency theory notion that incentives and supervision are substitutes for one another, given that having high levels of both was less productive in this study.

As would be predicted from expectancy theory and various theories of group performance (e.g., free riding, social loafing), improvements in group outcomes would be expected to decline as group size increased. Indeed, this appears to be the case. Specifically, Kaufman (1992) reported that doubling the number of employees covered by a gainsharing plan, from around 200 to 400, was associated with a reduction in the expected productivity gain of almost 50%.

In addition to group size, a number of other issues appear to complicate the interpretation of what seem to be primarily positive findings about gainsharing effectiveness. One such issue concerns whether it is gainsharing per se that is the key driver or rather other initiatives, such as employee involvement, often associated with gainsharing plans (Hammer, 1988; Mitchell, Lewin, & Lawler, 1991). For example, Milkovich and Wigdor (1991) suggest that "Many beneficial effects attributed to gainsharing—including productivity effects—may be as much due to the contextual conditions as to the introduction of gainsharing" (p. 87). Moreover, it may well be that contextual conditions are themselves determinants of whether or not gainsharing programs survive (Kim, 1999) or are adopted in the first place. For example, Collins, Hatcher, and Ross (1993) found that among all the employers that expressed preliminary interest in implementing gainsharing systems, only those that already had compatible structures and values were likely to actually adopt such systems.

Still, empirical evidence with respect to the importance of contextual factors is somewhat mixed. For example, Schuster (1990) has argued that gainsharing plans have often worked well even in cases where the main (or entire) focus was on the monetary aspect, unaccompanied by employee involvement. Consistent with this argument, a study of several Improshare plans (see Fein, 1981), which emphasize pay but not employee involvement, found positive effects on performance (Kaufman, 1992). Of course, simply finding positive effects for pay alone does not imply that effects would not be even greater if other innovations were adopted concurrently.

In a study that sought to speak directly to such concerns, Cooke (1994) examined the relationships between the joint effects of group-based incentives (profit sharing or gainsharing), employee participation programs (work teams), and productivity (value added per employee) in a sample of 841 Michigan manufacturing firms.[15] He hypothesized that "The potential performance gains from combining [employee participation] and group-based incentives may exceed the potential gains of either by itself" (p. 597). Following Levine and Tyson's (1990) logic, he argued that employees need to have both the motivation to put their knowledge to use and the opportunity to do so (e.g., through involvement programs).

Cooke's (1994) results, however, provided little support for the hypothesized interaction in either union or nonunion firms. In nonunion firms, the existence of group-based incentives alone was associated with a productivity increase of 18.3%, while the existence of teams alone had no real association with productivity. The existence of both group incentives *and* work teams was associated with an increase in productivity of 20.7%, which, although somewhat greater than the simple sum of the main effects (thus supporting the synergy idea), was not so different as to suggest that group-based incentives can succeed only if combined with work teams.

The pattern of Cooke's (1994) results in the nonunion setting provides stronger evidence of the potential importance of context, but the interaction was in the opposite direction from what was hypothesized. Specifically, the existence of work teams alone was associated with roughly 20% higher productivity, while group-based incentives alone were associated with only 6% higher productivity. Moreover, the combination of group-based incentives and work teams was associated with only about 5% higher productivity; thus, in this case, the whole seemed to be *less* than the sum of the parts. As an explanation, Cooke seems to suggest that having both teams and group incentives created too much mutual monitoring by employees, thus resulting in conflict rather than cooperation. Overall, though, his results support the effectiveness of gainsharing programs (across different contexts). His results are also consistent with work showing that employee involvement can have a substantial payoff (e.g., Appelbaum, Bailey, Berg, & Kalleberg, 2000; MacDuffie, 1995). His study, though, does not support the positive-synergy hypothesis.

There are certainly examples where the financial and employee involvement aspects of gainsharing seem to combine very effectively (be it in synergistic or additive fashion). For example, open-book management (OBM), which gives employees significant incentives and "joint responsibility for moving the numbers in the right direction" (Case, 1997, p. 124), has been successful at companies such as Whole Foods, where store managers share detailed information with worker teams regarding sales, product costs, wages and salaries, and operating profits for all stores. This information is shared because these factors determine profitability at each store, which in turn drives employee compensation. In the case of Whole Foods, "The company shares so much information so widely that the SEC has designated all 6,500 employees 'insiders' for stock-trading purposes" (Fishman, 1996). Other successful case applications of OBM have been reported at Springfield Remanufacturing, now SRC Holdings Corporation (Stack, 1992, 2002), and Southwest Airlines (Freiberg & Freiberg, 1996).

A second issue of interpretation has to do with the survival of gainsharing programs (Gerhart et al., 1996). In a number of cases where large positive effects of gainsharing have been reported, the programs have nevertheless been discontinued. This is true, for example, of the Petty et al. (1992) study described earlier. In that case, the initial problem was that the unionized employees in other divisions felt inequitably treated because they were not covered by the plan and thus did not receive payouts. However, when approached about being covered by the plan, the union's position was that all employees, regardless of pay or job level, should receive the same flat bonus payout. In contrast, management wanted the bonus to be a flat percentage of salary, resulting in larger payouts for higher-paid employees. Because the two sides were unable to reach agreement on these types of issues, the plan was discontinued.

As another example, Pritchard, Jones, Roth, Stuebing, and Ekeberg (1988) conducted an investigation of the effects of incentives, goal setting, and feedback on productivity at an air force base over almost a 2-year period. Despite productivity gains of up to 75% when compared with baseline levels, the program was discontinued. The authors cited the arrival of a new manager who was philosophically opposed to such a system as a reason for the program's withdrawal. Specifically, the new manager was "opposed to the use of incentives, especially when used for some units under his command and not for others" (p. 353). There was also resistance from people who believed that "Personnel should not get something for doing what they were already supposed to do" (p. 354) and from some supervisors who felt such an incentive system "would undermine their power and prerogatives to reward individuals and units informally" (p. 354).

The Kaufman (1992) study described earlier provides evidence on survival rates across multiple companies. Of 104 responding companies that had implemented Improshare programs between 1981 and 1988, 23% had discontinued the plans by the time of his study. In addition, another 163 companies that were known to have implemented Improshare plans during the period did not return the survey. We suspect that an even larger percentage of that group had discontinued the plan. Kim (1999) reports similar findings as well as interesting evidence on determinants of survival, one of which is employee involvement.

In summary, the evidence on gainsharing seems to tell us at least two things. First, group compensation interventions *can,* like individual incentives, result in significantly higher productivity. Second, however, as with individual incentives, administrative or contextual factors can nevertheless result in such programs being unacceptable to one or more of the involved parties.

Based on agency theory, a key consideration here is the degree of risk in the plan and how employees perceive risk as a function of variability of plan performance measures and payout formulae (Gomez-Mejia, Welbourne, & Wiseman, 2000). Schuster (1984b) drew similar conclusions, noting that management adjustment of payout formulas without worker input is likely to cause problems. He also reported evidence to suggest that plantwide plans may be better than group-specific plans because perceived inequities may arise when groups receive different levels of bonus payments.

A different type of perceived inequity—namely, that high performers may feel underrewarded—is something that will also need to be examined. A study by Weiss (1987) at AT&T, for example, found that extreme performers (at both the top and bottom) were more likely to leave under gainsharing plans. This goes back to our earlier discussion about the balancing of individual and group-based pay for performance, as well as the consequences for the composition of the workforce (i.e., sorting effects), and more specifically, the potential effects of group-oriented programs on individual high performers.

Profit Sharing

A profit-sharing plan pays out on the basis of meeting a profitability target (e.g., return on assets or net income). Thus, it is a results-oriented plan that depends on collective performance. Profit sharing can be either deferred (i.e., to fund retirement) or paid in cash. Payouts may be formula based (e.g., a fixed percentage of net income) or discretionary.

Weitzman and Kruse (1990) examined attitudes toward profit sharing and found that employers believed that profit sharing had positive effects on productivity and company performance. Although they also reported generally positive employee attitudes toward profit sharing, the evidence was more sparse and "tempered . . . by the risk of fluctuating income" (p. 123). They referred specifically to a U.S. Bureau of National Affairs (1988) survey showing that most employees prefer straight wages or salaries (63%), followed by individual incentives (22%), and companywide incentives (12%). In other words, consistent with agency theory, employees prefer to avoid risk in their pay. In addition, if they are to assume risk, they want it to be based on their own performance, not the performance of the company. These findings have been replicated by Cable and Judge (1994), who found the same preference hierarchy in a sample of college students.

With respect to productivity, Weitzman and Kruse (1990) concluded that "Evidence on the connection between profit sharing and productivity is not definitive. Yet it is also not neutral—many sources point toward a positive link; the only quarrel seems to be over magnitudes" (p. 139). Weitzman and Kruse estimated that the mean effect of profit sharing on productivity is 7.4% (median = 4.4%).

Other evidence on profit sharing comes from a meta-analysis conducted by Doucouliagos (1995). His study also focused on productivity (typically defined as value added or sales per employee) as the dependent variable. Based on 19 studies and 32,752 firms, he reported a correlation between profit sharing and productivity of .05. However, the correlation ($r = .26$) was higher in employee-managed firms than in more traditional firms ($r = .04$), suggesting that providing both an incentive and an opportunity to have influence has a larger impact than providing only an incentive. We note, however, that his definition of profit sharing included other plans such as gainsharing. Thus, it is possible that plans covering smaller employees (such as gainsharing) may have partly driven the results. Furthermore, given that the number of employees was not controlled in the study, differences in size might also be partly responsible for the larger correlation in employee-managed firms if such firms were smaller.

In perhaps the most extensive study to date, Kruse (1993) surveyed 275 firms employing a total of approximately 6 million employees. In firms having profit sharing, an average of 79% of employees were covered by the plan. Kruse found that productivity growth in profit-sharing companies was 3.5% to 5.0% higher than in companies not using profit sharing. However, there were some important contingency factors. First, it was important to distinguish between deferred (51% of profit-sharing companies) and cash profit-sharing plans (38%; remaining plans were either combination plans or not classified). As would be expected, cash plans exhibited substantially higher productivity growth than deferred plans, particularly in within-industry models.

Second, Kruse (1993) also found that size was an important contingency factor. Annual productivity growth in companies having fewer than 775 employees was 11% to 17%, far larger than productivity growth in companies having 775 employees or more (0%–6.9%). This finding fits well with our emphasis on the motivational challenges that arise in moving from the individual to the small-group to the large-group level of analysis (see also Kaufman, 1992). A third contingency factor, formula versus discretionary, indicated an advantage for discretionary plans, particularly using within-industry models. Kruse suggests that such plans probably require trust and a positive employee relations climate to be effective.

Kruse (1993) also looked at the statistical interactions between profit sharing and the following variables: information sharing with employees, use of attitude surveys, job enrichment, use of autonomous work teams, employment security, suggestion systems, and gainsharing. He concluded from these analyses that there is only "weak" (p. 87) evidence of an interaction with information sharing and "very little support" (p. 89) for interactions between profit sharing and the other human resource variables. This is not to say these practices should be ignored. To the contrary, these practices may well be beneficial (Huselid, 1995). But the research suggests that their effects are additive; that is, lack of such practices does not constrain the impact of profit sharing, nor does their presence magnify its effects. Indeed, many organizations do use these types of practices in conjunction with profit sharing and other group-based plans.

There are, of course, methodological concerns with this profit-sharing research, which Kruse (1993) and others have identified. One concern is selection bias. We are more likely to observe successful profit-sharing plans because the unsuccessful plans are less likely to survive. A second possibility is reverse causality; profit-sharing plans may be more likely to be adopted by companies that are more productive or more profitable in the first place. Third, profit sharing may be confounded with other positive management practices. If these other practices are not in the models, the coefficients for profit sharing may be inflated by omitted variable bias.

A fourth concern is the typical measure of productivity, value added, which is a measure of the extent to which the price (or value) of a product exceeds (or adds to) the cost of the factor inputs (labor, capital) rather than a measure of physical productivity (e.g., units produced). Obviously, the price of a product can be influenced by many factors other than productivity (e.g., product market competition, industry trends, marketing). Thus, finding a relation between profits distributed per worker (profit sharing) and value added does not necessarily mean that profit sharing causes higher productivity. (Using a dummy variable for profit sharing reduces this concern, but the previous caveats still apply.)

For example, consider profit-sharing payments in U.S. automobile companies, which began in 1988. Profit-sharing payouts in early 2000 (based on 1999 profits) for hourly union employees were $8,100 for the Chrysler side of Daimler-Chrysler, $8,000 at Ford, and $1,775 at GM, the highest in the history of the plan (Stamborski, 2000). Why were the payouts so much lower at GM? One possibility is that GM does have a less productive workforce. It is certainly true that GM has had far worse labor relations problems in terms of work stoppages, which have decreased profits by billions of dollars in recent years. However, a look at profit-sharing payouts at Chrysler over time is also informative.

Profits Year	*Payout*
1991	$0
1992	$429
1993	4,300
1994	8,000
1995	3,200
1996	7,900
1997	4,600
1998	7,400
1999	8,100
2000	375

Although it is possible that the productivity of the workforce fluctuated to this degree from year to year, an alternative explanation is that other factors (e.g., product design, general demand for automobiles, Daimler-Benz and Chrysler merger problems) had a more important influence on profits and profit-sharing payments. As noted previously, the motivational effects of incentive plans are expected to diminish rapidly as the number of employees increases, a consideration that seems quite relevant to the automobile company plans. This suggests that an alternative explanation, the goal of making labor costs more variable, may be a more important consideration. The average automobile worker earns an hourly wage of about $42,000 per year (without overtime). Thus, a profit-sharing payout of $8,000 results in annual compensation of about $50,000, 16% of which is a variable rather than fixed cost. As noted earlier, this variable aspect tends to be better received when there are payouts. A sustained period of no payouts can sometimes result in a plan being significantly modified (e.g., the Saturn experience) or eliminated (e.g., the DuPont Fibers experience).

Indeed, Kim's (1998) empirical study found that labor costs were considerably higher in profit-sharing companies than in other companies, suggesting that the agency theory prediction of a compensating differential is supported (for a similar finding, see also Mitchell et al., 1990). In addition, when Kim used a simultaneous equations model to control for reverse causality and profits, he found that the positive effect of profit sharing on profits disappeared.[16]

This leaves us with three conclusions regarding profit sharing. First, it almost certainly results in higher labor costs. Second, it may or may not have a positive causal effect on productivity. In fact, in large groups (broadly defined to include organizations), such an effect seems doubtful, particularly when payouts are deferred until retirement. (In larger groups, there is a greater risk of free riding. Deferring payouts weakens instrumentality perceptions.) Third, the supposed advantage of making labor costs variable is real only if the plan survives years when no payouts are made. Fourth, as with any plan based on group performance, sorting effects are potentially important.

Finally, we should emphasize that the preceding discussion and summary of empirical evidence is not necessarily applicable to executives, who are typically covered by different plans (having few participants) and who have a much more direct line of sight between their actions and firm performance. Under these conditions, profit sharing may be more likely to have its hypothesized positive effects (Abowd, 1990; Gerhart & Milkovich, 1990).

Stock Plans

Stock plans are based on a results-oriented measure at a collective level (stock price appreciation or stock price appreciation plus dividends). A

Table 6.4 Stock Plans, by Employee Level (Companies Using Stock-Based Plans)

Employee Level	*Stock Purchase*	*Stock Option*	*Stock Grant*	*Phantom Stock*	*Company Stock Through 401k*
Nonexempt[a]	51%	23%	6%	1%	60%
Exempt	54%	66%	18%	6%	63%
Officers/Executives	56%	92%	40%	14%	62%

SOURCE: Parus and Handel (2000).
NOTE: Sample size ranges from 715 to 1057. Note that 56.1% of companies use at least one stock-based plan. The table entries pertain *only* to those companies.
[a] Nonunion employees only.

major development in compensation has been the substantial growth in stock plans. According to the National Council on Employee Ownership Web site (NCEO, 2002), as of 2001, "Employees own or have options to own stock worth about $800 billion, or about 8% of all the stock in the U.S."[17] This 8% compares with just 1% to 2% only a decade earlier. In terms of number of employees covered, the NCEO estimates that broad-based stock options plans (i.e., those covering 50% or more of employees in a firm) cover 7 to 10 million employees, employee stock ownership plans (ESOPs) cover 8.5 million, and stock purchase plans cover 15.7 million. Thus, as many as 34 million employees, or about one third of all private sector employees, appear to have some degree of ownership in their employing companies. We focus our attention below on stock option and ESOP plans.

Table 6.4 shows that different types of stock plans tend to be used for different employee groups. For example, stock purchase plans and provision of company stock through 401(k) plans are roughly equally prevalent across employee categories. In contrast, stock options are still heavily weighted toward officers and executives, although less so than in the past. Outright stock grants and phantom stock plans (where pay is linked to stock performance but with no actual option or ownership) are also far more likely to be used for executives than for other groups.

Stock Options

How do stock options work? An option is the right to purchase a fixed number of shares of stock during a fixed time period at a fixed price (referred to as the *exercise price, option price,* or *strike price*), regardless of how high (or low) the actual stock price eventually goes. The more the eventual stock price exceeds the option price the greater the payoff. For example, consider an employee who receives options on 100 shares of stock that at the time of issue are trading at $50 per share. So, the strike price is set at $50. Three years later, the stock is trading at a price of $100 per share. At this point, the employee may wish to exercise the option (at a cost of 100 × $50 = $5,000), which can then be sold for 100 × $100, or $10,000. Thus, the employee realizes a pretax gain of $5,000.[18] Stock options often vest gradually over a 3- to 5-year period, and only those options that are vested can be exercised. In addition, options often expire after a fixed amount of time (e.g., 10 years) or when the employee leaves the company. As such, they can also serve as a retention device.

Of course, the retention effect is strongest if the options are "in the money" (i.e., stock price exceeds strike price) or expected to be so. In the case of *underwater options* (where stock price is less than the strike price), options have a lower current value and are thus less likely to provide desired incentive effects. (Note that even an underwater option ordinarily has a nonzero value as long as there is some possibility for the strike price to rise above the option price.) In such cases, firms must decide whether or not to reprice options (i.e., reduce the strike price) in order to enhance incentive and retention effects. This choice will determine whether or not options are used as true variable-pay programs, in that repricing effectively eliminates any downside risk to the holder and any variable component of labor cost to the company. As we shall see later, the effects of repricing options are complex and have been vigorously debated.

Stock options have received far more attention than any other type of pay program in recent years. One reason for this interest has been the tremendous growth in the granting of stock options. As Figure 6.1 shows, in 2001, 54% of large U.S. companies had stock options plans in which at least one half of all employees were eligible to receive option grants, up from 17% of companies in 1993. Likewise, across all companies, 22% of employees received grants in 2001, up from 6% in 1993. Another study of large U.S. employers reported that the percentage of all outstanding shares of stock allocated to employee and management stock option plans increased from 5.4% in 1990 to 14.6% in 2000 (Whiteley, 2001). A study of 125 large nonfinancial firms in the S&P 500 reported that the value of stock options granted per employee per

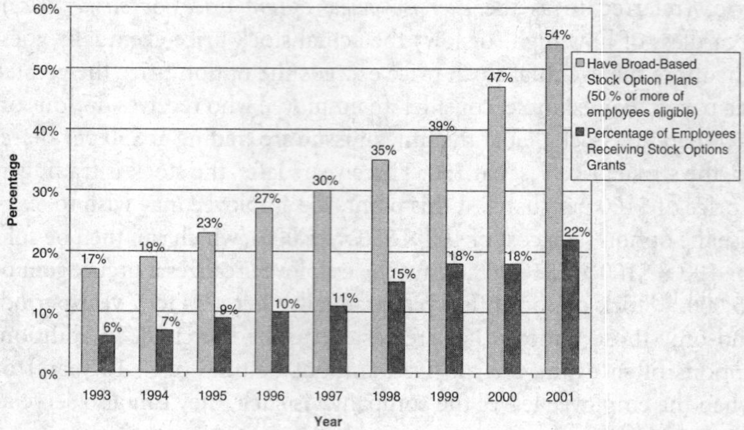

Figure 6.1 Percentage of Companies Having Broad-Based Stock Option Programs and Percentage of Employees in (All) Companies Receiving Grants

SOURCE: Mercer (2001).

year rose from approximately $600 in 1994 to over $1,600 in 1998 (Cohn, 1999). Similarly, a Watson Wyatt survey of 1,352 employers reported that 19% of workers in the United States were eligible for stock options in 1999, up from 12% only 1 year earlier (Watson Wyatt Worldwide, 1999). Finally, the NCEO (2002) estimated that in 1990, there were approximately 1 million options holders, compared with 7 to 10 million by 2001. Thus, although estimates vary somewhat across samples and surveys, there is little doubt that the growth in employee stock options has been fairly dramatic.

A second reason for the attention received by stock options is that they have translated into great wealth, not just for their traditional recipients (top executives) but also for an increasingly wide spectrum of other employees. At one time, providing stock options for nonexecutives was a strategy most likely to be found among technology companies such as Microsoft or small start-up firms. However, that has changed somewhat, as companies as diverse as Procter & Gamble, PepsiCo, DuPont, Delta Airlines, Wendy's International, and many others have implemented stock option plans that cover all employees.

As an example of the kind of wealth that can be generated, as we noted earlier, the Microsoft stock option plan has created over 10,000 millionaires. As another example, consider the experience of secretary D'Anne

Table 6.5 Average Executive Compensation Among Large U.S. Companies

Year	*Salary & Bonus*	*Long-Term Pay*	*Total Pay*	*Change*
2001	Not reported	Not reported	$11.0 million	−16%
2000	$2.7 million[a]	$10.4 million[a]	$13.1 million	6%
1999	$2.3 million	$10.1 million	$12.4 million	17%
1998	$2.1 million	$8.5 million	$10.6 million	36%
1997	$2.2 million	$5.6 million	$7.8 million	35%
1996	$2.3 million	$3.2 million	$5.8 million	54%

SOURCE: Date gathered from *Business Week*, annual issues on executive pay: April 19, 1999, p. 72; April 17, 2000, p. 100; and April 15, 2002, p. 80.
[a] Estimated.

Schjerning, who in 1994 earned an annual salary of $53,000 working for James Clark at Silicon Graphics (Prsager, 1999). When Clark decided to leave to start a new company, Mosaic, he asked Ms. Schjerning to join him. He offered her the same annual salary but also 10,000 stock options per year, which entitled her to purchase Mosaic shares at a half penny apiece. Ms. Schjerning reports that "I didn't know what a stock option was," but she admired her boss and thought it would be a good move to follow him. Later that year, Mosaic changed its name to Netscape and then went public. On the day it went public, Netscape closed at $54 per share and Ms. Schjerning was worth $1.08 million. She retired in 1997 and is now "free to spend her days golfing, driving her Dodge Durango and watching the financial news on CNBC."[19]

Still, by far the most fortunate beneficiaries of stock options continue to be top executives. For example, in the late 1990s, the highest-paid executives earned as much as $600 million in one year, the great bulk of which came from exercising stock options. Table 6.5 clearly shows that as the stock market rose through the late 1990s, so did average executive pay, going from $5.8 million in 1996 to $13.1 million in 2000. Likewise, Table 6.5 shows that as the stock market(s) declined in 2001, executive compensation also declined.

What can we say about the effectiveness of stock options from the company's point of view? As we shall see, this is a very complex question involving a variety of factors. In addition, the fact that we have had only a short period of experience with such extensive use of stock options means that existing empirical investigations are limited in their ability to reveal longer-term effects. Perhaps not surprisingly, then, there is considerable controversy surrounding the overall effects of stock options, as well as the various contingencies that might affect their usefulness.

Early research provided positive evidence on the effectiveness of stock plans, at least among the top five executives (for which public data are readily available). Based on data on 39 firms in three industries (electronics, aerospace, and chemicals) over the 1947 to 1966 time period, Masson (1971) reported that firms placing greater emphasis on stock-based compensation had higher shareholder return than did other firms. Brickley, Bhagat, and Lease (1985), using a sample of 83 firms from multiple industries and an event study methodology, found that the stock market reacted positively to the announcement of long-term compensation plans, with the abnormal cumulative return (i.e., the estimated added increase in shareholder wealth) for companies announcing these plans being 2.4%.[20]

In a study cited earlier in our book, Gerhart and Milkovich (1990) moved beyond studying only the top five managers and examined the relationship between the percentage of top- and middle-level managers (within six levels of the board of directors) eligible for stock options in a firm and the firm's return on assets. Their results suggested that a company having 20% of managers eligible for stock options had a predicted return on assets of 5.5%, compared with a predicted return on assets of 6.8% (or roughly 25% higher) for companies having 80% of managers eligible. However, because these findings pertain to relatively high-level and highly paid managers, results might be weaker for plans covering a broader range of employees, particularly in larger firms.

Indeed, despite the positive results experienced by companies such as Microsoft and the generally positive results from academic studies, recent fluctuations in the U.S. stock market (particularly on the NASDAQ exchange) have focused attention on the potential drawbacks and challenges of using stock-based compensation. For example, although stock options have no downside risk per se, there is nevertheless an opportunity cost when a job with lower base pay and benefits was accepted because of the upside wealth potential associated with stock options. For this reason, companies that rely heavily on stock options to attract and retain talent can suddenly become seriously disadvantaged in the labor market if stock values decline. Thus, a dramatic drop in stock prices presents such companies with the important dilemma of whether or not to reprice their options.

Repricing is thus a complicated, high-stakes decision whose overall effects are not well understood. Not surprisingly, then, two major "camps" (pro and con) have emerged. Those against repricing argue that since executives have been very handsomely rewarded during times of strong stock performance, they should not be "rescued" from poor performance when stocks go down. To do so, they argue, is to weaken the instrumentality link between performance and pay by reducing the penalties for poor performance.

Beyond the motivational arguments, others have raised equity concerns based on the rapidly increasing income inequality generated in large part by stock options (recall Table 6.5). For example, while executive compensation increased 114% between 1996 and 2000 (Reingold, 2000), earnings for production and nonsupervisory private sector employees grew by only 17% over that same time period. Based on such comparisons, there have been countless stories asking whether these levels of executive pay are "fair,"[21] particularly given that it has not been all that difficult to find cases where executive rewards have been very high, even in the face of mediocre or suboptimal firm performance (e.g., Crystal, 1991). In such cases, companies also have to factor in the motivational effects on nonexecutive employees, particularly if feelings of unfairness cause workers to be dissatisfied with their leadership as well as with their pay (recall Chapter 3).

Despite these concerns about repricing, a substantial number of boards of directors have indeed decided to reprice executive options. They argue that if total compensation is diminished too dramatically, executives will move to other firms that have higher base salaries or that have repriced their options. At that point, the board will need to hire another executive, which raises a host of other questions: Will there be a large pool of talent willing to take a job at a firm where the stock price is on a downward trajectory? What compensation package will it take to attract a new executive? Will the strike price on the options in this package be any different from the strike price that would have been offered to the previous executive after repricing?

In addition, boards argue that options that are hopelessly underwater have little incentive effect on executives and other option holders. Much as a piece rate worker will goldbrick if the standard is set too high to realistically earn much incentive money, an executive who sees little chance of driving up the stock price to obtain a reasonable return is unlikely to be maximally motivated. Alternatively, much like a gambler who has just lost a big stake at Vegas, such an executive may engage in much more risky behavior than owners might prefer, taking the view that "I have nothing to lose, anyway" (Asch & Quandt, 1988; Wiseman,

Gomez-Mejia, & Fugate, 2000). Sanders (2001, p. 487) has used the analogy of a lottery to describe this situation.

Although these are the justifications given by boards for repricing their options, a more skeptical view holds that boards reprice options at least in part because of the substantial power that many CEOs have to influence their own compensation packages (e.g., Crystal, 1991; Wade, O'Reilly, & Chandratat, 1990). Experts in this camp see repricing as a breakdown in the agency relationship (Chance, Kumar, & Todd, 2000), such that repricing decisions are driven not entirely by efficiency but also by the relative power of the CEO vis-à-vis outside stockholders, as well as the visibility of the company and its CEO.[22] Although power and politics likely play a role, it is not clear whether that role is primary or secondary. Unless variables that accurately capture both political and market (including incentive) factors are simultaneously included in econometric models, this question cannot be answered empirically. Logically, although the market for executive talent is certainly less than perfect, executives on the whole are quite visible and mobile, suggesting that market factors will play a major role in repricing decisions just as they do in other compensation decisions.[23]

Another major source of debate about the effects of stock options concerns the fact that current accounting treatments may cause firms to "overuse" options, thus setting up conflicts of interest between executives and employees on one hand and outside shareholders on the other. Under current accounting rules, stock option grants that have an option price equal to or greater than the current stock price create no compensation expense for a company when they are granted—only when they are eventually exercised. This rule, Accounting Principles Board Opinion (APB) 25, uses what is known as the *intrinsic value* approach to valuing options. Thus, although options clearly have value to employees, firms do not incur any accounting costs when they are issued. The fact that accounting profits are unaffected by issuing stock options creates a considerable temptation for firms to use this type of compensation in the short run, deferring the consequences to some later period when (or if) the options are exercised.

Despite what accounting rules have permitted, the fact of the matter is that stock options do eventually have an economic cost. Two types of data help illustrate this point. First, one can examine the *overhang* of stock and stock options, which is defined as the percentage of stock and options allocated to compensation plans as a percentage of all stock and options. As Table 6.6 shows, an increasing percentage of stock and stock

Table 6.6 Stock Shares and Stock Options Reserved for Compensation Plans as a Percentage of All Stock Shares and Stock Options ("Overhang" or Potential Dilution)

	S&P 1500	*S&P 500*	*S&P Small Capitalization*	*Internet Companies*
2000	14.6	13.1	16.8	
1999	13.4	11.4	16.3	23
1998		10.5	15.5	
1997		10.0	13.8	
1996				
1995		9.2		

SOURCE: S&P 1500: Investor Responsibility Research Center (2001); S&P Small Capitalization and Internet Companies: Howe (2000).

options have been allocated to compensation plans in recent years, with the largest grants observed in small and/or Internet companies where the overhang is as high as 23%. When options are eventually exercised, the company must either use funds to purchase existing stock shares or create new shares. Because either action entails substantial costs, the value of existing shares is diluted (overhang is also known as *potential dilution*), thus to some extent rewarding employees at the expense of other shareholders.

Indeed, Table 6.7 provides a second type of evidence on economic costs, specifically, the change in profitability that would take place if stock options were recognized as an expense when granted. In 1999, for example, net income in S&P 500 firms would have been 6% lower had stock options been recognized as an expense. Consistent with the evidence on overhang or potential dilution, the impact on profitability differs by industry, with the largest effects on health care services (38%) and computer networking (24%). In looking at specific companies, we see that Yahoo, Peoplesoft, and Micron Technology, for example, would have actually had their net income swing from positive to negative (i.e., a loss) if stock options were to be recognized as an expense.

Recently, the Financial Accounting Standards Board issued FAS 123, which recommends a "fair-value" approach to valuing stock options. Although companies are still permitted to report net income and earnings per share under the assumption that stock options create no expense, they are also required to provide a footnote that reports what

Table 6.7 Estimated Reduction in Net Income When Stock Options Are Recognized as an Expense

S&P 500 Year	*Reduction*	
1999	6%	
1998	4%	
1997	3%	
By Industry, 1999	*Reduction*	
Health care services	38%	
Computer networking	24%	
Commercial & consumer services	21%	
Communications equipment makers	19%	
Company Examples (2001)	*Net Income Using Current Accounting Standard*	*Net Income Using New Fair-Value Accounting Standard*
Yahoo	$21 million	−$1.9 billion
Peoplesoft	$104 million	−$43 million
Novell	$16 million	−149 million

SOURCE: Hitt and Schlesinger (2002); Morgenson (2000).

net income and earnings per share would have been using the fair-value approach to stock options. In 2002, high-profile accounting scandals, involving companies such as Enron and Worldcom, together with stock prices that continued to weaken (or collapse in the cases of Enron and Worldcom) placed additional pressure on companies to justify their accounting practices, including those for options. In response, several companies (e.g., GM, GE, and Coca-Cola) began to use the fair-value method, incorporating the cost of stock options into their earnings reports. However, in most of the companies making this switch, including the cost of options has had little effect on earnings.

One key argument against fair-value treatment of options is that it is difficult to estimate fair value. There are several alternative approaches, of which the Black-Scholes model of options pricing is the most widely used. Without going into the details of the statistical model (which is described in most finance texts), we can make a few general statements regarding the determinants of stock option value. In the typical case

Table 6.8 Effect of Volatility and Dividend Rate on Option Value (as percentage of stock price)

	Volatility			
Dividend Rate	*10%*	*30%*	*50%*	*70%*
0%	.45	.56	.69	.81
4%	.15	.29	.41	.51
8%	.02	.14	.24	.32

SOURCE: Adapted from Hall (2000).
Option value is stated as a fraction of stock price.
Volatility is the annual standard deviation of the company's stock price returns.
Assumes a 10-year at-the-money option with a risk-free (10-year) bond rate of 6%.
For *Fortune 500*, 30% volatility is about average.

where the option price is equal to the stock price on the day of the grant, one key factor is the dividend rate. Under the assumption that higher dividends are associated with lower stock price appreciation, an option is most valuable when there are no dividends.

A second key factor is volatility, which is essentially the variance of the stock price over time. At first blush, one might assume that less volatility is better, but in fact, just the opposite is true. Because there is no downside risk in an option that is granted at no cost to an employee, the effect of greater variance is to increase the probability that the price will spike to a high level at some point during the option period. Thus, options to buy volatile stocks are more valuable. Table 6.8 shows how the dividend rate and volatility influence the fair value of a stock option.

In addition to the substantial cost of stock options (which, as we have seen, is not accurately captured by current accounting treatments), there is also some question as to the value of stock options to employees. Hall and Murphy (2000) argue that the cost of options as estimated by Black-Scholes fails to take into account three key factors that do not affect cost, but do affect the value to the employee: initial wealth, diversification of investments, and risk aversion.[24] Specifically, as wealth and diversification of investments decreases and risk aversion increases, the value of options decreases. Using additional results provided to them by Hall and Murphy, an article in *Business Week* reported that including these factors would suggest that an option grant costing a company $3.3 million would have a value to a typical S&P 500 executive of $1.1 million, only one third of the cost to the company (Coy, 2001).[25]

In summary, stock options have surfaced as one of the most interesting areas in the study of compensation. Their growth can be attributed in large part to the fact that current accounting rules permit companies to issue stock options without immediately recognizing them as an expense, despite their clear economic cost. When used to compensate executives, there is disagreement as to whether stock options help solve agency problems (e.g., by aligning interests) or are instead a sure sign that such problems are out of hand, particularly when executive options pay off handsomely (or are repriced) in the absence of strong firm financial performance. This concern has taken on added relevance as executives at some companies have appeared to enjoy wealth accumulated as executives (sometimes in alleged illegal ways) while other stockholders have seen their investment wealth disappear. One response was the passage of the 2002 Sarbanes-Oxley Act, which, among other things, reduces the time allowed to report insider trading from as much as 40 days to 2 days. It also doubles the maximum prison sentence for violating securities laws to 20 years.

There are also questions about whether executives place enough value on options to make them worth the cost and whether line of sight for nonexecutives is sufficient for options to have an influence, especially in large companies. In sum, there are many opportunities for researchers to pursue here.

Employee Stock Ownership Plans

Like stock option plans, ESOPs have also grown significantly in recent years. For example, while only 248,000 employees were covered by ESOPs in 1975, by 2002 that number had grown to 8.8 million (NCEO, 2002). However, the two types of plans actually operate quite differently.

In contrast to stock option plans (where employees can cash out stock gains immediately), an ESOP is a retirement plan. ESOPs are *tax-qualified* plans, meaning that the employer receives tax advantages if certain rules are met. (This is also true of deferred profit-sharing plans.) One such rule is that the plan be broad based, rather than being limited to a select group of employees such as executives. An ESOP trust owns company stock on behalf of employees, who receive the vested stock when they leave the company. If the stock is not publicly traded, the company must offer to purchase the company stock from the departing employee.

One key issue with ESOPs is diversification and risk from the employee's point of view.[26] By law, an ESOP must invest at least 51% of its assets in the company's stock. Thus, it is impossible for an employee to achieve the degree of diversification necessary to reduce risk to desired levels. In companies that invest all ESOP assets in the company stock, this problem is exacerbated. As a partial remedy for this problem, the law requires that once an employee reaches age 55, with 10 years of coverage, he or she must be permitted to invest up to 50% of accumulated ESOP assets into investments other than company stock over the subsequent 6 years.

From an agency theory perspective, the investment risk borne by employees would suggest that ESOPs must pay a compensating risk differential. Free-rider issues may also be a concern in larger plans. From an expectancy theory point of view, not being able to access one's assets until retirement raises further questions about motivational impact. Of course, as an employee accumulates many years with a company and sizable assets in its ESOP, motivation to help the company succeed may grow substantially.

It is generally assumed that whatever effect ESOPs might have on firm performance is likely to be mediated through employee attitudes. Klein (1987) hypothesized that ESOPs might affect employee attitudes and motivation in three ways. First, she speculated that any degree of ownership, independent of the financial aspect, might create a different mentality among employees, a sort of "pride of ownership" effect. Beyond that, however, she hypothesized that employee attitudes would also be positively correlated with the size of the employer's contribution to their accounts. In addition, she speculated that there might be increased two-way communication with ESOP plans, thus providing a more effective means for employees to have a meaningful influence on company decisions and outcomes.

To test her hypotheses, Klein (1987) obtained data on 2,804 employees in 37 ESOPs. In addition, she also obtained data from key managerial respondents in each firm pertaining to the extent to which the ESOP was a core part of management's philosophy, as well as the resources devoted to ESOP communication.

Klein's (1987) empirical findings did not support the first hypothesis (mere pride of ownership), but did support the second and third. Specifically, the R^2 between size of employer financial contribution and organizational commitment was .17, while the R^2 with turnover intention was .25 (higher contributions were associated with lower intentions). Adding the management philosophy and ESOP communication variables increased the R^2 to .30 for organizational commitment and .39

for turnover intentions. There was also support for a relationship between perceived worker influence on decisions and employee commitment but not with turnover intentions. (It should be noted that the perceived influence relationships were estimated without controlling for employer financial contribution.)

A final observation about Klein's study is that it included only companies having ESOPs. As such, there was no comparison between ESOP and non-ESOP employees. Thus, her results may underestimate differences between employees' attitudes under ESOPs versus those not in ESOPs.

Most other studies of ESOPs have examined their effects on productivity or financial outcomes rather than attitudes. One of the largest such studies was conducted by Blasi, Conte, and Kruse (1996), who examined 562 employee ownership firms (EOFs) and compared their financial performance with 4,716 firms without such plans. To qualify as an EOF, employees (not counting top executives) had to own 5% or more of the market value of outstanding shares in 1990, and the plan had to "comprise substantially more than top and middle management." About half the employee stock ownership plans in their sample consisted of ESOPs, while the other half were either other types of retirement plans (e.g., 401(k) plans) or employee stock purchase plans. The median percentage of company stock held by employees was 10% (mean = 13.2%). The performance-dependent variables included the profitability and price/earnings *(P/E)* ratio.[27]

For the most part, there was no main effect for EOFs on the performance-dependent variables. The authors also conducted a test of whether this finding would change if the sample were restricted to firms where employee ownership was higher (i.e., 10% or more) and found that it did not. Instead, the relationship between EOF and performance depended to a "striking" degree on firm size (Blasi et al., 1996, p. 75). This, of course, is very consistent with the earlier results for profit sharing and with theories that focus on free-rider and large-group problems. Specifically, Blasi et al. found that for the smallest quartile on firm size (maximum firm size = 1,015 employees), EOF firms were 1.3 percentage points higher on return on assets (ROA) and 1.5 percentage points higher on *P/E* ratio ($p < .10$). In contrast, in the quartile between 3,014 to 12,700 employees, EOF firms had ROAs that were 1.9 percentage points lower ($p < .10$) and *P/E* ratios that were 1.6 percentage points lower ($p < .10$). Thus, the coefficients, while not always statistically significant, generally revealed a declining pattern of returns by firm size.

Other evidence on worker ownership comes from the meta-analysis conducted by Doucouliagos (1995). Based on 17 studies and 31,323 firms, a weighted mean correlation of .03 was found between employee ownership and productivity. Thus, this study further suggests that the typical effects of ESOPs on firm productivity are very modest.

In all likelihood, these small overall effects reflect the fact that most companies adopt such plans for their financial, tax, retirement benefit, and takeover defense advantages rather than as motivational plans designed to induce employees to "act like owners." Nevertheless, results from Klein (1987) and Blasi et al. (1996) suggest that ESOPs *can* have a positive impact on firm performance under the right conditions (i.e., small company size, strong two-way communications and employee participation, and high financial pay-in by employers).

Summary

As we have seen, every pay program has its advantages and disadvantages. For example, programs differ in their sorting and incentive effects; the degree to which they support teamwork and cooperation; the amount of informativeness or lack of measurement error (and thus, the degree to which pay-performance sensitivity can be supported); their tendencies to encourage employees to take a broad work focus; whether program costs vary with ability to pay; their susceptibility to large-scale employee relations problems (which affects risk); and finally, tax and accounting advantages (e.g., stock options). Some general conclusions about the pros and cons of various programs noted in this chapter are summarized in Table 6.9.

Because of the limitations of any single pay program, it is common for organizations to use a portfolio of programs, which may provide a means of reducing the risks of particular pay strategies while garnering most of their benefits (Gerhart et al., 1996). For example, using only an individual incentive program could result in unacceptably high levels of competitive behavior and too narrow a focus among employees. On the other hand, relying exclusively on gainsharing could result in the underrewarding (and potential turnover) of high-performing individuals. Similarly, paying executives largely on the basis of short-term profits could lead to manipulation of accounting returns and to underinvestment in product research and employee development. However, offering a mix of these different programs offers the possibility that the advantages of each could be captured while minimizing the disadvantages.

Table 6.9 Pay Programs for Nonexecutives: Advantages and Disadvantages

	Strong Incentive Intensity?	*Positive Sorting Effect?*	*Encourage Cooperation?*	*Informativeness? (i.e., low error?)*	*Avoid Narrow Focus Problems?*	*Cost Varies With Ability To Pay?*	*Avoid Employ Relations Problems?*	*Tax Accounting Advantage(s)?*
Individual incentives	Good	Good	Poor	Good	Poor	No	Poor	No
Merit pay	Medium	Medium	Medium	Medium	Medium	No	Medium	No
Gainsharing	Medium[a]	Medium[a]	Good	Good	Good	Depends	Neutral[b]	No
Profit sharing	Poor[a]	Poor[a]	Good	Good	Good	Yes	Neutral[b]	Yes
Stock plans	Poor[a]	Poor[a]	Good	Good	Good	Yes	Neutral[b]	Yes
Hybrids	Poor to Good	Poor to Good	Poor to Good	Poor to Good	Poor to Good	Depends	Poor to Good	Depends

[a] This can be "Good" if the plan covers a small number of people.

[b] This can be "Poor" if the plan is sufficiently risky.

For example, consider again the case of Lincoln Electric, a company well-known for its very intensive use of individual incentives. However, in addition to its individual piece rates, Lincoln also uses a bonus system, with pool size based on overall profitability and payouts based on ratings of individual performance on dimensions such as cooperation and quality. In addition, Lincoln employees also own a substantial portion of the company's stock. Thus, although an individual incentive program alone might cause many problems, by using it as one piece of a portfolio, Lincoln seems to have been able to reap considerable benefits, while avoiding the major pitfalls.

Another example of a portfolio approach is to use a "balanced scorecard," a concept developed by Kaplan and Norton (1996). At the executive level, their idea is to "track financial results while simultaneously monitoring progress in building the capabilities and acquiring the intangible assets [needed] for future growth" (p. 75). Whirlpool, for example, measures and compensates executive performance on three major dimensions (Gubman, 1998): shareholder value (assessed by economic value added, earnings per share, cash flow, and total cost productivity); customer value (measured by quality, market share, and customer satisfaction); and employee value (measured by scores on a high-performance culture index, high-performance culture deployment, and training and development diversity). In this way, executives are encouraged not to mortgage the future in favor of short-term performance and not to unduly favor shareholders at the expense of customers or employees.

Future Research

Throughout this chapter, we have offered suggestions for future research with respect to particular types of pay programs (e.g., merit or incentive pay). At a more holistic level, however, we believe that the main challenge for researchers will be to better align the policies they study with the policy choices faced by managers. For example, to the extent that organizations use a mix of pay programs, it would be more informative to study the impact of hybrid pay programs than to study the effects of "pure" gainsharing or pure profit-sharing plans. Similarly, studies of programs such as gainsharing often treat gainsharing as a dichotomous variable (i.e., an organization either has gainsharing or it does not). However, in attempting to determine the relative effects of gainsharing, it is crucial to know what kinds of alternative compensation programs these "other" companies have. Without such information, we may not be capturing the degree to which organizations have chosen pay programs or hybrids that are optimally aligned with their goals and strategies.

Another issue is one that we have raised previously. To show that profit sharing is associated with higher profits is interesting, but not persuasive with respect to causal processes. Far more persuasive would be to show that employees under profit sharing think and behave differently than other employees. That is, to show causal processes—as well as to provide guidance about how best to implement various pay programs—researchers need to begin measuring mediating variables such as employee suggestions and turnover rates. To date, few studies have simultaneously measured pay policy, employee reactions or behaviors, and unit/organization performance (but for some welcome exceptions, see Arthur & Aiman-Smith, 2001; Petty et al., 1992).

A final suggestion is to build on the progress that has been made in integrating individual difference factors into pay research. In particular, we encourage additional work that investigates the distinction between incentive and sorting effects, which appears to be very important, judging from the limited work available (Cable & Judge, 1994; Lazear, 1999; Schwab, 1991; Trevor et al., 1997).

In addition, we encourage increased attention to individual differences in risk aversion or, more broadly, how people perceive risk. Despite the fact that risk is a central factor in agency theory, little attention has been given to its measurement beyond using measures of pay variability or pay-performance sensitivity. The work by Hall and Murphy (2000) and Wiseman et al. (2000) provides a glimpse of how important risk can be in affecting employee perceptions of value. The rapid growth of "risky" pay in combination with the dramatic fluctuations in stock values and profits in recent years suggests that this may be an individual difference variable of considerable research importance.

Notes

1. The *Wall Street Journal* reported that at some of its hospitals, the percentage of Medicare cases having complications (which carry higher reimbursements) was 95% to 100% on an ongoing basis, in comparison with 40% to 60% in the typical community hospital (Lagnado, 1997). Much of the blame was placed on how hospitals and their managers were evaluated and rewarded. Specifically, a scorecard was used that included measures of admissions, earnings, supply costs, and "case mix index improvement," a variable that measured the percentage of Medicare cases having complication rates. Thus, higher complication rates were alleged to have translated directly into larger bonus payments for administrators.

2. Agency theory is often interpreted as predicting that if managers' compensation is the main component of their income, they will be more risk averse than shareholders who are better able to diversify their investments (and hence risks). As a consequence, top managers may bypass worthwhile investments because of risk concerns (Beatty & Zajac, 1994; Wright, Ferris, Sarin, & Awasthi, 1996). On the other hand, we also know, as shown later in our discussion of the Black-Scholes options pricing model, that the value of stock options held by a manager, ceteris paribus, is higher as the variance in stock price (i.e., risk) increases (e.g., Agrawal & Mandelker, 1987). As such, at some level of compensation risk, managers may shift from risk averse to risk seeking or "risk loving" (Asch & Quandt, 1988; see discussion in Wiseman et al., 2000), which is another potential problem from the perspective of shareholders.

Another potential consequence of risk, now thinking of the risk of job loss (and thus income loss), is that managers will overinvest in projects that they are uniquely qualified to oversee in an effort to entrench themselves and thus make their jobs more secure (Shleifer & Vishny, 1989). Risk aversion and concern for job security may also drive managerial resistance to takeover bids that would actually increase shareholder value. A "golden parachute" is an example of a plan that seeks to reduce entrenchment by granting a substantial payout to managers when there is a change in control of the company.

3. Saturn's collective-bargaining agreement with the UAW originally specified three components of pay (the source for the information in this note is Bohl, 1997). First, base pay was set approximately 12% lower than what UAW workers at other General Motors (GM) plants received. Second, a 12% at-risk component was added, based on training (5%), quality (5%), and team skills (2%). If these goals were met, workers at Saturn would earn the same as other GM workers. Third, Saturn had a variable-reward component (linked to scheduling, productivity, and quality goals) that provided considerable upside opportunity. For example, in 1995 and 1996, bonuses at Saturn averaged roughly $10,000 per worker, bringing total pay to several thousand dollars more than at other GM counterparts. The bonuses were so popular that a nearby competitor (Nissan) found itself fending off a UAW organizing drive where one of the key recruiting themes was "Join the UAW and get bonuses like the UAW workers at Saturn."

However, when the variable-pay plan at Saturn became "variable downward," things changed. In 1997, facing decreased demand for cars and resulting cutbacks in production, Saturn announced that bonuses would average only $2,000 (approximately $4,000 less than other GM workers). Not surprisingly, Saturn employees—who tended to define pay fairness in relation to their UAW peers in other plants—began to raise concerns about the equity of their compensation. Shortly thereafter, Saturn workers held a referendum to decide whether to keep the unique collective-bargaining contract (with its lower base pay) or change to the more traditional contract covering all other UAW members at GM.

In March 1998, Saturn workers voted by a 2-to-1 margin to keep their unique contract. This margin was significantly closer than during a similar vote held in 1992 (where the margin was 4 to 1) and would have been even smaller (or perhaps even negative) without an important renegotiation before the vote. Specifically, the UAW was able to renegotiate the production goal down from 310,000 to 280,000 vehicles, thus increasing the likelihood that the 1998 payout would be higher than in 1997. Subsequently, further changes were made to the compensation plan to reduce the variable-pay component and move it closer toward the UAW contract at other GM plants.

4. The *prisoner's dilemma* in game theory is similar to a social dilemma but differs in important respects (see Schroeder, 1995, pp. 7-8).

5. Pfeffer's recommendation—that organizations use group-based rewards more frequently—appears to rest on his interpretation of the classic empirical work of Gerald Marwell and his colleagues (summarized in Marwell, 1982). The method used by Marwell and Ames (1979) was to contact high school students over the phone and inform them that by participating in an experiment, they would receive a certain number of tokens (average of 225 per subject). Their choice was to invest the tokens either in an "individual exchange" or a "group exchange." They would receive with certainty 1¢ for each token invested in the former. However, by investing in the group

exchange, they could earn more than 1¢ per token—but only if enough others chose the same investment strategy. Subjects were told that they were members of groups having a total of either 4 (small) or 80 subjects (large). At no time did they meet other "group" members, and at no time (until the experiment was over) did they receive information on the investment choices of the others. In small groups, subjects invested an average of about 145 tokens in the group exchange, compared with 115 in the large groups, a difference of about 26%. According to Marwell and Ames, strong support for the free-rider hypothesis would have occurred if no investments had been made in the group exchange. Given this framing, their interpretation emphasized that their findings did not support free-ridership.

However, one could establish a different but equally valid anchor: that the most efficient outcome would have been for subjects to invest all their tokens in the group exchange. The fact that there is essentially no more effort required of each individual to do so (unlike in a work setting or even a social-loafing experiment) suggests that free riding should have been minimal here. Yet, individuals still underinvested in the group exchange. Moreover, this underinvestment was smaller in larger groups, just as the theory predicts (see Shepperd, 1993). Although the work by Marwell and his colleagues showed that the free-rider phenomenon was not as dominant as earlier conceptual work might have implied, we interpret his work to show that the free-rider effect is nevertheless important.

6. There has been experimental work in economics as well. A recent study by Nalbantian and Schotter (1997) is a good example. They set up a payoff structure for subjects working in groups of 6 (again, as with the Marwell research, there was no actual interaction between group members), where subjects could earn more money as group revenue increased. However, to increase group revenue, they had to devote more effort, and the relationship between effort and cost of effort was convex. In other words, doubling effort from 50 to 100 was more expensive than doubling effort from 25 to 50. Therefore, subjects would be tempted to free ride by choosing lower effort levels in the hope that other group members would exert sufficiently high effort to offset their own personal choices. Nalbantian and Schotter designed the payoff matrix such that the efficient effort level of each individual under a revenue-sharing pay system would be 75, but with pure free riding, it would be 12.5. What they actually observed is that in early rounds of their experiment, effort was approximately 34. By round 25, it had decreased to approximately 18. They describe their findings as being consistent with previous research (see Ledyard, 1995) showing that effort typically starts out at around 50% of the efficient (pareto-optimal) level and then decreases to approximately 11% in later rounds. Although effort level in the Nalbantian and Schotter study did not decrease by quite this much, the evidence of a free-rider effect was nevertheless quite strong.

7. We observe that pay is variable under results-oriented plans and becomes part of base pay under behavior-oriented plans. Therefore, we believe that the fixed-versus-variable pay dimension is largely captured by our framework. One exception would be the merit bonus, which is based on a performance rating but must be re-earned.

8. In Year 3 of Kopelman and Reinharth's (1982) study, the bank shifted to a more aggressive form of merit pay, whereby raises could range from 0% to 12%, with no guaranteed cost-of-living increment. This compared with merit increases of 0% to 6% in the prior 2 years, with across-the-board cost-of-living increases of 6.5% and 5.0% in each of the 2 years. The authors reported,

> Results were uniformly and very strongly supportive of the idea that an expanded range of possible merit salary increases yields a higher level of overall performance. In *all* branches, even those with a weak performance-reward tie, average levels of performance were substantially improved after the range of possible salary increases was expanded. (p. 34)

9. This study had several attractive features: a control plant with almost identical conditions except the removal of merit pay, separate analyses for production workers and supervisors, a carefully developed performance appraisal scale that was tailored to the unique characteristics of the industry and jobs, and separate analyses for high versus low performers. On the less positive side,

the measures of performance were individual performance ratings as opposed to objective or group level measures, although the ratings for supervisors were conducted by more than one person.

10. There have been some exceptions in the federal government, however, which has had notorious problems implementing merit systems (e.g., R. Heneman, 1992).

11. To be complete, this example would factor in taxes (which would diminish the performance payoff) and benefits (which would enhance the performance payoff).

12. In goal-setting terms, one might describe this as a lack of goal commitment. From an expectancy theory perspective, the instrumentality of high performance is mixed, in that both positive and negative valence outcomes are possible. Agency theory suggests that a compensating differential for risk is necessary for an incentive plan to take root.

13. White (1979) studied 22 Scanlon Plans (a form of gainsharing), of which 9 plans had been "abandoned." However, data on the variables he used as predictors of survival (e.g., size, managerial attitudes) were collected after survival or failure was observed. This lack of time precedence leaves open the question of whether these "predictors" truly have predictive power.

14. Anecdotal evidence against incentive plans can be found in practitioner journals such as *Harvard Business Review* (e.g., Kohn, 1993) and books, which are not subject to peer review.

15. Although Cooke was unable to distinguish between gainsharing and profit-sharing plans, we include his study in this section because we calculate that the mean number of employees in his sample companies was 112, indicating that the plans he observed covered a relatively small number of employees, a key attribute of gainsharing-type plans.

16. One concern with Kim's study is some ambiguity regarding which variables he used as instruments and the degree of explanatory power of those instruments (i.e., the R^2 for that equation). Without such information, it is difficult to judge whether the estimates using instrumental variables are better than the estimates based on ordinary least squares.

17. NCEO also estimates the value of stock associated with each plan. ESOPs are estimated to hold $500 billion in stock and $250 billion in 401(k) plans. The value of stock from stock purchase plans was not estimated. NCEO also reports that stock option plans have $500 billion in stock or stock rights. It appears that most of this amount was excluded from the total value of employee stock plans given in the text, $800 billion. This may be because NCEO observes that most of the stock option value is held by executives. NCEO's $800 billion overall estimate appears to be aimed at broad-based employee stock programs.

18. The employee may wish to hold the purchased shares for a longer period of time to take advantage of the lower capital gains tax rate. However, the advantage of this strategy depends on whether the stock price remains higher.

In many cases, companies permit this process to be "cashless." In other words, the employee does not necessarily need to actually come up with the cash to purchase the stock or then sell it.

19. Is this efficient for the economy? There are also a host of stories about executives retiring after making their fortunes. Although the press loves such stories (as do employees and prospective employees of such companies), how should stockholders feel when they lose executive talent because of such large earnings? Economic theory tells us that a firm maximizes profits by hiring workers until the last worker hired has a marginal product equal to his or her wage. How does the story of the secretary conform to this model? It does not. Although many of us know all too well the value of an outstanding secretary, it is difficult to justify earnings of this magnitude in terms of marginal products. Is this type of compensation system more like a tournament or more like a lottery? (On the role of luck in compensation systems, see Lawler, 1971, Lazear, 1995b, p. 29.)

20. Brickley et al. (1985) did not limit long-term compensation plans to pure stock-based plans, but approximately 70% of the plans they studied were either entirely or partly stock based. There were also a substantial number of performance plans, which typically depend on meeting long-term profit goals.

21. Often, the ratio of top executive pay to the pay of rank-and-file workers is compared. Thus, using $13.1 million from Table 6.5 for top executives at large companies and comparing this to the $30,139 average cash compensation for the average private sector worker implied by Table 2.2 (see our Chapter 2), we obtain a ratio of 435.

22. Based on a sample of firms in the computer industry, Pollock, Fisher, and Wade (in press) provide some support for this argument. Specifically, they found that negative spreads between option prices and stock prices were less likely to lead to repricing of CEO options when institutional ownership was high, but more likely to result in repricing when the CEO was also chairman of the board. Together, these findings suggest that repricing is more likely when CEO power is high and less likely when institutional investor power is high. Brenner, Sundaram, and Yermack (2000) reach a similar conclusion, that is, that repricing "represents a windfall for poorly performing managers rather than a necessary adjustment in incentives or a device for retaining talent" (p. 123).

23. Although Brenner et al. (2000) argue that executive retention is not an important factor, by their own admission, they did not examine any data on executive retention (nor on incentive effects, for that matter). So, their pessimistic conclusion may be somewhat premature. Indeed, at least two recent studies suggest that market factors do play a primary role in options repricing. For example, Chidambaran and Nagpurnanand (in press) found that firms that repriced options had had "abnormally high CEO turnover rates" prior to the repricing. Moreover, those that repriced did not have "low institutional ownership or more diffuse ownership of equity." Thus, they concluded, "Our evidence provides little support for the view that repricing primarily reflects managerial entrenchment or ineffective governance in firms." One other noteworthy finding was that stock options accounted for a larger share of total compensation in firms that repriced than in firms that did not. In such firms, a drop in stock price leads to total pay being farther below the market than it would be in firms that rely less on stock options. This would bring more pressure to reprice if a firm wishes to maintain total compensation at or near the market level.

Similarly, a study by Carter and Lynch (2001) also suggests the importance of competitive labor market factors over politics. They report that in addition to the spread between the current stock price and option price positively influencing repricing, repricing is also more common in young firms in high-technology industries that have poor firm-specific performance (i.e., worse than their industry). They also find that political factors (e.g., executive participation on the compensation committee) do not influence the likelihood of repricing. Their interpretation is that "To restore incentive effects of options and to discourage management from going to work for other firms, young, high-technology firms operating in competitive labor markets reprice as firm-specific performance deteriorates and options become out of the money" (p. 224). Of course, labor market competition was not measured directly in this study, so it remains to be seen whether this interpretation will stand up in future research.

24. Note also that an employee stock option cannot be traded, thus decreasing its value relative to options not having this restriction.

25. The value that employees give to options also depends on how well they understand them. Not surprisingly, given the complexities of valuing options even in the finance and accounting professions, evidence shows that employee decisions regarding option exercise are often inconsistent with financial theory. One implication is that employers need to do more to educate employees if they wish to maximize their value (Heath, Huddart, & Lang, 1999).

26. Diversification (or lack thereof) is also a major issue in 401(k) retirement plans. A Hewitt Associates survey reports that many companies use their own stock in lieu of cash to make matching contributions to 401(k) plans and about one half restrict sales of company stock, thus making it difficult to diversify (Schultz & Francis, 2001). For example, employees at Enron were not permitted to move their money out of Enron stock until they reached age 50. Thus, during the 2001 decline in Enron stock from about $84 per share to less than $1 per share, most employees watched the bulk of their retirement savings disappear and were unable to do anything about it.

27. Blasi et al. also examined changes in these dependent variables from 1980 to 1990. However, because the EOF independent variable was measured in 1990, these change dependent variables were actually measured prior to the independent variable, which is inconsistent with the time precedence assumption required to establish causality (Cook & Campbell, 1979). Therefore, we do not highlight the change results.

7 Pay Strategy

Managers of companies with a "loyalty" strategy have internalized . . . the belief that they have to attract people, hold people, recognize and reward people, motivate people, and serve and satisfy people. . . . Once they have built the foundation for a cash-flow surplus by acquiring a base of loyal customers, their first investment priority is to allocate some of that surplus to recruit and retain the best possible employees. And the best employees, like the best customers, are those who get swept up in a kind of value-and-loyalty spiral. Specifically, the best employees are those with the talent and motivation to raise their own productivity (and consequently their own incomes) swiftly enough to fuel their motivation further still, producing even greater improvements in service and productivity and therefore a growing surplus of value for company and customers.

—Reichheld (1996)

In the above quotation, Frederick Reichheld of Bain and Company hints at how performance-based compensation is a fundamental ingredient of the successful implementation of a business strategy that is based on customer loyalty. According to one of the predominant views of strategy today, when properly designed, human resource (HR) practices (including compensation) are capable of creating a "virtuous cycle" of employee motivation, customer satisfaction, and organizational profitability that continues to "feed on itself" to produce ever-higher levels of customer satisfaction, revenues, and profits. (For an example of such a virtuous cycle in one organization, see Exhibit 7.1.) However, to do so, it is presumed that compensation practices must be aligned with the business strategy as well as with other HR practices. In this chapter, we review models and evidence relevant to the role of compensation strategy in the formulation and execution of an organization's strategy (and vice versa). In previous chapters, we have seen how

Exhibit 7.1 Example of a Virtuous Cycle of Employee Motivation and Productivity at Springfield Remanufacturing Corporation

Springfield Remanufacturing Company (SRC) has emerged from the most highly leveraged buyout in American history (89:1 debt-to-equity ratio, with an 18% interest rate) to a company that multiplied the value of its stock 18,300% within its first 6 years. According to David Bollier (1996),

> [SRC's] workers and management together invented a highly original way of running a business that combines business education for all employees with active participation and employee stock ownership. The heart of the system is what Jack Stack (SRC's president) calls "open-book management" (OBM), in which every numerical assessment of every part of the business is made available to every employee. The radically decentralized system has not only helped SRC to constantly improve its performance, but has turned the company into a cohesive community that thrives on enthusiasm, hard work, and *fun.* (p. 170)

Internally, OBM became known as "The Great Game of Business," so named because SRC employees are "part of the business game, rather than getting kicked around in it" (Stack, 1992, p. 122). The extent to which Stack was willing to share both information and profits with employees has led to some amazing stories of employee contributions to SRC's success. For example, Stack tells the story of how a worker in the fuel injection department walked up to him and said,

> You guys are always teaching us business and financials. I was looking at the balance sheet the other day and 76% of your receivables are in one marketplace, and that marketplace typically has a recession every seven years. If you really believe in job security, what are you going to do about it? (Bollier, 1996, p. 180)

Another worker asked,

> You know, we've got an ESOP program here, and I've heard that eventually you've got to pay off an ESOP program. And in order to pay off an ESOP, you've got to sell the company or take the company public. So how are you going to pay off the ESOP? (Bollier, 1996, pp. 180–181)

In another case, everyone at SRC had gone without a bonus for six consecutive quarters. The latest quarterly statistics were within thousandths of a decimal point of meeting the bonus goal, and SRC's executives were inclined to pay the bonus. However, when the matter was put to the employees, they almost unanimously voted against making the payout lest it jeopardize the end-of-the-year ESOP contribution (Stack, 1992).

From revenues of $16 million in 1983, the company's business grew to more than $120 million in 2002. Approximately 35% of the company's stock is owned by the ESOP, while the original 13 manager-investors hold another 59%. As a result of employee initiative, SRC has spawned 22 additional spin-off businesses. One of the most successful of these is *The Great Game of Business,* a consulting book that helps other companies convert to OBM principles (Stack, 1992).

pay level, pay structure, and pay basis decisions separately influence effectiveness outcomes via motivational and workforce sorting effects. Here, we focus more explicitly on understanding how these pay decisions *jointly* influence the fit (or alignment) of the pay strategy with the organization's goals and strategies.

As a first step in understanding the importance of pay strategy in organizational strategy, it is necessary to review some basic aspects of organizational strategy. Three fundamental decisions are made in the organizational strategy process. First, an organization must decide what—and how many—businesses it wants to be in. For example, General Electric (GE) has chosen to operate in a variety of product markets, including plastics, lighting, appliances, medical systems, financial services, and entertainment (NBC). This is the *corporate strategy* decision.[1]

Second, after an organization decides what product market(s) to enter, it must decide how it will compete and make money in each product market. This is the *business strategy* decision, which is addressed in frameworks developed by Porter (1980, 1981) and Miles and Snow (1978).[2] For example, in its automobile business unit, Hyundai competes by being a cost leader (low-cost producer), whereas

BMW competes in the same industry by using a differentiation strategy (advanced technology, high performance, luxury, customer service).

Third, while the corporate and business strategy decisions pertain mainly to strategy formulation, a good plan adds no value until it is successfully implemented or executed. This rests on having successful *functional strategies* in place, including those having to do with compensation and other HR issues.

Our focus in the present chapter is primarily on this third aspect of the strategy process: the role that compensation (and other HR) strategies play in the execution of organizational strategy and achievement of business objectives. Although strategy is typically conceptualized as a macro field, what actually happens in an organization (i.e., strategy execution) depends on a great number of decisions made by individuals at the micro level, as well as their ability to execute those decisions. Successful strategy execution depends on choices and actions taken at all levels of the organization, from executives to front-line workers. For strategy implementation to succeed, the pay strategy must elicit supportive choices at each organizational level and ensure that the "right" people join and stay with the organization (i.e., both incentive and sorting effects). Similarly, on the strategy formulation side, incentives for executives must be correctly formulated to insure that they, in turn, design appropriate incentives for other employees.

Before proceeding, we observe that our discussion is shaped to an important degree by what previous researchers have chosen to study. For example, although we see both incentive and workforce sorting effects as being important to organizational outcomes, the bulk of attention in the pay strategy literature has been directed toward incentive effects alone. That is, studies typically examine how pay strategies influence goal choices, effort, or actions rather than workforce characteristics. As a consequence, the bulk of the present chapter deals with incentive-related effects.

Similarly, we pay relatively little attention to benefits in strategy formulation, largely because few prior researchers have addressed this question. Clearly, benefits are a nontrivial component of total compensation (about 27% in large companies; U.S. Chamber of Commerce Research Center, 2000), so lack of research cannot be attributed to a lack of importance. More likely is the fact that benefits plans are generally complex and difficult to value relative to monetary compensation (e.g., Gerhart & Milkovich, 1992). A second explanation is that some benefits have as their main purpose providing security to employees (e.g., medical coverage, disability insurance) and are thus explicitly not linked to any type of performance measure. Nevertheless, as our later discussion of the resource-based view (RBV) will suggest, benefits may be quite relevant for firms that wish to distinguish themselves from other labor market competitors.

In addition, the vast majority of studies that have looked at relationships between various types of strategic alignment, pay policies, and organizational performance have focused solely on executive compensation. Although some recent evidence suggests that organization strategy may influence the pay of *all* employees and not just executives (Boyd & Salamin, 2001), the influence does appear to lessen at lower job levels. Thus, generalizability below the executive level is also uncertain at this point in time.

Finally, this is a chapter on strategy, so our focus is on how firms differ, not on how they are similar. Thus, while we recognize that competitive (product market, labor market) and institutional (e.g., DiMaggio & Powell, 1983; Meyer & Rowan, 1997; Scott, 1995; Zucker, 1987) forces create important pressures on firms to be similar to other firms, our focus here is on the discretion (Hambrick & Finkelstein, 1987) firms have in choosing different pay strategies (e.g., Gerhart & Milkovich, 1990; Haire, Ghiselli, & Gordon, 1967; Pfeffer & Davis-Blake, 1987) that support their own firm-specific corporate and business strategies.

Below, after a brief description of what we mean by *alignment,* or *fit,* we introduce and describe the central concepts of this chapter: organization strategy and pay strategy. We have, of course, covered many of the key elements of pay strategy in the preceding chapters, but separately. Here, we look at how these elements can be combined into an overall pay strategy framework. Third, we discuss three aspects of pay strategy alignment or fit (Gerhart, 2000): *vertical alignment* with organizational strategy (i.e., corporate and business strategy); *horizontal alignment* (between pay strategy and other dimensions of HR management); and *internal alignment* between different dimensions of pay strategy (e.g., pay level and pay basis).

Strategic Fit and Alignment

What do we mean by alignment, synergy, or fit in a system of practices? Broadly speaking, we use these terms to refer to the case where effects (of pay, in this case) are *nonadditive and dependent on contextual factors.* For example, a pay strategy based heavily on stock options may be associated with 10% better financial performance when used in conjunction with business Strategy A, but with 10% lower performance when used with business Strategy B. Alternatively, a gainsharing program alone may result in an average performance increase of 10%, while a suggestion system alone may result in an average performance increase of 10%. Alignment would not be an issue if their effects were additive; that is, if, when used in combination, their total effect is 20%. In contrast, if combined pay-plus-suggestion programs result in a 30% increase in performance, their effects are nonadditive and depend positively on the presence of the other element in the HR system. By the same token, misfits and "negative synergies" are also possible (Gerhart, Trevor, & Graham, 1996) and in our example would be indicated by the joint effect of the two programs being (significantly) less than 20%. To the extent that the effects of various strategies are interdependent, their effects are said to be *contingent* on other contextual features.

At the outset, it is necessary to recognize that this alignment hypothesis, while intuitively appealing to many of us, has received mixed compelling empirical support. Indeed, there is a good deal of evidence that for one key dimension of pay strategy, pay-for-performance linkage, being somewhat above the population mean is usually better than being below the population mean, regardless of context (see Chapter 6 of this book; Gerhart, 2000; Gerhart, et al., 1996). Thus, to some extent, pay for performance may be a best practice. Nevertheless, there is also some empirical evidence, particularly in studies of executives and managers, to suggest that aligning pay strategy with the context *can* yield still greater effectiveness than ignoring context (Bloom & Milkovich, 1998; Rajagopalan, 1996; for reviews, see Gerhart, 2000 and Gomez-Mejia & Balkin, 1992a).

Moreover, even when such context effects are not observed in empirical studies, this may be due to the possibility that the consequences of poor alignment are serious enough in some cases that firms or units do not survive to be observed without making changes (Hannan & Freeman, 1977; Welbourne & Andrews, 1996). Thus, it is possible that only firms and units that achieve some minimal level of alignment survive. If so, alignment may be so important that it is almost impossible to observe substantial departures from it. In this case, restricted range in alignment would reduce the statistical power available to observe a relationship between alignment and performance.

Of course, one reason for the intuition that context matters is that there are well-known examples of pay strategies not succeeding, and the presumed culprit, almost by definition, is usually some contextual factor. For instance, although Lincoln Electric's compensation strategy has worked well for many years in the United States, its former chief executive officer (CEO) reported that it did not work at all well when Lincoln attempted to transplant it to Western Europe (Hastings, 1999). A small example of how context differs between the two parts of the world is that the International Labour Office reported in 2001 that German workers work, on average, 500 hours (or about 13 weeks) less per year than their U.S. counterparts. In France, it is now illegal to average more than 35 hours of work per week. Lincoln, by contrast, regularly has its employees working well beyond 40 hours per week when business is good. Indeed, this is a key to its record of no layoffs. It can reduce labor costs during difficult economic times by reducing the workweek from, say, 45 or 50 hours to 35 hours. Obviously, this doesn't work in a country like France.

In Chapter 6, we described the employee relations problems that arose in connection with the compensation plan at Saturn, which linked a significant part of employee pay to company performance. Fluctuations in company performance caused fluctuations in pay, and in poor years, Saturn employees were paid less than their counterparts at other General Motors (GM) operations. The reactions of Saturn employees are consistent with a key contingency hypothesis of agency theory: that the benefits of incentive pay gradually give way to the risk-bearing costs as variance in company performance (i.e., risk) increases (see also Bloom & Milkovich, 1998).

In studying pay alignment, a distinction is typically drawn between *internal* and *external* fit (Baird & Meshoulam, 1988; Huselid, 1995), or what we prefer to call horizontal and vertical alignment. The vertical-alignment question asks whether effectiveness depends on the alignment between pay strategy and organizational strategy (see next section). Horizontal alignment focuses on the relationship between pay strategy and other aspects of HR strategy, such as staffing, development, and employee influence. A third type of alignment has to do with the relationships between different dimensions of pay strategy (e.g., pay level, structure, and basis), which we call *internal compensation* alignment.

The dominant focus of the pay strategy literature has been on vertical alignment with organizational strategy. This is where we begin our discussion of the three types of alignment.

Vertical Alignment With Organizational Strategy

As indicated at the beginning of this chapter, organizational strategy consists of three separate "levels": corporate, business, and functional (e.g., Barney, 1997). Because functional strategies are discussed in relation to horizontal and internal strategies, we begin the present discussion with corporate strategy and then move to business strategy.

Corporate Strategy

The corporate strategy decision involves choices about which industries to compete in. As indicated earlier, GE is diversified in a wide range of industries, while Southwest Air is concentrated in a single industry. Over the years, a variety of typologies have been developed to help managers analyze the prospects for profitability in new or existing lines of business (e.g., Bain, 1956, 1968; Mason, 1939) or the consequences of staying in a single industry versus branching out to related or entirely new ones (e.g., Rumelt, 1974).

In the best-known example of this approach, Porter (1980, 1981) provided a framework, generally known as the "five forces," that describes industry structure in terms of five fundamental competitive forces: rivalry between existing firms, threat of new entrants, bargaining power of suppliers, bargaining power of buyers, and threat of substitute products or services. These forces can be used to identify industries where economic rents can more easily be realized. Specifically, industries are expected to offer better opportunities for profitability to the extent that these threats or forces can be kept at low levels.

Bain (1968) described approaches such as Porter's as being external, or focused on factors outside the firm. That is, in Porter's (and Bain's) typologies, the primary unit of analysis is an industry or group of firms rather than an individual firm (Hoskisson, Hitt, Wan, & Yiu, 1999). As such, external or corporate approaches largely ignore the role of firm-specific variables, on the assumption that firms in the same industry control roughly the same resources and follow generally the same strategies as other firms in their industry. Furthermore, these models assume resource mobility, such that firms are able to neutralize any firm-specific competitive advantage that temporarily materializes by simply acquiring new resources.

Previous research has demonstrated that there are indeed differences in average profitability across industries (e.g., Schmalensee, 1985). Moving closer to the pay arena, it has also been shown that aspects of corporate strategy (such as the process, degree, and type of diversification) are associated with different compensation strategies (Gomez-Mejia, 1992; Kerr, 1985; Pitts, 1976), suggesting some degree of contingency between corporate and compensation strategy formulation. For example, pay tends to be tied more closely to business unit performance in more highly diversified firms, but more strongly linked to corporate performance in firms that are either less diversified or in which business units require greater coordination.

These findings fit nicely with an agency theory perspective. As firms diversify into unrelated product markets, corporate directors have less expertise regarding such product markets, thus reducing their ability to monitor the behaviors of business unit managers. Thus, an alternative contracting arrangement is to more strongly link managers' pay to formula-driven, outcome-based plans that depend on business unit performance.

Another element of corporate strategy that has been found to be associated with compensation plans is the firm's life cycle. During start-up and growth stages, firms may need to conserve cash for investments in product development and marketing, leaving less money available for cash compensation and benefits (Ellig, 1981). Thus, growth firms, especially those in the early stages, may find it more effective to keep fixed costs (e.g., base pay and benefits) below market but to provide long-term earnings opportunities through, for example, stock plans that can lead to total-compensation levels well above market. Indeed, this was a primary element of the early compensation strategy employed by Microsoft and is a general pattern that has been supported by empirical research (Balkin & Gomez-Mejia, 1987).

In addition to demonstrating linkages between pay strategies and corporate strategies, a few studies have also suggested that there are performance implications of such linkages. For example, Balkin and Gomez-Mejia (1987) found that growth firms did better with an incentive-based strategy. Gomez-Mejia (1992) found that the effectiveness of an incentive-based strategy depended on the level of diversification. Reviews of these and related studies are available in Gomez-Mejia and Balkin (1992a) and Gerhart (2000).

Business Strategy

In a retrospective interview about the genesis of his five forces model (Argyres & McGahan, 2002), Porter indicated that after outlining the five forces, he also recognized the need for a discussion of alternative strategies that might be used by different firms *within* a given industry. Thus, he developed a typology of three such strategies, which he termed differentiation, cost leadership, and focus. In *differentiation*, a firm seeks to distinguish its product from all others on the basis of features that particular market segments will find attractive. Thus, for example, Apple has differentiated its personal computers on the basis of ease of use and stylish design. In contrast, Dell emphasizes economies of scale, routinization, and efficiencies in order to develop a *cost leadership* (i.e., low-cost) position in its industry. Finally, some firms *focus* on a particular market segment, seeking to provide a range of related products or services that will prove attractive to, say, upper-income individuals over 50 years of age.

A second business strategy typology that has attracted considerable research attention (particularly in relation to HR strategies) was developed by Miles and Snow (1978). In their framework, firms following a *prospector* strategy generally seek to be first to market with product or service innovations, hoping to capture first-mover advantages in attracting new consumers. In contrast, those following a *defender* strategy tend to stay in the same industry and product lines, continually refining production and marketing processes to lower costs and maintain profits. Somewhere in between are *analyzer* firms, which scan the environment to find new products and processes (often developed by prospectors), which they then attempt to produce more efficiently than the original innovator. (Microsoft is a classic analyzer, having been the original inventor of very few products but doing an excellent job of refining the ideas of others into highly profitable product lines.)

Porter's differentiation and cost leadership strategies have much in common with Miles and Snow's prospector and defender categories. For example, under a cost leadership or defender strategy, firms tend toward centralized decision making, limited and stable product lines, and an emphasis on cost-efficiency through high volume and market penetration. In contrast, prospector or differentiation strategy firms are characterized by broad, changing product lines that require decentralized decision making to facilitate innovation, flexibility, and rapid response to changing conditions. Following this through to HR practices, Olian and Rynes (1984) suggested that prospectors would be more likely than defenders to pursue external hiring at all levels of the organization, less likely than defenders to provide specific functional training, and less likely to use pay policies that emphasized internal hierarchical differentiation.

Gomez-Mejia and Balkin (e.g., Balkin & Gomez-Mejia, 1987, 1990; Gomez-Mejia, 1992; Gomez-Mejia & Balkin, 1989, 1992a) proposed and proceeded to test a typology of two generic pay strategies that they felt were likely to be compatible with defender and prospector strategies, respectively. Specifically, defender firms were hypothesized to use *algorithmic* pay strategies, while prospectors were assumed to use *experiential* ones. As shown in Table 7.1, relative to algorithmic firms,

Table 7.1 Strategic Pay Choices

Algorithmic	*Experiential*
	Basis for Pay
Job	Skills
Membership	Performance
Individual performance	Aggregate performance
Short-term orientation	Long-term orientation
Risk aversion	Risk taking
Corporate performance	Division performance
Internal equity	External equity
Hierarchical	Egalitarian
Qualitative performance measures	Quantitative performance measures
	Design Issues
Salary and benefits above market	Salary and benefits below market, Salary + incentives above market
Emphasis on salary and benefits	Emphasis on incentives
Infrequent rewards	Frequent rewards
Emphasis on intrinsic rewards	Emphasis on extrinsic rewards
	Administrative Framework
Centralized	Decentralized
Pay secrecy	Pay openness
Managers make pay decisions	Employees participate in decisions
Bureaucratic	Flexible

SOURCE: Gomez-Mejia and Balkin (1992a).

experiential strategy firms are expected to have lower base pay (but higher total pay potential) and lower benefits. Experiential firms are also hypothesized to place a stronger emphasis on long-term incentives, risk taking, and decentralized decision making (to permit paying each person based on his or her relevant labor market, as opposed to emphasizing internal consistency across divisions and skill areas). In contrast, given the central importance of coordination and efficiency to defenders and cost leaders as well as their tendency to be located in more mature markets, Gomez-Mejia and Balkin predicted that above-market base pay and benefits and centralized and consistent pay policies would be optimal for defenders.

The empirical literature is mostly supportive of the above contingency hypotheses (e.g., Balkin & Gomez-Mejia, 1987, 1990; Gomez-Mejia, 1992;

Gomez-Mejia & Balkin, 1989, 1992a; Rajagopalan, 1996; for a review, see Gerhart, 2000). Rajagopalan, for example, examined 235 observations over a 5-year period on a sample of 50 investor-owned electric utility firms. Working primarily from an agency theory perspective, he argued that incentive alignment issues and managerial discretion would differ across prospector and defender firms. For example, in a prospector firm, there is greater uncertainty due to the focus on new products and markets. This translates into more managerial discretion (Hambrick & Finkelstein, 1987) and more difficulty in specifying desired managerial behaviors before the fact. Thus, he argued that there would be more emphasis in prospector firms than in defender firms on managerial incentives, especially long-term incentives linked to stock performance, in order to align interests, to promote risk taking, and to encourage a long-term perspective. Rajagopalan found no main effects for pay strategy. However, consistent with the contingency approach, he reported that prospectors had better financial performance in cases where long-term stock plans were emphasized and that defenders did better when they put more relative emphasis on short-term bonus plans. The Rajagopalan study is part of a broader trend to use discretion (and related concepts such as information-processing requirements; Henderson & Fredrickson, 1996) as a central variable in studies of top executive pay (Finkelstein & Boyd, 1998; Magnan & St-Onge, 1997).

To this point, we have talked primarily about the influence of business strategy on pay strategy. However, there is considerable evidence that pay strategy (particularly the pay strategy for executives) also has an effect on organizational and business strategies. For example, Carpenter (2000) showed that changes in executive pay strategies are likely to induce changes in organizational strategy. More generally, Gerhart's (2000) review found that a wide range of strategic decisions appear to be influenced by compensation design, including staffing patterns (Gerhart & Trevor, 1996); diversification (Hitt, Hoskisson, Johnson, & Moesel, 1996; Phan & Hill, 1995); research and development investment (Galbraith & Merrill, 1991; Hill & Snell, 1989); capital investment (Larcker, 1983); and reaction to takeover attempts (Buchholtz & Ribbens, 1994; Kosnik, 1992; Mallette & Fowler, 1992). Likewise, over time, organizational strategy is more likely to change when executive pay strategy changes (Carpenter, 2000). Thus, there is consistent evidence that pay strategy does influence managerial goal choice.

Another developing stream of work on nonexecutives at the business unit level focuses on the alignment between pay strategy and manufacturing strategy (Shaw, Gupta, & Delery, 2002; Snell & Dean, 1994). For example, Shaw et al. (in press) examined the fit between two dimensions of integrated manufacturing—advanced manufacturing technology and total quality management—and pay strategy. They hypothesized that individual incentives and seniority-based pay would reduce the effectiveness of integrated manufacturing, whereas skill-based pay and team incentives would increase its effectiveness. Using the population of member plants of the American Concrete Pipe Association and seven measures of effectiveness (e.g., labor hours per ton, customer satisfaction), they found only limited support for their alignment predictions. Of 56 cross-products, only 13 were statistically significant. These, for the most part, demonstrated support for the impact of individual and team incentives. For example, labor hours per ton were lower (i.e., better) when team incentives were used with a total quality management manufacturing strategy, but higher (i.e., worse) when individual incentives were used with the total quality management strategy.

Horizontal Alignment

A number of authors have made the case that looking at individual HR practices alone may give misleading results because it is not possible to judge the effectiveness of a practice in isolation from the web of interrelated HR practices, employee characteristics, and corporate/business strategies. The argument takes three forms (Gerhart et al., 1996).[3] First, studying only one practice may result in omitted-variable bias, whereby coefficients for the examined practice are confounded with the effects of unexamined ones and thus overestimated (MacDuffie, 1995). For example, a pay program such as gainsharing may be found to have a positive effect on productivity, but part of that effect may in fact be due to other related, but unmeasured, aspects of the HR system, such as employee advisory councils, empowerment, or cross-training.

An alternative argument suggests the opposite possibility. Specifically, if there are synergies to be gained by designing a system of complementary HR practices, then we will *underestimate* the influence of HR as a whole if we simply take the sum of the individual HR practice effects (Doty, Glick, & Huber, 1993; Dyer & Kochan, 1995; Ichniowski, Shaw, & Prennushi, 1993; MacDuffie, 1995). A third variant argues that whether the effect of pay is over- or underestimated

Table 7.2 Employment System Ideal Types

	Market-Type System	*Internal System*
Results-oriented performance appraisals	High	Low
Profit sharing	High	Low
Job descriptions tightly defined	Low	High
Employment security	Low	High
Internal career opportunities & promotion from within	Low	High
Training & firm-specific Socialization	Low	High
Participation in decisions	Low	High

SOURCE: Adapted from Delery and Doty (1996).

depends on whether fit exists with the internal and external contexts. Whatever the situation, the general point is that if a contingency model is indeed correct, then studying only main effects is likely to yield misleading results.

Note that the different conceptual approaches also imply different estimation strategies. The first suggests that contextual factors be treated as controls and their effects partialed out to obtain accurate estimates of the effect of pay. In contrast, the second and third variants suggest that partialing will yield misleading estimates because it is the overall *system*, which is more than the sum of the parts, that matters. Hence, the employment of statistical interactions would be necessary to account for a pay program's total impact (i.e., main effects plus interactions).

One example of how pay strategy dimensions are hypothesized to relate to other dimensions of HR strategy has been provided by Delery and Doty (1996), who, in turn, drew on earlier work by others (Kerr & Slocum, 1987; Osterman, 1987; Sonnefeld & Peiperl, 1988). As Table 7.2 indicates, greater incentive intensity (or risk sharing) is part of the market-type system they define. Relative to internally oriented systems, market-type systems are associated with less opportunity for internal promotion (more hiring is done from the outside), less employment security, lower investment in people, and less employee influence.

Is this an accurate portrayal of the way that pay and other HR policies tend to cluster in organizations? To our knowledge, little empirical data are available to help answer this basic question. With the exception of work by Arthur (1994), who used cluster analysis (see also

Table 7.3 Alignment between Compensation and other Human Resource Policies

Alignment of Compensation With	*Managerial/Professional Employees* *Mean*	*# Negative*	*Hourly Employees* *Mean*	*# Negative*
Training and development	0.5	(5)	0.6	(2)
Performance appraisal	1.4	(3)	0.2	(6)
Recruiting and selection	1.3	(3)	1.0	(3)
Teams and employee involvement	0.8	(3)	0.6	(2)
Mean across rows	1.0		0.6	
Number of respondents	41		34	

SOURCE: Wright, McMahan, Snell, and Gerhart (n.d.).
NOTE: Scale: −3=practices get in the way of one another, 0=practices are unrelated, +3=practices complement one another.

Thompson & Heron, 2002), most other work is either purely conceptual or treats alternative parts of the HR system as additive (e.g., Huselid, 1995). Likewise, there is little evidence on whether practices that tend to occur together *should* go together. As such, greater use of techniques such as cluster analysis would be helpful in our understanding of how HR practices typically covary (or not) in organizations (see also Becker & Gerhart, 1996).

In any event, the modest evidence that exists concerning the degree of actual alignment between pay and other HR strategy dimensions suggests that there is less alignment than one might wish. For example, Table 7.3 shows the results from one small survey of HR executives, who were asked to assess the degree to which pay and other HR practices complemented each other (as opposed to getting in the way of one another). With +3 describing the case where the practices perfectly complement or fit with one another and -3 describing a worst-case scenario of working entirely at cross-purposes, the mean for policies regarding managerial and professional employees was 1.0, and the mean for hourly employees was 0.6. Both are some distance away from the ideal +3 case. Note also that there were a number of negative responses, especially regarding the (mis)alignment of compensation with training and development among managerial/professional employees and the (mis)alignment of compensation with performance appraisal among hourly employees.

Thus, from an effectiveness point of view, there is obviously considerable room for improvement. From a research point of view, however, the bright spot is that there appears to be ample variance in perceived alignment, which suggests that there is probably the necessary variance in alignment to study its importance.

Clearly, there are companies where alignment is much stronger than what was found in the preceding study (Wright et al., n.d.). We have, for example, talked about companies such as Lincoln Electric, SAS, and Southwest Airlines, which seem to have created close alignment between pay and other aspects of HR strategy. In the case of Southwest Airlines, we noted that its employees own a substantial share of company stock. However, that alone is not enough to make a company successful, as we can easily see by looking at another company in the same industry, United Airlines. Despite the fact that United employees own roughly 55% of its shares, that high degree of ownership has not resulted in a more positive employee relations climate or turned United into a more successful airline. (Indeed, United, as well as US Airways, discussed in Chapter 4, were operating under bankruptcy court protection as this book went to press in early 2003.) In contrast, Southwest Airlines has built a more productive relationship with its employees over time because it treats employees as a key business capability. For example, even after the attacks on the Pentagon and the World Trade Center, on September 11, 2001, although most airlines made substantial workforce reductions, Southwest did not.

In summary, empirical research has not squarely addressed the question of how different pay strategies align with other aspects of HR strategy. There is suggestive evidence from case studies of single firms, but little in the way of comprehensive multifirm evidence. As an important and underresearched question, there is ample opportunity for a program of research to make an important contribution.

Internal Alignment Within Pay Strategy

The third and final type of fit that we address is the fit between various subdimensions of pay strategy, or internal alignment. Here, research has been hampered by the absence of a well-validated measure of pay strategy. The main candidate at this point is the typology (and corresponding measure) created by Gomez-Mejia and Balkin (see Table 7.1, described earlier). This model depicts the multiple pay strategy choices as falling cleanly into two possible generic strategies, algorithmic or experiential. As such, it has the clear advantage of parsimony.

Unfortunately, however, there is not a great deal of evidence to support the assumption that the 17 different dimensions load in a simple linear fashion on one factor (Gerhart, 2000; Thompson & Heron, 2001). Although the single-factor hypothesis has not been rejected, the alternative hypothesis—that these dimensions do not necessarily covary together in so simple a fashion—is also plausible. For example, Lincoln Electric has some elements of algorithmic systems (e.g., emphasis on individual and corporate performance) and some elements of experiential systems (e.g., use of quantitative performance measures, emphasis on incentives and extrinsic rewards). Similarly, Southwest Airlines also mixes algorithmic components (e.g., emphasis on intrinsic rewards and corporate performance) with experiential (emphasis on aggregate performance, pay openness, and employee participation in decisions).

Indeed, there may be good reasons for organizations not to design pay strategies that are too single-minded in their focus. In other words, perhaps there can be too much alignment (Gerhart et al., 1996). The evidence reviewed throughout this book demonstrates that pay programs can have powerful effects on behaviors. As such, a major challenge is to avoid the potential problems that can arise from incentives that motivate "too well."

As one example, too much emphasis on individual pay for performance may harm cooperation and teamwork. In this circumstance, one potential solution is to give a major role to individual incentives in the compensation strategy but to temper the potential for negative effects by also having a component of pay that is based on cooperation and teamwork. This can be done by incorporating aspects of teamwork into individual appraisals, as is done at Lincoln Electric and GE. In some sense, the two components can be viewed as being misaligned with one another horizontally, in that the unit-based and individual-based components are encouraging different performance goals. However, the combination of individual and team-based pay for performance may be an effective hedging strategy that balances risks and helps to achieve vertical alignment. Another alternative is to use group performance targets as a minimal threshold before individual incentives can be paid, which is also done at GE. Of course, even these kinds of checks and balances will be ineffective in the face of a culture that encourages "making the numbers" at any cost, such as the one that was apparently in operation at Enron (Raghavan, Kranhold, & Barrionuevo, 2002).

Beyond Generic Strategies: The Resource-Based View of the Firm

The dominant focus in the pay strategy literature has been on the fit between pay strategy and *generic* business strategies. For example, researchers have used Porter's differentiation, cost leadership, and focus strategies or Miles and Snow's prospector, analyzer, and defender categories to derive prescriptive models of how pay and other HR strategies should be designed in order to best support the chosen business strategy (e.g., Olian & Rynes, 1984; Schuler & Jackson, 1987). Although these models move beyond the assumption that all businesses within a particular industry face roughly the same external conditions and resource constraints (and thus require similar strategies), they still tend to assume that organizations using the same business strategy will benefit from using similar compensation and other HR strategies.

By contrast, the resource-based view (RBV) of the firm emphasizes how firms "look inside" for resources that are rare and difficult to imitate and that can be leveraged to build sustained competitive advantage. Industry characteristics and business strategy are still important under the RBV because they place some limits on managerial discretion. However, within these limits, firms are viewed as having considerable discretion in how they compete.

Indeed, the RBV of the firm draws an important distinction between competitive parity and competitive advantage (Barney, 1991; Rumelt, 1984; Wernerfelt, 1984). Parity is achieved by choosing and executing a business strategy comparable to that of competing firms (e.g., those in the same industry). Generic business strategy models are seen as leading to parity with the competition. By contrast, competitive advantage requires that firms be unique by developing and deploying resources in unique ways that add value and are difficult to imitate.

According to RBV, a company's resources include all input factors owned and controlled by the firm that enable it to develop strategies to improve its economic status (Amit & Schoemaker, 1993; Daft, 1983). Barney (1991) classified the critical resources for developing unique competitive advantage as physical capital (Williamson, 1975), human capital (Becker, 1975), and organizational capital (Tomer, 1987). The last of these categories includes controlling and coordinating systems such as compensation and other HR functions, as well as related concepts such as social capital, culture, and organizational knowledge (e.g., Coleman, 1990; Kogut & Zander, 1996; Nooteboom, Berger, & Noorderhaven, 1997; T. Stewart, 1997). To the degree that pay strategy helps a firm to leverage rare and valuable resources in a manner that is difficult to imitate (e.g., by creating a unique and valuable culture), pay strategy should contribute to sustained competitive advantage.

What are the key factors that make it difficult to imitate a firm's internal capabilities? Barney (1999) provides a helpful summary. First, there is a firm's historical context. Creating firm capabilities may depend on being at the right place at the right time. Second, the concept of path dependence suggests that a firm may need to follow a long, difficult learning process to create a capability, because there are no short-cuts; competing firms cannot hope to duplicate such an experience. Third, social complexity refers to the fact that a capability may be difficult to create, even when the actions used successfully by other firms in doing so are visible and understood.

Finally, the sources of a firm's success may not be easily grasped, let alone implemented. This is because the causal relationships between specific actions and eventual success are difficult to discern, particularly when there are many different policies and actions as well as multiple outcomes. In such cases, causal ambiguity is common.[4]

The RBV presents an interesting challenge for conventional pay practice, where benchmarking against what other firms are doing weighs heavily in the way firms set their own pay strategies (e.g., Crystal, 1991; Gerhart et al., 1996; Weber & Rynes, 1991). According to the RBV, merely imitating what other firms do can generate competitive parity but not competitive advantage.

In this sense, the RBV has the potential to give a greater role to HR and pay strategy decisions than is the case with generic strategy frameworks. From a generic strategy framework, the most prominent sources of competitive advantage are believed to include product and process technology, protected markets, access to financial resources, and economies of scale (Porter, 1980). However, these and other sources of competitive advantage have diminished in importance, in part because over time they have become more imitable or easily substituted for by other firms (Pfeffer, 1994). For example, protected markets are declining, economies of scale are diminishing in many industries, and technological advantages are becoming more easily imitated through processes such as reverse engineering. As a result, other sources of competitive advantage—particularly HR systems—are increasingly being recognized as important.

To examine the potential value of incorporating firm-specific (or idiosyncratic) factors, Hansen and Wernerfelt (1989) compared the predictive power of economic (i.e., industry level) factors with organizational models of firm performance and found that organization level factors explained more variance in business performance than did more traditional economic determinants.[5] Using a 5-year average return on assets as the dependent variable, they found that the economic model, which included industry profitability, relative market share, and size (factors relevant to Porter's five forces), accounted for 14% of the variance in firm performance. The organizational model, which measured two aspects of organizational climate—average employee perceptions of emphasis on HR and emphasis on goal accomplishment—explained an additional 32% of the variance in firm performance. These findings suggest, first, that firms similarly positioned within their respective industries can have very different organizational climates and second, that such differences in climate may be important in explaining firm performance differences.

In fact, the "source of value creation" in today's economy has been described as having shifted "from bricks and mortar to brains" (Litan, 2000, p. 15). McKinsey & Company's "War for Talent" study of nearly 6,000 managers also makes the case for the critical role of effective HR practices. Specifically, their study concluded that "talent" will be *the* most important firm resource over the next 20 years: "Talented people, in the right kind of culture, have better ideas, execute those ideas better and even develop other people better" (Fishman, 1998, p. 104). In contrast, traditional sources of competitive advantage do not provide the same edge they once did: "Capital is accessible today for good ideas and good projects. Strategies are transparent: even if you've got a smart strategy, others can simply copy it. And the half-life of technology is growing shorter all the time" (Fishman, 1998, p. 104).

In sum, the RBV of organizational strategy proposes a key role for internal resources that differentiate a firm from other firms within its product market. As such, the task of pay strategy under the RBV is not only to help create value but also to do so in a way that is difficult for the competition to imitate. Both value and inimitability are likely to depend to an important degree on how well aligned the pay strategy is from both vertical and horizontal perspectives (Gerhart et al., 1996). Thus, issues of fit play a key, rather than secondary, role in the RBV.

Pay Strategy and the RBV

Just as the RBV presents challenges to pay strategy *practice*, it also presents challenges to pay strategy *research*. To our knowledge, there has been no systematic research linking RBV concepts of strategy with pay strategy nor any study of the consequences of such linkages. Such research would presumably be designed to show how an HR strategy, including pay strategy, would support the RBV focus on creating value in a manner that is nonsubstitutable and inimitable.[6]

Indeed, it is difficult to envision how conclusive RBV research might be conducted. It seems likely that such work may have to proceed using more of a case study methodology, as opposed to the large-scale, multi-firm, quantitative approach that has been used to study vertical alignment with generic strategies. Or perhaps (multiple) expert raters can be used to evaluate the degree to which pay strategies appear to be aligned with firm objectives and then assess whether subsequent performance is higher in firms where this perceived alignment is stronger.

In the meantime, we are limited to applying RBV concepts to a few well-known case studies of firms that do not appear to follow the types of pay strategies that would be suggested by generic models such as the ones proposed by Balkin and Gomez-Mejia (1987) or Olian and Rynes (1984). For example, in the paragraphs that follow, we use an RBV approach to analyze the case of Lincoln Electric, the subject of one of the Harvard Business School's classic case studies and a company often studied by those with an interest in pay for performance.

Over the years, Lincoln's bonus payouts to employees have averaged between 78% and 129% of base pay. In a 1992 *60 Minutes* video, some production workers were earning $85,000 per year, or about $120,000 in 2001 dollars. This fact alone very likely qualifies its pay strategy as rare.

Lincoln Electric was founded in 1895 by John Lincoln, who was later joined by his brother, James, who played the lead role in developing Lincoln Electric's management philosophy. In 1911, Lincoln developed an early technical edge in welding machines that it has never relinquished. Its competitive strategy was to build quality equipment more efficiently than its competitors, thus enabling it to continuously lower prices. GE and Westinghouse subsequently entered the market but eventually exited, presumably because Lincoln Electric was too strong a competitor. Scientific management principles, including extensive division of labor and the use of incentives, perhaps contributed to Lincoln Electric's early productivity advantage.

However, unlike most advocates of scientific management (who believed that managers should do the thinking while workers do the working), as early as 1914, James Lincoln created an employee advisory board that met semimonthly with the CEO. James Lincoln also believed in competition and "survival of the fittest." He placed his stamp on Lincoln Electric's culture and management system and wrote about his philosophy in books.

While Lincoln's management system retains much of its early character to this day, one can also identify the unique path it took with respect to the learning process that is consistent with the RBV of developing unique competitive advantage. For example, Lincoln did not put its bonus system into place until 1934 and did so at the request of its *employees,* who proposed it as a way of raising wages without putting the company in financial jeopardy. Similarly, the company implemented a guaranteed continuous employment plan (no layoffs, 30-hour-minimum workweek) in 1958.[7] In other words, even Lincoln Electric, with its well-known strong culture, learned as it proceeded and responded with changes to its management approach along the way.

In summary, even though Lincoln Electric is well studied, discussed, and perhaps understood (relative to most companies), it continues to be unique both in terms of its success and in the extent to which it pays for performance. It is also again interesting to note that it does not appear to fit well with the generic model of vertical alignment developed by Gomez-Mejia and Balkin (1992a; see Table 7.1). Specifically, although Lincoln's business strategy is best described as defender, many aspects of its pay system are experiential rather than algorithmic.

For example, with respect to pay basis, Lincoln pay is based on performance rather than membership, on aggregate performance as well as individual performance, and on quantitative measures more than qualitative ones. With respect to pay design, Lincoln's base salary and benefits are *below* rather than above market (although salary plus incentives are *above* market), and there is an emphasis on frequent, extrinsic rewards. Finally, with respect to the administrative framework, pay decisions are open and include employee participation. These "inconsistencies" again raise the possibility that companies may do well to avoid too much alignment between different aspects of pay strategy. For another example of a company, SAS, where pay strategy does not appear to be aligned with business strategy in the way that the literature suggests, see Exhibit 7.2.

Can competitors imitate Lincoln Electric or SAS? In a *60 Minutes* video, Lincoln workers seem to believe that the answer is "no," at least

Exhibit 7.2 SAS as a Successful Example of Prescriptively "Nonaligned" Pay Practices

Like Lincoln Electric, SAS is another example of a company where pay strategy does not appear to be aligned with business strategy in the way that the prescriptive literature would suggest. SAS is in the software industry, where continuous innovation (i.e., prospecting) is crucial. Indeed, SAS has been reported to spend 30% of its revenues on research and development. Thus, SAS appears to be a *prospector* in the Miles and Snow typology or to follow a *differentiation* strategy under the Porter typology. As such, an experiential pay strategy would be expected to be most effective for SAS.

Yet, in contrast to prescriptive typologies, SAS has a conscious strategy of deemphasizing pay. There are no stock options and no major pay-for-performance plans. There are not even commissions for salespeople. In fact, SAS's rewards are mostly linked to *membership* in the form of an extensive benefits package. As noted earlier, SAS's business strategy is built on long-term relationships with its customers, which it also seeks to duplicate on the employee side. Thus, the long-term employment relationship combined with the deemphasis on individual differences in performance are consistent with SAS's goal of building an environment where employees share information freely to foster innovation, rather than closely holding information to "out-compete" other employees in the reward process. This produces a result similar to the virtuous cycle mentioned in the opening paragraphs of this chapter, although in this case, it appears to be accomplished primarily through membership and lifestyle benefits rather than opportunities to increase direct pay.

for existing organizations with an already established culture. Their view is consistent with our preceding analysis, which shows that the culture at Lincoln Electric has emerged from strong founding values and a well-entrenched process of learning and improvement over time, a path-dependent course that would probably be difficult to recreate.

In addition, it is difficult to imagine other organizations duplicating Lincoln's achievement of having established more than 70,000 piece rates over its history yet somehow managing to avoid the type of burdensome negotiation and renegotiation of piece rates that can easily cause such large and complex systems to fail. Indeed, Wiley (1993) reports that Lincoln Electric workers challenge fewer than one fifth of 1% of all piece work changes! Certainly, the stable nature of its technology and product markets is likely to be helpful in maintaining the piece rate system. Nevertheless, there also appears to be something much deeper that is difficult to explain and that raises social complexity, causal ambiguity, and implementation issues for any organization that would like to duplicate its success.

More generally, however, whether or not a competitor can imitate another company probably depends on what we mean by *imitate.* Specifically, consistent with Pfeffer (1994), Becker and Gerhart (1996) proposed that the seeming dilemma between a best practice and a firm-specific point of view is that there may be best practices at broad conceptual levels (what they termed the "organizational architecture"), but *differentiation* with respect to design and implementation of these practices at the firm level. For example, they suggested that pay for performance appears to be a general best practice but that it might be most effectively operationalized in the form of individual incentives at one firm (e.g., Lincoln Electric), but stock options (e.g., Microsoft) or profit sharing (e.g., Southwest Airlines) at another. Thus, a firm could imitate Lincoln Electric at a very general level but differ greatly at the more concrete level of implementation.

In addition, imitation may be easier in some areas than in others. For example, firms operating in similar product and labor markets may find that it is a straightforward matter to imitate (or stay in-line) with competitors with respect to pay level via the use of widely used pay surveys. Moreover, they may also find that it is generally efficient as well. As we noted earlier, paying too much for labor makes it difficult to compete in product markets because, all else being equal, higher labor costs raise product prices. Paying too little, by contrast, risks not being able to attract and retain talent, which is increasingly seen as the key to competitive advantage as the economy becomes more knowledge based. Therefore, it is not always necessarily good to be unique. In some aspects of pay strategy, perhaps it makes sense to be like everyone else.

However, even in making decisions about how *much* to pay, there may be strategic reasons that argue in favor of being somewhat unique. If so, then pressures to be consistent with other firms must be balanced against the need to tailor pay strategy to the strategy of the firm (Carpenter, Sanders, & Gregersen, 2001; Carpenter & Wade, 2002; Pfeffer & Davis-Blake, 1987). The Pfeffer and Davis-Blake (1987) study we discussed earlier, for example, suggested that organizations within a particular industry (higher education, in their study) may choose to deviate from market rates in selected cases to recognize that certain occupations may be more critical to strategy execution than others. In other cases (such as Southwest Airlines or SAS), firms may deviate substantially from industry practice across most or all occupations.

When it comes to *how* an organization pays (e.g., its use of incentives), imitation may be both more difficult and more risky. For example, an organization that wishes to pay on the basis of group, unit, or firm performance must deal with agency costs. Agency theory tells us that agents are risk averse and that to shift risk to employees, higher pay (a compensating differential) is needed. Employee relations problems with such plans are not uncommon (e.g., Slichter et al., 1960), and many individual incentive plans have been abandoned because of high administrative costs (see Chapter 6). In addition, information asymmetries mean that it is all too easy to design pay plans that overpay or that unduly focus the attention of agents on certain aspects of performance at the expense of others, sometimes causing great problems for the organization (see Chapter 6).

Still, organizations appear to have greater flexibility with respect to how they pay than how much they pay. Moreover, although following a unique strategy with respect to the basis for pay may be risky, the returns may also be correspondingly higher (Gerhart et al., 1996; Gerhart & Milkovich, 1990). Thus, a well-designed and well-executed pay-for-performance plan may be sufficiently rare (and valuable) to meet the RBV test. Taking it a step further, such plans may be all the more rare, valuable, and difficult to imitate when they are well aligned with other key organizational characteristics, including culture and business strategy. Thus, at least conceptually, synergies have the potential both to create value beyond that generated by lone HRM programs (e.g., pay) and to do so in a way that is not easily imitated by competitors (Gerhart et al., 1996).

Beyond Direct Earnings: Total Rewards

Finally, it is important in discussing pay strategy to recognize that although pecuniary rewards continue to receive the lion's share of attention in the pay research literature (and in this book), pay is not all that matters in thinking about how to use rewards to motivate people. Earlier in our book (Chapter 5), we noted that a number of prominent psychologists (e.g., Deci & Ryan, Maslow, Herzberg) have, in fact, accorded a secondary status to money as a motivator, focusing instead on factors that are deemed relevant to so-called higher-order needs. Although we see little evidence to support the notion that money is of secondary importance as a motivator, there is nevertheless ample evidence that money is not the only reward that motivates.

In addition to nonpecuniary rewards, a total-compensation perspective must also recognize the importance of benefits programs such as retirement, health care, and vacation plans. As noted earlier, these and other benefits programs account for roughly 27% of total compensation among larger employers. Historically, these types of compensation have been most strongly linked to organizational membership (i.e., attraction and retention), and there is solid evidence that certain benefits (e.g., defined-benefit retirement plans) are associated with substantially lower turnover rates (Gustman, Mitchell, & Steinmeir, 1994; Ippolito, 1987; Mitchell, 1982; for a partial review, see Broderick & Gerhart, 1997). In the now familiar case of the SAS Institute, we have noted that SAS has an extensive package of benefits. Perhaps not coincidentally, SAS also has an annual turnover rate in recent years of approximately 4%, a rate that appears to be much lower than that in the software industry generally. This means not only that SAS saves a considerable amount of money on turnover costs but also that its long-service employees are well positioned to help SAS carry out its "loyalty" business strategy of building long-term customer relationships.

Nevertheless, conventional wisdom is that most benefits are not linked to (and thus do not influence in any meaningful way) company performance. For example, the benefits employees receive under a traditional defined-benefit retirement plan (or under a typical health care plan) do not ordinarily depend on the company's stock price or profitability. However, some companies use defined-contribution plans to link retirement benefits to firm performance by basing contributions to retirement plans on company profits or by making contributions in the form of company stock.

One advantage of taking a broader total-rewards perspective is that it may better capture the range of observed differences between firms in compensation strategy. We have already noted that many firms differ quite substantially (e.g., in their emphasis on cash in compensation; for example, Microsoft versus SAS). More broadly, the recent McKinsey

"War for Talent" study (Fishman, 1998; Michaels, Handfield-Jones, & Axelrod, 2001) suggested that there are four general types of successful HR strategies. "Go with a Winner" is for people who want a high-performing company where they will get lots of advancement opportunities (e.g., Microsoft). "Big Risk, Big Reward" is for people who want an environment where they are challenged either to do exceptionally well (for high compensation) or to leave (e.g., McKinsey). "Save the World" can be used to attract people who want a company with an inspiring mission and an exciting challenge but generally not high pay levels or high pay for performance (e.g., not-for-profit organizations). "Lifestyles" is for people seeking companies that offer them more flexibility and better lifestyle benefits, such as child care, a good location, or flexible or limited work hours (e.g., SAS).

In summary, many factors contribute to a job's attractiveness (or its total compensation, broadly defined). We have also noted previously that individual differences in values, preferences, personality, and ability play a role in determining how people respond to job attributes, including compensation. The role of these individual difference factors is highlighted in overarching models of organizational composition, such as Schneider's (1987) attraction-selection-attrition framework. Individual differences are also central to various sorting models from the economics literature, although considerably less attention is given to the precise nature of relevant individual differences.

Summary and Future Research

We began this chapter by arguing that pay strategy can have a major influence on both organizational strategy formulation and strategy execution. Ample evidence reviewed briefly here and in more detail elsewhere (Gerhart, 2000) provides strong support for this argument. We also noted that in both the organizational strategy and pay strategy literatures, there has been an important shift in focus away from industry characteristics as the primary driver of firm actions to a view that incorporates both industry and firm level characteristics. On the organizational strategy side, the RBV of the firm has emphasized the importance of heterogeneity of firms' resources and demonstrated that such resources (e.g., HR and pay strategy, culture) are not necessarily tradable. On the pay strategy side, there has likewise been a focus on how firms differentiate themselves, especially in terms of how they pay (pay basis).

Despite the progress made on these fronts, three pertinent research questions remain almost completely unexamined at this juncture. First, what role does pay strategy play in increasing the effectiveness of the strategy process, especially the execution phase? We have seen some work on the vertical-alignment dimension of this issue, but little on the horizontal-alignment dimension. For example, which pay and staffing strategies tend to go together? Which pay and staffing strategies *should* go together? How does pay strategy contribute to an organization's ability to capitalize on its rare and inimitable resources? Second, the study of these types of questions rests on the assumption that pay strategy can be measured with validity. There has been some initial work done on this front (e.g., Gomez-Mejia & Balkin, 1992a), but it strikes us that more attention needs to be given to the dimensionality of such measures as well as to the question of whether different dimensions of pay strategy combine in an additive or multiplicative fashion. In addition, any research that measures key constructs via self-reports would do well to avoid single-rater designs, which have been shown to introduce unacceptable levels of measurement error (Gerhart, Wright, McMahan, & Snell, 2000).

Third, our confidence in the interpretation of observed relationships between pay strategy and outcomes such as business performance rests not only on the construct validity of pay strategy (and business strategy) measures but also on our ability to flesh out the intervening variables that link pay and business strategies to organizational outcomes (Gerhart, 2000). As is true more generally of the literature on HR practices and business performance (Becker & Gerhart, 1996), there is essentially no research to show that pay strategy influences business performance by changing employee perceptions or behaviors. Until such intervening processes are documented, we will have less confidence than we would like in the observed relationships between organizational strategy, pay strategy, HR strategy, and business performance. This, in turn, limits our ability to confidently draw policy implications for organizations.

Finally, we close by emphasizing that the issues raised above need to be addressed at both the executive and nonexecutive levels. Too often, pay strategy research is operationalized as research on the determinants and consequences of how the top five executives in the firm are paid. Although top executives are important, as recognized by the upper echelons framework (Hambrick & Mason, 1984) and indicated by the extensive attention devoted to top executive compensation in both the research literature and popular press, the success of an organization hinges on the contributions of all members. Therefore, additional research that attempts to examine the consequences of pay policies at all levels would be most useful.

Notes

1. There are also a variety of broader market or environmental factors—beyond corporate strategy—that may influence compensation strategy and firm outcomes, such as technology, unionization, or the regulatory environment. However, we do not discuss these factors in any detail here.

2. In Chapter 2, we discussed how the field of economics has slowly moved from an emphasis solely on market factors (and a belief in the "law of one price") to a recognition of the importance of organizational differences both across and within industries (e.g., Boyer & Smith, 2001). A somewhat similar evolution has occurred in the field of strategy. Although early case-based research suggested that managerial actions and decisions could have important effects on organizational performance (e.g., Chandler, 1962), this view was overshadowed for several decades by the structure-conduct-performance paradigm (also known as the Bain/Mason paradigm; Bain, 1956, 1968; Mason, 1939), which viewed firm performance primarily as a function of the industry in which the firm chose to compete, a theme also reflected in Porter's five forces framework (Hoskisson et al., 1999). However, in recent years, strategy researchers have increasingly talked about "looking inside" for sources of competitive advantage (e.g., Prahalad & Hamel, 1990), as discussed later in this chapter, under the resource-based view of the firm (Barney, 1991; Rumelt, 1984; Wernerfelt, 1984).

3. This section draws freely on Gerhart, Trevor, and Graham (1996).

4. It is often hard to comprehend the dynamics of a particular company and how it operates because the way people are managed often fits together in a system. It is easy to copy one thing but much more difficult to copy numerous things. This is because the change needs to be more comprehensive and also because the ability to understand the system of management practices is hindered by its very extensiveness. (Pfeffer, 1994, p. 15)

Clearly, if such attributes cannot be observed and described, it will be difficult to imitate them. Itami (1987) uses the concept of "invisible assets" to characterize the unspoken or tacit capabilities that enable firms to accomplish their goals. Barney (1999) illustrates these points using the "visionary" firms described by Collins and Poras in their 1994 book, *Built to Last.* Although these firms share core elements, such as their commitment to employees, customers, and suppliers, it is one thing to understand how these elements contribute to the success of these firms and quite another to design a strategy that successfully executes plans in these areas with the same degree of success. Thus, firms that effectively develop these invisible assets are likely to have an enduring advantage over their competition. HR strategy, including pay strategy, can play a central role in creating this difficult-to-imitate advantage.

5. Several empirical studies have sought to estimate the relative influence of industry and firm characteristics on firm performance. As noted previously, Schmalensee (1985) reported that industry was the dominant determinant of firm performance. Later research, in contrast, found that firm effects were larger than industry effects (Hawawini, Subramanian, & Verdin, 2003; Mauri & Michaels, 1998; Rumelt, 1991). Of interest, however, is that Mauri and Michaels (1998) found strategy-related variables, such as research and development (R&D) intensity and advertising intensity, to be better explained by industry than by firm. Therefore, they suggested that "Firm-level proxies like R&D and advertising expenditures do not capture idiosyncratic resources that provide competitive advantage" (p. 217). This would seem to reinforce the need to "look inside

firms" for competitive advantage, even if data on the relevant attributes, such as HR strategy (e.g., Barney & Wright, 1998), pay strategy, climate, and culture (e.g., Barney, 1986), are more difficult to collect than publicly available data (e.g., R&D expenditures and so forth).

6. Although we do not know of any study showing that adopted pay strategies are difficult to imitate and substitute, there is one study (Collins, Hatcher, & Ross, 1993) showing that executives were more likely to adopt gainsharing plans when they felt that gainsharing was likely to be compatible with the existing organizational culture (e.g., high employee participation, positive labor relations).

7. Although several other well-known companies (e.g., IBM, Xerox, Kodak) also adopted employment security policies, nearly all deemed it necessary to retract them as business conditions declined during the 1980s. Lincoln Electric, however, has kept its guarantee in place.

8 Toward the Future

Several broad goals have guided the development of this book. First, we sought to summarize the current status of theory and research on compensation and its effects on individuals and organizations. While doing so, our second goal was to integrate developments from multiple disciplines in the hope of directing researchers to relevant work in areas other than their own. To that end, we have drawn from psychology, economics, management, and to a lesser degree, sociology. Our third goal has been to use the current status of research and theory as a departure point for suggesting the most likely ways of advancing the field through future research.

We began our book by raising a number of key questions that guided us in our examination of pay practices and effects. How important is money as a motivator? Is it better to have high pay differentials across and within job categories, or egalitarian pay throughout? Does paying higher wages lead to more productive workforces? Are there general "best practices" in compensation, or do appropriate compensation practices depend on a variety of contextual conditions?

Our analysis suggests that the answers to these questions are often ambiguous but that we are closer to answers in some areas than others. For example, with respect to the question of the importance of pay, theory and evidence leave little doubt that pay is, in fact, a very important motivator. To say that money does not motivate or that it is of secondary importance as a motivator (as some prominent people continue to argue; e.g., Pfeffer, 1998a, 1998b) is to ignore a vast amount of compelling evidence to the contrary. Indeed, we have noted that one problem with monetary incentives is that they can motivate "too well" in some cases, particularly where highly contingent rewards are involved. Thus, the real challenge is to design pay practices so that key goals (e.g., profits, stock price) are achieved but not at the expense of legal compliance and other important goals (customer satisfaction or employee morale).

Similarly, the evidence now seems conclusive that the use of extrinsic rewards does *not,* on average, decrease intrinsic motivation. Evidence against the "antagonistic" effects of extrinsic and intrinsic rewards is particularly strong in the context of real, ongoing work organizations, as opposed to laboratory experiments with child subjects (Eisenberger & Cameron, 1996). For example, Fang and Gerhart (2002) found *higher* intrinsic motivation among employees covered by pay-for-performance plans, as well as *lower* feelings of being "externally controlled" by managers (one of the hypothesized "demotivators" of pay-for-performance schemes; Deci & Ryan, 1985). More generally, research suggests that the two types of motivation are essentially independent of one another (Amabile, Hill, Hennessey, & Tighe, 1994). Nevertheless, strong claims to the contrary continue to receive coverage in prestigious, widely read (although not peer-reviewed) outlets (e.g., Kohn, 1993; Pfeffer, 1998b). As such, our analysis lends credibility to Steers's (2001) contention that "Motivation theories that were discredited long ago still permeate current textbooks" (p. 686), not to mention popular trade books and journals.

Similarly, our review of the evidence related to pay dispersion raises serious questions about previous interpretations of the effects of within-group pay dispersion on group performance. Specifically, previous authors (e.g., Bloom, 1999; Pfeffer & Langton, 1993) have argued that within-job group pay dispersion is associated with lower group performance. However, reinterpretation of their data suggests that dispersion due to differential performance is *positively* associated with group performance, although dispersion that is *not* related to performance (e.g., due to favoritism or error) is negatively related. Still, at this point in time, not enough studies have been done to firmly settle this particular issue, so future research (with appropriate distinctions between performance-based and other sources of pay dispersion) is still warranted. Similarly, the question of whether higher or lower pay differentials *across* job levels are more effective has received surprisingly little attention.

In sum, although we have been able to reach relatively well-supported conclusions in some areas (e.g., pay importance), very important questions remain seriously underexplored (effects of pay structure) or have produced ambiguous findings (e.g., pay strategy). Thus, there are many opportunities for future compensation researchers to make important contributions to knowledge. In each of the preceding chapters, we have made suggestions concerning the types of research that might prove useful. Here, we focus on a few broad areas that we consider most essential for making further progress (see Table 8.1).

Table 8.1 Major Categories of Future Research Needs

Additional research on the effects of pay dispersion (both performance based and non–performance based), within and across organizational levels
Greater attention to *sorting* or *selection effects* of compensation, on the *types* of individuals attracted and retained (e.g., ability, competencies, values)
Research on *intervening processes* between pay policies and organizational outcomes (e.g., sorting and motivational effects)
Pay strategy: Tensions between fit and differentiation
Attraction, retention, and motivational effects of *total compensation:* simultaneous consideration of direct pay, benefits, nonmonetary rewards, and sanctions

Future Research

One of the most important priorities for future research is to learn much more about the attitudinal and, especially, behavioral implications of differing types and degrees of pay differentiation, both within and across job levels. At present, we have a much clearer understanding of the effects of pay levels and pay contingencies than of relative pay and pay comparisons. Yet we have known for a long time that the motivational effects of pay operate in nontrivial ways through comparative processes (Adams, 1963; Frank, 1985).

As we move ahead with research on pay differentiation, we believe it is very important to measure both process and outcome variables in the same study. This is because perceptions of fairness (and hence potential motivation) contain both procedural and distributive elements that may operate rather independently of one another. For example, employees might be perfectly content with a pay system in which a chief executive officer (say, Microsoft CEO Bill Gates) earns far more than they do, because the *procedures* for determining pay are basically the same for everyone. That is, as Microsoft's stock price rises, so does the compensation of all employees, although more so at top levels. This is in clear contrast to procedurally unjust systems such as Enron's, where executives were presumably allowed to unload stock on the basis of inside information, while other employees were prohibited from doing so. We suspect that differences in pay *amounts* across levels are much more readily accepted when everyone in an organization is playing by roughly the same (procedural) rules than when they are not.

In addition, as our earlier analysis indicates, it is crucial to determine the *bases* on which pay distinctions are made, particularly the extent to which they are due to differences in performance versus differences in other factors (e.g., seniority or favoritism). Consistent with previous theorizing in both economics (Milgrom & Roberts, 1992) and psychology (Vroom, 1964), we tentatively propose that (a) pay differentiations will be more motivational to the extent that differences in performance are clearly detectable and measurable and (b) observed pay differentiations are correlated with those differences. Conversely, to the extent that performance differences are obvious, measurable, and *unrewarded,* demotivation or turnover is likely to be observed among the group where it hurts the most, that is, in high-performing individuals (Trevor, Gerhart, & Boudreau, 1997).

A second research need is to pay much more attention to the *sorting* or *selection* effects of different compensation practices. To date, by far the most attention has been paid to the *incentive* effects of various pay practices. However, the limited available evidence suggests that the sorting effects may be every bit as important (e.g., Lazear, 1999). Fortunately, the resurgence of interest in personality and other individual differences in psychology has begun to make a small dent in psychological research on the effects of different pay systems. Specifically, the applied psychology literature has begun to recognize both the sorting effects of individual differences (Bretz, Ash, & Dreher, 1989; Cable & Judge, 1994; Harrison, Virick, & William, 1996; Trevor et al., 1997) as well as their role in moderating incentive effects (G. Stewart, 1996).

For the most part, the same cannot be said of the economics literature, however. To the extent that sorting is addressed by economists, the focus is typically only on ability, which is almost always inferred or assessed via proxies rather than directly measured. Having said that, Lazear's 1999 study (in which he shows the sizable impact of changes in pay-for-performance systems on performance-related employee turnover) makes a substantial contribution to the literature in providing one of the clearest demonstrations for the importance of measuring not just *how many* people join or leave, but *what kinds.*

Third, like others before us (e.g., Becker & Gerhart, 1996), we suggest additional research on the *intervening processes* between pay policies and organizational outcomes. Although there is a fair amount of psychological research addressing mediating effects at the individual level of analysis (see Chapter 5), attention to mediating processes is far less common at the group and organizational levels of analysis. Because observed relationships between pay and performance outcomes vary across studies, without measuring intervening variables, it is difficult to identify characteristics of either the pay design or context that contribute to such variance. Similarly, not being able to document intervening processes makes it difficult to have much faith in any single causal interpretation of observed relationships which, in turn, makes it difficult to develop confident policy recommendations.

The paucity of mediating process models at the organizational level of analysis is almost certainly due to the difficulties of getting such intensive data from multiple organizations. However, many of the most important questions about compensation cannot be resolved without such multilevel data. As such, we encourage researchers to ally themselves with organizations that have access to the necessary types of data, such as consulting firms (e.g., see Fulmer, Gerhart, & Scott, 2002; Harter, Schmidt, & Hayes, 2002) or professional associations such as World at Work (American Compensation Association).

A fourth challenge concerns research on pay strategy. In particular, there is a need to reconcile the traditional emphasis of compensation practice on benchmarking (e.g., salary surveys) and best practices, both of which are forms of "looking outside," with the resource-based view's emphasis on capitalizing on internal resources ("looking inside") to become different from others as a means of achieving competitive advantage. This same tension between *fit* and *differentiation* appears in the broader strategy literature, where pressures both to conform (to achieve legitimacy) and to be different (which can reduce competition and provide unique comparative advantage) have been examined in recent research (e.g., Deephouse, 1999).

At present, most organizations' compensation practices appear to mimic those of other organizations, particularly those that are believed to be part of their "competitor" group (Crystal, 1991). However, recent evidence is at least suggestive that firms might achieve greater competitive advantage by being "as different as legitimately possible" (e.g., Deephouse, 1999) or employing a "rare human capital structure" (Sherer, 1995; see also Cappelli & Crocker-Hefter, 1996). Case examples of the deeply embedded and integrated human resource practices of such firms have been provided throughout this book (e.g., Lincoln Electric, Southwest Airlines, Springfield Remanufacturing Company).

A final challenge, also noted by others before us (e.g., Gerhart & Milkovich, 1992), is to improve the conceptualization and measurement of total compensation by more effectively integrating both benefits and nonmonetary aspects of reward systems. Although we have shown that pay is undoubtedly a central motivator, it is clear that many

Table 8.2 Needed Methodological Enhancements

Improved construct validity and operationalization of measures (essential for avoiding misleading conclusions)
Increased use of multilevel designs (especially helpful for studying processes and mediating variables)
Increased use of multisource, multimethod data sets (increased reliability, validity, and generalizability)
Increased attention to effect sizes and practical significance of findings
Longitudinal research needed to reduce selection biases (due to censoring of unsuccessful programs and organizations) and to illuminate underlying processes

other factors influence motivation, as well as performance, attraction, retention, and effectiveness. What is needed is a more refined understanding, from an organization's point of view, of the most efficient investment of total resources in making organizational membership both attractive and motivating to the types of people it needs. Field experiments appear to present particularly promising opportunities in this regard, as would alliances with compensation consulting firms or research consortia such as the Mayflower Group.

Methodological Recommendations

In addition to the substantive areas mentioned above, there is also a need for improvements on the methodological front. Here, we make five recommendations that we believe apply to many of the substantive areas discussed in this book (see Table 8.2). First, we recommend *improved construct validity* in investigations of pay-outcome relationships. Although construct validity is an important consideration in any research area (Schwab, 1980a), we believe that failure to attend to basic construct validity issues may have caused serious misinterpretations of data in several areas of compensation research.

For example, in the case of merit pay, construct validity principles require that to study its effectiveness, one must first establish the extent to which merit pay is actually practiced and not just "claimed" on paper (Chapter 6). Similarly, if one wishes to study the impact of pay dispersion on organizational or work unit effectiveness, one must take care to distinguish between dispersion that is due to performance differences and dispersion that is not (Chapter 4). Although we raise these points as methodological concerns, we are really talking about a broader process of developing careful and well-reasoned *theory* about the nature of the construct, followed by the development of measures that truly reflect the underlying theory. As we have seen, unless constructs are clearly defined and measured in ways commensurate with the theory, interpretation of findings can be inaccurate or even seriously misleading.

A second change that will be required in order to more fully unlock the mysteries of compensation is the more frequent application of multi-level designs. For example, to explore the attitudinal links between pay strategy and organizational performance, pay strategy and performance must be measured at the organizational level, and employee attitudes measured at the individual level. Thus, appropriate statistical tools are needed for combining these different levels of data. Fortunately, there has been considerable progress in this arena, so much so that Shadish (2002) has proclaimed, "The unit of analysis problem is dead: Long live multi-level modeling!" (p. 7). Statistical models (complete with software) such as hierarchical linear modeling (HLM; Raudenbush & Bryk, 2002) are now available for such situations.

A related issue is the need to obtain *multisource data* whenever possible. One reason is that single-source data often suffer from common-method variance, which generally works to considerably inflate observed relationships (Doty & Glick, 1998). A second problem is that different individuals in the same organization often have differing views of the extent to which various policies (e.g., merit pay) are actually in operation, as well as their effectiveness (e.g., Gerhart, Wright, McMahan, & Snell, 2000; H. Heneman, Huett, Lavigna, & Ogsten, 1995). As such, data from a single subject may be neither reliable nor valid as a representation of a particular phenomenon. A third problem is that single-source data, for example, on employee perceptions of pay for performance, do not tell us how these perceptions relate to pay policies such as merit pay, gainsharing, and so forth, which organizations hope to use to influence these perceptions.

Whatever the design or statistical analyses used, we would also like to see researchers devote more attention to interpreting the *practical significance* of their results. In compensation literature (as in others), one too often finds researchers interpreting their results solely by looking at statistical significance levels. However, we seldom are interested only in whether or not an effect is different from zero, particularly given that the assumptions underlying significance testing are rarely met in practice anyway (Schmidt, 1996). Instead, as we have attempted to do in this book, one must look at the magnitude of effect sizes in a way that sheds light on practical significance. If, for example, the dependent variable has a natural metric, such as dollars or unit labor costs, then interpretation of results should include the predicted value of the dependent variable (e.g., in dollar terms) at different levels of the independent variables (e.g., ±1 standard deviation).

A final methodological plea is to increase the use of *longitudinal designs* in pay research. This would be helpful in at least two ways. First, cross-sectional research on pay outcomes has the potential for severe selection bias, since such studies typically observe only the organizations and pay programs that have survived (Gerhart, Trevor, & Graham, 1996). By omitting unsuccessful programs or organizations, research is likely to overestimate the average returns to existing pay programs. For example, if cross-sectional research shows an average return of 20% to a particular pay program, but approximately half of all such programs are started and then abandoned, the average expected return may be significantly lower than 20% (or even negative). Selection bias due to elimination of poor performers is also associated with restriction of range, which makes it more difficult to detect true causes or correlates of success.

Second, longitudinal research can often be very helpful in determining the underlying causes of pay program effects. For example, Wagner, Rubin, and Callahan (1988) were able to rule out an initial burst of enthusiasm as the cause of productivity increases under the group incentive program discussed in Chapter 6, because productivity continued to increase steadily for 83 months following implementation. As such, the authors concluded that employees were continuing to learn more effective ways of working throughout the entire time period. Similarly, by following the implementation of a piece rate incentive over a 12-month period, Lazear (1999) was able to decompose the 44% overall productivity increase into the portion due to sorting (i.e., increased quits by low-performing employees and reduced quits by high performers) versus the portion due to incentive effects (increases in output among those who stayed throughout the entire period). For these reasons, longitudinal research that tracks the initiation and survival of programs would be very helpful for eliminating selection bias, decreasing range restriction, and improved understanding of underlying processes.

In summary, our book has reviewed theory and evidence on the link between pay decisions and effectiveness. There are many claims and counterclaims regarding the consequences of pay programs and strategies in organizations. We have sought to address these issues in a systematic and research-based manner. Much is known about the likely consequences of different pay strategies and the risks and opportunities associated with each. Of course, much remains to be done. We hope that our book will prove useful in inspiring and guiding these future research efforts.

References

Abelson, R. (2001, March 19). Companies turn to grades, and employees go to court. *The New York Times,* p. A1.

Abowd, J. M. (1989). The effect of wage bargains on the stock market value of the firm. *The American Economic Review, 79,* 774–800.

Abowd, J. M. (1990). Does performance-based managerial compensation affect corporate performance? *Industrial and Labor Relations Review, 43,* 52S-73S.

Adams, J. S. (1963). Toward an understanding of inequity. *Journal of Abnormal Psychology, 67,* 422–436.

Adams, J. S. (1965). Inequity in social exchange. In L. Berkowitz (Ed.), *Advances in experimental social psychology.* New York: Academic Press.

Aggarwal, R. K., & Samwick, A. A. (1999). The other side of the trade-off: The impact of risk on executive compensation. *Journal of Political Economy, 107,* 65–105.

Agrawal, A., & Mandelker, G. N. (1987). Managerial incentives and corporate investment and financing decisions. *Journal of Finance, 42,* 823–837.

Akerlof, G. A. (1984). Gift exchange and efficiency-wage theory: Four views. *American Economic Review, 74,* 79–83.

Albanese, R., & Van Fleet, D. D. (1985). Rational behavior in groups: The free-riding tendency. *Academy of Management Review, 10,* 244–255.

Alchian, A. A., & Demsetz, H. (1972). Production, information costs, and economic operations. *American Economic Review, 62,* 777–795.

Allen, N. J., & Meyer, J. P. (1990). The measurement and antecedents of affective, continuance, and normative commitment to the organization. *Journal of Occupational Psychology, 63,* 1–18.

Althauser, R. P., &. Kalleberg, A. L. (1981). Firms, occupations, and the structure of labor markets: A conceptual analysis. In Ivar Berg (Ed.), *Sociological perspectives on labor markets* (pp. 119–149). New York: Academic Press.

Amabile, T. M., Hill, K. G., Hennessey, B. A., & Tighe, E. M. (1994). The work preference inventory: Assessing intrinsic and extrinsic motivational orientations. *Journal of Applied Psychology, 66,* 950–967.

Ambrose, M. L., & Kulik, C. T. (1999). Old friends, new faces: Motivation research in the 1990s. *Journal of Management, 25,* 231–292.

Amit, R., & Schoemaker, P. J. (1993). Strategic assets and organizational rent. *Strategic Management Journal, 14,* 33–46.

Anderson, E., & Oliver, R. L. (1987). Perspectives on behavior-based versus outcome-based salesforce control systems. *Journal of Marketing, 51,* 76–88.

Antle, R., & Smith, A. (1986). An empirical investigation of the relative performance evaluation of corporate executives. *Journal of Accounting Research, 24,* 1–39.

Appelbaum, E., Bailey, T., Berg, P., & Kalleberg, A. L. (2000). *Manufacturing advantage: Why high-performance work systems pay off.* Ithaca, NY: Cornell University Press.

Argyres, N., & McGahan, A. M. (2002). An interview with Michael Porter. *Academy of Management Executive, 16*(2), 43–52.

Arthur, J. B. (1994). Effects of human resource systems on manufacturing performance and turnover. *Academy of Management Journal, 37,* 670–687.

Arthur, J. B., & Aiman-Smith, L. (2001). Gainsharing and organizational learning: An analysis of employee suggestions over time. *Academy of Management Journal, 44,* 737–754.

Arthur, J. B., & Jelf, G. S. (1999). The effects of gainsharing on grievance rates and absenteeism over time. *Journal of Labor Research, 20,* 133–145.

Asch, P., & Quandt, R. (1988). Betting bias in exotic bets. *Economic Letters, 28,* 215–219.

Bain, J. S. (1956). *Barriers to new competition.* Cambridge: Harvard University Press.

Bain, J. S. (1968). *Industrial organization* (2nd ed.). New York: Wiley.

Baird, L., & Meshoulam, I. (1988). Managing two fits of strategic human resource management. *Academy of Management Review, 13,* 116–128.

Baker, G., Gibbs, M., & Holmstrom, B. (1994a). The internal economics of the firm: Evidence from personnel data. *Quarterly Journal of Economics,* 881–919.

Baker, G., Gibbs, M., & Holmstrom, B. (1994b). The wage policy of a firm. *Quarterly Journal of Economics,* 921–955.

Baker, G. P. (1992). Incentive contracts and performance measurement. *Journal of Political Economy, 100,* 598–614.

Balkin, D. B., & Gomez-Mejia, L. R. (1987). Toward a contingent theory of compensation strategy. *Strategic Management Journal, 8,* 169–182.

Balkin, D. B., & Gomez-Mejia, L. R. (1990). Matching compensation and organizational strategies. *Strategic Management Journal, 11,* 153–169.

Bandura, A. (1986). *Social foundations of thought and action: A social cognitive view.* Upper Saddle River, NJ: Prentice Hall.

Banker, R. D., Lee, S-Y., Potter, G., & Srinivasan, D. (1996). Contextual analysis of performance impacts of outcome-based incentive compensation. *Academy of Management Journal, 39,* 920–948.

Barber, A. E. (1998). *Recruiting employees: Individual and organizational perspectives.* Thousand Oaks, CA: Sage.

Barber, A. E., & Bretz, R. D. Jr. (2000). Compensation, attraction and retention. In S. L. Rynes & B. Gerhart (Eds.), *Compensation in organizations* (pp. 32–60). San Francisco: Jossey-Bass.

Barber, A. E., & Roehling, M. V. (1993). Job postings and the decision to interview: A verbal protocol analysis. *Journal of Applied Psychology,* 845–856.

Barnard, C. I. (1951). *The functions of the executive.* Cambridge, MA: Harvard University Press.

Barney, J. B. (1986). Organizational culture: Can it be a source of sustained competitive advantage? *Academy of Management Review, 11,* 656–665.

Barney, J. B. (1991). Firm resources and sustained competitive advantage. *Journal of Management, 17,* 99–120.

Barney, J. B. (1997). *Gaining and sustaining competitive advantage.* Reading, MA: Addison-Wesley.

Barney, J. B. (1999). How a firm's capabilities affect boundary conditions. *Sloan Management Review, 40*(3), 137–145.

Barney, J. B., & Wright, P. M. (1998). On becoming a strategic partner: The role of human resources in gaining competitive advantage. *Human Resource Management, 37*(1), 31–46.

Barrick, M. R., & Mount, M. K. (1991). The big five personality dimensions and job performance: A meta-analysis. *Personnel Psychology, 44,* 1–26.

Barrick, M. R., Stewart, G. L., Neubert, M. J., & Mount, M. K. (1998). Relating member ability and personality to work-team processes and team effectiveness. *Journal of Applied Psychology, 83,* 377–391.

Barron, J. M., Bishop, J., & Dunkelberg, W. C. (1985). Employer search: The interviewing and hiring of new employees. *Review of Economics and Statistics, 67,* 43–52.

Barry, B., & Stewart, G. L. (1997). Composition, process, and performance in self-managed groups: The role of personality. *Journal of Applied Psychology, 82,* 62–78.

Bartol, K. M., & Locke, E. A. (2000). Incentives and motivation. In S. L. Rynes & B. Gerhart (Eds.), *Compensation in organizations.* San Francisco: Jossey-Bass.

Batt, R. (2001). Explaining wage inequality in telecommunications services: Customer segmentation, human resource practices, and union decline. *Industrial and Labor Relations Review, 54,* 425–449.

Bayard, K., & Troske, K. R. (1999). Examining the employer-size wage premium in the manufacturing, retail trade, and service industries using employer-employee matched data. *The American Economic Review, 89,* 99–103.

Beatty, R., & Zajac, E. (1994). Managerial incentives, monitoring, and risk bearing: A study of executive compensation, ownership, and board structure in initial public offerings. *Administrative Science Quarterly. 39,* 313–335.

Becker, B., & Gerhart, B. (1996). The impact of human resource management on organizational performance: Progress and prospects. *Academy of Management Journal, 39,* 779–801.

Becker, B. E., & Huselid, M. A. (1992). The incentive effects of tournament compensation systems. *Administrative Science Quarterly, 37,* 336–350.

Becker, B. E., & Olson, C.A. (1992). Unions and firm profits. *Industrial Relations, 31,* 395–415.

Becker, G. (1975). *Human capital: A theoretical and empirical analysis, with special reference to education* (2nd ed.). Chicago: University of Chicago Press.

Behling, O. (1998). Employee selection: Will intelligence and conscientiousness do the job? *Academy of Management Executive, 12,* 77–86.

Berger, C. J., Olson, C. A., & Boudreau, J. W. (1983). Effects of unions on job satisfaction: The role of work-related values and perceived rewards. *Organizational Behavior and Human Performance, 32,* 289–324.

Bishop, J. (1984). The recognition and reward of employee performance. *Journal of Labor Economics, 5,* S36-S56.

Blasi, J., Conte, M., & Kruse, D. (1996). Employee stock ownership and corporate performance among public companies. *Industrial and Labor Relations Review,* 50, 60–79.

Blinder, A. S. (1990). Introduction. In A. S. Blinder (Ed.), *Paying for productivity.* Washington, DC: Brookings Institution.

Blinder, A. S., & Choi, D. H. (1990). A shred of evidence on theories of wage stickiness. *Quarterly Journal of Economics, 105,* 1003–1015.

Bloom, M. (1999). The performance effects of pay dispersion on individuals and organizations. *Academy of Management Journal, 42,* 25–40.

Bloom, M., & Milkovich, G. T. (1998). Relationships among risk, incentive pay, and organizational performance. *Academy of Management Journal, 41,* 283–297.

Bohl, D. L. (1997, November/December). Saturn Corp.: A different kind of pay. *Compensation and Benefits Review,* pp. 51–56.

Bok, D. C. (1993). *The cost of talent: How executives and professionals are paid and how it affects America.* New York: Free Press.

Bollier, D. (1996). When workers play the numbers game. In D. Bollier (Ed.), *Aiming higher.* New York: AMACOM.

Bommer, W. H., Johnson, J. L., Rich, G. A., Podsakoff, P. M., & MacKenzie, S. B. (1995). On the interchangeability of objective and subjective measures of employee performance: A meta-analysis. *Personnel Psychology, 48,* 587–606.

Boudreau, J. W. (1991). Utility analysis in human resource management decisions. In M. D. Dunnette & L. M. Hough (Eds.), *Handbook of industrial and organizational psychology* (2nd ed., pp. 621–745). Palto Alto, CA: Consulting Psychologists Press.

Boudreau, J. W., & Berger, C. J. (1985). Decision-theoretic utility analysis applied to employee separations and acquisitions. *Journal of Applied Psychology, 70,* 581–612.

Boudreau, J. W., Sturman, M. C., Trevor, C. O., & Gerhart, B. (1999). *Is it worth it to win the talent war: Using turnover research to evaluate the utility of performance-based pay* (Working Paper No. 99–06). Cornell University, Center for Advanced Human Resource Studies, Ithaca, NY.

Boyd, B., & Salamin, A. (2001). Strategic reward systems: A contingency model of pay system design. *Strategic Management Journal, 22,* 777–792.

Boyer, G. R., & Smith, R. S. (2001). The development of the neoclassical tradition in labor economics. *Industrial and Labor Relations Review, 54,* 199–223.

Brenner, M., Sundaram, R. K., & Yermack, D. (2000). Altering the terms of executive stock options. *Journal of Financial Economics, 57,* 103–128.

Bretz, R. D., Ash, R. A., & Dreher, G. F. (1989). Do people make the place? An examination of the attraction-selection-attrition hypothesis. *Personnel Psychology, 42,* 561–581.

Bretz, R. D. Jr., Boudreau, J. W., & Judge, T. A. (1994). Job search behavior of employed managers. *Personnel Psychology, 47,* 275–301.

Bretz, R. D. Jr., & Judge, T. A. (1994). The role of human resource systems in job applicant decision processes. *Journal of Management, 20,* 531–551.

Bretz, R. D. Jr., & Thomas, S. L. (1992). Perceived equity, motivation, and final-offer arbitration in major league baseball. *Journal of Applied Psychology, 77,* 280–287.

Brickley, J., Smith, C., & Zimmerman, J. (1997). *Managerial economics and organizational architecture.* Chicago: Irwin.

Brickley, J. A., Bhagat, S., & Lease, S. C. (1985). The impact of long-range management compensation plans on shareholder wealth. *Journal of Accounting and Economics, 7,* 115–129.

Broderick, R., & Gerhart, B. (1997). Nonwage compensation. In D. J. B. Mitchell, D. Lewin, & M. A. Zadi (Eds.), *The human resource management handbook* (pp. 145–173), JAI.

Brown, C., & Medoff, J. (1989). The employer size-wage effect. *Journal of Political Economy, 97,* 1027–1059.

Brown, K. A., & Huber, V. L. (1992). Lowering floors and raising ceilings: A longitudinal assessment of the effects of an earnings-at-risk plan on pay satisfaction. *Personnel Psychology, 45,* 279–311.

Bryk, A. S., & Radenbush, S. W. (1992). *Hierarchical linear models.* Newbury Park, CA: Sage.

Buchholtz, A. K., & Ribbens, B. A. (1994). Role of chief executive officers in takeover resistance: Effects of CEO incentives and individual characteristics. *Academy of Management Journal, 37,* 554–579.

Bunnell, D. (2000). *Making the Cisco connection.* New York: John Wiley.

Cable, D. M., & Judge, T. A. (1994). Pay preferences and job search decisions: A person-organization fit perspective. *Personnel Psychology, 47,* 317–348.

Cain, G. G. (1976). The challenge of segmented labor market theories to orthodox theory: A survey. *Journal of Economic Literature, 14,* 1215–1258.

Campbell, J. P., & Pritchard, R. D. (1976). Motivation theory in industrial and organizational psychology. In M. Dunnette (Ed.), *Handbook of industrial and organizational psychology.* Chicago: Rand McNally.

Cappelli, P. (1999). *The new deal at work: Managing the market-driven workforce.* Boston: Harvard Business School Press.

Cappelli, P. (2000, Feb/June). A market-driven approach to retaining talent. *Harvard Business Review, 78,* 103–111.

Cappelli, P., & Chauvin, K. (1991, August). An interplant test of the efficiency wage hypothesis. *Quarterly Journal of Economics, 106*(3), 769–787.

Cappelli, P., Crocker-Hefter, A. (1996 Winter). Distinctive human resources are firms' core competencies. *Organizational Dynamics, 24,* 7–22.

Carpenter, M. A. (2000). The price of change: The role of CEO compensation in strategic variation and deviation from industry strategy norms. *Journal of Management, 26,* 1179–1198.

Carpenter, M. A., Sanders, W. G., & Gregersen, H. B. (2001). Bundling human capital with organizational context: The impact of international assignment experience on multinational firm performance and CEO pay. *Academy of Management Journal, 44,* 493–511.

Carpenter, M. A., & Wade, J. B. (2002). Micro-level opportunity structures as determinants of non-CEO executive pay. *Academy of Management Journal, 45,* 1085–1103.

Carroll, S. J. (1986). Management by objectives: Three decades of research and experience. In S. L. Rynes & G. T. Milkovich (Eds.), *Current issues in human resources management* (pp. 295–312). Plano, TX: Business Publications.

Carter, M. E., & Lynch, L. J. (2001). An examination of executive stock option repricing. *Journal of Financial Economics, 61,* 207–225.

Case, J. (1997, March-April). Opening the books. *Harvard Business Review,* pp. 118–127.
Case, J. (1998). *The open-book experience.* Reading, MA: Addison-Wesley.
Chance, D. M., Kumar, R., & Todd, R. B. (2000). The 'repricing' of executive stock options. *Journal of Financial Economics, 57,* 129–154.
Chandler, A. D. Jr. (1962). *Strategy and structure.* Cambridge: MIT Press.
Chidambaran, N. K., & Nagpurnanand, R. P. (in press). Executive stock option repricing, internal governance mechanisms, and management turnover. *Journal of Financial Economics.*
Coase, R. (1998). The new institutional economics. *AER Papers and Proceedings, 88,* 72–74.
Coase, R. H. (1937). The nature of the firm. *Economica, 4,* 386–406.
Coff, R. W. (1999). When competitive advantage doesn't lead to performance: The resource-based view and stakeholder bargaining power. *Organization Science, 10,* 119–133.
Cohn, L. (1999, December 6). The hidden costs of stock options. *Business Week,* p. 44.
Coleman, J. S. (1990). Social capital in the creation of human capital. *American Journal of Sociology, 94,* s95-s120.
Collins, D., Hatcher, L., & Ross, T. L. (1993). The decision to implement gainsharing: The role of work climate, expected outcomes, and union status. *Personnel Psychology, 46,* 77–104.
Collins, J. C., & Porras, J. (1994). *Built to last.* New York: HarperCollins.
Colvin, G. (2001, June 25). The great CEO pay heist. *Fortune, 143*(14), pp. 64–70.
Conlon, E. J., & Parks, J. M. (1990). Effects of monitoring and tradition on compensation arrangements: An experiment with principal-agent dyads. *Academy of Management Journal, 33,* 603–622.
Conyon, M. J., Peck, S. I., & Sadler, G. V. (2001). Corporate tournaments and executive compensation: Evidence from the U.K. *Strategic Management Journal,* 22, 805–815.
Cook, T. D., & Campbell, D. T. (1979). *Quasi-experimentation: Design and analysis issues for field settings.* Boston: Houghton Mifflin.
Cooke, W. N. (1994). Employee participation programs, group-based incentives, and company performance: A union-nonunion comparison. *Industrial and Labor Relations Review,* 47, 594–609.
Cooper, C. L., Dyck, B., & Frohlich, N. (1992). Improving the effectiveness of gainsharing: The role of fairness and participation. *Administrative Science Quarterly, 37,* 471–490.
Costa, P. T., Jr. & McCrae, R. R. (1992). *Revised NEO-Personality inventory (NEO PI-R) and NEO five-factor inventory (NEO-FFI) professional manual.* Odessa, FL: Psychological Assessment Resources.
Cowherd, D. M., & Levine, D. I. (1992). Product quality and pay equity between lower-level employees and top management: An investigation of distributive justice theory. *Administrative Science Quarterly, 37,* 302–320.
Coy, P. (2001, January 15). Funny money, or real incentive? *Business Week,* pp. 71–72.
Cronbach, L. J., Gleser, G. C., Nanda, H., & Rajaratnam, N. (1972). *The dependability of behavioral measurements: Theory of generalizability of scores and profiles.* New York: John Wiley.
Crystal, G. S. (1991). *In search of excess: The overcompensation of American executives.* New York: Norton.
Cummings, L. L., & Schwab, D. P. (1973). *Performance in organizations.* Glenview, IL: Scott, Foresman.
Daft, R. L. (1983). *Organization theory and design.* New York: West.
Daley, K. (2001, February 26). Balk out of turn: Many stars griping about contracts after A-Rod's deal. *Dallas Morning News,* p. 12B.
Davy, J. A., & Shipper, F. (1993). Voter behavior in union certification elections: A longitudinal study. *Academy of Management Journal, 36,* 187–199.
Dawes, R. M. (1975). Formal models of dilemma in social decision making. In M. Kaplan & S. Schwartz (Eds.), *Human judgment and decision processes: Formal and mathematical approaches.* New York: Academic Press.
Dawes, R. M. (1980). Social dilemmas. *Annual Review of Psychology, 31,* 169–193.
Dawis, R. V. (1991). Vocational interests, values, and preferences. In M. D. Dunnette & L. M. Hough (Eds.), *Handbook of industrial and organizational psychology* (2nd Ed., Vol. 2). Palo Alto, CA: Consulting Psychologists Press.

Dawis, R. V., Lofquist, L. H., & Weiss, D. J. (1968). A theory of work adjustment: A revision. *Minnesota Studies in Vocational Rehabilitation, 23,* University of Minnesota, Industrial Relations Center.

Deci, E. L. (1975). *Intrinsic motivation.* New York: Plenum.

Deci, E. L., Koestner, R., & Ryan, R. M. (1999). A meta-analytic review of experiments examining the effects of extrinsic rewards on intrinsic motivation. *Psychological Bulletin, 25,* 627–668.

Deci, E. L., & Ryan, R. M. (1985). *Intrinsic motivation and self-determination in human behavior.* New York: Plenum.

Deckop, J. R., Mangel, R., & Cirka, C. C. (1999). Getting more than you pay for: Organizational citizenship behavior and pay-for-performance plans. *Academy of Management Journal,* 42, 420–428.

Deephouse, D. L. (1999). To be different, or to be the same? It's a question (and theory) of strategic balance. *Strategic Management Journal, 20,* 147–166.

Delery, J. E., & Doty, H. D. (1996). Modes of theorizing in strategic human resource management: Tests of universalistic, contingency, and configurational performance predictions. *Academy of Management Journal, 39,* 802–835.

Deming, W. E. (1986). *Out of the crisis.* Cambridge: MIT, Center for Advanced Engineering Study.

Digman, J. M. (1990). Personality structure: Emergence of the five-factor model. *Annual Review of Psychology, 41,* 417–440.

DiMaggio, P. J., & Powell, W. W. (1983). The iron cage revisited: Institutional isomorphism and collective rationality in organizational fields. *American Sociology Review, 48,* 147–160.

Doeringer, P. B., & Piore, M. J. (1971). *Internal labor markets and manpower analysis.* Lexington, MA: D.C. Heath.

Doty, D. H., & Glick, W. H. (1998). Does common methods variance really bias results? *Organizational Research Methods, 1,* 374–406.

Doty, D. H., Glick, W. H., & Huber, G. P. (1993). Fit, equifinality, and organizational effectiveness: A test of two configurational theories. *Academy of Management Journal, 36,* 1196–1250.

Doucouliagos, C. (1995). Worker participation and productivity in labor-managed and participatory capitalist firms: A meta-analysis. *Industrial and Labor Relations Review, 49,* 58–77.

Dreher G. F., Ash, R. A., & Bretz, R. D. (1988). Benefit coverage and employee cost: Critical factors in explaining compensation satisfaction. *Personnel Psychology, 41,* 237–254.

Dreher, G. F., & Cox, T. H. Jr. (2000). Labor market mobility and cash compensation: The moderating effects of race and gender. *Academy of Management Journal, 43,* 890–900.

Dunham, R. B. (1984). *Organizational behavior.* Homewood, IL: Irwin.

Dunlop, J. T. (1957). The task of contemporary wage theory. In G. W. Taylor & F. C. Pierson (Eds.), *New concepts in Wage Determination,* 117–139. New York: McGraw-Hill.

Dyer, L. & Kochan, T. A. (1995). Is there a new HRM? In B. Downie & M. Coates (Eds.), *Managing human resources in the 1990s and beyond: Is the workplace being transformed?* (pp. 132–163). Kingston, Ontario: IRC Press, Queen's University.

Dyer, L., & Theriault, R. (1976). The determinants of pay satisfaction. *Journal of Applied Psychology, 61,* 596–604.

Ehrenberg, R. G., & Bognanno, M. L. (1990). Do tournaments have incentive effects? *Journal of Political Economy, 98,* 1307–1324.

Ehrenberg, R. G., & Smith, R. S. (1982). *Modern labor economics.* Glenview, IL: Scott, Foresman.

Ehrenberg, R. G., & Smith, R. S. (1988). *Modern labor economics.* Homewood, IL: Irwin.

Eisenberger, R., & Cameron, J. (1996). Detrimental effects of rewards: Reality or Myth? *American Psychologist, 51,* 1153–1166.

Eisenhardt, K. M. (1988). Agency- and institutional-theory explanations: The case of retail sales compensation. *Academy of Management Journal, 31,* 488–511.

Eisenhardt, K. M. (1989). Agency theory: An assessment and review. *Academy of Management Review, 14,* 57–74.

Ellig, B. R. (1981). Compensation elements: Market phase determines the mix. *Compensation Review,* (Third Quarter), 30–38.

Eriksson, T. (1999). Executive compensation and tournament theory: Empirical tests on Danish data. *Journal of Labor Economics, 17,* 262–280.

Eskew, D., & Heneman, R. L. (1994). A survey of merit pay plan effectiveness: End of the line for merit pay or hope for improvement? *Human resource planning, 19*(2), 12–19.

Estrine, D. (1998, June 22). The Jordan effect. *Fortune, 137*(12), 124–138.

European Parliament. (1999). *Labour costs and wage policy within EMU.* Luxembourg, Belgium: Directorate-General for Research, Economic Affairs Series, ECON 111 EN.

Fang, M. Y., & Gerhart, B. (2002). *Does pay for performance diminish intrinsic interest? A workplace test using cognitive evaluation theory and the attraction-selection-attrition model* (Working Paper). University of Wisconsin-Madison, School of Business.

Feldman D. C., & Arnold, H. J. (1978). Position choice: Comparing the importance of organizational and job factors. *Journal of Applied Psychology, 63,* 706–710.

Fein, M. (1981). *Improshare: An alternative to traditional managing.* Norcross, GA: Institute of Industrial Engineers.

Finkelstein, S., & Boyd, B. K. (1998). How much does the CEO matter? The role of managerial discretion in the setting of CEO compensation. *Academy of Management Journal, 41,* 179–199.

Fishman, C. (1996, April/May). Whole Foods is all teams. *Fast Company,* p. 103.

Fishman, C. (1998, August). The war for talent. *Fast Company, 16,* p. 104. (Available on the World Wide Web at: http://www.fastcompany.com/online/16/mckinseyhtml.)

Folger, R., & Konovsky, M. A. (1989). Effects of procedural and distributive justice on reactions to pay raise decisions. *Academy of Management Journal, 32,* 115–130.

Frank, R. H. (1985). *Choosing the right pond: Human behavior and the quest for status.* New York: Oxford University Press.

Frank, R. H., & Cook, P. J. (1995). *The winner-take-all society: How more and more Americans compete for ever-fewer and bigger prizes, encouraging economic waste, income inequality, and an impoverished cultural life.* New York: Free Press.

Freeman, R. B. (1980). The exit-voice tradeoff in the labor market: Unionism, job tenure, quits, and separations. *Quarterly Journal of Economics, 94,* 643–673.

Freeman, R. B, & Medoff, J. L. (1984). *What do unions do?* New York: Basic Books.

Freiberg, K., & Freiberg, J. (1996). *Nuts! Southwest Airlines' crazy recipe for business and personal success.* Austin, TX: Bard.

Fulmer, I. (2003, January). *Executive pay and the labor market.* Michigan State University, School of Business, East Lansing. Unpublished manuscript.

Fulmer, I. S., Gerhart, B., & Scott, K. S. (2002). *Are the 100 best better? An empirical investigation of the relationship between being a "great place to work" and firm performance.* Michigan State University, Broad School of Management, East Lansing. Unpublished manuscript.

Galbraith, C. S., & Merril, G. B. (1991). The effect of compensation program and structure of SBU competitive strategy: A study of technology-intensive firms. *Strategic Management Journal, 12,* 353–370.

Garen, J. E. (1994). Executive compensation and principal-agent theory. *Journal of Political Economy, 102,* 1175–1200.

General Electric. (2000). Letter to shareholders. *GE 2000 annual report.* Retrieved from the World Wide Web on January 7, 2003, at: http://www.ge.com/annual00/index.html.

Gerhart, B. (1987). How important are dispositional factors as determinants of job satisfaction? Implications for job design and other personnel programs. *Journal of Applied Psychology, 73,* 154–162.

Gerhart, B. (1990). Gender differences in current and starting salaries: The role of performance, college major, and job title. *Industrial and Labor Relations Review, 43,* 418–433.

Gerhart, B. (2000). Compensation strategy and organizational performance. In S. L. Rynes & B. Gerhart (Eds.), *Compensation in organizations.* San Francisco: Jossey-Bass.

Gerhart, B., & Milkovich, G. T. (1989). Salaries, salary growth, and promotions of men and women in a large, private firm. In R. Michael, H. Hartmann, & B. O'Farrell (Eds.), *Pay equity: Empirical inquiries.* Washington, DC: National Academy Press.

Gerhart, B., & Milkovich, G. T. (1990). Organizational differences in managerial compensation and financial performance. *Academy of Management Journal, 33,* 663–691.

Gerhart, B., & Milkovich, G. T. (1992). Employee compensation: Research and practice. In M. D. Dunnette & L. M. Hough (Eds.), *Handbook of industrial and organizational psychology* (2nd ed.). Palo Alto, CA: Consulting Psychologists Press.

Gerhart, B., Milkovich, G. T., & Murray, B. (1992). Pay, performance, and participation. Under preparation for D. Lewin, O. Mitchell, & P. Sherer (Eds.), *Research Frontiers in Industrial Relations.* Madison, WI: Industrial Relations Research Association.

Gerhart, B., Minkoff, H., & Olsen, R. (1995). Compensation and reward systems. In G. R. Ferris, S. D. Rosen, & D. T. Barnum (Eds.), *Handbook of human resource management.* Cambridge, MA: Blackwell.

Gerhart, B., Trevor, C., & Graham, M. (1996). New directions in employee compensation research. In G. R. Ferris (Ed.), *Research in personnel and human resources management,* pp. 143–203.

Gerhart, B., & Trevor, C. O. (1996). Employment variability under different managerial compensation systems. *Academy of Management Journal, 39,* 1692–1712.

Gerhart, B., Wright, P. M., McMahan, G., & Snell, S. (2001). Measurement error in research on human resource decisions and firm performance: How much error is there and how does it influence effect size estimates? *Personnel Psychology, 53,* 855–872.

Gibbons, R. (1998). Incentives in organizations. *Journal of Economic Perspectives, 12,* 115–132.

Gibbons, R., & Murphy, K. J. (1990). Relative performance evaluations for chief executive officers. *Industrial & Labor Relations Review, 43,* 30–51.

Gibbons, R., & Waldman, M. (1999). A theory of wage and promotion dynamics inside firms. *Quarterly Journal of Economics,* 1321–1358.

Gomez-Mejia, L. R. (1992). Structure and process of diversification, compensation strategy, and firm performance. *Strategic Management Journal, 13,* 381–397.

Gomez-Mejia, L. R., & Balkin, D. B. (1989). Effectiveness of individual and aggregate compensation strategies. *Industrial Relations, 28,* 431–445.

Gomez-Mejia, L. R., & Balkin, D. B. (1992a). *Compensation, organizational strategy, and firm performance.* Cincinnati, Ohio: Southwestern Publishing.

Gomez-Mejia, L. R., & Balkin, D. B. (1992b). Determinants of faculty pay: An agency theory perspective. *Academy of Management Journal, 35,* 921–955.

Gomez-Mejia, L. R., Tosi, H., & Hinkin, T. (1987). Managerial control, performance, and executive compensation. *Academy of Management Journal, 30,* 51–70.

Gomez-Mejia, L. R., Welbourne, T. M., & Wiseman, R. M. (2000). The role of risk sharing and risk taking under gainsharing. *Academy of Management Review, 25,* 492–507.

Goodman, P. S. (1974). An examination of referents used in the evaluation of pay. *Organizational Behavior and Human Performance, 12,* 170–195.

Gray, J. A. (1973). Causal theories of personality and how to test them. In J. R. Royce (Ed.), *Multivariate analysis and psychological theory* (pp. 409–464). New York: Academic Press.

Greenberg, J. (1987). Reactions to procedural injustice in payment distributions: Do the means justify the ends? *Journal of Applied Psychology, 72,* 55–61.

Greenberg, J. (1990). Employee theft as a reaction to underpayment of inequity: The hidden cost of pay cuts. *Journal of Applied Psychology, 75,* 561–568.

Greenberg, J. (1993). Stealing in the name of justice: Informational and interpersonal moderators of theft reactions to underpayment inequity. *Organizational Behavior and Human Decision Processes, 54,* 81–103.

Greene, C. N., & Podsakoff, P. M. (1978). Effects of the removal of a pay incentive: A field experiment. *Academy of Management Proceedings, 34th Annual Meeting,* 206–210.

Groshen, E., & Krueger, A. B. (1990). The structure of supervision and pay in hospitals. *Industrial and Labor Relations Review, 43,* S134-S146.

Groshen, E. L. (1988). Why do wages vary among employers? *Economic Review, 24,* 19–38.

Groshen, E. L. (1991). Sources of intra-industry wage dispersion: How much do employers matter? *Quarterly Journal of Economics, 106,* 869–885.

Gubman, E. L. (1998). *The talent solution.* New York: McGraw-Hill.

Gunther, M. (2001, July 9). God and business: The surprising quest for spiritual renewal in the American workplace. *Fortune, 144*(1), 59–80.

Gustman, A. L., Mitchell, O. S., & Steinmeir, T. L. (1994). The role of pensions in the labor market: A survey of the literature. *Industrial & Labor Relations Review, 47,* 417–438.

Guzzo, R. A., & Bondy, J. S. (1983). *A guide to worker productivity experiments in the United States 1976–1981.* New York: Pergamon.

Guzzo, R. A., Jette, R. D., & Katzell, R. A. (1985). The effects of psychologically based intervention programs on worker productivity: A meta-analysis. *Personnel Psychology, 38,* 275–291.

Hackman, J. R., & Oldham, G. R. (1976). Motivation through the design of work: Test of a theory. *Organizational Behavior and Human Performance, 16,* 250–279.

Haire, M., Ghiselli, E. E., & Gordon, M. E. (1967). A psychological study of pay [Monograph]. *Journal of Applied Psychology 51,* 1–24.

Hall, B. J. (2000, March-April). What you need to know about stock options. *Harvard Business Review, 78,* pp. 121–129.

Hall, B. J., & Murphy, K. J. (2000). *Stock options for undiversified executives* (Working Paper No. w8052). National Bureau of Economic Research. Retrieved from the World Wide Web on December 1, 2001, at www.nber.org.

Hall, D. T., & Nougaim, K. E. (1968). An examination of Maslow's need hierarchy in an organizational setting. *Organizational Behavior and Human Performance,* 3, 12–35.

Hallock, K. F., & Murphy, K. J. (1999). *The economics of executive compensation.* Cheltenham, UK: Edward Elgar.

Hambrick, D., & Mason, P. (1984). Upper echelons: The organization as a reflection of its top managers. *Academy of Management Journal, 15,* 514–535.

Hambrick, D. C., & Finkelstein, S. (1987). Managerial discretion: A bridge between polar views on organizations. In L. L. Cummings & B. M. Staw (Eds.), *Research in Organizational Behavior, 9,* 369–406.

Hammer, T. H. (1988). New developments in profit sharing, gainsharing, and employee ownership. In J. P. Campbell, R. J. Campbell, & Associates (Eds.), *Productivity in organizations.* San Francisco: Jossey-Bass.

Hamper, B. (1991). *Rivethead: Tales from the assembly line.* New York: Warner Books.

Hannan, M., & Freeman, J. (1977). The population ecology of organizations. *American Journal of Sociology, 82,* 929–964.

Hansen, G. S., & Wernerfelt, B. (1989). Determinants of firm performance: The relative importance of economic and organizational factors. *Strategic Management Journal, 10,* 399–411.

Hardin, G. (1968). The tragedy of the commons. *Science, 162,* 1243–1248.

Harrison, D. A., Virick, M., & William, S. (1996). Working without a net: Time, performance, and turnover under maximally contingent rewards. *Journal of Applied Psychology, 81,* 331–345.

Harter, J. K., Schmidt, F. L., & Hayes, T. L. (2002). Business-unit-level relationships between employee satisfaction, employee engagement, and business outcomes: A meta-analysis. *Journal of Applied Psychology, 87,* 268–279.

Hastings, D. F. (1999). Lincoln Electric's harsh lessons from international expansion. *Harvard Business Review, 77,* 162–173.

Hatcher, L., & Ross, T. L. (1991). From individual incentives to an organization-wide gainsharing plan: Effects on teamwork and product quality. *Journal of Organizational Behavior, 12,* 169–183.

Hawawini, G., Subramanian, V., & Verdin, P. (2003). Is performance driven by industry- or firm-specific factors? A new look at the evidence. *Strategic Management Journal, 24,* 1–16.

Hay Group. (1994). *The Hay report: Compensation and benefit strategies for 1995 and beyond.* Philadelphia: Author.

Heath, C., Huddart, S., & Lang, M. (1999). Psychological factors and stock option exercise. *Quarterly Journal of Economics,* 601–627.

Henderson, A. D., & Fredrickson, J. W. (1996). Information-processing demands as a determinant of CEO compensation. *Academy of Management Journal, 39,* 575–606.

Heneman, H. G., III. (1985). Pay satisfaction. *Research in Personnel and Human Resource Management, 3,* 115–139.

Heneman, H. G., III, Huett, D. L., Lavigna, R. J., & Ogsten, D. (1995). Assessing managers' satisfaction with staffing services. *Personnel Psychology, 53,* 803–834.

Heneman, H. G., III, & Judge, T. A. (2000). Compensation attitudes. In S. L. Rynes & B. Gerhart (Eds.), *Compensation in organizations,* 61–103. San Francisco: Jossey-Bass.

Heneman, H. G., III, & Schwab, D. P. (1985). Pay satisfaction: Its multidimensional nature and measurement. *International Journal of Psychology, 20,* 129–141.

Heneman, R. L. (1986). The relationship between supervisory ratings and results-oriented measures of performance: A meta-analysis. *Personnel Psychology, 39,* 811–826.

Heneman, R. L. (1990). Merit pay research. *Research in Personnel and Human Resource Management, 8,* 203–263.

Heneman, R. L. (1992). *Merit pay: Linking pay increases to performance ratings.* New York: Addison-Wesley.

Heneman, R. L., Ledford, G. E., Jr., & Gresham, M. T. (2000). The changing nature of work and its effects on compensation design and delivery. In S. L. Rynes & B. Gerhart (Eds.), *Compensation in organizations.* San Francisco: Jossey-Bass.

Herzberg, F. (1966). *Work and the nature of man.* Cleveland: World Publishing Company.

Herzberg, F. (1987, September-October). One more time: How do you motivate employees? *Harvard Business Review,* 5–16. (Reprint 87507).

Hildreth, A. K. G., & Oswald, A. J. (1997). Rent-sharing and wages: Evidence from company and establishment panels. *Journal of Labor Economics, 15,* 318–337.

Hill, C. W. L., & Snell, S. A. (1989). Effects of ownership structure and control on corporate productivity. *Academy of Management Journal, 32,* 25–46.

Hirsch, B. T., & Morgan, B. A. (1994). Shareholder risks and returns in union and nonunion firms. *Industrial and Labor Relations Review, 47,* 302–318.

Hitt, G., & Schlesinger, J. M. (2002, March 26). Perk police: Stock options come under fire in wake of Enron's collapse. *Wall Street Journal,* p. A1.

Hitt, M. A., Hoskisson, R. E., Johnson, R. A., & Moesel, D. D. (1996). The market for corporate control and firm innovation. *Academy of Management Journal, 39,* 1084–1119.

Hodgetts, R. M. (1997). Discussing incentive compensation with Donald Hastings of Lincoln Electric. *Compensation and Benefits Review, 29,* 60–66.

Hollenbeck, J. R., & Klein, H. J. (1987). Goal commitment and the goal-setting process: Problems, prospects, and proposals for future research. *Journal of Applied Psychology, 72,* 212–220.

Holmstrom, B. (1982). Moral hazard in tams. *Bell Journal of Economics, 13,* 324–340.

Holmstrom, B., & Milgrom, P. (1991). Multi-task principle-agent analysis: Incentive contracts, asset ownership, and job design. *Journal of Law, Economics, and Organization, 7,* 24–52.

Holzer, H. J. (1990). Wages, employer costs, and employee performance in the firm. *Industrial & Labor Relations Review, 43,* 147–164.

Hoskisson R. E., Hitt, M. A., Wan, W. P., & Yiu, D. (1999). Theory and research in strategic management: Swings of a pendulum. *Journal of Management, 25,* 417–456.

House, R. J., & Wigdor, L. A. (1967). Herzberg's dual-factor theory of job satisfaction and motivation: A review of the evidence and a criticism. *Personnel Psychology, 20,* 369–389.

Howe, P. J. (2000, August 22). Taking a cue from the old economy once again, money has the last word in uncertain market, stock options losing favor, study says. *Boston Globe,* p. C1. (Original data from PriceWaterhouse Coopers survey.)

Hulin, C. (1991). Adaptation, persistence and commitment. In M. D. Dunnette & L. M. Hough (Eds.), *Handbook of industrial and organizational psychology* (2nd ed., Vol. 2, pp. 445–505). Palo Alto, CA: Consulting Psychologists Press.

Hunter, L. W. (2000). What determines job quality in nursing homes? *Industrial and Labor Relations Review, 53,* 463–481.

Huselid, M. A. (1995). The impact of human resource management practices on turnover, productivity, and corporate financial performance. *Academy of Management Journal, 38,* 635–672.

Ichniowski, C., Shaw, K., & Prennushi, G. (1997). The effects of human resource management practices on productivity: A study of steel finishing lines. *American Economic Review, 87,* 291–313.

Idson, T. L., & Oi, W. Y. (1999). Workers are more productive in large firms. *The American Economic Review, 89,* 104–108.

Investor Responsibility Research Center. (2001, February 6). *Losing value.* Retrieved from the World Wide Web on December 1, 2001, at: www.irrc.org.

Ippolito, R. A. (1987). Why federal workers don't quit. *Journal of Human Resources, 22,* 281–299.

Itami, H. (1987). *Mobilizing invisible assets.* Cambridge, MA: Harvard University Press.

Janakiraman, S. N., Lambert, R. A., & Larcker, D. F. (1992). An empirical investigation of the relative performance evaluation hypothesis. *Journal of Accounting Research, 30,* 53–69.

Jaques, E. (1991). *Equitable payment.* New York: John Wiley.

Jasinowski, J., & Hamrin, R. (1995). *Making it in America.* New York: Simon & Schuster.

Jenkins, D. G. Jr., Mitra, A., Gupta, N., & Shaw, J. D. (1998). Are financial incentives related to performance? A meta-analytic review of empirical research. *Journal of Applied Psychology, 83,* 777–787.

Jensen, M. C. (2001, April). *Paying people to lie: The truth about the budgeting process* (Working Paper No. 01–072). Cambridge, MA: Harvard Business School.

Jensen, M. C., & Meckling, W. H. (1976). Theory of the firm: Managerial behavior, agency costs, and ownership structure. *Journal of Financial Economics, 3,* 305–360.

Jensen, M. C., & Murphy, K. J. (1990). Performance pay and top management incentives. *Journal of Political Economy, 98*(2), 225–264.

Judge, T. A. (1993). Validity of the dimensions of the pay satisfaction questionnaire: Evidence of differential prediction. *Personnel Psychology, 46,* 331–355.

Judiesch, M. K. (1994). *The effects of incentive compensation systems on productivity, individual differences in output variability and selection utility.* Unpublished doctoral dissertation, University of Iowa.

Jurgensen, C. E. (1978). Job preferences (What makes a job good or bad?). *Journal of Applied Psychology, 63,* 267–276.

Kahn, L. M., & Sherer, P. D. (1990). Contingent pay and managerial performance. *Industrial and Labor Relations Review, 43,* 107S-120S.

Kanfer, R. (1990). Motivation theory and industrial and organizational psychology. In M. D. Dunnette & L. M. Hough (Eds.), *Handbook of industrial and organizational psychology* (2nd ed.). Palo Alto, CA: Consulting Psychologists Press.

Kanfer, R., & Ackerman, P. L. (1989). Motivation and cognitive abilities: An integrative/aptitude-treatment interaction approach to skill acquisition. *Journal of Applied Psychology, 74,* 657–690.

Kanter, R. M. (1977). *Men and women of the corporation.* New York: Basic Books.

Kaplan, R. S., & Norton, D. P. (1996, January-February). Using the balanced scorecard as a strategic management system. *Harvard Business Review,* 75–85.

Katz, H. C., & Kochan, T. A. (1992). An introduction to collective bargaining and industrial relations. New York: McGraw Hill.

Katzell, R. A., Bienstock, P., & Faerstein, P. H. (1977). *A guide to worker productivity experiments in the United States 1971–1975.* New York: New York University Press.

Kaufman, B. E. (1999). Expanding the behavioral foundations of labor economics. *Industrial and Labor Relations Review, 52,* 361–392.

Kaufman, R. T. (1992). The effects of Improshare on productivity. *Industrial and Labor Relations Review, 45,* 311–322.

Keith, K., & McWilliams, A. (1999). The returns to mobility and job search by gender. *Industrial and Labor Relations Review, 52,* 460–477.

Kerr, C. (1954). The balkanization of labor markets. In E. W. Bakke (Ed.), *Labor mobility and economic opportunity* (pp. 92–110). New York: John Wiley.

Kerr, J., & Slocum, J. W. Jr. (1987). Managing corporate culture through reward systems. *Academy of Management Executive, 1*(2), 99–108.

Kerr, J. L. (1985). Diversification strategies and managerial rewards: An empirical study. *Academy of Management Journal, 28,* 155–179.

Kidwell, R. E., & Bennett, N. (1993). Employee propensity to withhold effort: A conceptual model to intersect three avenues of research. *Academy of Management Review, 18,* 429–456.

Kim, D. (1999). Determinants of the survival of gainsharing programs. *Industrial and Labor Relations Review, 53,* 21–42.

Kim, S. (1998). Does profit sharing increase firms' profits? *Journal of Labor Research, 19,* 351–370.

Klaas, B. S., & McClendon, J. A. (1996). To lead, lag, or match: Estimating the financial impact of pay level policies. *Personnel Psychology, 49,* 121–141.

Klaas, B. S., & Ullman, J. C. (1995). Sticky wages revisited: Organizational responses to a declining market-clearing wage. *Academy of Management Review, 20, 281*–310.

Klein, H. J. (1989). An integrated control theory of work motivation. *Academy of Management Review, 14,* 150–172.

Klein, H. J., Wesson, M. J., Hollenbeck, J. R., & Alge, B. J. (1999). Goal commitment and the goal-setting process: Conceptual clarification and empirical synthesis. *Journal of Applied Psychology, 84,* 885–896.

Klein, K. J. (1987). Employee stock ownership and employee attitudes: A test of three models [Monograph]. *Journal of Applied Psychology, 72,* 319–332.

Klein, K. J., Dansereau, F., & Hall, R. (1994). Levels issues in theory development, data collection, and analysis. *Academy of Management Review, 19,* 195–229.

Klein, K. J., & Kozlowski, S. W. J. (Eds.). (2000). *Multilevel theory, research, and methods in organizations.* San Francisco: Jossey-Bass.

Kochan, T. A., & Cappelli, P. (1984). The transformation of the industrial relations and personnel function. In P. Osterman (Ed.), *Internal labor markets.* Cambridge: MIT Press.

Kochan, T. A., & Osterman, P. (1994). *The mutual gains enterprise: Forging a winning partnership among labor, management and government.* Boston: Harvard Business School Press.

Kogut, B., & Zander, U. (1996). What do firms do? Coordination, identity, and learning. *Organization Science, 7,* 502–518.

Kohn, A. (1993, September-October). Why incentive plans cannot work. *Harvard Business Review,* pp. 54–63.

Konrad, A. M., & Pfeffer, J. (1990). Do you get what you deserve? Factors affecting the relationship between productivity and pay. *Administrative Science Quarterly, 35,* 258–285.

Kopelman, R. E. (1976). Organizational control system responsiveness, expectancy theory constructs, and work motivation: Some interrelations and causal connections. *Personnel Psychology, 29,* 205–220.

Kopelman, R. E., & Reinharth, L. (1982). Research results: The effect of merit-pay practices on white-collar performance. *Compensation Review, 14*(4), 30–40.

Koslowsky, M., Sagie, A., Krausz, M., & Singer, A. D. (1997). Correlates of employee lateness: Some theoretical considerations. *Journal of Applied Psychology, 82,* 79–88.

Kosnik, R. D. (1992). Effects of board demography and directors' incentives on corporate greenmail decisions. *Academy of Management Journal, 33,* 129–150.

Kristof-Brown, A., Barrick, M. R., & Stevens, C. K. (2001). *Opposites attract: A multi-sample demonstration of complementary person-team fit on extraversion.* University of Iowa, Tippie College of Business. Unpublished manuscript.

Krueger, A. B. (1988). The determinants of queues for federal jobs. *Industrial & Labor Relations Review, 41,* 567–581.

Krueger, A. B., & Summers, L. H. (1988). Efficiency wages and the inter-industry wage structure. *Econometrica, 56,* 259–293.

Kruse, D. L. (1993). *Profit sharing: Does it make a difference?* Kalamazoo, MI: Upjohn Institute.

Kuethe, J. L., & Levenson, B. (1964). Conceptions of organizational worth. *American Journal of Sociology, 70,* 342–348.

Lagnado, L. (1997, May 30). Columbia/HCA graded its hospitals on severity of their Medicare cases. *The Wall Street Journal,* p. A6.

Lakhani, H. (1988). The effect of pay and retention bonuses on quit rates in the U.S. Army. *Industrial & Labor Relations Review, 41*, 430–438.

Lambert, R., Larcker, D., & Weigelt, K. (1993). The structure of organizational incentives. *Administrative Science Quarterly, 38*, 438–461.

Larcker, D. (1983). The association between performance plan adoption and corporate capital investment. *Journal of Accounting and Economics, 5*, 3–30.

Latané, B., Williams, K., & Harkins, S. (1979). Many hands make light the work: The causes and consequences of social loafing. *Journal of Personality and Social Psychology, 37*, 822–832.

Lavelle, L. (2001, April 16). Executive pay. *Business Week*, p. 76.

Lawler, E. E. (1968). Equity theory as a predictor of productivity and work quality. *Psychological Bulletin, 70*, 596–610.

Lawler, E. E., III. (1971). *Pay and organizational effectiveness: A psychological view.* New York: McGraw-Hill.

Lawler, E. E., III. (1990). *Strategic pay: Aligning organizational strategies and pay systems.* San Francisco: Jossey-Bass.

Lawler, E. E., III, & Suttle, J. L. (1972). A causal correlational test of the need hierarchy concept. *Organizational Behavior and Human Performance, 7*, 265–287.

Lazear, E. P. (1979). Why is there mandatory retirement? *Journal of Political Economy, 87*, 1261–1264.

Lazear, E. P. (1986). Salaries and piece rates. *Journal of Business*, 59, 405–431.

Lazear, E. P. (1989). Pay equality and industrial politics. *Journal of Political Economy, 97*, 561–580.

Lazear, E. P. (1995a). A jobs-based analysis of labor markets. *American Economic Review, 85*, 260–265.

Lazear, E. P. (1995b). *Personnel economics.* Cambridge: MIT Press.

Lazear, E. P. (1998). *Personnel economics for managers.* New York: John Wiley.

Lazear, E. P. (1999). Personnel economics: Past lessons and future directions. *Journal of Labor Economics, 17*, 199–236.

Lazear, E. P., & Rosen, S. (1981). Rank order tournaments as an optimum labor contract. *Journal of Political Economy, 89*, 841–864.

Ledyard, J. O. (1995). Public goods: A survey of experimental research. In J. H. Kagel (Ed.), *Handbook of experimental economics.* Princeton, NJ: Princeton University Press.

Leonard, J. S. (1987). Carrots and sticks: Pay, supervision, and turnover. *Journal of Labor Economics, 5*, s136-s152.

Leonard, J. S. (1989). Wage structure and dynamics in the electronics industry. *Industrial Relations, 28*, 251–275.

Leonard, J. S. (1990). Executive pay and firm performance. *Industrial & Labor Relations Review, 43*, 13S-29S.

Lepper, M., Greene, D., & Nisbett, R. (1973). Undermining children's intrinsic interest with extrinsic reward. *Journal of Personality and Social Psychology, 28*, 129–37.

Lester, R. A. (1946). Wage diversity and its theoretical implications. *Review of Economics and Statistics, 28*, 152–159.

Lester, R. A. (1952). A range theory of wage differentials. *Industrial & Labor Relations Review, 5*, 483–500.

Levine, D. I. (1993a). Fairness, markets, and ability to pay: Evidence from compensation executives. *American Economic Review, 83*, 1241–1259.

Levine, D. I. (1993b). What do wages buy? *Administrative Science Quarterly, 38*, 462–463.

Levine, D. I., & Tyson, L. D. (1990). Participation, productivity, and the firm's environment. In A. S. Blinder (Ed.), *Paying for productivity.* Washington, DC: Brookings Institution.

Litan, R. E. (2000, May 25). Corporate disclosure in the internet age. *Financial Times.*

Livernash, E. R. (1957). The internal wage structure. In G. W. Taylor & F .C. Pierson (Eds.), *New concepts in wage determination.* New York: McGraw-Hill.

Locke, E. A. (1968). Toward a theory of task motivation and incentives. *Organizational Behavior and Human Performance, 3*, 157–189.

Locke, E. A. (1976). The nature and causes of job satisfaction. In M. D. Dunnette (Ed.), *Handbook of industrial and organizational psychology* (pp. 1297–1349). Chicago: Rand McNally.

Locke, E. A. (1986). *Generalizing from laboratory to field settings.* Lexington, MA: Lexington Books.

Locke, E. A., Feren, D. B., McCaleb, V. M., Shaw, K. N., & Denny, A. T. (1980). The relative effectiveness of four methods of motivating employee performance. In K. D. Duncan, M. M. Gruenberg, & D. Wallis (Eds.), *Changes in working life* (pp. 363–388). New York: Wiley.

Locke, E. A., & Latham, G. P. (1984). *Goal setting: A motivational technique that works!* Englewood Cliffs, NJ: Prentice Hall.

Locke, E. A., & Latham, G. P. (1990). *A theory of goal-setting and task performance.* Englewood Cliffs, NJ: Prentice Hall.

Locke, E. A., & Latham, G. P. (2002). Building a practically useful theory of goal-setting and task motivation. *American Psychologist, 57,* 705–717.

Longenecker, C. O., Sims, H. P., & Gioia, D. A. (1987). Behind the mask: The politics of employee appraisal. *Academy of Management Executive, 1,* 183–193.

Lum, S. K. S., Moyer, B. C., & Yuskavage, R. E. (2000, June). Improved estimates of gross product by industry for 1947–98. *Survey of Current Business,* pp. 24–54.

Luthans, F., Hodgetts, R. M., & Rosenkrantz, S. A. 1988. *Real managers.* Cambridge, MA: Ballinger.

MacDuffie, J. P. (1995). Human resource bundles and manufacturing performance: Organizational logic and flexible production systems in the world auto industry. *Industrial & Labor Relations Review, 48,* 197–221.

Magnan, M. L., & St-Onge, S. (1997). Bank performance and executive compensation: A managerial discretion perspective. *Strategic Management Journal, 18,* 573–581.

Mahoney, T. A. (1979a). *Compensation and reward perspectives.* Homewood, IL.: Richard D. Irwin.

Mahoney, T. A. (1979b). Organizational hierarchy and position worth. *Academy of Management Journal, 22,* 726–737.

Mahoney, T. A., & Weitzel, W. (1978). Secrecy and managerial compensation. *Industrial Relations, 17,* 245–251.

Main, B., O'Reilly, C., III, & Wade, J. (1993). Top executive pay: Tournament or teamwork? *Journal of Labor Economics, 11,* 606–628.

Mallette, P., & Fowler, K. J. (1992). Effects of board composition and stock ownership on the adoption of poison pills. *Academy of Management Journal, 35,* 1010–1035.

March, J. G., & Simon, H. A. (1958). *Organizations.* New York: Wiley.

Martin, J. (1981). Relative deprivation: A theory of distributive injustice for an era of shrinking resources. In L. L. Cummings & B. M. Staw (Eds.), *Research in organizational behavior* (Vol. 3, pp. 53–107). Greenwich, CT: JAI.

Martin, J. (1982). The fairness of earnings differentials: An experimental study of the perceptions of blue-collar workers. *Journal of Human Resources, 17,* 110–122.

Marwell, G. (1982). Altruism and the problem of collective action. In V. J. Derlega & J. Grzelak (Eds.), *Cooperation and helping behavior: Theories and research.* New York: Academic Press.

Marwell, G., & Ames, R. E. (1979). Experiments on the provision of public goods I: Resources, interest, group size, and the free-rider problem. *American Journal of Sociology, 84,* 1135–1360.

Maslow, A. H. (1943). A theory of human motivation. *Psychological Review, 50,* 370–396.

Mason, E. S. (1939). Price and production policies of large scale enterprises. *American Economic Review, 29,* 61–74.

Masson, R. T. (1971). Executive motivations, earnings, and consequent equity performance. *Journal of Political Economy, 79,* 1278–1292.

Mauri, A. J., & Michaels, M. P. (1998). Firm and industry effects within strategic management: An empirical examination. *Strategic Management Journal, 19,* 211–219.

McAdams, J. L. (1995, March-April). Design, implementation, and results: Employee involvement and performance reward plans. *Compensation and Benefits Review,* pp. 45–55.

McCartney, S. (2002, October 9). Southwest sets standard on costs. *Wall Street Journal,* p. A2.

McGregor, Douglas. (1960). *The human side of enterprise.* New York: McGraw-Hill.

McKenzie, R. B., & Lee, D. R. (1998). *Managing through incentives.* New York: Oxford University Press.

McNulty, P. J. (1966). Labor market analysis and the development of labor economics. *Industrial & Labor Relations Review, 19,* 538–548.

Medoff, J. L., & Abraham, K. G. (1981). Are those paid more really more productive? The case of experience. *Journal of Human Resources, 16,* 186–216.

Mellow, W. (1982). Employer size and wages. *The Review of Economics and Statistics, 64,* 495–501.

Mercer, W. M. (2001). *Broad-based stock options—2001 update.* New York: William M. Mercer Consulting Firm.

Meyer, H. H., Kay, E., & French, J. (1965). Split roles in performance appraisal. *Harvard Business Review, 43,* 123–129.

Meyer, J. W., & Rowan, B. (1977). Institutionalized organizations: Formal structure as myth and ceremony. *American Journal of Sociology, 83,* 340–363.

Michaels, E., Handfield-Jones, H., & Axelrod, B. (2001). *The war for talent.* Boston: Harvard Business School Press.

Miles, R. E., & Snow, C. C. (1978). *Organizational strategy, structure, and process.* New York: McGraw-Hill.

Milgrom, P., & Roberts, J. (1992). *Economics, organization & management.* Englewood Cliffs, NJ: Prentice Hall.

Milkovich, G. T. (1988). A strategic perspective on compensation management. *Research in Personnel and Human Resources Management, 6,* 263–288.

Milkovich, G. T., & Newman, J. M. (1999). *Compensation* (6th ed.). New York: Irwin/McGraw-Hill.

Milkovich, G. T., & Newman, J. M. (2002). *Compensation* (7th ed.). New York: Irwin/McGraw-Hill.

Milkovich, G. T., & Wigdor, A. K. (1991). *Pay for performance.* Washington, DC: National Academy Press.

Miller, D. J. (1995). CEO salary increases may be rational after all: Referents and contracts in CEO pay. *Academy of Management Journal, 38,* 1361–1385.

Mills, D. Q. (1985). Seniority versus ability in promotion decisions. *Industrial & Labor Relations Review, 8,* 421–425.

Mincer, J. (1974). *Schooling, experience, and earnings.* New York: National Bureau of Economic Research.

Mincer, J., & Polachek, S. (1974). Family investments in human capital: Earnings of women. *Journal of Political Economy, 82,* S76-S108.

Miner, J. B. (1980). *Theories of organizational behavior.* Hinsdale, IL: Dryden.

Mitchell, D. J. B., Lewin, D., & Lawler, E. E. III. (1990). Alternative pay systems, firm performance, and productivity. In A. S. Blinder (Ed.), *Paying for productivity.* Washington, DC: Brookings Institution.

Mitchell, O. S. (1982). Fringe benefits and labor mobility. *Journal of Human Resources, 17,* 286–298.

Mitchell, T. (1974). Expectancy models of job-satisfaction, occupational preference and effort: A theoretical, methodological and empirical appraisal. *Psychological Bulletin, 81,* 1053–1077.

Mitchell, T. R. (1997). Matching motivational strategies with organizational contexts. *Research in Organizational Behavior, 19,* 57–149.

Morganti, A. (2001, July 2). *A cap on top?* (ESPN on-line). Retrieved from the World Wide Web on July 3, 2001, at: http://espn.go.com/nhl/columns/morganti_al/.

Morgenson, G. (2000, August 29). Market place: Investors may now eye costs of stock options. *The New York Times,* C1.

Motowidlo, S. J. (1983). Predicting sales turnover from pay satisfaction and expectation. *Journal of Applied Psychology, 68,* 484–489.

Mowday, R. T. (1996). Equity theory predictions of behavior in organizations. In R. M. Steers, L. W. Porter, & G. A. Bigley (Eds.), *Motivation and leadership at work* (pp. 53–71). New York: McGraw-Hill.

Murphy, K. J. (1999). *Handbook of labor economics* (Vol. 3b). O. C. Ashenfelter & D. Card (Eds.). New York: Northolland.

Murphy, K. R. (1986). When your top choice turns you down: The effect of rejected offers on the utility of selection tests. *Psychological Bulletin, 99,* 133–138.

Murphy, K. R., & Cleveland, J. N. (1995). *Understanding performance appraisal.* Thousand Oaks, CA: Sage.

Murray, B. (1993). *Organizational outcomes from the introduction of a skill-based pay program.* Unpublished doctoral thesis, Cornell University, Ithaca, NY.

Murray, B. C., & Gerhart, B. (1998). An empirical analysis of a skill-based pay program and plant performance outcomes. *Academy of Management Journal, 41*(1), 68–78.

Myers, C. A., & Shultz, G. P. (1951). *The dynamics of a labor market.* New York: Prentice Hall.

Nalbantian, H. R., & Schotter, A. (1997). Productivity under group incentives. *American Economic Review, 87,* 314–341.

National Center for Employee Ownership. (1999, June 21). *Employee ownership update.* Retrieved from the Worldwide Web on January 16, 2003, at: http://www.nceo.org/columns/cr69.html.

National Center for Employee Ownership. (2002). *A statistical profile of employee ownership.* Retrieved from the Worldwide Web on January 15, 2002, at: http://www.nceo.org/library/eo_stat.html.

Neal, D. (1993). Supervision and wages across industries. *The Review of Economics and Statistics, 75,* 409–417.

Noe, R. A., Hollenbeck, J. R., Gerhart, B., & Wright, P. M. (2000). *Human resource management: Gaining a competitive advantage* (3rd ed.). Boston: Irwin/McGraw-Hill.

Nooteboom, B., Berger, H., & Noorderhaven, N. G. (1997). Effects of trust and governance on relational risk. *Academy of Management Journal, 40,* 308–338.

Oi, W. (1962). Labor as a quasi-fixed factor. *Journal of Political Economy, 70,* 538–555.

Olian, J. D., & Rynes, S. L. (1984). Organizational staffing: Integrating practice and strategy. *Industrial Relations,* 23, 170–183.

Olian, J. D., & Rynes, S. L. (1991). Making total equality work: Aligning organizational processes, performance measures and stakeholders. *Human Resource Management, 30,* 303–333.

Oliver, R. L., & Anderson, E. (1994). An empirical test of the consequences of behavior- and outcome-based sales control systems. *Journal of Marketing, 58,* 53–67.

Olson, M. (1965). *The logic of collective action: Public goods and the theory of groups.* Cambridge, MA: Harvard University Press.

Opshal, R. L., & Dunnette, M. D. (1966). The role of financial incentives in industrial motivation. *Psychological Bulletin, 66,* 95–116.

Orbell, J., & Dawes, R. (1981). Social dilemmas. In G. Stephenson & H. H. Davis (Eds.), *Progress in applied social psychology* (Vol. 1, pp. 37–65). New York: Wiley.

O'Reilly, C., & Chatman, J. (1986). Organizational commitment and psychological attachment: The effects of compliance, identification, and internalization. *Journal of Applied Psychology, 71,* 492–499.

O'Reilly, C., Main, B. S., & Crystal, G. (1988). CEO compensation as tournaments and social comparisons: A tale of two theories. *Administrative Science Quarterly, 33,* 257–274.

O'Reilly, C. A., & Pfeffer, J. (2000). *Hidden value: How great companies achieve extraordinary results with ordinary people.* Boston: Harvard Business School.

O'Shea, J., & Madigan, C. (1997). *Dangerous company: The consulting powerhouses and the businesses they save and ruin.* New York: Times Business.

Osterman, P. (1987). Choice of employment systems in internal labor markets. *Industrial Relations, 26,* 46–67.

Ostroff, C. (1993). Comparing correlations based on individual-level and aggregated data. *Journal of Applied Psychology, 78,* 569–582.

Parks, J. M., & Conlon, E. J. (1995). Compensation contracts: Do agency theory assumptions predict negotiated agreements? *Academy of Management Journal, 38,* 823–838.

Parsons, D. O. (1977). Models of labor market turnover: A theoretical and empirical survey. *Research in Labor Economics,* 185–223.

Parus, B., & Handel, J. (2000, September). 2000–2001 total salary increase budget survey results. *World at Work, 43*(9), pp. 17–21.

Pearce, J. L., Stevenson, W. B., & Perry, J. L. (1985). Managerial compensation based on organizational performance: A time series analysis of the effects of merit pay. *Academy of Management Journal, 28,* 261–278.

Petty, M. M., Singleton, B., & Connell, D. W. (1992). An experimental evaluation of an organizational incentive plan in the electric utility industry. *Journal of Applied Psychology, 77,* 427-436.

Pfeffer, J. (1994). *Competitive advantage through people.* Boston: Harvard Business School Press.

Pfeffer, J. (1998a). *The human equation: Building profits by putting people first.* Boston: Harvard Business School.

Pfeffer, J. (1998b). Six dangerous myths about pay. *Harvard Business Review, 76,* 108–120.

Pfeffer, J. (1998c). *Case HR-6.* SAS Institute. Cambridge, MA: Harvard Business School.

Pfeffer, J., & Davis-Blake, A. (1987). Understanding organizational wage structures: A resource dependence approach. *Academy of Management Journal, 30,* 437–455.

Pfeffer, J., & Davis-Blake, A. (1992). Salary dispersion, location in the salary distribution, and turnover among college administrators. *Industrial and Labor Relations Review, 45,* 753–770.

Pfeffer, J., & Langton, N. (1993). The effect of dispersion on satisfaction, productivity, and working collaboratively: Evidence from college and university faculty. *Administrative Science Quarterly, 38,* 382–407.

Phan, P. H., & Hill, C. W. (1995). Organizational restructuring and economic performance in leveraged buyouts: An ex post study. *Academy of Management Journal, 38,* 704–739.

Pinder, C. C. (1998). *Work motivation in organizational behavior.* Upper Saddle River, NJ: Prentice Hall.

Pink, D. H. (1998, August). The talent market. *Fast Company, 16,* pp. 87–116.

Pitts, R. A. (1976). Diversification strategies and organizational policies of large diversified firms. *Journal of Economics and Business, 8,* 181–188.

Platt. (1964). Strong inference. *Science, 146,* 347–353.

Pollock, T. G., Fisher, H. M., & Wade, J. B. (2002). The role of politics in repricing executive options. *Academy of Management Journal, 45,* 1172–1182.

Porac, J. F., Wade, J. B., & Pollock, T. G. (1999). Industry categories and the politics of comparable firm in CEO compensation. *Administrative Science Quarterly, 44,* 112–144.

Porter, M. E. (1980). *Competitive strategy.* New York: Free Press.

Porter, M. E. (1981). The contribution of industrial organization to strategic management. *Academy of Management Review,* 6, 609–620.

Powell, I., Montgomery, M., & Cosgrove, J. (1994). Compensation structure and establishment quit and fire rates. *Industrial Relations, 33,* 229–248.

Prahalad, C. K., & Hamel, G. (1990, May-June). The core competence of the organization. *Harvard Business Review,* pp. 79–83.

Prendergast, C. (1999). The provision of incentives in firms. *Journal of Economic Literature, 37,* 7–63.

Prendergast, C. (2000). What trade-off of risk and incentives? *American Economic Review* (Papers and Proceedings), *92,* 421–425.

Prince, J. B., & Lawler, E. E. (1986). Does salary discussion hurt the developmental performance appraisal? *Organizational Behavior and Human Decision Processes, 37,* 357–376.

Pritchard, R. D., Jones, S. D., Roth, P. L., Stuebing, K. K., & Ekeberg, S. E. (1988). Effects of group feedback, goal setting, and incentives on organizational productivity [Monograph]. *Journal of Applied Psychology, 73,* 337–358.

Proctor, P. (1999, November 1). High salaries keep pilot pipeline flowing. *Aviation Week & Space Technology, 151*(18), p. 44.

Prsager, J. H. (1999, April 21). Joining the ranks of rich secretaries in the Internet age. *Wall Street Journal,* p. A1.

Raff, D. M. G., & Summers, L. H. (1987). Did Henry Ford Pay efficiency wages? *Journal of Labor Economics, 5,* S57-S86.

Raghavan, A., Kranhold, K., & Barrionuevo, A. (2002, August 26). How Enron bosses created a culture of pushing limits. *Wall Street Journal,* pp. A-1, A-7.

Rajagopalan, N. (1996). Strategic orientations, incentive plan adoptions, and firm performance: Evidence from electric utility firms. *Strategic Management Journal, 18,* 761–785.

Rappaport, A. (1999, March-April). New thinking on how to link executive pay with performance. *Harvard Business Review,* pp. 91–101.

Raudenbush, S. W., & Bryk, A. S. (2002). *Hierarchical linear models: Applications and data analysis methods* (2nd ed.). Newbury Park, CA: Sage.

Rebello, K. (1992, February 24). How Microsoft makes offers people can't refuse. *Business Week,* p. 65.

Rees, A. (1973). *The economics of work and pay.* New York: Harper & Row.

Rees, A. (1979). *The economics of work and pay* (pp. 65–66). New York: Harper Row.

Reichheld, F. F. (1996). *The loyalty effect.* Boston: Harvard Business School Press.

Reilly, K. F. (1995). Human capital and information: The employer size-wage effect. *The Journal of Human Resources, 30,* 1–18.

Reingold, J. (2000, April 17). Executive pay. *Business Week,* p. 100.

Reingold, J., Melcher, R. A., & McWilliams, G. (1998, April 20). Executive pay: Stock options plus a bull market made a mockery of many attempts to link pay to performance. *Business Week,* pp. 64–70.

Reynolds, L. G. (1951). *The structure of labor markets: Wages and labor mobility in theory and practice.* Westport, CT: Greenwood.

Rice, R. W., Phillips, S. M., & McFarlin, D. B. (1990). Multiple discrepancies and pay satisfaction. *Journal of Applied Psychology, 75,* 386–393.

Richter, A. S. (1998). Paying the people in black at Big Blue. *Compensation and Benefits Review, 30,* 51–59.

Rodgers, R., & Hunter, J. E. (1991). Impact of management by objectives on organizational productivity. *Journal of Applied Psychology, 76,* 322–326.

Roethlisberger F., & Dickson, W. (1939). *Management and the worker.* Cambridge: Cambridge University Press.

Rosen, C. (2002). National Center for Employee Ownership. *Update for October 29, 2002.* Retrieved from the World Wide Web on January 12, 2003, at: http://www.nceo.org/columns/cr126.html.

Rosenbaum, J. E. (1984). *Career mobility in a corporate hierarchy.* London, England: Academic Press.

Ross, A. M. (1957). The external wage structure. In G. W. Taylor & F. C. Pierson (Eds.), *New concepts in wage determination.* New York: McGraw-Hill.

Rottenberg, S. (1956). On choice in labor markets. *Industrial & Labor Relations Review, 9,* 183–199.

Rousseau, D. (1985). Issues of level in organizational research: Multilevel and cross-level perspectives. In L. L. Cummings & B. M. Staw (Eds.), *Research in organizational behavior* (Vol. 7, pp. 1–37). Greenwich, CT: JAI.

Rousseau, D. (2000). Multilevel competencies and missing linkages. In K. J. Klein & S. W. J. Kozlowski (Eds.), *Multilevel theory, research, and methods in organizations.* San Francisco: Jossey-Bass.

Rousseau, D. M., & Ho, V. T. (2000). Psychological contract issues in compensation. In S. L. Rynes & B. Gerhart (Eds.), *Compensation in organizations.* San Francisco: Jossey-Bass.

Rumelt, R. P. (1974). *Strategy, structure, and economic performance.* Cambridge, MA: Harvard University Press.

Rumelt, R. P. (1984). Toward a strategic theory of the firm. In R. Lamb (Ed.), *Competitive strategic management* (pp. 556–570). Englewood Cliffs: NJ: Prentice Hall.

Rumelt, R. P. (1991). How much does industry matter? *Strategic Management Journal,* 12, 167–185.

Ryan, R. M., Mims, V., & Koestner, R. (1983). Relation of reward contingency and interpersonal context to intrinsic motivation: A review and test using cognitive evaluation theory. *Journal of Personality and Social Psychology, 45,* 736–750.

Ryan, T. A. (1958). Drives, tasks, and the initiation of behavior. *American Journal of Psychology, 71,* 74–93.

Rynes, S. L. (1987). Compensation strategies for recruiting. *Topics in Total Compensation, 2,* 185–196.

Rynes, S. L., & Barber, A. E. (1990). Applicant attraction strategies: An organizational perspective. *Academy of Management Review, 15,* 286–310.

Rynes, S. L., & Bono, J. E. (2000). Psychological research on determinants of pay. In S. L. Rynes & B. Gerhart (Eds.), *Compensation in organizations* (pp. 3–31). San Francisco: Jossey-Bass.

Rynes, S. L., & Gerhart, B. (2000). *Compensation in organizations: Current research and practice.* San Francisco: Jossey-Bass.

Rynes, S., & Lawler, J. (1983). A policy-capturing investigation of the role of expectancies in decisions to pursue job alternatives. *Journal of Applied Psychology, 68,* 620–631.

Rynes, S. L., & Milkovich, G. T. (1986). Wage surveys: Dispelling some myths about the "market wage." *Personnel Psychology, 39,* 71–90.

Rynes, S. L., Schwab, D. P., & Heneman, H. G., III. (1983). The role of pay and market pay variability in job application decisions. *Organizational Behavior and Human Performance, 31,* 353–364.

Saari, L. M., & Latham, G. P. (1982). Employee reactions to continuous and variable ratio reinforcement schedules in involving a monetary incentive. *Journal of Applied Psychology, 67,* 506–508.

Salop, J., & Salop, S. (1976). Self-selection and turnover in the labor market. *Quarterly Journal of Economics, 90,* 619–627.

Samuelson, P. A. (1951). Economic theory and wages. In D. M. Wright (Ed.), *The impact of the union* (pp. 312–342). Freeport, NY: Books for Liberty Press.

Sanders, W. G. (2001). Behavioral responses of CEOs to stock ownership and stock option pay. *Academy of Management Journal, 44,* 477–492.

Schmalensee, R. (1985). Do markets differ much? *American Economic Review, 75,* 341–351.

Schmidt, F. L. (1996). Statistical significance testing and cumulative knowledge in psychology: Implications for training of researchers. *Psychological Methods, 1,* 115–129.

Schmidt, F. L., & Hunter, J. E. (1998). The validity and utility of selection methods in personnel psychology: Practical and theoretical implications of 85 years of research findings. *Psychological Bulletin, 124,* 262–274.

Schneider, B. (1987). The people make the place. *Personnel Psychology, 40,* 437–453.

Schneider, B., Smith, D. B., & Sipe, W. P. (2000). Personnel selection psychology: Multilevel considerations. In K. J. Klein & S. W. J. Kozlowski (Eds.), *Multilevel theory, research, and methods in organizations.* San Francisco: Jossey-Bass.

Schneider, B., Smith, D. B., Taylor, S., & Fleenor, J. (1998). Personality and organizations: A test of the homogeneity of personality hypothesis. *Journal of Applied Psychology, 83,* 462–470.

Schroeder, D. A. (1995). An introduction to social dilemmas. In D. A. Schroeder (Ed.), *Social dilemmas: Perspectives on individuals and groups.* Westport, CT: Praeger.

Schuler, R. S., & Jackson, S. E. (1987). Linking competitive strategies with HRM practices. *Academy of Management Executive, 1,* 207–220.

Schultz, E. E., & Francis, T. (2001, November 27). Fair shares? Why company stock is a burden for many—and less so for a few. *Wall Street Journal,* p. A1.

Schultz, T. (1963). *The economic value of education.* New York: Columbia University Press.

Schuster, M. H. (1984a). The Scanlon plan: A longitudinal analysis. *Journal of Applied Behavioral Science, 20,* 23–28.

Schuster, M. H. (1984b). *Union-management cooperation: Structure, process, and impact.* Kalamazoo, MI: Upjohn Institute.

Schuster, M. H. (1990, March). *Gainsharing: Current issues and research needs* [Workshop]. Cornell University, School of Industrial and Labor Relations, Ithaca, NY.

Schwab, D. P. (1973). Impact of alternative compensation systems on pay valence and instrumentality perceptions. *Journal of Applied Psychology, 58,* 308–312.

Schwab, D. P. (1980a). Construct validity in organizational behavior. In L. L. Cummings and B. M. Staw (Eds.), *Research in organizational behavior* (Vol. 2). Greenwich, CT: JAI.

Schwab, D. P. (1980b). Job evaluation and pay-setting: Concepts and practices. In E. R. Livernash (Ed.), *Comparable worth: Issues and alternatives.* Washington, DC: Equal Employment Advisory Council.

Schwab, D. P. (1991). Contextual variables in employee performance-turnover relationships. *Academy of Management Journal, 34,* 966–975.

Schwab, D. P., & Cummings, L. L. (1970). Theories of performance and satisfaction: A review. *Industrial Relations, 9,* 408–430.

Scott, W. R. (1995). *Institutions and organizations.* Thousand Oaks, CA: Sage.

Segal, M. (1986). Post-institutionalism in labor economics: The forties and fifties revisited. *Industrial & Labor Relations Review, 39,* 388–403.

Shadish, W. R. (2002). Revisiting field experimentation: Field notes for the future. *Psychological Methods, 7,* 3–18.

Shaw, J. D., Delery, J. E., Jenkins, G., & Gupta, N. (1998). An organization-level analysis of voluntary and involuntary turnover. *Academy of Management Journal, 41,* 511–525.

Shaw, J. D., Gupta, N., & Delery, J. E. (2002). Pay dispersion and workforce performance: Moderating effects of incentives and interdependence. *Strategic Management Journal, 23,* 491–512.

Shepperd, J. A. (1993). Productivity loss in performance groups: A motivation analysis. *Psychological Bulletin, 113,* 67–81.

Sherer, P. D. (1995). Leveraging human assets in law firms: Human-capital structures and organizational capabilities. *Industrial & Labor Relations Review, 48,* 671–691.

Shleifer, A., & Vishny, R. W. (1989). *Journal of Financial Economics, 25,* 123–139.

Simon, H. A. (1957a). *Models of man.* New York: John Wiley.

Simon, H. A. (1957b). The compensation of executives. *Sociometry, 20,* 32–35.

Simon, H. A. (1979). Rational decision making in business organizations. *American Economic Review, 69,* 493–513.

Slichter, S., Healy, J., & Livernash, E. R. (1960). *The impact of collective bargaining on management.* Washington, DC: Brookings Institution.

Slichter, S. H. (1950). Notes on the structure of wages. *Review of Economics and Statistics, 32,* 80–91.

Slovic, P., & Lichtenstein, S. (1971). Comparison of Bayesian and regression approaches to the study of information processing in judgment. *Organizational Behavior and Human Performance, 6,* 649–744.

Smith, A. (1976). *An inquiry into the nature and causes of the wealth of nations.* Dunwoody, GA: Norman S. Berg. (Original work published 1776).

Snell, S. A., & Dean, J. W. Jr. (1994). Strategic compensation for integrated manufacturing: The moderating effects of jobs and organizational inertia. *Academy of Management Journal, 37,* 1109–1140.

Sonnefeld, J. A., & Peiperl, M. A. (1988). Staffing policy as a strategic response: A typology of career systems. *Academy of Management Review, 13,* 588–600.

Southwest Airlines. (2001). *Southwest annual report, 2001.* Retrieved from the World Wide Web January 2003 at: http://www.southwest.com/investor_relations/annual_reports.html.

Spaulding v. University of Washington, 35 FEP Cases 1140–1147 (1984).

Stack, J., & Burlingham, B. (1992). *The great game of business.* New York: Currency Doubleday.

Stack, J., & Burlingham, B. (2002). *A stake in the outcome.* New York: Currency Doubleday.

Stajkovic, A. D., & Lee, D. (2001). *A meta-analysis of the relationship between collective self-efficacy and group performance.* Unpublished manuscript, School of Business, University of Wisconsin-Madison.

Stajkovic, A. D., & Luthans, F. (1997). A meta-analysis of the effects of organizational behavior modification on task performance, 1975–1995. *Academy of Management Journal, 40,* 1122–1149.

Stajkovic, A. D., & Luthans, F. (1998a). Self-efficacy and work-related performance: A meta-analysis. *Psychological Bulletin, 124,* 240–261.

Stajkovic, A. D., & Luthans, F. (1998b, Spring). Social cognitive theory and self-efficacy: Going beyond traditional motivational and behavioral approaches. *Organizational Dynamics.*

Stamborski, A. (2000, January 28). Ford workers will average $8,000 in profit sharing. *St. Louis Dispatch,* p. E2.

Staw, B. M. (1977). Motivation in organizations: Toward synthesis and redirection. In B. M. Staw & G. R. Salancik (Eds.), *New directions in organizational behavior* (pp. 55–95). Chicago: St. Clair.

Steers, R. M. (2001). Call for papers: The future of work motivation theory. *Academy of Management Review, 26,* 686–687.

Steers, R. M., & Porter, L. W. (1975). *Motivation and work behavior.* New York: McGraw-Hill.

Stewart, G. L. (1996). Reward structure as a moderator of the relationship between extraversion and sales performance. *Journal of Applied Psychology, 81,* 619–627.

Stewart, T. A. (1996). Watch what we did, not what we said. *Fortune, 133*(9), 140–141.

Stewart, T. A. (1997). *Intellectual capital: The new wealth of organizations.* New York: Doubleday/Currency Publishers.

Stigler, G. (1962). Information in the labor market. *Journal of Political Economy, 70,* 94–105.

Stigler, G. J. (1974). Free riders and collective action: An appendix to theories of economic regulation. *Bell Journal of Economics and Management Science, 5,* 359–365.

Strauss, G. (2001, August 2). Companies know where to go for a CEO. *USA Today,* p. B1.

Swoboda, F. (1995, February 5). So, you think you're top dog in the corporate hierarchy? *The Washington Post,* p. H6.

Takao, S. (1998). *The multidimensionality of organizational commitment* [Research series, No. 1]. Japan: Keio University Sangyo Kenkyujo Organization.

Tannen, M. B. (1987). Is the army college fund meeting its objectives? *Industrial & Labor Relations Review, 41,* 50–62.

Taylor, M. S., & Collins, C. J. (2000). Organizational recruitment: Enhancing the intersection of research and practice. In C. L. Cooper & E. A. Locke (Eds.), *Industrial and organizational psychology: Linking theory with practice* (pp. 304–340). Oxford: Blackwell.

Terborg, J. R., & Miller, H. E. (1978). Motivation, behavior and performance: A closer examination of goal setting and monetary incentives. *Journal of Applied Psychology, 63,* 29–39.

Thompson, P., & Heron, M. (2001). *Searching for complementaries: Compensation strategies, HR practices and firm performance.* Oxford University, Templeton College. Unpublished manuscript.

Thurow, L. (1975). *Generating inequality.* New York: Basic Books.

Tomer, J. F. (1987). *Organizational capital: The path to higher productivity and well-being.* New York: Praeger.

Tosi, H. L., & Gomez-Mejia, L. R. (1989). The decoupling of CEO pay and performance: An agency theory perspective. *Administrative Science Quarterly, 34,* 169–189.

Tosi, H. L., Werner, S., Kats, J. P., & Gomez-Mejia, L. R. (2000). How much does performance matter? A meta-analysis of CEO pay studies. *Journal of Management, 26,* 301–339.

Trank, C. Q., Rynes, S. L., & Bretz, R. D. Jr. (2001). Attracting applicants in the war for talent: Differences in work preferences among high achievers. *Journal of Business and Psychology, 16,* 331–345.

Treiman, D. J., & Hartmann, H. I. (Eds.). (1981). *Women, work and wages: Equal pay for jobs of equal value.* Washington, DC: National Academy Press.

Trevor, C., & Graham, M. E. (2000). Deriving the market wage: Three decision areas in the compensation survey process. *World at Work Journal, 9*(4), 69–77.

Trevor, C. O., Gerhart, B., & Boudreau, J. W. (1997). Voluntary turnover and job performance: Curvilinearity and the moderating influences of salary growth and promotions. *Journal of Applied Psychology, 82,* 44–61.

Tsui, A. S., Pearce, J. L., Porter, L. W., & Tripoli, A. M. (1997). Alternative approaches to the employee-organization relationship: Does investment in employees pay off? *Academy of Management Journal, 40,* 1089–1121.

Turban, D. B., & Keon, T. L. (1993). Organizational attractiveness: An interactionist perspective. *Journal of Applied Psychology, 78,* 184–193.

Tversky, A., & Kahneman, D. (1981). The framing of decisions and the psychology of choice, *Science, 211,* 453–457.

US Airways. (2001). *US Airways annual report,* 2001. Retrieved from the World Wide Web January 2003 at: http://www.usairways.com/about/investor_relations/reports/report_2001.pdf.

U.S. Bureau of Labor Statistics. (2000, March). *Employer costs for employee compensation summary.* Retrieved from the World Wide Web January 2003 at: www.bls.gov/news.release/ecec.nr0.htm.

U.S. Bureau of Labor Statistics. (2001a). *Productivity and costs.* Retrieved from the World Wide Web January 2003 at: http://www.bls.gov/lpc/peoplebox.htm.

U.S. Bureau of Labor Statistics. (2001b). *Hourly compensation costs in U.S. dollars.* Retrieved from the World Wide Web January 2003 at: http://www.bls.gov/news.release/ichcc.t02.htm.

U.S. Bureau of Labor Statistics. (2001c). *National compensation survey.* Retrieved from the World Wide Web January 2003 at: http://www.bls.gov/oes/2001/oes_5360.htm.

U.S. Bureau of Labor Statistics. (2001d). *Current population survey.* Retrieved from the World Wide Web January 2003 at: http://www.bls.gov/cps/home.htm.

U.S. Bureau of Labor Statistics. (2002, January). *National compensation survey: Evaluating your firm's jobs and pay.* Washington, DC: Author.

U.S. Bureau of National Affairs. (1988). *Changing pay practices: New developments in employee compensation.* Washington, DC: Author.

U.S. Chamber of Commerce Research Center. (2000). *Employee benefits 2000.* Washington, DC: Author.

van Ark, B., & McGuckin, R. H. (1999, July). International comparisons of labor productivity and per capita income. *Monthly Labor Review,* pp. 33–41.

Van Eerde, W., & Thierry, H. (1996). Vroom's expectancy models and work-related criteria: A meta-analysis. *Journal of Applied Psychology, 81,* 575–586.

Viswesvaran, C., & Barrick, M. R. (1992). Decision-making effects on compensation surveys. *Journal of Applied Psychology, 77,* 588–597.

Viswesvaran, C., Ones, D. S., & Schmidt, F. L. (1996). Comparative analysis of the reliability of job performance ratings. *Journal of Applied Psychology, 81,* 557–574.

Vroom, V. H. (1964). *Work and motivation.* New York: Wiley.

Wade, J., O'Reilly, C. A., & Chandratat, I. (1990). Golden parachutes: CEOs and the exercise of social influence. *Administrative Science Quarterly, 35,* 587–603.

Wagner, J. A. III. (1995). Studies of individualism-collectivism: Effects on cooperation in groups. *Academy of Management Journal, 38,* 152–172.

Wagner, J. A. III, Rubin, P., & Callahan, T. J. (1988). Incentive payment and nonmanagerial productivity: An interrupted time series analysis of magnitude and trend. *Organizational Behavior and Human Decision Processes, 42,* 47–74.

Warren, K. (2000, October 31). Pronger keeps everybody happy: The NHL and the NHLPA like what they see in $29.5-million contract, and that's good news with 2004 fast approaching. *Ottawa Citizen,* p. B6.

Watson Wyatt Worldwide. (1999). *1999/2000 survey of top management compensation.* Washington, DC: Author.

Weber, C. L., & Rynes, S. L. (1991). Effects of compensation strategy on job pay decisions. *Academy of Management Journal, 34,* 86–109.

Weiss, A. (1987). Incentives and worker behavior: Some evidence. In H. R. Nalbantian (Ed.), *Incentives, cooperation and risk taking.* Lanham, MD: Rowman & Littlefield.

Weitzman, M. L., & Kruse, D. L. (1990). Profit sharing and productivity. In A. S. Blinder (Ed.), *Paying for productivity.* Washington, DC: Brookings Institution.

Welbourne, T., & Andrews, A. (1996). Predicting the performance of initial public offerings: Should human resource management be in the equation? *Academy of Management Journal, 39,* 891–919.

Welbourne, T. M., & Gomez-Mejia, L. (1995). Gainsharing: A critical review and a future research agenda. *Journal of Management, 21,* 559–609.

Wernerfelt, B. (1984). A resource-based view of the firm. *Strategic Management Journal, 5,* 171–180.

White, J. K. (1979). The Scanlon plan: Causes and correlates of success. *Academy of Management Journal, 22,* 292–312.

Whiteley, P. (2001, June 7). Overhang threatens "candy" handouts. *The Times.*

Whyte, W. F. (1955). *Money and motivation.* New York: Harper Brothers.

Wiley, C. (1993). Incentive plan pushes production. *Personnel Journal, 72*(8), 86–91.

Williams, M. L., & Dreher, G. F. (1992). Compensation system attributes and applicant pool characteristics. *Academy of Management Journal, 35,* 571–595.

Williamson, O. E. (1975). *Markets and hierarchies: Analysis and antitrust implications.* New York: Free Press.

Williamson, O. E. (1996). *The mechanisms of governance.* New York: Oxford University Press.

Williamson, O. E., Wachter, M. L., & Harris, J. E. (1975). Understanding the employment relation: The analysis of idiosyncratic exchange. *Bell Journal of Economics, 6,* 250–280.

Wilson, N., & Peel, M. J. (1991). The impact on absenteeism and quits of profit-sharing and other forms of employee participation. *Industrial and Labor Relations Review, 44,* 454–468.

Wiseman, R. M., Gomez-Mejia, L. R., & Fugate, M. (2000). Rethinking compensation risk. In S. L. Rynes & B. Gerhart (Eds.), *Compensation in organizations.* San Francisco: Jossey-Bass.

Wood, R., & Bandura, A. (1989). Social cognitive theory of organizational management. *Academy of Management Review, 14,* 361–383.

Wood, R. E., Atkins, P. W. B., & Bright, J. E. H. (1999). Bonuses, goals, and instrumentality effects. *Journal of Applied Psychology, 84,* 703–720.

Woodyard, C. (1998, June 19). Global GM plants at strike's center. *USA Today,* p. 3B.

Wright, P., Ferris, S. P., Sarin, A, & Awasthi, V. (1996). Impact of corporate insider, blockholder, and institutional equity ownership on firm risk taking. *Academy of Management Journal, 39,* 441–563.

Wright, P. M., George, J. M., Farnsworth, R., & McMahan, G. C. (1993). Productivity and extra-role behavior: The effects of goals and incentives on spontaneous helping. *Journal of Applied Psychology, 78,* 374–381.

Wright, P. M., McMahan, G., Gerhart, B., & Snell, S. A. (n.d.). *Building human capital and organizational capability* (Technical Report). Cornell University, Center for Advanced Human Resource Studies, Ithaca, NY.

Yellen, J. L. (1984). Efficiency wage models of unemployment. *American Economic Review, 74,* 200–205.

Yukl, G. A., Latham, G. P., & Pursell, E. D. (1976). The effectiveness of pay incentives under continuous and variable ratio schedules of reinforcement. *Personnel Psychology, 29,* 221–231.

Yukl, G. A., Wexley, K. N., & Seymore, J. D. (1972). Effectiveness of pay incentives under variable ratio and continuous reinforcement schedules. *Journal of Applied Psychology, 56,* 19–53.

Zajac, E. J. (1995). Agency theory. In N. Nicholson (Ed.), *The Blackwell encyclopedic dictionary of organizational behavior.* Cambridge, MA: Blackwell.

Zedeck, S. (1977). An information-processing model and approach to the study of motivation. *Organizational Behavior and Human Performance, 18,* 47–77.

Zucker, L. G. (1987). Institutional theories of organization. *American Review of Sociology, 13,* 443–464.

Index

A. G. Edwards:
  pay practices, 5, 103, 110
  pay strategy, 30
Abelson, R., 184
Ability-to-pay model/theory, 6, 25–26. *See also* Rent-sharing model
Abowd, J. M., 69, 205, 259
Abraham, K. G., 191
Accounting Principles Board Opinion (APB) 25, 212
Ackerman, P. L., 129
Adams, J. S., 25, 61, 71, 107
Adverse selection model, 23
Agency costs, 140
  behavior-based contracts, 140, 142, 151, 161
  outcome-based contracts, 140–142, 151, 161
  See also Merit pay
Agency theory, 8, 120, 121, 138–151, 161, 166, 173, 175, 198, 201, 202, 205, 217, 222, 235, 238, 251
  adverse selection and, 139–140
  goal incongruence and, 139
  information asymmetry and, 139
  moral hazard and, 140, 174
  pay-for-performance empirical tests, 142–144, 148–151
  postcontractual opportunism, 174
  risk and pay-for-performance, 144–145
  See also Organizational commitment; Relative performance evaluation (RPE)
Aggarwal, R. K., 144, 145, 147, 148, 149, 163, 173
Agrawal, A., 173, 223
Aiman-Smith, L., 196, 222
Akerlof, G. A., 25
Akibia, 129
Albanese, R., 178, 179
Alchian, A. A., 177
Alge, B. J., 126, 127, 128
Alignment, 8, 231–233, 238. *See also* Fit; Pay strategy alignment
Allen, N. J., 151
Althauser, R. P., 88
Amabile, T. M., 153, 258
Ambrose, M. L., 51, 123
American Compensation Association (ACA), 86, 261
Ames, R. E., 179, 223
Amit, R., 244
Amoco Canada, 130
Andersen Accounting, 172
Anderson, E., 149
Andrews, A., 232
Antle, R., 145
Appelbaum, E., 199
Apple computer, 235
Argyres, N., 235
Arnold, H. J., 58, 65
Arthur, J. B., 196, 222, 240
Asch, P., 173, 211, 223
Ash, R. A., 78, 119, 154, 260
AT&T, 201
Atkins, P. W. B., 123, 127, 128
Attraction-selection-attrition (ASA) model, 119, 151, 153–154, 158, 160, 180
Awasthi, V., 173, 223
Axelrod, B., 253

Bailey, T., 199
Bain, J. S., 229, 234, 255
Bain and Company, 227
Baird, L., 233
Baker, G. P., 89, 171
Balkin, D. B., 58, 59, 148, 149, 232, 235, 236, 237, 238, 242, 247, 248, 254
Bandura, A., 118, 132, 133, 162
Banker, R. D., 197
Barber, A. E., 64, 65, 66, 123, 162
Barnard, C. I., 92, 138
Barney, J. B., 123, 229, 233, 244, 245, 246, 255, 256
Barrick, M. R., 32, 35, 153, 155, 157
Barrionuevo, A., 244
Barron, J. M., 65
Barry, B., 157
Bartol, K. M., 3, 127, 131, 132, 161
Bayard, K., 23
Beatty, R., 145, 173, 223
Becker, B. E., 69, 105, 106, 111, 162, 241, 250, 254, 260
Becker, G., 23, 30, 84, 85, 88, 244
Behavior-based pay:
  versus results-based pay, 166–175
Behavior-based performance measures, 166, 167–170, 172
  advantages, 167–168
  disadvantages, 168–170
Behling, O., 161
Ben and Jerry's:
  pay practices, 103
  pay strategy, 30
Bennett, N., 177
Berg, P., 199
Berger, C. J., 61, 73, 89, 113
Berger, H., 245
Bhagat, S., 209, 210, 225
Bienstock, P., 117
Big Five personality classification, 153, 155
  agreeableness, 153
  conscientiousness, 153, 155
  emotional stability, 153
  extraversion, 153, 157
  openness to experience, 153
"Big Risk, Big Reward" HR strategy, 253
Bishop, J., 65, 180
Blasi, J., 218, 219, 226
Blinder, A. S., 1, 38, 39, 43
Bloom, M., 104, 145, 173, 182, 232, 233, 258
Bognanno, M. L., 105, 106
Bohl, D. L., 173, 223
Bok, D. C., 104, 108
Bollier, D., 228
Bommer, W. H., 167
Bondy, J. S., 117
Bono, J. E., 31
Boudreau, J. W., 61, 63, 67, 71, 73, 74, 75, 76, 79, 89, 113, 119, 190, 191, 192, 222, 260
Boyd, B., 231
Boyd, B. K., 238
Boyer, G. R., 21, 44, 46, 229, 255
Brenner, M., 212, 226
Bretz, R. D. Jr., 55, 62, 64, 65, 67, 77, 78, 119, 123, 154, 155, 176, 192, 260
Brickley, J. A., 55, 122, 159, 209, 210, 225
Bright, J. E. H., 123, 127, 128
Broadbanding, 112
Broderick, R., 252
Brown, C., 22, 23, 45
Brown, K. A., 63, 135
Bryk, A. S., 161, 263
Buchholtz, A. K., 238
Bunnell, D., 167
Business strategy, pay rates and, 27, 30–31. *See also* Business strategy decision
Business strategy decision, 229–230, 233, 235–239
  analyzer, 236, 244
  cost leadership, 235–236, 237, 244
  defender, 236, 237, 238, 244, 248
  differentiation, 235–236, 244, 250, 261
  focus, 235, 236, 244
  pay strategy and, 238
  prospector, 236, 238, 244

Cable, D. M., 55, 119, 154, 155, 176, 202, 222, 260
Cain, G. G., 44, 46

Callahan, T. J., 131, 197, 264
Cameron, J., 52, 258
Campbell, D. T., 78, 218, 226
Campbell, J. P., 25, 50, 123, 137
Cappelli, P., 15, 41, 45, 68, 69, 90, 93
Carpenter, M. A., 31, 101, 238, 251
Carroll, S. J., 131
Carter, M. E., 212, 226
Case, J., 130, 170, 195, 196, 200
Cendant, 172, 175
Chance, D. M., 212
Chandler, A. D. Jr., 229, 255
Chandratat, I., 212
Chatman, J., 150
Chauvin, K., 68, 69
"Cheap riders," 178
Chick-Filet:
  pay strategy, 30
Chidambaran, N. K., 212, 226
Choi, D. H., 38, 39, 43
Chrysler, 34
  profit-sharing payouts, 204
Cirka, C. C., 129, 151
Cisco Systems, 184
Clark, J., 208–209
Cleveland, J. N., 168
Coase, R. H., 44, 46, 91
Coca-Cola:
  pay level decision making, 32, 33, 136
  stock options fair-value approach, 214
Coff, R. W., 26
Cognitive evaluation theory (CET), Deci and Ryan's, 53, 252
  overjustification effect, 51
  versus compensation as motivation, 49, 51–53
Cohn, L., 208
Coleman, J. S., 245
Collective action, 138
Collective bargaining contracts, pay rates and, 17, 18
Collins, C. J., 162
Collins, D., 198, 247, 256
Columbia/HCA, 172, 173
Colvin, G., 102, 108
Common-resource problem, 177
Commons, J. R., 16, 44
Compensating differentials, 39
Compensating wage differential, 12
Compensation theory, 15
  future research needs, 259–262
  methodological recommendations, 262–265
Competency-based pay, 8
Conlon, E. J., 150, 173
Connell, D. W., 197, 200, 222
Conte, M., 218, 219, 226
Contracts:
  behavior-based, 140, 142, 151, 161
  outcome-based, 140–142, 157, 161
Convex job level-pay relationships, 95, 97
Conyon, M. J., 97, 107, 110
Cook, P. J., 22, 70, 98, 99, 100, 102, 104, 108, 123, 134
Cook, T. D., 78, 218, 226
Cooke, W. N., 199
Cooper, C. L., 179
Cooperative theories, 7
Corporate strategy decision, 229, 230, 233, 234–235
  degree, 234
  diversification type, 234
  firm's life cycle and, 235
  Porter's "five forces" framework, 234, 235, 246
  process, 234
Cosgrove, J., 66
Cost leadership position, 236
Cowherd, D. M., 81, 107, 108, 109, 110, 114
Cox, T. H., Jr., 59
Coy, P., 215
Cronbach, L. J., 94, 114
Crystal, G. S., 15, 32, 36, 97, 102, 104, 108, 111, 134, 137, 141, 211, 212, 245, 261
Cummings, L. L., 50, 171

Daft, R. L., 244
Daley, K., 136

Dansereau, F., 161
Davis-Blake, A., 31, 100, 101, 231, 251
Davy, J. A., 62
Dawes, R. M., 177, 178
Dawis, R. V., 152
Dean, J. W. Jr., 239
Deci, E. L., 49, 51, 52, 53, 138, 252, 258
Deckop, J. R., 129, 151
Declining marginal utility principle, 56
Deephouse, D. L., 261
Delery, J. E., 66, 183, 239, 240
Dell, 235–236
Delta Airlines:
  stock options, 208
Deming, W. E., 175, 179
Demsetz, H., 177
Denny, A. T., 48, 49, 117, 118, 170, 175, 192
Dickson, W., 121
Digman, J. M., 153
DiMaggio, P. J., 7, 231
Doeringer, P. B., 30, 41, 87, 88, 89, 91, 113
Donnelly, 130
Doty, D. H., 239, 240, 263
Doucouliagos, C., 202, 219
Dreher, G. F., 59, 66, 73, 78, 119, 154, 260
Dunham, R. B., 53
Dunkelberg, W. C., 65
Dunlop, J. T., 6, 14, 16, 17, 21, 42, 85, 86
Dunnette, M. D., 39, 56, 57, 137
DuPont:
  stock options, 208
DuPont Fibers Division, 175, 205
  incentive program, 174
Dyck, B., 179
Dyer, L., 60, 62

Efficiency wage models, 20, 69. *See also* specific efficiency wage models; Efficiency wage theory
Efficiency wages, 39. *See also* Lincoln Electric Company
Efficiency wage theory, 6, 21–25, 26, 27, 31, 32, 36, 39, 67, 73, 74, 98, 119, 122, 152. *See also* Efficiency wage models
Effort withholding, 138
Egalitarian theories, 7
Egon Zehnder International:
  pay practices, 2
Ehrenberg, R. G., 13, 43, 44, 66, 84, 105, 106
Eisenberger, R., 52, 258
Eisenhardt, K. M., 149, 150, 173
Ekeberg, S. E., 130, 200
Employee attraction and retention, pay level and, 64–67
Employee behavior, compensation decisions and, 151–152. *See also* Incentive effects; Sorting effects
Employee effort and performance, pay level and, 67–71
Employee ownership firms (EOFs), 218
Employee Stock Ownership Plans (ESOPs), 206, 216–219, 228, 229
  employee attitudes/motivation and, 217–218
  productivity and, 218
Enclosure movement, 41
Enron, 172, 175, 259
  accounting scandal, 214
Equal compensation principle, 129, 172
Equilibrium wage, 13
Equity theory, 7, 50, 61, 64, 107, 120, 135–138, 180
Eriksson, T., 96, 107, 110, 114
Eskew, D., 187
Estrine, D., 99
European Parliament, 1
Expectancy theory, 7, 120, 123–125, 133, 134, 151, 153, 186, 198
  expectancy in, 124
  expectancy perceptions and, 128
  individual incentive systems and, 124
  instrumentality in, 123, 124
  motivational force in, 123–124, 128
  outcome attractiveness and, 128
  valence in, 124
Extensive information, 41

Faerstein, P. H., 117
Fang, M. Y., 53, 258
Farnsworth, R., 129
Feldman, D. C., 58, 65
Feren, D. B., 48, 49, 117, 118, 170, 175, 192
Ferris, S. P., 173, 223
Financial Accounting Standards Board 123, 213
Finkelstein, S., 231, 238
Fischer, H. M., 212, 226
Fishman, C., 200, 246, 253
Fit, 8, 231–233, 246. *See also* Alignment; Pay strategy alignment
Fleenor, I., 153, 154
Folger, R., 62
Ford, 67, 184, 261
  pay level decision making, 32, 33–34, 136
  profit-sharing payouts, 204
Fowler, K. J., 238
Francis, T., 216, 226
Frank, R. H., 22, 70, 98, 99, 100, 102, 104, 108, 123, 134, 259
Fredrickson, J. W., 22, 89, 113, 238
Freeman, J., 232
Freeman, R. B., 66, 73, 79
Free-rider problem, 156, 177, 179, 217, 218
  unions and, 178
Free riding, 177–178, 180, 198
Freiberg, J., 83, 200
Freiberg, K., 83, 200
French, J., 131
Frohlich, N., 179
Fugate, M., 173, 212, 222, 223
Fulmer, I. S., 146, 162, 261
Functional strategies, 230, 233

Gainsharing, 7, 8, 113, 166, 167, 199, 202, 203, 263. *See also* Gainsharing plans
Gainsharing plans, 184, 185, 195–201, 219, 220, 232, 239
  advantages, 195–196
  "pure," 221
  survival of, 200–201
  See also Gainsharing
Galbraith, C. S., 238
Gallup:
  pay strategy, 30
Garen, J. E., 145
Gates, B., 259
General Electric (GE), 22, 47, 78, 130, 143, 184, 234, 243, 247
  corporate strategy decision, 229
  pay practices, 2, 6, 110
  stock options fair-value approach, 214
General Motors (GM), 29, 34
  profit-sharing payouts, 204
  stock options fair-value approach, 214
George, J. M., 129
Gerhart, B., 3, 18, 20, 30, 31, 42, 46, 53, 63, 64, 65, 71, 73, 75, 76, 86, 90, 95, 96, 108, 111, 112, 113, 116, 119, 131, 151, 159, 162, 167, 176, 188, 190, 191, 192, 195, 196, 200, 205, 210, 219, 222, 230, 231, 232, 235, 238, 239, 241, 242, 243, 245, 246, 250, 251, 252, 253, 254, 255, 258, 260, 261, 263, 264
Ghiselli, E. E., 20, 115, 231
Gibbons, R., 89, 113, 145, 146, 147, 148, 171, 173
Gibbs, M., 89
Gift exchange model, 25
Gioia, D. A., 168, 186
Gleser, G. C., 94, 114
Glick, W. H., 239, 263
Global Crossing, 172, 175
Goal-setting theory (GST), 7, 120, 121, 125–132, 151, 160
  in field settings, 128–131
  management by objectives research and, 131–132
  support for, 132
Goldbricking, 174, 194, 211
Gomez-Mejia, L. R., 58, 59, 140, 143, 144, 148, 149, 173, 196, 201, 212, 222, 223, 232, 234, 235, 236, 237, 238, 242, 247, 248, 254

Goodman, P. S., 137
Goods-producing industries, pay rates and, 17, 18
Gordon, M. E., 20, 115, 231
"Go with a Winner" HR strategy, 253
Graham, M. E., 35, 36, 45, 176, 195, 200, 219, 232, 239, 243, 245, 246, 251, 255, 264
Gray, J. A., 155
Great Depression, 16
Greenberg, J., 62, 63, 110, 111
Greene, C. N., 189
Greene, D., 51
Gregersen, H. B., 251
Gresham, M. T., 31, 111, 112, 132, 195
Groshen, E. L., 18, 19, 23, 42, 46, 67, 68, 79
Group-based pay plans, 179
  limitations, 179–180
Group incentive pay plans, 185
Gubman, E. L., 221
Gunther, M., 53, 79
Gupta, N., 66, 118, 165, 170, 175, 183, 192, 239
Gustman, A. L., 252
Guzzo, R. A., 117, 118, 170, 192

Hackman, J. R., 53
Haire, M., 20, 115, 231
Hall, B. J., 215, 222
Hall, D. T., 50, 51
Hall, R., 161
Hallock, K. F., 142
Hambrick, D. C., 231, 238, 254
Hamel, G., 229, 255
Hammer, T. H., 198
Hamper, B., 194
Hamrin, R., 1, 129, 170
Handel, J., 206
Handfield-Jones, H., 253
Hannan, M., 232
Hansen, G. S., 246
Hardin, G., 177
Harkins, S., 178
Harris, J. E., 91, 92, 89, 113, 114
Harrison, D. A., 119, 195, 260
Harter, J. K., 261
Hartmann, H. I., 11, 17
Hastings, D. F., 233
Hatcher, L., 196, 198, 247, 256
Hawawini, G., 246, 255
Hayes, T. L., 261
Hay Group, 168, 186, 191
Health South, 143
Healy, J., 124, 251
Heath, C., 215, 226
Henderson, A. D., 22, 89, 113, 238
Heneman, H. G. III, 39, 46, 58, 60, 62, 63, 64, 65, 168, 263
Heneman, R. L., 31, 111, 112, 118, 132, 167, 187, 189, 195, 225
Hennessey, B. A., 153, 258
Heron, M., 241, 243
Herzberg, F., 39, 46, 49, 50, 53, 120, 138, 252
High-performance work systems (HPWS), 53
Hildreth, A. K. G., 26
Hill, C. W. L., 238
Hill, K. G., 153, 258
Hinkin, T., 140
Hirsch, B. T., 69
Hitt, G., 214
Hitt, M. A., 229, 234, 238, 255
Ho, V. T., 93
Hodgetts, R. M., 76, 77, 135
Hollenbeck, J. R., 126, 127, 128, 131
Holmstrom, B., 89, 146, 171
Holzer, H. J., 65, 67
Horizontal alignment, 8, 231, 233, 239–242
Hoskisson, R. E., 229, 234, 238, 255
House, R. J., 50
Howe, P. J., 213
Huber, G. P., 239
Huber, V. L., 63, 135
Huddart, S., 215, 226
Huett, D. L., 263
Hulin, C., 70
Human capital literature, 70
Human capital theory, 23–24, 84–85, 97, 119
Hunter, J. E., 73, 152

Hunter, J. E., 131
Hunter, L. W., 27
Huselid, M. A., 105, 106, 203, 233, 241
Hyundai:
  business strategy decision, 229–230

IBM, 90
Ichniowski, C., 239
Improshare plans, 198–199, 201
Incentive effects, 22, 59, 70, 71, 119–120, 151, 159, 160, 170, 184, 219, 230, 260
  pay-for-performance plans and, 116, 119
  versus sorting effects, 119, 161, 222
Incentive intensity, 175–176
Individual contracting, 167
Individual incentive pay programs, 179, 184, 192–195, 219, 220, 221
Individual incentives, 31, 167
Industrial feudalism, 41
Informativeness principle, 169, 173, 176
Institutional theory, 7, 231
Intel, 143
Intensive information, 41
Internal alignment, 8, 231, 233
  within pay strategy, 242–244
Internal labor markets (ILMs), 87–90, 91, 92, 93, 104, 112
  key feature, 87
International Labour Office, 233
Investor Responsibility Research Center, 213
Ippolito, R. A., 252
Itami, H., 245, 255

Jackson, S. E., 224
Janakiraman, S. N., 147, 163
Jaques, E., 95
Jasinowski, J., 1, 129, 170
Jelf, G. S., 196
Jenkins, D. G. Jr., 66, 118, 165, 170, 175, 192
Jensen, M. C., 131, 138, 139, 142, 143, 144
Jette, R. D., 117, 118, 170, 192
Job enrichment movement, Herzberg's motivation-hygiene theory and, 53
Job evaluation, 85
Johnson, J. L., 167
Johnson, R. A., 238
Jones, S. D., 130, 200
Jordan, M., 99
Judge, T. A., 55, 60, 62, 63, 64, 67, 119, 154, 155, 168, 176, 202, 222, 260
Judiesch, M. K., 118, 170, 192
Jurgensen, C. E., 58
Justice theory, 62

Kahn, L. M., 186
Kahneman, D., 39, 46
Kalleberg, A. L., 88, 199
Kanfer, R., 25, 50, 51, 53, 79, 123, 129, 134
Kanter, R. M., 94
Kaplan, R. S., 221
Kats, J. P., 143, 144
Katz, H. C., 16
Katzell, R. A., 117, 118, 170, 192
Kaufman, B. E., 16, 158
Kaufman, R. T., 198, 199, 201, 203
Kay, E., 131
Keith, K., 58
Kelleher, H., 78
Keon, T. L., 154
Kerr, C., 16, 40, 41, 88
Kerr, J. L., 234, 240
Kidwell, R. E., 177
Kim, D., 198, 201
Kim, S., 205
Klaas, B. S., 43, 66, 73, 74, 75
Klein, H. J., 126, 127, 128
Klein, K. J., 110, 161, 162, 217, 218, 219
Kochan, T. A., 15, 16, 45, 150
Koestner, R., 51, 52
Kogut, B., 245
Kohn, A., 52, 53, 120, 165, 195, 225, 258
Konovsky, M. A., 62
Konrad, A. M., 191, 192
Kopelman, R. E., 187, 189, 190, 224
Koslowsky, M., 62
Kosnik, R. D., 238

Kozlowski, S. W. J., 162
Kranhold, K., 244
Krausz, M., 62
Kristof-Brown, A., 157
Krueger, A. B., 14, 22, 26, 65, 67, 68, 79
Kruse, D. L., 202, 203
Kruse, D., 218, 219, 226
Kuethe, J. L., 95
Kulik, C. T., 51, 123
Kumar, R., 212

Labor market, 40–44
Lagnado, L., 172, 222
Lakhani, H., 66
Lambert, R. A., 95, 147, 163
Lang, M., 215, 226
Langton, N., 175, 180, 181, 258
Larcker, D. F., 95, 147, 163, 238
Latane, B., 178
Latham, G. P., 118, 126, 127, 128, 131, 134
Lavelle, L., 104
Lavigna, R. J., 263
Lawler, E. E., III, 3, 39, 49, 51, 55, 56, 57, 60, 61, 77, 115, 123, 131, 137, 162, 169, 170, 171, 198, 205, 209, 225
Lawler, J., 125
Layoff decisions, 88
Lazear, E. P., 24, 30, 81, 84, 85, 93, 94, 96, 97, 98, 107, 119, 151, 159, 160, 168, 175, 191, 192, 205, 222, 225, 260, 264
Lease, S. C., 209, 210, 225
Ledford, G. E. Jr., 31, 111, 112, 132, 195
Ledyard, J. O., 179, 224
Lee, D., 133
Lee, D. R., 91, 179
Lee, S-Y., 197
Leonard, J. S., 18, 19, 66
Lepper, M., 51
Lester, R. A., 11, 16, 17, 21, 26, 43
Letterman, D., 22
Levenson, B., 95
Levine, D. I., 38, 69, 81, 107, 108, 109, 110, 114, 199
Lewin, D., 198, 205
Lichtenstein, S., 39, 46, 57
"Lifestyles" HR strategy, 253
"Lifetime employment," 90
Lincoln, James, 247, 248
Lincoln, John, 247
Lincoln Electric Company, 129, 158, 170–171, 172, 221, 242, 243, 247–250
  administrative framework, 248
  compensation strategy, 232–233
  efficiency wage, 76–77
  HR practices, 261
  management system, 248
  pay basis, 248
  pay design, 248
  pay level, 31
  pay practices, 1–2, 5, 119
Litan, R. E., 246
Livernash, E. R., 85, 86, 124, 251
Locke, E. A., 3, 48, 49, 60, 117, 118, 124, 125, 126, 127, 128, 130, 131, 132, 134, 137, 162, 170, 175, 192
Lofquist, L. H., 153
Longenecker, C. O., 168, 186
Lum, S. K. S., 14, 44
Luthans, F., 117, 118, 133, 135, 162, 170, 175, 192
Lynch, L. J., 226

MacDuffie, J. P., 53, 199, 239
MacKenie, S. B., 167
Madigan, C., 110
Magnan, M. L., 238
Mahoney, T. A., 14, 95
Main, B., 96, 97, 106, 107, 108, 110, 111
Mallette, P., 238
Management by objectives (MBO), 131–132, 161
  goal-setting theory and, 131
Mandelker, G. N., 173, 223
Mangel, R., 129, 151
Manufacturing industries, wage variance in, 18–19
March, J. G., 70, 71, 75

Market wage, 5, 16
Mars Candy:
  pay practices, 5
  pay strategy, 30
Marshall, A., 29
Martin, J., 102, 107
Marwell, G., 179, 223
Maslow, A. H., 39, 46, 49, 50, 53, 120, 138, 252
Mason, E. S., 229, 234, 255
Mason, P., 254
Masson, R. T., 210
Mauri, A. J., 246, 255
Mayflower Group, 111, 262
McAdams, J. L., 197
McCaleb, V. M., 48, 49, 117, 118, 170, 175, 192
McCartney, S., 83
McClendon, J. A., 66, 73, 74, 75
McFarlin, D. B., 60
McGahan, A. M., 235
McGregor, D., 53
McGuckin, R. H., 28, 45
McKenzie, R. B., 91, 179
McKinsey "War for talent" study, 252–253. *See also* HR strategies, successful
McMahan, G. C., 129, 241, 242, 254, 263
McNulty, P. J., 16, 45
McWilliams, A., 58
McWilliams, G., 104
Meckling, W. H., 138, 139
Medoff, J. L., 22, 23, 45, 66, 79, 191
Medtronics, 143
Melcher, R. A., 104
Mellow, W., 23
Mercer, W. M., 208
Merit bonuses, 8
Merit increase grids, 168–169
Merit pay, 7, 8, 113, 116, 166–167, 263
  bonuses, 186
  increases, 186
  research, 4
  See also Merit pay programs
Merit pay programs, 184, 185–192, 220, 221
  advantages, 186, 189
  weaknesses, 186, 189
  See also Merit pay
Merril, G. B., 238
Meshoulam, I., 233
Meyer, H. H., 131
Meyer, J. P., 151
Meyer, J. W., 231
Michaels, E., 253
Michaels, M. P., 246, 255
Micron Technology, 213
Microsoft, 143, 252, 259
  business strategy, 236
  HR strategy, 253
  pay practices, 2, 5, 165–166, 184, 235
  stock options, 208, 210, 250
Miles, R. E., 123, 229, 236, 249
Milgrom, P., 26, 45, 129, 140, 159, 169, 171, 172, 174, 176, 177, 260
Milkovich, G. T., 3, 15, 18, 20, 22, 30, 32, 40, 42, 46, 63, 64, 65, 73, 76, 81, 86, 95, 96, 101, 108, 112, 114, 116, 119, 151, 173, 188, 190, 191, 192, 196, 205, 210, 230, 231, 232, 233, 251, 261
Miller, D. J., 145
Miller, H. E., 118
Mills, D. Q., 88
Mims, V., 51
Mincer, J., 23, 55, 84
Miner, J. B., 49, 50, 51, 79, 137
Minkoff, H., 190
Mitchell, D. J. B., 198, 205
Mitchell, O. S., 252
Mitchell, T. R., 123, 125, 153
Mitra, A., 118, 165, 170, 175, 192
Moesel, D. D., 238
Montgomery, M., 66
Morgan, B. A., 69
Morganti, A., 183
Morgenson, G., 214
Motivation-hygiene (two factor) theory, Herzberg's, 49–50, 53–54, 252
  job enrichment movement and, 53

versus compensation as motivation, 49–50
Motowidlo, S. J., 60
Mount, M. K., 153, 155, 157
Mowday, R. T., 137
Moyer, B. C., 14, 44
Multitasking, 171
Murphy, K. J., 142, 143, 144, 145, 146, 147, 148, 163, 215, 222
Murphy, K. R., 74, 168
Murray, B. C., 108, 113
Myers, C. A., 16, 40

Nagpurnanand, R. P., 212, 226
Nalbantian, H. R., 179, 224
Nanda, H., 94, 114
National Center for Employee Ownership, 165, 206, 208, 216
National War Labor Board, 16
Neal, D., 68
Needs hierarchy theory, Maslow's, 53, 54, 56, 252
versus compensation as motivation, 49, 50
Neoclassical economic theory, 6, 11, 12–16, 23, 24, 40, 42, 44, 84, 85
Netscape, 209
Neubert, M. J., 157
Newman, J. M., 22, 81, 86
Nisbett, R., 51
Noe, R. A., 131
Noncontingent high-pay levels, 55
Noorderhaven, N. G., 245
Nooteboom, B., 245
Norton, D. P., 221
Nougaim, K. E., 50, 51

Ogsten, D., 263
Oi, W., 88, 89
Oldham, G. R., 53
Olian, J. D., 30, 236, 244, 247
Oliver, R. L., 149
Olsen, R., 190
Olson, C. A., 61, 69
Olson, M., 177, 178
Ones, D. S., 169
Open-book management (OBM), 200, 228, 229
Opshal, R. L., 39, 56, 57, 137
Orbell, J., 178
Oregon Steel Mills, 170
O'Reilly, C. A., III, 96, 97, 106, 107, 108, 110, 111, 159, 161, 212
Organizational architecture, 250
decision rights assignment, 159
performance evaluation, 159
rewards, 159
Organizational commitment, 150–151
compliance dimension, 151
identification dimension, 150–151
internalization dimension, 150
Organizational size, pay rates and, 17, 18
Organizational strategy, 229, 231
pay strategy and, 238, 253
vertical alignment with, 233–239
See also Business strategy decision; Corporate strategy decision; Functional strategies
Organization for Economic Cooperation and Development (OECD), 28
O'Shea, J., 110
Osterman, P., 150, 240
Ostroff, C., 161
Oswald, A. J., 26
Outsourcing, 167
Overreward inequity, 25

Parks, J. M., 150, 173
Parsons, D. O., 66, 79
Partial gift exchange model, 25
Parus, B., 206
Pay:
as demotivator, 131
changes in, 5
Pay basis, 48, 63, 78, 115–116, 233, 253
future research, 160–162
See also Agency theory; Equity theory; Expectancy theory; Goal-setting theory; Pay-for-performance

relationship theories; Pay-for-performance system; Social cognition theory
Pay delivery, 8
Pay delivery systems, 7. *See also specific pay delivery systems*
Pay dispersion, within-group, 180–184
consequences, 180
major league baseball example, 182
national hockey league example, 182–183
Pay dissatisfaction, 138
Pay-for-group-based outcomes, 8
Pay form, 39, 48
Pay-for-outcome systems, individual, 8
Pay-for-performance programs, 115–116, 124, 188, 232, 258
demotivators, 258
future research, 221–222
See also Gainsharing; Individual incentive pay programs; Merit pay; Profit sharing plans; Stock plans
Pay-for-performance relationship theories, 119–120. *See also* Pay basis
Pay-for-performance system, 8, 32, 71, 75, 76
Pay importance, theories of, 258
contingency, 4, 6, 54–56
empirical evidence, 56–59
general, 6, 48–54
individual differences contingency, 54–56
market-based contingency, 54, 56
Pay increases, across-the-board, 7
Pay level, 5, 8, 11, 31, 39–44, 115, 116, 119, 135, 233
across different jobs, 29–31
across-nation differences, 17, 27–29
future research on, 77–78
overall utility and, 71–76
pay policies and, 76–77
versus pay structure, 30
See also Ability-to-pay model; Efficiency wage theory; Neoclassical economic theory; Pay level decision making, research on; Pay levels, high; Post-institutional economics; Rent-sharing model
Pay level decision making, research on, 31–39
Coca-Cola example, 32, 33
Ford example, 32, 33–34
Proctor & Gamble example, 34
Pay level effects, 47–48, 59–77. *See also* Cognitive evaluation theory (CET), Deci and Ryan's; Motivation-hygiene (two factor) theory, Herzberg's; Needs hierarchy theory, Maslow's; Pay importance, theories of; Pay level; Pay levels, high
Pay levels, high:
employee performance and, 59, 60
possible consequences of, 60
work attitudes and, 59
work effort and, 59, 60
See also Employee attraction and retention; Employee effort and performance; Pay satisfaction
Pay-plus-suggestion program, 232
Pay practices, issues relating to:
researcher disagreement about, 3
Pay satisfaction:
pay level and, 60–64
voting for union representation and, 62
Pay strategy, 39, 219, 227–231, 253–255, 258
business strategy and, 238
future research, 254–255
managerial goal choice and, 238
manufacturing strategy and, 239
organizational strategy and, 238
RBV and, 247–251
Pay strategy alignment, 8, 231, 233. *See also* Alignment; Fit; Horizontal alignment; Internal alignment; Vertical alignment
Pay structure, 5, 39, 48, 77, 81–84, 103–105, 115, 135, 233, 258
differences in, 30

empirical research on effects of, 105–108
future research, 108–113
jobs/job evaluation in, 84–87
theories of differences in, 87–97
versus pay level, 30, 81
work-life incentives, 97–105
Pay systems, 48
Pearce, J. L., 93, 187, 188, 189, 190
Peck, S. I., 97, 107, 110
Peel, M. J., 66
Peoplesoft, 213
PepsiCo:
stock options, 208
Performance-contingent pay, 31
Periperl, M. A., 240
Perry, J. L., 187, 188, 189, 190
Personnel economics, 21, 85, 159–160
Petty, M. M., 197, 200, 222
Pfeffer, J., 1, 3, 31, 47, 48, 52, 53, 100, 101, 103, 159, 161, 171, 175, 179, 180, 181, 191, 192, 231, 245, 250, 251, 255, 257, 258
Phan, P. H., 238
Phillips, S. M., 60
Piece rates, 8
Pinder, C. C., 51
Pink, D. H., 167
Piore, M. J., 30, 41, 87, 88, 89, 91, 113
Pitts, R. A., 234
Platt, 111
Podsakoff, P. M., 167, 189
Polachek, S., 23, 55, 84
Pollock, T. G., 36, 37, 38, 212, 226
Porac, J. F., 36, 37, 38
Porter, L. W., 50, 93
Porter, M. E., 229, 234, 236, 245
Post-institutional economics, 16–21, 32, 39, 56, 85
Post-institutional economics, research findings on:
actual wage patterns and compensating wage differentials assumptions, 43
employers and rate necessary to attract labor, 42–43
imperfect information, 41
imperfect mobility of labor, 40–41
internal labor markets, 41
lack of utility-maximizing worker behavior, 41–42
pay levels and employer profitability, 42
pay setting based on relative rates, 42
rule-based constraints to mobility, 41
wages are sticky, 43
weak labor supply/pay rates links, 42
Potter, G., 197
Powell, I., 66
Powell, W. W., 7, 231
Prahalad, C. K., 229, 255
Pratt and Whitney, 112
Prendergast, C., 171, 173, 176
Prennushi, G., 239
Price takers, 14
Price theory, 23
Prince, J. B., 131, 162
Pritchard, R. D., 25, 50, 123, 130, 137, 200
Proctor, P., 82
Proctor & Gamble:
pay level decision making, 34, 136
stock options, 208
Profit sharing, 7, 8, 31, 32, 113, 166, 167, 199, 222. *See also* Profit sharing plans
Profit sharing plans, 184, 185, 195, 201–205, 220, 250
cash payout, 202, 203
company size and, 203
deferred, 202, 203, 216
discretionary payout, 202, 203
formula-based payout, 202, 203
"pure," 221
See also Profit sharing
Promotion ladders, 88
Prsager, J. H., 208
Public-goods problem, 177
Pursell, E. D., 118

Quandt, R., 173, 211, 223

Raff, D. M. G., 66, 67
Raghavan, A., 244

Rajagopalan, N., 232, 238
Rajaratnam, N., 94, 114
Rappaport, A., 147
Raudenbush, S. W., 161, 263
Rebello, K., 2
Rees, A., 14, 41, 44
Reichheld, F. F., 30, 41, 227
Reilly, K. F., 23
Reingold, J., 104, 211
Reinharth, L., 189, 190, 224
Relative performance evaluation (RPE), 145–148
Renegotiation behaviors, 138
Rent, 25–26
Rent-sharing model/theory, 6, 25–26. *See also* Ability-to-pay model
Reservation wage, 56
Resource-based view (RBV) of firm, 231, 244–251, 253
  historical context, 245
  human capital, 244
  organizational capital, 244–245
  path dependence, 245
  pay strategy and, 247
  physical capital, 244
  social complexity, 245
Resource dependence theory, 6, 7, 31
Results-based pay:
  versus behavior-based pay, 166–175
  See also Gainsharing; Individual incentives; Profit sharing; Stock options
Results-oriented performance measures, 166, 170–175, 176
  advantages, 170–171
  disadvantages, 171–175
  incentive effects, 170
Retention, worker:
  pay structure differences and, 30
Reynolds, L. G., 15, 16, 21, 36, 40, 41, 42, 56, 135
Ribbens, B. A., 238
Rice, R. W., 60
Rich, G. A., 167
Richter, A. S., 90
Roberts, J., 26, 45, 129, 140, 159, 169, 172, 174, 176, 177, 260
Rodgers, R., 131
Rodriquez, A., 136
Roehling, M. V., 65
Roethlisberger, F., 121
Rosen, C., 82
Rosen, S., 30, 85, 93, 94
Rosenbaum, J. E., 76, 94
Rosenkrantz, S. A., 135
Ross, A. M., 41, 43
Ross, T. L., 196, 198, 247, 256
Roth, P. L., 130, 200
Rottenberg, S., 13, 48, 49, 54, 65
Rousseau, D., 161, 162
Rousseau, D. M., 93
Rowan, B., 231
Rubin, P., 131, 197, 264
Rumelt, R. P., 229, 234, 244, 246, 255
Ryan, R. M., 49, 51, 52, 53, 252, 258
Ryan, T. A., 125
Rynes, S. L., 15, 30, 31, 32, 39, 46, 55, 58, 65, 77, 86, 87, 101, 114, 119, 125, 151, 162, 176, 192, 236, 244, 245, 247

Saari, L. M., 118
Sadler, G. V., 97, 107, 110
Sagie, A., 62
Salamin, A., 231
Salop, J., 98
Salop, S., 98
Samuelson, P. A., 43, 44
Samwick, A. A., 144, 145, 147, 148, 149, 163, 173
Sanders, W. G., 212, 251
Sarbanes-Oxley Act, 216
Sarin, A., 173, 223
SAS Institute, 158, 242, 248, 251
  benefits package, 119, 249, 252
  business strategy, 249
  HR strategy, 253
  nonaligned pay practices, 249
  pay level, 31
  pay practices, 2, 6, 103, 110, 165, 166
  virtuous cycle, 249

Saturn (division of GM), 175, 205, 233
United Auto Workers and, 173
"Save the World" HR strategy, 253
Schjerning, D., 208–209
Schlesinger, J. M., 214
Schmalensee, R., 234, 246, 255
Schmidt, F. L., 4, 73, 152, 169, 261, 264
Schneider, B., 110, 119, 151, 153, 154, 158, 159, 161, 253
Schoemaker, P. J., 244
Schotter, A., 179, 224
Schroeder, D. A., 177, 223
Schuler, R. S., 224
Schultz, E. E., 216, 226
Schultz, G. P., 16, 40
Schultz, T., 84
Schuster, M. H., 195, 198, 201
Schwab, D. P., 39, 46, 50, 51, 58, 63, 65, 70, 75, 85, 86, 124, 171, 222, 262
Scott, K. S., 261
Scott, W. R., 251
Sears auto repair centers, 172, 173
Segal, M., 16, 43, 45
Seniority-based pay, 7
Seymore, J. D., 118
Shadish, W. R., 263
Shaw, J. D., 66, 118, 165, 170, 175, 183, 192, 239
Shaw, K., 239
Shaw, K. N., 48, 49, 117, 118, 170, 175, 192
Shepperd, J. A., 178, 179, 224
Sherer, P. D., 186, 261
Shipper, E., 62
Shirking, 22, 39, 98, 177
avoiding, 121
controlling, 26
discouraging, 25
Shirking/monitoring model, 24, 69. *See also* Efficiency wage model
Shleifer, A., 173, 223
Silicon Graphics, 208
Simon, H. A., 42, 70, 71, 75, 92, 95, 138
Sims, H. P., 168, 186
Singer, A. D., 62
Singleton, B., 197, 200, 222
Sipe, W. P., 161
Skill-based pay, 8
Slichter, S., 21, 124, 251
Slichter, S. H., 11, 17, 36, 42, 71, 135
Slocum, J. W. Jr., 240
Slovic, P., 39, 46, 57
Smith, A., 12, 145
Smith, C., 55, 122, 159
Smith, D. B., 153, 154, 161
Smith, R. S., 13, 21, 43, 44, 46, 66, 84, 229, 255
Snell, S. A., 238, 239, 241, 242, 254, 263
Snow, C. C., 123, 229, 236, 249
Social cognition theory (SCT), 7, 120, 121, 132–135
observational learning in, 121
self-efficacy in, 132–133, 160
self-mastery in, 121
Social cohesion theory, 4
Social dilemma, 177
Social loafing problem, 156, 178, 198
Sonnefeld, J. A., 240
Sorting by ability, 23
Sorting effects, 22, 59, 70, 71, 119, 120, 151–152, 158, 159–160, 184, 219, 230
versus incentive effects, 119, 161, 222
Southwest Airlines, 78, 83, 129, 158, 200, 234, 242, 243, 251
business strategy, 82–83
HR practices, 261
pay practices, 6, 103, 110
profit sharing, 250
Spaulding v. University of Washington, 11, 14
Springfield Remanufacturing Company (SRC), 170, 200, 228–229
HR practices, 261
pay practices, 103
See also SRC Holdings Corporation
SRC Holdings Corporation, 200. *See also* Springfield Remanufacturing
Srinivasan, D., 197
Stack, J., 228, 229
Stajkovic, A. D., 117, 118, 133, 162, 170, 175, 192

Stamborski, A., 204
Staw, B. M., 53
Steers, R. M., 50, 258
Steinmeir, T. L., 252
Stevens, C. K., 157
Stevenson, W. B., 187, 188, 189, 190
Stewart, G. L., 155, 157, 260
Stewart, T. A., 135, 245
Stigler, G., 41
Stigler, G. J., 178
Stock awards, 166
Stock grants, 7, 113, 206
Stock options, 7, 113, 166, 167, 206–216, 219, 231, 250
  Black-Scholes model of pricing, 214–215
  economic costs, 212–213
  exercise price, 207
  growth in, 208
  option price, 207
  overhang of stock and, 212–213
  overusing, 212
  recognized as expense when granted, 213
  repricing, 210–212
  strike price, 207
  top executives and, 209–210
  underwater, 174, 207, 211
  valuing, 212
Stock ownership, 116
Stock plans, 8, 31, 184, 185, 195, 205–219, 220
  balanced scorecard, 221
  401(k) plans, 206
  phantom, 206
  stock purchase plans, 206
  See also Employee Stock Ownership Plans (ESOPs), Stock awards; Stock grants; Stock options
St-Onge, S., 238
Strauss, G., 184
Stuebing, K. K., 130, 200
Sturman, M. C., 75, 76
Subramanian, V., 246, 255
"Sucker effect," 178
Summers, L. H., 14, 22, 26, 66, 67
Sunbeam, 172, 175
Sundaram, R. K., 212, 226
Suttle, J. L., 51
Swoboda, F., 135

Takao, S., 150
Tannen, M. B., 70
Taylor, M. S., 162
Taylor, S., 153, 154
Temporary employment, 167
Terborg, J. R., 118
Theriault, R., 60, 62
Thierry, H., 124, 125
Thomas, F., 136, 137
Thomas, S. L., 62
Thompson, P., 241, 243
Thurow, L., 41, 88, 89, 92, 113
Tighe, E. M., 153, 258
Todd, R. B., 212
Tomer, J. F., 244
Tosi, H. L., 140, 143, 144
Total compensation, 40, 252–253
Total utility, 12
Tournament model, 30, 100, 102, 104, 105–107. *See also* Tournament theory
Tournament theory, 4, 7, 85, 93–97, 98, 105, 111, 151. *See also* Tournament model
Trank, C. Q., 55, 77, 176, 192
Transaction cost economics (TCE), 21, 85, 91–93, 104
Treiman, D. J., 11, 17
Trevor, C. O., 35, 36, 45, 63, 71, 75, 76, 119, 176, 190, 191, 192, 195, 200, 219, 222, 232, 238, 239, 243, 245, 246, 251, 255, 260, 264
Tripoli, A. M., 93
Troske, K. R., 23
Tsui, A. S., 93
Turban, D. B., 154
Turnover, 138
Turnover models/theories, 24, 70
Tversky, A., 39, 46
Tyson, L. D., 199

U.S. Bureau of Labor Statistics, 1, 17, 18, 19, 24, 36, 45, 86
U.S. Bureau of National Affairs, 202
U.S. Chamber of Commerce Research Center, 230
Ullman, J. C., 43
Underreward inequity, 138
Unemployment, work incentives and, 25
Unions, 41, 113
  declining membership, 69
  free rider problem and, 178
United Airlines, 242
US Airways, 83–84, 242
Utility theory, 24, 71–76, 119, 152

van Ark, B., 28, 45
Van Eerde, W., 124, 125
Van Fleet, D. D., 178, 179
Verdin, P., 246, 255
Vertical alignment, 8, 231, 233, 247
Virick, M., 119, 195, 260
Virtuous cycle of employee motivation/customer satisfaction/organizational profitability, 227
  examples, 228–229, 249
Vishny, R. W., 173, 223
Viswesvaran, C., 32, 35, 169
Vroom, V. H., 123, 260

Wachter, M. L., 91, 92, 89, 113, 114
Wade, J. B., 31, 36, 37, 38, 96, 97, 101, 106, 107, 108, 110, 212, 226, 251
Wage differentials, geographic, 19
Wage rate, 31
Wage takers, 11
Wagner, J. A., III, 131, 155, 156, 157, 197, 264
Waldman, M., 89, 113
Wan, W. P., 229, 234, 255
Warren, K., 183
Watson Wyatt Worldwide, 208
Weber, C. L., 86, 87, 245
Weigelt, K., 95
Weiss, A., 201
Weiss, D. J., 153
Weitzel, W., 95
Weitzman, M. L., 202
Welbourne, T., 232
Welbourne, T. M., 196, 201
Welch, J., 78, 143, 184
Wendy's International, 208
Werner, S., 143, 144
Wernerfelt, B., 229, 244, 246, 255
Wesson, M. I., 126, 127, 128
Wexley, K. N., 118
Whirlpool, 170, 221
White, J. K., 195, 225
Whiteley, P., 207
Whole Foods, 200
Whyte, W. F., 121, 124, 174, 193, 194, 195
Wigdor, A. K., 185, 196, 198
Wigdor, L. A., 50
Wiley, C., 172, 250
William, S., 119, 195, 260
Williams, K., 178
Williams, M. L., 66, 73, 78
Williamson, O. E., 85, 91, 92, 89, 113, 114, 244
Wilson, N., 66
Winner-take-all theory, 7
Wiseman, R. M., 173, 201, 211, 222, 223
Within-group pay differential research, 4–5
Wood, R. E., 123, 127, 128, 132, 133
Woodyard, C., 29
Work adjustment:
  Dawis model, 160
  Minnesota model, 152–153
Workforce composition, pay decisions and, 152–158
Workforce composition effect, 76
Work-life incentives, 97–105
  equity/relative deprivation models, 102–103, 104, 107, 111
  resource-dependence models, 100–102
  winner-take-all models, 98–100, 104
  See also Equity theory
Work teams, 199
World at Work, 261

Worldcom accounting scandal, 214
World Trade Center/Pentagon attacks, 242
Wright, P., 173, 223
Wright, P. M., 129, 131, 241, 242, 246, 254, 256, 263

Xerox Customer, 47

Yahoo, 213
Yellen, J. L., 24, 25, 45
Yermack, D., 212, 226
Yiu, D., 229, 234, 255
Yukl, G. A., 118
Yuskavage, R. E., 14, 44

Zajac, E., 139, 145, 173, 223
Zander, U., 245
Zedeck, S., 65, 125
Zimmerman, J., 55, 122, 159
Zucker, L. G., 231

About the Authors

Barry Gerhart is Professor of Management and Human Resources and the John and Barbara Keller Distinguished Chair of Business, School of Business, University of Wisconsin-Madison. Previously, he held the Frances Hampton Currey Professorship and served as Chairman of the Organization Studies area at Vanderbilt University's Owen Graduate School of Management. Earlier, he also served as Chairman of the Department of Human Resource Studies, Cornell University. His major fields of interest are human resource management and strategy, compensation, and business performance. He received his B.S. in Psychology from Bowling Green State University and his Ph.D. in Industrial Relations from the University of Wisconsin-Madison. Current and past editorial board appointments include the *Academy of Management Journal, Administrative Science Quarterly, Industrial & Labor Relations Review, the International Journal of Human Resource Management, the Journal of Applied Psychology, and Personnel Psychology.* He has been a course designer and faculty member for the American Compensation Association. In 1991, he received the Scholarly Achievement Award from the Human Resources Division, Academy of Management. He is also a Fellow of the American Psychological Association and of the Society for Industrial and Organizational Psychology. He is coeditor of the recent book, *Compensation in Organizations,* and coauthor of *Human Resource Management: Gaining a Competitive Advantage,* now in its fourth edition.

Sara L. Rynes is the John F. Murray Professor and Chair of the Department of Management and Organizations at the University of Iowa. Before moving to Iowa, she was on the faculties of Cornell University and the University of Minnesota. She is currently Associate Editor for *Academy of Management Journal* and an editorial board member of *Academy of Management Learning and Education.* She previously served on the boards of *Journal of Applied Psychology, Personnel Psychology, Quality Management Journal,* and *Frontiers in Industrial and*

Organization Psychology. Her research interests include compensation, staffing, field influences on higher education, and knowledge sharing and transformation between academics and practitioners. She has been a course designer and faculty member for the American Compensation Association and Cornell University's Institute for College Relations and Recruiting, and is co-editor of two previous books, *Compensation in Organizations* and *Current Issues in Human Resource Management.* She is a fellow of the American Psychological Association and the Society for Industrial and Organizational Psychology. She received her M.S. and Ph.D. degrees in Industrial Relations from the University of Wisconsin.